NOW THE DRUM OF WAR

Fatal Mountaineer

Cuervo Tales

Mexico Days

On Spider Creek

Royo County

The Trespassers

In Caverns of Blue Ice

NOW THE DRUM OF WAR

Walt Whitman and His Brothers
in the Civil War

ROBERT ROPER

Walker & Company
New York

Published by Walker Publishing Company, Inc., New York

ART CREDITS

Courtesy of Trent Collection, Duke University: p. 3. Library of Congress: pp. 10, 20, 72, 96, 106, 150, 155,
162, 169, 171, 180, 195, 211, 250, 252, 264, 265, 292, 341, 349, 360. photobucket.com: p. 22. Ed Folsom collection
p. 32. Courtesy of Walt Whitman House: p. 56. Courtesy of the George Peabody Library, Johns Hopkins University: p. 59. New York Public Library: pp. 64, 208. Reproduced from *The Brooklyn Water Works and Sewers: A
Descriptive Memoir*: p. 87. Courtesy of Orchard House and the Louisa May Alcott Memorial Association: p. 101.
National Archives: pp. 103, 340. Courtesy of Clara Barton National Historic Site, National Park Service: p. 127.
United States Army Military History Institute: pp. 139, 236, 261, 267, 270, 300, 306. genealogyandmore.com:
p. 310. Bayley Collection, Ohio Wesleyan University: p. 378.

LIBRARY OF CONGRESS CATALOGING-IN-PUBLICATION DATA HAS BEEN APPLIED FOR.

ISBN-10: 0-8027-1553-2
ISBN-13: 978-0-8027-1553-1

Visit Walker & Company's Web site at www.walkerbooks.com

First U.S. edition 2008

1 3 5 7 9 10 8 6 4 2

Typeset by Westchester Book Group
Printed in the United States of America by Quebecor World Fairfield

For Bob Spertus: eloquent friend

*My ties and ballasts leave me....I travel....I sail....my elbows
rest in the sea-gaps,
I skirt the sierras....my palms cover continents,
I am afoot with my vision.*

LIST OF ILLUSTRATIONS

THE SCENT OF pennyroyal, crushed by soldiers' shoes, remained intense as a false twilight came.[1] A large force of Union troops had been stymied all day by rebels holding the high ground, and as the sun set early behind the wooded Maryland ridge, a shadowy time of error and anxiety arrived.

A Union brigade under Colonel Edward Ferrero, a former New York dancing instructor, spent the afternoon of September 14, 1862, in fair safety, downslope from the fighting in a cornfield. Three hundred yards away, some of the fiercest exchanges of musket fire yet heard in the Civil War rattled and clacked. Yet here in the cornfield, and in the nearby woods, Ferrero's men lay around and waited, their only job the guarding of nearby artillery. It was the Lord's day. Some Ohio troops had assembled that morning in an outdoor prayer session, led by a chaplain in a recitation out of Psalms: "Bow down thy ear, O Lord, hear me: for I am poor and needy . . . In the day of my trouble I will call upon thee . . ." For most, though, the day had little of a Sabbath character. One of Ferrero's most battle-hardened units, the 51st New York Volunteers, grumbled as they waited: Orders had come to leave their knapsacks in the bushes, so as not to be encumbered when they entered the fight. At Second Bull Run two weeks before, they likewise had been made to leave their packs behind, and they had never recovered them.[2]

Clean drawers, socks, tobacco, writing materials . . . the articles lost were much prized, and hard to replace on the march. The knapsack belonging to one young lieutenant, George Washington Whitman, of

Brooklyn, probably contained a letter written by his mother, Louisa, on September 7 and another from his younger brother, Jeff, written September 8. Whitman treasured letters from home and begged for them with a frank desperation ("Mother why the deuce don't some of you write to a fellow"). He confessed to intense bouts of homesickness that made him "think quite strange." Given the uncertainties of mail delivery to soldiers on the march, he understood that more letters were probably being written than he received, yet his fierce longing led him to fantasize about his family back in Brooklyn ("ile bet now, that Mother is makeing pies . . . Mat is putting up shirt bosoms by the deuce . . . Sis is down stairs helping Mother mix the dough, Walt is up stairs writing, Jeff is down at the Office, Jess is pealing Potatoes for dinner, and Tobias has gone down cellar for a scuttle of coal").[3]

Although homesick and often afraid, George Whitman was living the adventure of his life. Battle thrilled him. In situations of mortal peril he became calmly intent. Other men followed him into combat willingly, even eagerly. Hardly more than a year into a savage war, Whitman and his fellows in the 51st New York had seen as much close-quarters fighting as any unit in the Federal army. Yet, on this temperate, blue-skied Sunday, the true darkening and deepening of their experience of war was about to begin.

Around seven P.M., Ferrero received orders to move his brigade uphill. A kind of darkness had fallen along the rugged north–south ridge called South Mountain. By clever maneuvering and brilliant fakery, a numerically inferior Confederate force had defended the mountain's passes all day. Rebel artillery had rained grape and canister downslope, and the Federal units now struggling uphill saw several surgeons at work at outdoor operating tables, with piles of severed feet and arms accumulating in the trampled corn and pennyroyal. Ferrero's brigade, numbering around two thousand men, included three veteran regiments plus one rank green one, the 35th Massachusetts. This being his largest unit (eight hundred men), Ferrero sent the 35th uphill first, and the sight of the Union wounded stumbling back downslope and of the field surgeries had an unsettling effect.

In this sector of the battle, near a mountain pass called Fox's Gap, rebel and Federal troops had exchanged close-range fire all day. There were many dead and maimed. A narrow lane along the summit, called the

George Whitman at about age thirty-two, during his first year of soldiering.

Wood Road, was full of bodies, and the soldiers of the 35th trod around them and through their copious blood. Enemy musket fire had lessened as twilight came. As they ranged over the pass and down into a forest to the west, the men of the 35th became separated into small groups of confused, noisily thrashing shadow figures. Sensing peril, their officers ordered them back uphill, closer to their supporting units.

Ferrero's more experienced forces, including Whitman's 51st New York, moved into position along the Wood Road meanwhile, sheltering in a field. As the disoriented 35th began straggling up out of the woods—still making noise and, at one point, lighting a lantern to show the way, despite the nearness of rebel sharpshooters—Union major general Jesse L. Reno, commander of 9th Corps, Ferrero's superior by several orders of rank and a beloved leader to the men, came up the road on a horse. One of the more competent Union generals, Reno was curious to see the disposition of forces at the end of this bloody day. Soldiers who recognized him in the dusk said he looked thoughtful. His escort consisted of two orderlies plus a staff surgeon, also on mounts. Reno rode just slightly ahead of the others, peering into the gloom.

A young soldier of the 35th, emerging from the woods, cried, "Rebel cavalry!" at the sight of the four horsemen. He leveled his musket and discharged it. Several other shots crackled almost simultaneously—the fire came from nearby, possibly from rebel troops about to counterattack. Reno slid from his horse. Moments before, he had told some soldiers he met to stack arms and brew coffee—the fighting appeared to be over for the night, and they deserved a rest.[4] Now he understood that he was badly wounded, indeed, that he was dying. "Willcox," he said to a friend, General Orlando Willcox, a few minutes later, having been carried back from the woodside ambuscade, "I am killed. Shot by our own men."[5]

In a newspaper dispatch he wrote soon afterward, George Whitman said of Reno's death, "[It] caused every one to look sad and melancholy, and many to shed tears. It could hardly be realized by the boys, even for days after."[6] Now, as rebel skirmishers again opened a concentrated fire, the 51st New York found itself pinned down in the dark field. "Our regt was ordered to lie close and not fire a shot untill the enemy advanced out of the woods," Whitman wrote his mother the next week.* "The regts on our right and left had a regular cross fire on the enemy and kept pouring the lead into them like rain. I had command of our Company . . . and I had mighty hard work to keep some of them from getting up and blazing away as they said they did not like to lay there like a lot of old women and be shot without fighting back."[7]

At last, "the order was given for us to open fire and you never saw men go to work with a better relish." Night had now fallen truly. Rifle

---

*All transcriptions of letters, journals, diaries, and other sources are as they originally appeared, without corrections to spelling or grammar except where necessary to avoid confusion.

flashes invited return fire, and there was much dying. The young recruits of the 35th Massachusetts, having mostly escaped the woods full of reenergized rebels, circled back behind the 51st New York and the other veteran units and, in a bid for glory, lustily opened fire, endangering the Union soldiers in front of them. "Cease firing! Cease firing!" roared the veterans, threatening to turn their guns backward, and eventually the rookies of the 35th crept away, to shelter in a nearby wood.

The next morning, September 15, 1862, "I took a walk over our part of the battle field," Whitman wrote his mother. "In some parts of the feild the enemys dead lay in heaps and in a road for nearly a quarter of a mile they lay so thick that I had to pick my way carefully to avoid stepping on them . . . I think judging from what I saw that the enemys loss was fully 8 times as great as ours and I am told that the slaughter was equally great" elsewhere on the mountain.[8] Ferrero's brigade had lost 150 men in only the last act of the fighting, lasting less than forty-five minutes. In two more days they would be at Antietam, for the bloodiest twenty-four hours in American history.

CHAPTER TWO

A SOLDIER WHO FOUGHT with Whitman at South Mountain, Corporal Elmer Bragg, of the 9th New Hampshire, later wrote, "You can form no idea of the harass of the Battlefield. It was only through excitement that I endured it."[1]

Whitman also seems to have endured through excitement. His many letters home, treasured and saved by his poet brother, are written in a vivid, pell-mell style, especially their accounts of actual combat. Describing an earlier battle (Roanoke Island, coastal North Carolina), George Whitman wrote, "We struck directly into the woods and soon heard the firing comence on the right of the first Brigade we were in a wagon path and all around us was a thick wood . . . we kept on, the first Brigade driving the enemy untill we got into a thick swamp where the mud and water was over the top of my boots . . . it was mighty trying to a fellows nerves as the balls was flying around pretty thick . . . As soon as our regt got sight of the [enemy gun emplacement] Gen Renno who is our Brigadeer General gave the order to charge and away we went the water flying over our heads as we splashed through . . . I heard the order to charge [and] when I reached the Battery our colors and the flag of the 9th New York and the 21st Mass were planted there ours were there first however."[2]

Aged thirty-two at the time of this fight, Whitman made some signal discoveries about himself. "I was as calm and cool during the whole affair as I am at any time," he wrote home, "and I was perfectly surprised to see how well our troops acted." Moreover, "it is a miracle to me that our loss was so small when I think how the bullets wized around our heads. The enemy had a great advantage in knowing the ground and could pick his position while we had to follow without knowing . . . they thought they would toll us up to the Bateries and then slaughter us . . . they did not think we would go in that water and fight."[3]

He was able to stand the fear and stress and still perform—a good thing to know about himself. Also, "it was rather a sickening sight to see the wounded brought along the road but I expected sutch things so that it did not effect me mutch and after a while we would pass them lying in the bushes and think nothing of it." "So Mammy," he concluded, "I think we done a pretty good days work yesterday marching 15 or 16 miles and fighting with boots filed with water for 4 hours . . . I wish Walt if he is home, or Jeff would send me some papers   often it is a great treat to get a sight of a New York paper   I should like one giveing a discription of the battle."[4]

A carpenter by trade, George Whitman enlisted soon after the firing on Fort Sumter, April 12, 1861. The rebellion was expected to last only a few weeks, and troops leaving New York marched down Broadway with lengths of rope attached to their rifle barrels—rope with which to tie up naughty Rebs and bring them north to justice. Whitman's first term of enlistment, with the 13th Regiment of New York Militia, was for one hundred days. Having seen scant action in that time, at the end of the summer he joined a New York infantry regiment then forming, for a period of service—three years—that by itself suggests a new estimate of Confederate power.

Those bad Johnnys had decidedly *not* been dragged home at the ends of ropes. The embarrassing rout of Union forces in the war's first major battle, Bull Run, July 21, 1861, gave evidence of something that looked disturbingly like tactical ability on the part of some rebel commanders, in particular General P. G. T. Beauregard and General Thomas J. Jackson, who stood "like a stone wall" to check the Union advance. The ordinary soldiers, of North and South alike, had shown themselves ill prepared and prone to confusion, but game enough for a fight. No, it was the Northern *commanders*, Lincoln included, who had pushed too soon for a kill-shot victory, one that proved beyond them, leading to widespread panic in Washington, only thirty miles from the rebel lines.

"Resolution, manliness, seem to have abandoned" the capital, Walt

Whitman wrote of the battle's aftermath. "The principal hotel, Willard's, is full of shoulder-straps . . . There you are, shoulder-straps!—but where are your companies? where are your men? . . . Sneak, blow, put on airs there in Willard's sumptuous parlors and bar-rooms . . . no explanation shall save you. Bull Run is your work; had you been half or one-tenth worthy of your men, this would never have happen'd."[5]

He continued, "One bitter, bitter hour—perhaps proud America will never again know such an hour . . . Those white palaces—the dome-crown'd capitol there on the hill, so stately over the trees—shall they be left—or destroy'd first? For it is certain that the talk among certain of the magnates and officers and clerks and officials . . . for twenty-four hours in and around Washington after Bull Run, was loud and undisguised for yielding out and out, and substituting the southern rule, and Lincoln promptly abdicating."[6]

George Whitman, who did not fight at First Bull Run, was made sergeant major in his new regiment. He was older than most of the other recruits, and his three months' prior service qualified as experience. He also simply looked like a soldier. Physically more robust than the average Civil War infantryman, who stood about five foot seven and weighed 147 pounds, he was large and thick boned and unhurried in his movements.[7] As a devoted niece said of him later, he "possessed the power of silence."[8] His piercing, pale blue-gray eyes had a benign but measuring cast: They seemed to see all, and to see things as they were.

War made sense to George. "I went down to one of their Batteries this afternoon," he wrote after storming the Confederate fortifications at Roanoke Island on February 8, 1862, "and was surprised to see how large and well aranged it was   it was made of turf   the parapet which shields the gunners being about 15 ft thick and 8 or 9 feet high with embrasures to rain the guns out   it mounted 10 guns   2 of them being 32 pound Parrot guns rifled and the others heavy smoothe bore guns."[9] Often he walked a battleground after the fight was over, to comprehend the complex interplay of influences that had led to a discrete outcome. His letters home to his mother—a poorly educated, stay-at-home woman whom Whitman biographers have woefully mischaracterized as ignorant, incurious, and "almost illiterate"[10]—are peppered with military terms of art that George, himself, must only recently have learned. The old mother back in her Brooklyn kitchen understood *everything*—this was the first fact of the Whitman family—Mrs. Whitman's power of understanding—and the reason why George addressed his detailed reflections on military strategy, his confessions of fear, his exaltations in victory, when he and his comrades did "terrible execution" upon the bodies of their enemy, to her.

All to her, and all *through* her. This soldier's letters assumed a strong-minded, unsanctimonious personage as correspondent, someone able to see to the marrow of things. The Victorian "angel in the home," the morally strenuous, socially anxious female paragon subject to fainting spells, was not here being addressed. By the same token, that other remarkable body of letters written by a Whitman son during the Civil War—Walt's—was addressed mainly to her as well, and assumed the same special qualities. The poet's most intimate correspondent for most of his life, until her death in 1873, Mrs. Whitman was his touchstone, his anchor. Her quicksilver intelligence and unostentatious decency made her invaluable as someone to whom he could describe in detail the perturbations of *his* Civil War—which, like his brother's, was physically dangerous, morally disorienting, and deeply thrilling.

Washington   June 30   1863

Dearest Mother,
Your letter with [sister Hannah's] I have sent to George, though whether it will find him or not I cannot tell, as I think the 51st must be away down at Vicksburgh . . . Mother, I have had quite an attack of sore throat & distress in my head for some days past . . . I have been about the city same as usual . . . to the Hospitals, &c . . . I am told that I hover too much over the beds of the hospitals, with fever & putrid wounds, &c. One soldier, brought here about fifteen days ago, very low with typhoid fever, Livingston Brooks, Co B 17th Penn Cavalry, I have particularly stuck to, as I found him in what appeared to be a dying condition . . . I called the doctor's attention to him, shook up the nurses, had him bathed in spirits, gave him lumps of ice . . . he was very quiet, a very sensible boy, old fashioned—he did not want to die.[11]

Whitman has been called a "nurse" to the soldiers. Indeed, like a nurse, he assisted at amputations, changed dressings over gangrenous wounds, and administered medicines. But he insisted on describing himself not as a nurse but as something simpler, a mere "visitor & consolatory," one who brought "soothing invigoration" to the sick and wounded.[12] He arrived on the wards most days toward evening, after working a few hours as a copyist in a Washington office. The clean drawers, tobacco, stamps, crackers, and whatnot to be found in the knapsack of a soldier had a correspondence in the items he pulled out of his capacious coat pockets: horehound candy,

Walt Whitman during his work in the hospitals in Washington. While he dated it 1864, he also identified another photograph from this session "taken from life 1863."

jam, magazines, brandy, lemons, oranges, loose change, jars of rice pudding. Whitman's now famous book, *Memoranda During the War: Written on the Spot in 1863–'65*, had its beginnings in notes he scribbled to himself during his visits to the hospitals, to bring particular gifts to particular men. This one might need a needle and thread, that one a nice ripe peach or a plum.

In the same letter to his mother, he wrote,

> The rule is to remove bad fever patients out from the main wards to a tent by themselves, & the doctor told me [Livingston] would have to be removed. I broke it gently to him, but the poor boy got it immediately in his head that he was marked with death, & was to be removed on that account . . . for three days he lay just about an even chance, go or stay, with a little leaning toward the first—But, mother, to make a long story short, he is now out of any immediate danger—he has been perfectly rational throughout—begins to taste a little food . . . & I will say, whether one calls it pride or not, that if he *does* get up & around again, it's me that saved his life.[13]

Over the course of four years, Whitman made more than six hundred visits to hospitals, tending, he claimed, to "80,000 to 100,000 of the wounded and sick, as sustainer of spirit and body in some degree, in time of need." This extraordinary claim owes a little to poetic inflation—but only a little. He was there; he did what he said. His vocation as healer to the wounded men had deep roots in his character, but the immediate inspiration was familial or, rather, brotherly. Hearing that George had been wounded at the Battle of Fredericksburg (December 13, 1862), Walt rushed south to the scene of that appalling slaughter, finding George pretty much in one piece (a shell fragment had pierced his cheek, rattling his teeth but doing no greater damage). Other soldiers were not faring as well. As the poet wrote to his mother, "One of the first things that met my eyes in camp, was a heap of [severed limbs] under a tree in front [of] a hospital, the Lacy house."[14] In *Memoranda*, he added more detail:

> [It was] a large brick mansion, on the banks of the Rappahannock . . . Seems to have receiv'd only the worst cases. Out doors . . . I

notice . . . amputated feet, legs, arms, hands, &c., a full load for a
one-horse cart . . . In the door-yard, towards the river, are fresh
graves, mostly officers, their names on pieces of barrel-staves or broken board, stuck in the dirt . . . I went through the rooms, downstairs
and up. Some of the men were dying. I had nothing to give at that
visit, but wrote a few letters to folks home, mothers, &c.[15]

The weather has been cold. It is December, after all:

[T]he Camp, Brigade, and Division Hospitals . . . are merely tents,
and sometimes very poor ones, the wounded lying on the ground,
lucky if their blankets are spread on layers of pine . . . No cots; seldom even a mattress . . . The ground is frozen hard, and there is occasional snow. I go around from one case to another. I do not see that
I do much good, but I cannot leave them. Once in a while some
youngster holds on to me convulsively, and I do what I can for him;
at any rate, stop with him and sit near him for hours, if he wishes it.[16]

Walt remained with his brother for nine days, sharing his life in the
rough military camp. When he returned to Washington, on December
28, 1862, he accompanied a party of wounded and sick men being sent
back to other hospitals—the trip, in open railroad cars, then in the open
air on the deck of a government steamer, was brutal. One man died en
route.[17] Whitman went among the thinly clad invalids. "Several wanted
word sent home to parents, brothers, wives, &c., which I did for them,
(by mail the next day from Washington.) On the boat I had my hands
full," he noted tersely.

Living with his brother for that week and two days, Whitman came to
see how raw and bitter was the lot of the ordinary soldier, but also how
vivid, and how full of comradely pleasures. Knowing his mother would
want as much frank detail as he could manage—this was a mother, after
all, who could safely be told about amputated hands in a pile—he described being jammed in a small tent with George and others ("there were
five of us altogether, to eat, sleep, write, &c. in a space twelve feet square,
but we got along very well"). "They have a kind of fire-place, and the
cook's fire is outside, on the open ground. George had very good times
while [his company commander, Captain Henry W.] Francis was away—

the cook, a young disabled soldier, Tom, is an excellent fellow, and a first-rate cook." Young Tom was so devoted to George that, hearing he had been wounded, he rushed onto the battlefield at Fredericksburg—one of the most dire killing fields of the entire war—to try to find him. About George's face wound, Walt told his mother, "You could stick a splint through into the mouth," but not to worry: It had already closed up.[18]

One lasting impression the poet took was of the soldiers' profound need for frequent word from home. "You can have no idea how letters from home cheer one up in camp," he wrote Mrs. Whitman, asking her to order his younger brother, Jeff, to write to George more often, and to enclose a few lines written by other family members when he did so. From the time of the first Battle of Fredericksburg until the end of the war, Whitman wrote to his soldier brother continually, often sending him newspapers from New York and Washington as well, including papers wherein were printed articles that Walt, himself, wrote about the war—articles that sometimes relied for color on George's firsthand accounts in *his* letters.

THE WHITMANS OF Brooklyn were a troubled, brilliant, poor, aspiring, declining, woefully afflicted, remarkably successful clan.
The darkest terrors of the nineteenth century shadowed their hearth.
Madness touched several of their number, and congenital disorders and in-
curable infections harrowed them. Yet some of them did rise and rise. The
second-oldest son, Walter, born 1819, the same year as Melville and two
years after Thoreau, became America's most original poet, author of the
most influential book of poetry in English of the last century and a half,
Leaves of Grass. That kind of anomaly begs explanation, almost: as well
try to explain the eyes of a tiger. But two other brothers, George, born in
1829, and Jeff, in 1833, were also specially gifted, and their accomplishments are likewise hard to explain. Jeff (born Thomas Jefferson Whitman)
received no formal education beyond about age fourteen, yet he competed
successfully with university-educated men and graduates of technical in-
stitutes, to become one of the nineteenth century's great engineers. He
built the Saint Louis waterworks, among other large projects. According
to one longtime colleague, Jeff depended less on "formulae and mathe-
matical deductions" than on an "intuitive mechanical insight" that found
the solution to maddeningly complex problems almost offhandedly.[1]

George was also unusually able—his gift being for war. He seems to
have followed a path ordained by capricious gods, who contrived over
and over to place him in situations of maximum peril, with only his wits
and his nerve to rely on. His behavior in battle led to promotions, and by
the time of his brother's visit to Fredericksburg he had been formally

promoted to captain, placed in charge of Company K, of the 51st New York Infantry. Although his regiment missed Gettysburg, they fought at many other great battles, often in the very thick of legendary passages of combat—on Burnside's Bridge, Antietam, before Marye's Heights at Fredericksburg, in the burning woods at the Wilderness. On March 16, 1865, Walt published an account of his brother's military career in the *Brooklyn Daily Union*—it was one of several articles he wrote about George and the 51st New York:

> Of the officers, in their original position, that went with the regiment, not a single one remains; and not a dozen out over a thousand of the rank and file. Most of his comrades have fallen by death. Wounds, imprisonment, exhaustion, &c., have also done their work . . . For three years and two months he has seen and been part of war waged on a scale of amplitude, with an intensity on both sides, that puts all past campaigning of the world into second class; and has had danger, hardship, and death for his companions by night and by day, in all their Protean forms.[2]

At Spotsylvania (May 10–12, 1864), three of George's men were shot dead by his side, and afterward he found his coat to be "riddled & wrinkled & slit in the most curious manner ever seen"—the result of having been raked by grapeshot (heavy, round shot from an exploding artillery shell).[3] At the Wilderness, five days before, the canteen he wore was shot in half, yet George emerged unharmed from a contest in which Union casualties exceeded seventeen thousand.[4] To his mother he wrote,

> I am all right so far. We had a pretty hard battle on the 6th. I don't know what the battle is called but it was about 5 miles from Germania Ford on the Rapidan River. our Regt. suffered severely loseing 70 in killed and wounded. I lost nearly half of my Co but we won the fight and the rebel loss was pretty heavy . . . there has been fighting going on every day . . . its my opinion that Genl Grant has got Lee in a pretty tight spot.[5]

One of George's fellow officers said of him, "George was just the luckiest man in the American army. Consider what tight skirmishes he has been in." In his *Daily Union* article, Walt reckoned up his brother's battles and tried to put them in some perspective:

> He has been in twenty-one general engagements or sieges, most of them first class of war, and skirmishing, &c., almost beyond count; has sailed the sea in long and severe storms, fought all over the blood-reddened soil of Virginia and Western Maryland, also in the Carolinas, also in Kentucky and Tennessee, also in Mississippi at Vicksburg and Jackson . . . and so to Petersburg and the Weldon road. He has marched across eighteen states . . . has journeyed as a soldier . . . over twenty thousand miles; and has fought under Burnside, McClellan, McDowell, Meade, Pope, Hooker, Sherman and Grant. Such has been the experience, beyond what any romance could tell or narrative comprise, of one of our Brooklyn soldiers.

Brooklyn was the cradle for them all, and out of it they made their way, not endlessly but certainly prolifically. There were nine Whitman children. One died in infancy but the rest survived into adulthood, an accomplishment for any cohort of siblings in that era of hapless doctoring and unchecked epidemics. Beginning in 1832, cholera took many lives in New York in the summer—in 1845, in one of his early published stories, Walt wrote about "God's angels," the men and women who did not flee the city when cholera first made its appearance, but instead "went out amid the diseased, the destitute, and the dying . . . wiping the drops from hot brows, and soothing the agony of cramped limbs."[6]

This sentimental story, called "Revenge and Requital; A Tale of a Murderer Escaped," is a strange foreshadowing of the poet's Civil War work in the hospitals. He wrote about a man who trod "softly from bedside to bedside—with those little offices which are so grateful to the sick . . . Wherever the worst cases of contagion were to be found, he also was to be found. In noisome alleys and foul rear-buildings, in damp cellars and hot garrets, thither he came with food, medicine, gentle words, and gentle smiles."[7] Whitman called this story a "fact-romance," and despite the sappy passages it gives a basically factual picture of parts of New York in the 1840s, when European immigrants, mostly Irish, were pouring into the teeming city. When he spoke of "God's angels" visiting the slums, Whitman may have been remembering visits he himself made: From an early age, he was attracted to the sick and the dying, to the victims of horse-cart smash-ups and shipwrecks, to broken bodies, especially male ones, lying helplessly in bed and needing a tender touch.

Brooklyn was the Whitman homeground. The life of Brooklyn Village (then Town, then City) shaped them, and the period of Whitman residence in Brooklyn was packed with furious change. When the family first arrived, May 1823, Dutch was still often heard on the streets. The old Dutch Church, near the site of modern-day Erasmus Hall High School, recalled the earliest period of settlement, when church fathers back in Amsterdam sent lay functionaries out to the New World trading posts—calling them, Whitmanesquely, "comforters of the sick."[8] A popular guidebook from 1818 speaks of the "narrow, dirty, and disagreeable streets of Brooklyn," a "huddle of taverns, stores, dwellings, and shanties near the [ferry] slip . . . crooked cartways . . . litter . . . odors from stables, tar sheds, tanneries, and slaughterhouses . . . motley throng of blacks . . . sailors, market men, and ragged urchins."[9]

New York streets were said to be the dirtiest in the country. It was because of the hordes of swine that roamed freely, encouraging citizens to toss their garbage in the streets to feed them. The Brooklyn of 1816, with a population of about four thousand, including scores of slaves, had an undeniably rural character. Small landholders, many of them Dutch, carted in produce from farms and kitchen gardens farther east on Long Island, for sale in the local market or across the East River, in Manhattan. Those families that owned land on the edge of, or within, the village proper often prospered mightily, as the local population increase took off: by 1820, to 7,200; by 1830, 15,500; by 1840, greater than 36,000.

The Whitmans moved to Brooklyn from West Hills, Long Island, near Huntington, coming from a background of long family catastrophe. The father, Walter Sr., born 1789, financed the move to the city by selling remnants of what had once been a considerable Whitman holding in fertile, well-watered farmland, the highest on Long Island. Whitmans had been a notable presence in the West Hills area since the 1650s. They had established themselves socially, and when Walt, in 1881, returned for a visit to the region, he noted more than fifty Whitman graves on the family burial site. But from being prosperous, acknowledged landowners they had declined over the course of generations, and by the time of the move to Brooklyn they were subsistence farmers—indeed, failed subsistence farmers.

Walter Sr., whose character has been the subject of much speculation among scholars, apprenticed himself in his youth to an older cousin, Jacob, a carpenter. Jacob Whitman had a workshop in New York City. For at least three years, young Walter lived in a boardinghouse in Manhattan, on his own in a way that might have seemed scandalously liberated to previous generations of Protestant landowning people. His older cousin made an able carpenter of him, but it can be doubted whether Jacob, who was the foreman of a shop that made venetian blinds, provided a moral example of the most stringent sort—he was an unconventional man who, when the owner of the blinds business died, opportunely married the widow, and when *she* died, married one of her daughters.

"[A]nd by her had quite a brood of children," Walt Whitman, who made meticulous notes about his ancestors, recorded some fifty years later.[10] This period of his father's youth, when he was living on his own in sometimes riotous New York, predicted and may have given license to the poet's own unsupervised years of apprenticeship, when he, too, lived on his own in New York boardinghouses, one of the thousands of nearly anonymous young men separated from their families and tasting the distractions of the city. The Manhattan of Walter Sr.'s youth partook of a certain atmosphere of loose living, by American standards: Following the Revolution, some of the constraints that had bound colonial society tight were relaxed, and Brooklyn, like Manhattan, was awash in grogshops, taverns, and groceries that sold liquor to children as well as adults. Hard public drinking was a feature of everyday behavior, not just Fourth of July celebrations, and even the Sabbath was not proof against noisy street scenes of a dissolute tone.[11]

Very soon this period of relative laxity would provoke a stern reaction: the Second Great Awakening of the 1820s and '30s, with its militant revivalism; its temperance campaigns; its social activism on many fronts, most notably, abolition. But Walter Sr. as a young man had taken on the coloration of the loosening, postrevolutionary moment. In his beliefs he was radical, being an acquaintance of Tom Paine and an ardent admirer of *The Age of Reason* and other iconoclastic, anticlerical works. George Whitman would later say of him, "Father did not go to church at all . . . There were, of course, no religious exercises or observances in the family at all."[12] Mrs. Whitman was slightly more of a churchgoer, it appears: "She went almost anywhere," George said, and, when the mood took her, "she pretended to be a Baptist." But the father born on the very day of the storming of the Bastille—July 14, 1789—bequeathed to his sons and daughters a certain radical élan.

As a master carpenter, probably a good one, Walter Sr. seemed poised to benefit from a period of expansion, with the building of hundreds, then thousands, of small, mostly white-painted frame houses on Brooklyn's unpaved streets. But in this expectation he had made a grievous error. The fifty years of Whitman residence in Brooklyn (1823–72, with a period during which they returned briefly to West Hills) were the ruination of New York's artisan class. Carpenters, tailors, shoemakers, printers, and all that group commonly referred to as "mechanics" suffered a bitter erosion of hopes and status. Wage labor in dynamic capitalist enterprises replaced independent craftwork, as the same immense swelling of population that was increasing demand for new furniture and shoes also flooded the labor market with skilled foreigners and rural Americans eager to work for rock-bottom wages.

Real wages fell for artisans in New York in the 1830s and '40s.[13] By the early 1850s, the average annual income for a skilled tradesman was about $300, while minimum living costs for an average family were over $500, and probably close to $600.[14] Families adapted by taking in piecework, apprenticing their children, and renting out spare rooms or floors. The Whitmans resorted to all these semidesperate shifts and probably to some others. In a photograph of Walter Sr. from about 1850, taken by F. Gutekunst, of Philadelphia, it may be possible to discern the effects of a lifetime of toil at a trade practiced under steadily eroding conditions, with one's pride on the line in the relentless struggle to feed a growing family. Reading character from a face is always an exercise in the higher conjecture—but this is quite a face. Some Whitman experts have argued that Walter Sr. was a cruel man, given to frequent rages and punishing silences. Almost the only evidence for such a guess comes from some early Whitman stories and from two famous lines in *Leaves of Grass*, in the poem called "There Was a Child Went Forth":

The father, strong, selfsufficient, manly, mean, angered, unjust,
The blow, the quick loud word, the tight bargain, the crafty lure

Walter Whitman Sr., about 1850.

This follows a description, in a very different key, of the woman of the house, Mrs. Whitman perhaps:

The mother at home quietly placing the dishes on the suppertable,
The mother with mild words....clean her cap and gown....a
    wholesome odor falling off her person and clothes as she walks by

George Whitman, in later years, said that Walt's relations with their father were "always friendly, always good." And Walt wrote about his father now and then in his journals, always with respect and quiet sympathy. In one notebook kept during the war, he mused about those early apprentice years, when Walter Sr. had boarded "steady for 3 years in New York in one place. He then went up around the Hills, and South, Long Island, and took contracts at building. He was a first-rate carpenter, did solid, substantial, conscientious work. I have heard mother say that he would sometimes lay awake all night planning out some unusually difficult plan in his building arrangements."[15]

This lying-awake calls to mind Walter Sr.'s second-youngest son Jeff's solving devilish problems in hydrodynamics in his head. Those building arrangements included plans for lifting the family out of poverty, back into the class of propertied folk from which they had come, by the common strategy of building residential houses on spec. A year and three months after their arrival in Brooklyn, Walter Sr. bought a small lot on the southeast corner of Washington and Johnson streets for $250, his aim being to erect a freestanding house upon it. Occupied by the Whitmans in May 1825, this no doubt modest, wood-frame, open-lot house was the family's third Brooklyn dwelling in only two years, the others being rentals. Walter Sr. bought the lot from an Evan M. Johnson, a minister, and his wife, Maria.[16] But following the purchase and the building there came an experience typical of the senior Whitman's attempts to build and sell: "[My] straightforward father was nearly swindled out of his boots," Walt later declared.

Of the house on Johnson Street, and another built soon after, "We occupied them, one after the other," Walt wrote, "but they were mortgaged, and we lost them."[17] In about ten years, the family lived in at least seven different places. By 1830 there were six children in the family (Jesse, the firstborn, Walt, Mary Elizabeth, Hannah, Andrew, and George). Frequent moves to new houses were probably made easier by having few belongings to transport. A new house might look or smell better (privies were in the backyard), might be roomier (but not by much), might have a new coat of paint or be located on a quieter street, or among more genteel-seeming neighbors; a family in which the principal breadwinner was in the building trade can be expected to have been attuned to slight advantages in circumstances and inclined to act on

Catharine Market, Brooklyn, New York, 1850.

them. But the father's schemes for building, occupying, then selling mostly drove their restlessness, and if they were rising economically throughout this period, that rise is hard to make out.

In these years, the ferries that ran between Brooklyn and Manhattan were converted to steam, thus increasing Brooklyn's ease of access and its desirability. Many streets of the town were still like country lanes, and although most were bare and dusty in dry weather, some were shaded by tall elms and willows. As it approached the year of its incorporation, 1834, Brooklyn took on a prosperous, moderately citified character. Still hugely dwarfed by Manhattan, which had become America's industrial as well as its commercial capital, Brooklyn had a robust manufacturing district of its own, busy shipyards, a neighborhood for the "quality" (Brooklyn Heights), and population numbers that put it among the twenty biggest cities in the country.

How Walter Sr. failed to grow well off, or just better off, during this boom in Brooklyn housing is a puzzle. A whole class of speculators,

builders, lawyers, insurers, and bankers had come into existence to exploit the opportunities, and despite brief depressions (1825–26, 1829)
and the much deeper economic dislocation of the panic of 1837, the
trend was strongly up. Those able to make small or large fortunes often
began with advantages, access to capital being the most important. Mr.
Whitman was disadvantaged by the thinness of his wallet and by meager
goods to offer as collateral, although the idea that he arrived in Brooklyn
owning nothing, having sold off all the ancestral lands, is wrong: In
1838, he and Mrs. Whitman signed a mortgage offering a "dwelling
house and tract of land situated in Huntington S. on the Neck of land" in
exchange for $600.[18] The tract was sizable, over forty-seven acres. Quite
probably it came from Mrs. Whitman's parents, the Van Velsors (a
clause added by the county clerk noted that he had interviewed the wife
and found her to be under no "fear or compulsion" from her husband).

To imagine that Walter Sr. failed because he was an alcoholic whose
drinking disabled him, as some Whitman scholars do, is unnecessary.
Probably he drank strong spirits, as workmen those days were expected
to—the theory being that drink fortified the body for hard physical
tasks—but an undercapitalized builder-owner, with a large, hungry
family, forced to live for periods in the houses he built, who from all his
extant property transfers appears never to have taken on a partner, thus
to spread the risk of speculative construction, had many ways to fail. A
better way to think of his business career is as a small success. By 1835
there were eight children, the last, Edward, born crippled and not right
in the head. None of them starved. None went without clothing or books
or some schooling. One even received a fashionable private education—
not the poet-to-be, and not George or Jeff, but one of their sisters, the
lovely, literary, sensitive, gray-eyed Hannah. There was always a house
to shelter in. Walt, when he became that poet, recorded for posterity's
sake all their various changes of address ("Front st . . . to Cranberry
st . . . Johnson St . . . Van Dyke's . . . to Adams St . . . to Tillary corner
Washington," and so forth), and although he noted trouble with some
creditors and neighbors, these changes are not a litany of suffering and
dislocation. The family was always *at home*, no matter the address, or
addresses.

Like other large families, the Whitmans achieved a certain critical
mass, and the evolving human oddity of it all captivated them, warmed

them for life. George writing letters home from the war, begging for news out of that Brooklyn kitchen; Jeff, aged fourteen, writing from New Orleans (where he worked as an office boy for Walt, who was briefly the editor of the *New Orleans Daily Crescent*) and confessing to an almost unbearable homesickness ("Do write to us, Father, even half a sheet . . . I go to the post office every day");[19] Walt in his faithful correspondence sending small gifts to everyone, always sending his mother the odd dollar, shouldering the care of his helpless brother Eddy when their mother passed away—these are not proofs of a cozy, picture-book home life overflowing with fun and good cheer, but they suggest something sustaining.

It was an era when many Americans forgot family—when they disappeared, in city as well as country. Long before the gold rush drew thousands to California, Americans in large numbers were migrating and losing touch, taking on the status of industrial wage-workers in cities that swarmed with refugees from villages and farms. A new class of clerks, earning money of their own and often far away from parents and other controlling figures, helped create a different sort of critical mass, of the engulfing and liberating urban crowd, in which they might lose and reinvent themselves.[20] But none of the Whitman children disappeared. Even the most troubled among them—and those were *very* troubled—did not vanish out west, or at sea.

Walter Sr. might himself have disappeared into that class of fallen craftsmen that was a feature of the period, skilled men forced to travel seasonally for menial work. He did travel, to take on construction jobs, but he was not, for instance, plowing pastures in Ohio for a farmer and mailing his wages home. He was mostly *present* in that home. What slight evidence exists suggests that he was sometimes a fond figure who discussed matters of interest with his children; for example, when Jeff, as an office boy, wrote home from Louisiana, he said, "Father, you wanted me to ask how much carpenter's wages were here. I am told they are from forty to fifty dollars a month and found [room and board], which I think is a pretty good sum, but every thing is so much here that you hardly know whether you get a good bargain or not."[21]

Describing a scary boat trip down the Ohio River, Jeff added, "Father can judge how fast we went, when I tell him it is a fall of twenty feet, within a space of three miles . . . It happened we got off with a little bump on each rock . . . The fun of the whole thing was, the *fright* we all had, some of the passengers . . . looking as gloomy as if they were going to be hung."[22]

Walt recalled being taken by his father to hear a famous religious speaker: "I can remember [Father] coming home toward sunset from his day's work as a carpenter, and saying briefly, as he throws down his armful of kindling-blocks with a bounce on the kitchen floor, 'Come, mother, Elias [Hicks, the radical Quaker] preaches tonight.' Then my mother . . . puts the two little ones to bed—and as I had been behaving well that day, as a special reward I was allow'd to go also."[23]

Walter Sr. did not abandon these children—not that that is a great accomplishment, but some other men might have. As a working-class American breadwinner in the 1820s, '30s, and '40s, his fortunes were typically, and radically, unstable; as with most such men and women, bankruptcy was always close, and the wages they earned as craftspeople were hardly higher than those paid to sewer diggers.[24] His buying of lots and building of houses, in addition to his regular carpenter's daywork, ruined him physically by his fifties, but he had bought time and scope for the family. In the next generation, some of his offspring would be healthy and hopeful enough to ascend into the class of the "middling sorts," the people who worked not for wages but for salaries, who acquired property and sometimes even managed to keep hold of it. They would join the "most valuable class in any community," as Walt Whitman said in a newspaper editorial in 1858: "the men of moderate means."[25]

So POTENT WAS the dream of building houses and making a tidy little fortune thereby that at least two of Walter Sr.'s sons spent years at it. George, when he returned from the Civil War, took on a partner and sank all of his resources, and more, into speculative building schemes that nearly ruined him. (But only nearly—he found a way to cheat disaster here, as on the battlefield.) And Walt, in the most mysterious and crucial period of his poetic life—when he was incubating the first, 1855, edition of *Leaves of Grass,* that outrageously sexualized, narcissistic, free-versifying little book, the "barbaric yawp" that caught the ear and stunned the eye of Emerson, no less, then of all the world—was a busy builder of houses.

"I Built the place 106 Myrtle av.," Walt wrote in one of his notebooks, "in winter of 1848-9, and moved in, latter part of April '49 . . . I Sold the Myrtle av. House in May, '52, and built in Cumberland street, where we moved Sept. 1st, '52." He continued, "Sold the two 3 story houses in Cumberland st. March 1853. moved into the little 2 story house Cumberland st. April 21st, '53 (lived there just one year exactly) . . . Built in Skillman st. and moved there May, 1854 . . . Moved in Ryerson st, May 1855.—lived in Classon from may 1st '56, '7 '8 '9."[1]

Like his father, Walt took tools in hand and did what came naturally, building houses that he planned to sell but that meanwhile the family could shelter in. Before he built at 106 Myrtle, he took over ownership of a property belonging to his parents, paying them $1,360.[2] Walt had been working since age eleven. He had been an office boy for some lawyers on

Fulton Street; the same for a doctor on the same street; the same for a printer, Samuel E. Clements, who edited a newspaper, the *Long Island Patriot*, in which Walt at age twelve or so published his first lines of prose.[3] When Clements fell into disgrace, after digging up the body of the recently dead Elias Hicks, the aim being to make a death mask and turn it into a salable sculpture, Walt went to work for other printers, learning the craft thoroughly at a time of great excitement and change in the profession. During these antebellum years, stereotyping replaced traditional compositor's work, yielding much faster press runs, but the introduction of steam-powered presses also caused thousands of printers to be thrown out of work.[4]

Like his father, who lived though an era of steady degrading of his craft, both in terms of wages offered and the nature of the work itself (house building being divided into many smaller, repetitive tasks, which were then subcontracted), Walt learned the fascinating and arcane craft of making printed text as it was becoming untenable as an independent occupation. Both men must have had, at times, a slipping-through-the-fingers feeling. Great opportunity was all around, and yet they could not seize it. The father never escaped his dilemma, but the son had learned a craft that also had a shadow side—printers often being writers or editors, and writing for publication being a craft not so readily undermined by technological progress.

It helped Walt, the son of a large, economically vulnerable family, that the society of his youth was print mad, that more newspapers and journals and books were offered for sale in America before the Civil War than in any other country in the world. Whitman would become a poet of economic vitality—a singer of hymns to work, of praise for blacksmiths, loggers, sailors, butchers, cart drivers, and cabinetmakers. As a self-anointed poet of democracy, he would argue for the dignity and meaning of ordinary American labor (and especially picturesque men's craftwork, the kind becoming obsolete even as he wrote about it). Such a focus is hard to conceive of in an era of overall economic stagnation or decline. America was booming—harshly, unevenly, cruelly booming—and although the Whitman family knew fear and deprivation, the overall thrust of things was clear.

The problem for the family was how to attach to this boom. What modes of work would provide health, prosperity, interest, a return (conceivably) to the ownership of substantial real property? The generation of Walter Sr.'s children faced this question more or less consciously, and more or less worked out a successful strategy. Walt's experience was the most varied, the most colorful, and although he became a great poet and therefore not very like anybody else, his upward struggle typified that of an entire class of Americans. He began by leaving school early (Brooklyn's District School No. 1, which was attended mostly by the children of paupers and free blacks).[5] He became a skilled artisan in time to feel the earth shift under his feet, as artisanship was devalued. By age sixteen, he had just about earned his journeyman printer's credential, and he had published a number of newspaper articles, including at least one in the *New York Mirror*, an important Manhattan daily.[6] But he had not secured a future.

He was a tall, good-looking young man, with pale blue eyes and an unhurried air. He was thoughtful—as George recalled, "His opinion was not only asked by the family, even when he was quite young, but by neighbors. We all deferred to his judgment—looked up to him."[7] In 1834, the family returned to Long Island, possibly for financial reasons but possibly because of a nervous breakdown or other illness suffered by Mrs. Whitman, who would soon give birth to her last, and severely disabled, child.[8] Walt stayed on in New York. Now he lived his own version of his father's apprentice years. He often went to the theater, "sometimes witnessing fine performances," as he wrote in *Specimen Days*, his autobiographical collection. He was on his own, and he encountered the hurly-burly of the Bowery and lower Broadway, where a sexual demimonde would soon draw the attention of newspapers with names such as the *Whip* and the *Rake*, which in the early 1840s attracted readers with lurid attacks on a supposed class of "sodomites" that preyed on innocent American boys.[9]

The years of Walt's late apprenticeship, 1833 to '36, were years of inflation in New York, of strikes and workers' riots. In 1834, an eight-day disturbance wrecked the home of a prominent financier, Lewis Tappan, and led to a rampage in the Bowery Theatre, where an English actor, George Farren, was appearing, annoying the audience with his effete foreign manner.[10] Walt knew this theater well. The realm of lower-class amusements, of crude sideshows, semilegal prostitution, and raucous "fire laddies" (volunteer firemen) was familiar to him, was at least partly *his* realm. Yet he was also, in this period, a "most omnivorous novel-reader" who "devour'd everything I could get," and he belonged to a number of formal debating societies—evenings of ordered debate being not the usual diversion favored by most Manhattan street-toughs.[11]

Where Walt stood class-wise had everything to do with how he saw himself, with his half-formed aspirations, with who his father was. A follower of the fiery Paine, a devotee of the atheistic, semisocialist radical reformer Frances Wright, Walter Sr. brought a stance of political defiance to the family circle—and of all his sons, Walt took on this legacy with the most energy. But the life of a worker in the industrializing city was a life subject to grave uncertainties, especially in this period. When a colossal fire destroyed fifty acres of commercial Manhattan in December 1835, hundreds of businesses failed, putting thousands out of work. The print industry had been hard hit by an earlier fire, and Walt, in early 1836, was forced to leave the city, to take up work as a country schoolteacher.

In the next six years he taught at eight village schools, often boarding with the parents of his pupils. The temper of these postings can perhaps be gauged from this description, written by another teacher, who worked at Smithtown, Long Island, a few years before Walt:

Preparations for supper—a tablecloth probably once washed . . . on which appeared a bone of beef, parts of a hogs head . . . Supper done, set down to the fireplace to read . . . Began to feel cold—looked at the fire—very little to be seen . . . half past seven thought would go to bed to keep warm . . . lay awhile—could not get warm—felt to see if the blankets were damp—could not tell.[12]

The schools themselves were primitive, one-room affairs, cheaply built (the one at Smithtown cost $110). The pupils sat on rough wooden slabs on three sides of the room, facing the walls. For a five-month session, in charge of upward of eighty students, Walt earned $72.20 in 1837 to '38—school met every day but Sunday (alternate Saturday afternoons also off), with no holiday at Christmas or New Year's. In winter, the students sometimes suffered from the cold—there was a fireplace but often the room was icy, and students begged permission to stand close to the fire, to warm up.

Walt's contemporaries Melville and Thoreau were also schoolteach-
ers in these years, also beset, fellow refugees from the economic down-
turn that preceded and followed the 1837 bank panic. Only seventeen
years old when he began in the schools, Walt might have gone to work
for his father instead, who was living then in Babylon, in southwest
Long Island, with the rest of the family, supporting them by subsistence
farming and odd-job carpentry, as well as by mortgaging Mrs. Whitman's real estate. But Walt was already beyond such labor. He had never
cared for farmwork, and he had forged a certain independence as a New
York apprentice, and so soon a return to the family fold might have been
an unhappy prospect. There may also have been some satisfaction in
having qualified as a teacher, for a youth with only four years of class-
room schooling himself. In the earliest extant letters he ever wrote, his
new worldliness strains to make itself felt, as does his New York remove
from his rustic surroundings:

I feel but little in the humour for writing any thing that will have the
stamp of cheerfulness.—Perhaps it would be best therefore not to
write at all, and I don't think I should, were it not for the hope of getting a reply.—I believe when the Lord created the world, he used up
all the good stuff, and was forced to form Woodbury [one of his
postings] . . . out of the fag ends, the scraps and refuse: for a more
unsophisticated race than lives hereabouts you will seldom meet
with.[13]

His correspondent, Abraham Paul Leech, of nearby Jamaica, Queens
County, presumably shared Walt's amusement at his surroundings:

Why the dickins did n't you come out to the whig meeting at the
court house, last Saturday week? . . . I daresay you would have been
much . . . astonished, for the orator of the day related facts, and cut
capers, which certainly never before met the eye or ear of civilized
man . . . Were you ever tried?—I don't mean tried before Squire
Searing or Judge Strong for breach of promise . . . but tried as they
try mutton fat, to make candles of—boiled down—melted into liq-
uid grease? . . . I have.—The scene was "Huckleberry plains," the
day Friday last . . . It was what the ladies and gentlemen of this truly

refined place call a party of *pleasure.*—Yes; it was delightful; fun to the back-bone.[14]

Even as he asserted his distance from them, Walt formed ties with the local gentry. In Smithtown, a farm village on the North Shore (citizen pop. 1,580, plus 4 paupers, 238 persons of color, and 7,000 head of cattle), Walt joined a local debating society, soon becoming its secretary.[15] He thus associated on terms of rough equality with the most prominent local citizens, among them judges, a congressman, physicians, justices of the peace, and a member of the New York legislature.[16] These social elements, no doubt Whiggish in their politics, some of them, would have been politically uncongenial to a son of Walter Whitman Sr., the radical democrat, but they were welcome as intellectual companions among whom to pass the often long, creeping hours.

At age eighteen, Walt's entrée into their society was a question mainly of intellect and comfort around the printed word. The fluidity of status enjoyed by a young white man who could read, write, and express himself in educated-sounding terms—let alone write letters that strained for the weary wit of Lord Chesterfield's *Letters to His Son*, which Walt had recently read—was definingly American. Rural Long Island society was not so rigid with marks and forms of class as to be impregnable, or even very formidable. Smithtown, in fact, was a scene of some economic dynamism—it was a hearty town with grist mills, textile makers, a sheep-shearing pool, and bountiful orchards. Surrounded by forest, it supported sawmills and sent lumber by sloop to New York City. There were rich shellfish beds nearby, and a clamming industry (one visitor complained, though, of the "fetor" of decaying fish used as fertilizer on the local farms).[17]

In the spring after his five-month term, Walt moved from Smithtown to Huntington, near West Hills—just short of his twentieth birthday, he declared himself the editor of a new newspaper, the *Long-Islander*, which he would write and print. An irregular weekly, the *Long-Islander* was successful in a modest way. The image of the future poet as dreamy loafer lying flat on his back looking up at the stars, or counting apple blossoms, first began to get established in these years, but what would actually mark his behavior now and at all stages of his professional life was efficient, varied, resourceful effort leading to financial success to some degree, over some

period of time. The paper, founded in an economic depression, with Walt
no doubt writing all or almost all the copy, and delivering issues to outly-
ing villages on horseback, lasted with him as editor for more than a
year—and then lasted, under many other editors, for the next 170.[18]

He only *seemed* lazy. He was lumbering and large, he spoke deliberately and was never particularly quick witted, and he did sometimes lie
out under a tree for a couple of hours when he was supposed to be at

*Walt Whitman as a young newspaper writer and editor. This print, from a lost
daguerreotype, may date from as early as 1840.*

work (or so complained the wife of his next employer, James J. Brenton, editor of the *Long Island Democrat*, where Walt worked after the *Long-Islander*).[19] But he took on large jobs of work and usually completed them. No doubt he had noted the mortgaging of his mother's property in January 1838. This property, in the very town where he established his newspaper, was probably lost (if not, no record remains of Whitmans later living on it, selling it, or passing it on to descendants). The economic plight of someone like his father, who was also a hard worker, but one bound within the possibilities of a defined social class, needed no more demonstrations.

In May 1841, Walt returned to New York City and began a meteoric rise as a journalist. He had been scribbling poetry and prose while in his teaching posts, and the *Long-Islander* had accustomed him to regular written work, as had his job at the *Democrat*. But now he became a professional. The details of his rise are curious and impressive, but most notable perhaps is his simple confidence, his stout belief in his own prospects, in his own *suitability* for such progress. New York journalism was a world, and New York journalists were a class, in no way beyond him. The straitened economics of the Whitman family did not disqualify him, nor did its obscurity. The early 1840s were a booming heyday of the one- and two-penny press in New York, with a class of noisy, aggressive, sensationalist editors inventing and discovering the possibilities of mass journalism. First as a printer, but almost immediately as a writer also, Walt found a paying niche among them. As a typesetter—a craftsman, a skilled handworker again, if only briefly—he gave a solid foundation to his economic enterprise: Printers were then in dependable demand in a way that even well-known writers were not.[20]

The combination of physical labor at a craft, leading to membership in a white-collar profession, became a Whitman family hallmark. Both George, the Civil War soldier, and Jeff, the engineer, were professionals in later years who began as laborers and who retained a fondness all their lives for rolling up their sleeves and getting dirty. George was a cabinetmaker, no doubt schooled by his father. After the war, he became a contractor and then a pipe inspector for Camden, New Jersey, and other East Coast cities, certifying foundry work for the sort of hydrological installations that his brother Jeff designed. Jeff had begun as a surveyor's apprentice (after work as a printer's devil). Like George, he found a way into the salaried middle class and made a large success, yet he enjoyed going down into the bowels of the Saint Louis waterworks, the most advanced system in North America at the time of its construction, to sense and gauge the enormous forces he had put under control.

Neither was a man entirely content with abstraction. They might have become clerks or storekeepers, thus achieving roughly the same rise in status, but they preferred working to physical exhaustion on occasion. (We know this from letters written by wives and other female relatives, worrying about their physical state.) Their older brother, the supposed loafer, who would one day become the poet of work, specifically skilled physical work, taught them by example. In his own negotiation of the assaultive, but promising, changes for working people of their era, he showed them a way through, one that yoked the force and dignity of their "hickory-souled father" to the complicated future.[21]

W ALT LIVED AT Mrs. Chipman's boardinghouse when he made his way back to New York in May 1841.[1] He was on his own again, set free in a riotous, sexually charged Manhattan whose engulfing life must have had an effect on him not unlike that of modern-day New York on a contemporary twenty-one-year-old.

The Bowery Theatre, where he had seen "fine performances" in the 1830s, was a scene of Rabelaisian energy and color. The large, gaslit house, with seats for three thousand, was closer in spirit to the theaters of Renaissance London than to today's stage venues. The house lights never went down at the Bowery. People of all classes, many dressed to the nines, mingled and displayed themselves, roaming the aisles during performances and in general creating a spectacle that sometimes rivaled the one onstage.[2]

In the lowest level of seats, the pit, women were excluded. Walt favored the hurly-burly fellowship of these ground-level spots. In the next tier up, the box seats, women were permitted to sit if accompanied by men. Higher up still, in the colorful third tier, unaccompanied prostitutes gathered in large numbers, to enjoy the show while making assignations for later in the evening. In the Bowery and also at the slightly more starchy Park Theatre, near City Hall, the thriving Manhattan sex trade received a kind of semiofficial blessing. Although required to enter the building by special doors, and to keep clear of the lobby unless accompanied, "women of the town" were free of police harassment, and they were actively welcomed by theater managers, who reasoned that their presence would swell the numbers of unattached men.[3]

In 1834 or '35, Walt had seen a performance at the Bowery that he would remember all his life. Sitting in the pit, in a seat "pretty well front," as he later wrote, he saw the elder Booth (Junius Brutus) in *Richard III*, acting with such "electric personal idiosyncrasy" that the packed audience was moved to a kind of ecstasy. The "alert, well dress'd, full-blooded young and middle-aged men" plus assorted women were held in "an indescribable, half-delicious, half-irritating suspense" until moved to erupt in "one of those long-kept-up tempests of hand-clapping peculiar to the Bowery." This was mesmerizing tragedy, "one of the most marvelous pieces of histrionism ever known." The applause was "no dainty kid-glove business," either, "but electric force and muscle from perhaps 2000 full-sinew'd men."[4]

By the early 1840s, such performances were rare. "Cheap prices and vulgar programmes came in," Walt wrote, and "people who of after years saw the pandemonium of the pit and the doings on the boards must not gauge by them" what had been seen only six years before. The audience was not any worse educated in 1841. There were still unrefined workingmen, "young ship-builders, cartmen, butchers, firemen," but now their ability to attend, to concentrate, seemed less. Or maybe the change was not in "the best average of American-born mechanics," as Walt characterized the bulk of the audience, but in what the cultural market was fashioning as entertainment.[5]

In the world of print, the world of his day job, competition was harsh among the dozens of one-, two-, and six-penny New York papers. Back in 1836, when he had been about to leave New York to teach, the sensational story of the murder of Helen Jewett, a high-class prostitute, broke, leading to a mad scramble to publish the most salaciously detailed accounts. James Gordon Bennett, editor of the *New York Herald*, dominated that particular press frenzy, and in 1841 Walt went to work for Bennett's enemy, the churlish Park Benjamin, editor of the *Evening Signal* and the weekly *New World*. Benjamin enjoyed a healthy secondary revenue stream via the pirating of new books by British writers, which were rushed across the Atlantic by steamship and set up in cheap editions overnight.[6] Walt thus went to work in the busiest print shop in New York, under one of the most aggressive publishers.

Six months later, his poetry began appearing in Benjamin's *New World*, a semiliterary journal. Walt's short stories had already been appearing in the *United States and Democratic Review*, the era's most prestigious publication. He was all of twenty-two. Hawthorne contributed to the *Democratic Review*, as did Poe, William Cullen Bryant, and John Greenleaf Whittier. (Emerson and Thoreau would contribute in later years.) Even more remarkable, in March 1842, Walt was named editor of a six-day-a-week paper owned by a group of experienced press entrepreneurs, the *Aurora*, which specialized in society reporting and accounts of murder trials.[7] He lasted as editor only about a month, but from the first day he fit the mold of the newspaperman—his writing shows an easy command of the arch, moralizing, local-color-loving style of other editors of the hour, and in appearance he was suddenly a man of some fashion, given to strolling down Broadway carrying a cane, dressed in a gray frock coat and a hat ("a plain, neat . . . one, from Banta's, 130 Chatham street"), with a flower in his buttonhole.[8]

Someone his age could only be pretending, yet the pretense was convincing and in some ways authentic. It bespoke years of preparation, of self-education through polymathic reading; an intense effort of imagining himself to be this particular thing, a literary man; and, again, a certain confidence of belonging. Just before taking over the *Aurora*, he published in its pages an attack on Park Benjamin, his former boss, that in style and temper was like the attacks that other New York editors were always making on each other, calling him a bamboozler, a "witless ape," a man of "impudence, conceit, and brazen assumption . . . who has, by some mistake, gained admittance into the society of decent and fashionable people."[9] Walt may have been thinking of himself when he accused Benjamin of jumping up in class, just as, a few months later, he may have been when he turned against the *Aurora*'s owners (now no longer his bosses), calling them "dirty fellows . . . able by the force of brass . . . and a coarse manner of familiarity, to push themselves among gentlemen."[10]

While at the *Aurora*, Walt cultivated a personal style heavy on nonchalance. He came to the office late, usually between eleven A.M. and noon, and then would set off down Broadway toward the Battery, "spending an hour or two amid the trees and enjoying the water view," a young printer in the office remembered, "returning . . . about 2 or 3 o'clock," after having had lunch at his boardinghouse. The *Aurora*'s owners

accused Whitman of being an outrageous loafer, saying in their pages
near the time of his departure, "There is a man about our office so lazy
that it takes two men to open his jaws when he speaks . . . *What* can be
done with him?"[11] But during Walt's time as freelancer and editor, the
paper appeared as scheduled, and it was stuffed full of articles he
wrote—over 180, plus some poetry.[12]

Whitman's journalistic career, which was to last another thirty years,
eventually involved a great deal of hackwork. But in this period of first
trying on the garb, and the attitudes, of a genuine Manhattan editor,
there was a kind of freshness, and many of his pieces remain vivid and
persuasive today. The daily strolls along Broadway were for self-
display, but they were also purposeful—something about the brash,
booming, gaudy city awoke his spirit, and the impressions he gathered as
he ambled downtown gave him urgent ideas.

On April 6, 1842, he reported on a walk taken the day before:

> Strangely enough, nobody stared at us with admiration—nobody
> said "there goes *the* Whitman, of Aurora!"—nobody ran after us to
> take a better . . . look—no beautiful ladies turned their beautiful
> necks and smiled . . . no apple women became pale with awe—no
> news boys stopped, and trembled . . .

Loving the "intoxicating sweetness" of the April day, he comes upon a
children's game in the park,

> some kind of a game which required that they should take each oth-
> ers' hand and spread themselves . . . to make a large ring. When we
> came up, they were just in the crisis of their game, and occupying
> clear across the walk. "Ah!" said one . . . , "we shall have to break
> the line. There comes a gentleman."

But the boy gives Walt "an arch confiding" look, as if he sees right through
him, and Walt himself steps aside.

Not long out of childhood himself, Walt sees in children

> all the freshness, the alertness of nature—the dew, the bloom upon
> them, as it were—how fond we have been of the mischief loving lit-

tle creatures! They are fresh from the hands of Him whose architecture is always perfect until desecrated by the conduct of the world.[13]

Declining into conventional sentiment, he soon goes all the way:

And the *death* of children—why do we never associate it with anything terrible and ghastly—as we do with the death of grown people? Perhaps it is that in the latter case we know . . . there was doubtless much guilt committed, either in disposition or in actual performance . . . While in the other instance, the very extremest wrongs ever done by the dead child, were but airy follies.[14]

Unlike when he was older, Whitman was then conventionally pious. When a deaf child asks him to explain a religious engraving, Walt does so:

[H]e came running in with a picture he had just found . . . which baffled him to comprehend. It was the crucifixion of Christ and the thieves. His head bound with thorns and leaning from the weight of his awful misery . . . the Man of Grief still bore upon his features the impress of a mighty and unconquerable . . . mind . . . We explained the scene as well as we could . . . that wicked men had seized on the person of the holy Teacher . . . that when the orb of day thrice crossed its circuit, the body of the murdered Nazarene [would] burst the cerements of the grave, and, throwing aside the bonds of death and decay, [rise] to life and glory.[15]

No doubt Whitman was writing things he expected would win favor with the audience the *Aurora* hoped to attract. His career as newspaperman would include stints as editor of several papers (most notably, the *Brooklyn Daily Eagle*, 1846–47), stints that usually ended with an angry debate over content, Walt refusing to trim his sails to suit the political or other beliefs of a paper's owners. So it seems unlikely that this fervent, indeed reverent, expression of Christological belief was entirely put on. In probably his most remarkable writing for the *Aurora*, he tackled another religious subject. Called "A Peep at the Israelites" (and continued for a second day under the title "Doings at the Synagogue"), it offers an account of Sabbath services at an Orthodox house of worship on Crosby Street. Walt takes a man-from-Mars approach, reporting exactly what he sees and hears, strange as it may seem to his mostly Christian readers. The result is an invaluable bit of religious ethnography, nearly unique in early nineteenth-century America:

> The congregation (we don't know what other word to use) were all standing, each one with his hat on. A white silken mantle, somewhat like a scarf, was worn . . . it encircled the neck, falling down the back, and the ends in front reaching to the floor. In the middle of the room was a raised platform about four yards square [upon which] was a figure which, by the voice coming from it, we knew to be a man. None of the lineaments of the human form, however, were visible; for one of the large silk mantles . . . was thrown over his head.[16]

The Jews go up to a kind of cabinet made of paneled wood, "which from the ornaments and expensive tracery . . . seemed intended to contain something . . . very valuable." He notes that

> the priest then raised aloft a large scroll of parchment . . . wafting it around so that the people could see it in all parts of the house. All this while he uttered a kind of chant . . . The main floor, on which we were, was occupied exclusively by men. There was a gallery over it filled with women—dark-eyed Jewesses, most of them dressed in black.[17]

Walt concludes,

> The people of Solomon and Saul, of Ruth and Mary Magdalene, of the very Christ himself—these were they who stood around. And they were speaking in the same tones as those which at night bade the shepherds to follow the guidance of the star in the east . . . which sounded out from the plaintive Hagar in the wilderness . . . the tones and the native language of the holy Psalmist . . . and the malignant Shylock of Shakespeare.[18]

In other ways, not just in his religiousness, Walt seems a conventional fellow at this point. His pose as young man-about-town implies a certain romantic quest, and the objects of that quest are decidedly female. The "dark-eyed Jewesses," he notes, are "by no means . . . unpleasing"; over and over they draw his eyes up toward the gallery, just as, in his loafing down Broadway, women in their sensual aspect are always capturing his attention. Walt says about himself, "We never professed to be very susceptible to the tender passion," but then adds, "we met a tall, pale, delicate girl, dressed fashionably . . . She had her veil only half drawn over her face; and as we looked, we beheld one of the most lovely, intellectually feminine countenances our sight was ever blessed with . . . those starlike eyes! and that queenly neck!" and although he may be pretending to feel an attraction, he seems to be *happy* with the pretense, in the mood for it.

This may have been his last—maybe his only—period of trying on heterosexuality as a possible mode for living. He had never before seemed inclined in that direction: One of his students on Long Island remembered that "the girls did not seem to attract him. He did not specially go anywhere with them or show any extra fondness for their company."[19] His brother George stated plainly the year after Walt's death, "I am confident I never knew Walt to fall in love with young girls or even to show them marked attention."[20]

Yet as a good-looking, well-dressed newspaperman, with money in his pocket and a romantic and enviable social role to play, why not? Why not display such susceptibility as he was able to summon? A slight heat of actual attraction seems to arise from some of his descriptions of women in the pages of the *Aurora*, for example, when recreating a scene at a New York market: "Notice that prim, red cheeked damsel, for whom is being weighed a small pork steak . . . How the young fellow who serves her, at the same time casts saucy, lovable glances at her pretty face; and she is nothing loth, but pleased enough . . . Cunning minx!"[21] Or: "Gods! What a glorious morning it was! Just enough of enervating, voluptuous heat . . . just enough sunshine to reflect a sparkle in the eyes of beautiful women . . . just enough people walking on the pave to make one continued, ceaseless, devilish . . . jam."[22] Or even: "The little girls would throw up their heads and shake their curling locks, and smile an apology for running against thoughtful old men . . . Now, a little nymph, with her white pantalettes, and . . . short frock, might be seen trundling her hoop, even among the dense human tide."[23]

The point is not that Walt Whitman had discovered little girls as erotic subjects. But there is a convincing susceptibility to the shapes and colors of real women and girls, along with a general absence of the sort of coded descriptions of men as erotic figures to be found later in *Leaves of Grass*. At least for one season, then—springtime, 1841—Walt seems to have recognized and warmly responded to what was female and lovely and pleasurably before his eyes.

A S   A   D W E L L E R in Manhattan rooming houses, Walt could not have missed the hearty banquet of sex on offer in New York. Not only in the raucous theaters, but in private dwellings and on the streets of prosperous neighborhoods he would have encountered the "monstrous tide of depravity and dissipation" that awaited men and boys who came to the city, according to one popular book of moral advice. According to another such book, William A. Alcott's *The Young Man's Guide*, "[T]he whole race of young men in our cities, of the present generation, will be ruined" by commerce with whores, which leads inevitably to "disease and premature death."[1]

Manhattan in the 1840s did, indeed, present temptation to young and not-so-young men. In the Fifth Ward, the area west of Broadway from Chambers Street up to Canal, well-appointed brothels could be found on residential blocks where some of the city's most respectable families lived.[2] East of Broadway, in the Sixth Ward (the Bowery), rougher establishments were densely clustered. Streetwalkers serviced customers down alleys and in the back rooms of bars. Walt's favorite theater was located at the very center of this rich swirl of sex business. Some estimates of the time put the number of prostitutes in New York City at ten thousand, in a total female population of seventy-five thousand aged fifteen to forty-five.[3]

The lurid sporting paper, the *Whip*, with its 1842 campaign against foreign sodomites, who supposedly preyed upon innocent American boys, was part of an antigenteel street culture strongly established in

Manhattan.[4] George Wilkes, publisher of the *Whip*, was about the same
age as Walt, another son of a working carpenter who grew up fast on
city streets. In 1841, when Walt was venturing into Manhattan journalism, Wilkes was also starting out as an editor—in addition to the *Whip*,
he worked for the *New York Flash*, the *Subterranean*, *New York As It Is*,
and the *National Police Gazette*.[5] Unlike Walt's more demure papers,
Wilkes's catered to men on the town, rakish or would-be rakish fellows
with money to burn on prostitutes and revels.

Walt's writing never leers, as Wilkes's always does; but the great
energy tied up in the enterprise of sex and in the implicit rejection
of American prudery strongly impressed him. When, in an action
unusual for the time, a New York law magistrate ordered the arrest
of fifty prostitutes operating on Broadway, Walt was outraged. On
March 24, 25, 26, and 30, 1842, he wrote editorials that thundered
against the arrests, calling them "a ruffianly, scoundrelly, villain-
ous, outrageous and high handed proceeding, unsanctioned by law,
justice, humanity, virtue, or religion." He apologized in one editorial for getting so hot under the collar, but insisted that the arrests
were tantamount to "the kidnapping of women . . . by the police
authorities."[6]

There were male prostitutes working Broadway, too. The *Whip* identified City Hall Park, Walt's backyard, as the local "Sodom" and referred
to young boys who might be picked up in the streets for sexual purposes.[7] It would be a mistake, probably, to infer from Walt's outspoken
attack on the arrests of some prostitutes a more personal motive, a private one. If he himself were a patron of prostitutes, either female or
male, no direct evidence remains of that fact (nor can it be expected to);
no doubt, the fierceness of his protest bespeaks his usual concern for
people without protection before the law, be they streetwalkers or the
ragged children who played in the city's parks, whom the police dis-
persed by beating them with sticks.[8]

Still, the intensity of his concern is remarkable, signaling an important dissent from conventional attitudes. The early 1840s were both the
heyday and the last hour of open prostitution in New York; already, a
reform movement was gaining traction that would soon drive prostitution underground, although without undermining it in a business
sense. Walt quite saw the uses of prostitution. In articles he wrote for

the *Brooklyn Times*, a paper he edited in 1857, he discussed the trade in the light of the sexual needs of unmarried people, and he seems to have been comfortable in an atmosphere leavened with sex, unlike many young men of his era. His brother George, after noting Walt's lack of interest in girls, added, "Nor was he qualmish, either," meaning that he was no prig. George's careful and amused observations about Walt and women give no hint of an awareness of his older brother's active homosexuality.* Yet the idea that George, who had been a soldier for four years, who was no doubt familiar, as were other Civil War veterans, with camp-follower prostitutes and "nancyboys," and with the phenomenon of love affairs that sometimes developed between comrades, somehow missed or failed to recognize his brother's nonstandard sexuality strains belief.

Earlier, though, in the early 1840s, Walt's behavior would have escaped his younger brother's notice; George was only twelve when Walt went to work on the *Aurora*, in a bustling city of 315,000 people, in a capacity that required him to range far and wide, in the nights and in the days. Something of his inner life, maybe even of a sex life, is suggested in the short fiction he wrote and published in this same period. "The Child's Champion," a story that appeared in Benjamin's *New World*, describes a young man from the city coming to the aid of a handsome country boy of twelve. "Oh, it is passing wondrous," Walt writes, "how in the hurried walks of life and business, we meet with young beings, strangers, who seem to touch the fountains of our love."[9] The boy, apprenticed to a farmer, passes by the open window of a tavern one night, and he sees inside a bunch of sailors engaged in a drunken frolic. "The men in the middle of the room were dancing," Walt writes, "that is, they were going through certain contortions and shufflings, varied occasionally by exceedingly hearty stamps upon the sanded floor."[10]

---

*The term *homo-sexual* appeared first in English in 1892, the year of Walt's death, in a translation of Krafft-Ebing's *Psychopathia Sexualis*. To speak of Walt's "active homosexuality" thus commits an anachronism. Walt and other men and women of the last half of the nineteenth century were aware of a lack of terminology for describing a way of being they felt themselves, sometimes, in whole or in part, to embody.

Among the sailors sits a different sort of man, one who "excited the boy's attention more than any other . . . He might have been twenty-one or two years old. His countenance was intelligent, and had the air of city life and society. He was dress'd not gaudily, but in every respect fashionably; his coat being of the finest broadcloth, his linen delicate and spotless."

A one-eyed sailor catches sight of the lad at the window. He drags the boy into the room, and then, "placing one of his tremendous paws on the back of the boy's head . . . he thrust the edge of the glass to his lips, swearing at the same time, that if he shook it so as to spill its contents the consequences would be . . . by no means agreeable to his back and shoulders." But the boy Charley does not want to drink. He has promised his mother not to sully his lips with spirits. He knocks the glass of brandy away, and the one-eyed sailor begins to beat him ("for the child hung like a rag in his grasp"), at which point the fashionable man from the city intervenes, punching the sailor in "a scientific manner."

This scene half-suggestive of forced oral sex emerges from Walt's moralistic tale with a bracing shock. Walt himself seems to be aware of having given something away: "The scene was a strange one," he writes, "and for the time quite a silent one. The company had started from their seats, and for a moment held breathless . . . strain'd positions." Things calm down, though, the boy sits down beside the gent from the city, and that night they sleep together at the inn ("That roof . . . sheltered two beings that night"). It's the beginning of a beautiful friendship—one "that grew not slack with time."[11]

In other stories of these years, Walt returned to some of these same themes: boys at risk, young men in moral peril (the gent in "The Child's Champion" has a drinking problem of his own, which meeting the boy helps him overcome). Other repeating elements in the stories are cruel, overbearing fathers and sensitive young sons cruelly denied the love they need. Whiskey-drinking is always bad, and in 1842 Walt wrote a baggy temperance novel, *Franklin Evans, or the Inebriate*, which was serialized in the *New World*, a book he later described as "rot of the worst sort," but which seems to have expressed a genuine dislike of drunkenness.

Even in this moralistic early writing, Walt sometimes cannot refrain from using vivid words that carry a sexual charge. Thus we have the girl in her "white pantalettes," comely boys "who touch the fountains of our love," and even male bed partners whose intimacy "grew not *slack* with time." These are signs of a fraught, personally risky labor taken on by the future author of *Leaves of Grass*, the reintroduction of the sexually awakened body into literary parlance. Most of his prose is suitably repressed, full of Victorian moral purpose, but now and then we get startling hints of the poet who in the next decade would write in *Leaves*,

> I am less the reminder of property or qualities, and more the
>   reminder of life,
> And go on the square for my own sake and for other's sake,
> And make short account of neuters and geldings, and favor men
>   and women fully equipped.[12]

He would also one day write of "libidinous prongs," of a "phallic procession" through the streets, and, famously, of "limitless limpid jets of love hot and enormous." He will allude casually in his verse to "a spirt of my own seminal wet"—surely a rawly abrupt answer to the prevailing literary mode of mid-nineteenth-century America.

In "Song of Myself," the 1855 version of the poem, he describes a night at the opera:

> I hear the trained soprano....she convulses me like the climax of my
>   love-grip;
> The orchestra whirls me wider than Uranus flies,
> It wrenches unnamable ardors from my breast,
> It throbs me to gulps of the farthest down horror,
> It sails me....
> I am exposed....
> Steeped amid honeyed morphine....my windpipe squeezed in the
>   fakes of death.[13]

Walt thus becomes unique among literary authors of the time in trying to say just what an orgasm feels like—and not only that, an orgasm brought on by the "love-grip" of the writer's own hand.

Walt at age twenty-two is unlikely to have been *less* captivated by sex than he was at thirty-six, when the first edition of *Leaves of Grass* saw print. Less experienced, of course; less able to seduce whom he wanted and to consummate his attractions at will; but just as "quivering" with sex feeling, just as painfully "swelling and deliciously aching."[14] No one has yet found any evidence of sexual attachments in these early years as a New York writer/editor, but the idea that Walt was too young or too pure of thought seems far-fetched. This was already his second spell of living on his own, and important elements of his sexual character were already in place. He enjoyed being unsupervised in a dense human setting full of variety, and he often disappeared for many hours. The pairing of older man and young lad strongly attracted him. ("Who can help loving a wild, thoughtless, heedless, joyous boy?" he wrote in a sketch published in 1844.) In the Civil War, when he visited thousands of young soldiers in the Washington hospitals, he did so in the guise of a fatherly man already gone gray of head (although he was only in his early forties), and the beauty and vulnerability of the suffering soldiers both excited him and broke his heart. His tender faithfulness as Civil War nurse thus expressed, emerged from, and consummated a long-lived erotic impulse—an impulse that survived the war and even the strokes he suffered afterward.

It need not diminish one of the most profoundly empathic gestures ever undertaken by an American, to see it so intertwined with sex. Walt's biographers since the 1890s have struggled with the question of his sex life, however, at first denying that he had one, then saying that he had one, but only with women (echoing Walt's cheeky claim to have fathered "six children—two are dead—One living southern grandchild, fine boy").[15] In the twentieth century, critics grudgingly allowed that he was probably a homosexual, although as recently as the last twenty-five years some of the best Whitman scholars have suggested that he was sexually inactive, too shy to take many lovers, or, alternatively, active but unhappy until he settled down, in the 1860s, with just one man.[16]

Gay literary scholars, also in the last twenty-five years, have posed another possibility. On the basis of some direct and much indirect evidence, they suggest that Walt probably had a rich and various love life, probably exclusively homosexual. Like most people's love life, it had its fertile and fallow periods, its desperately unhappy passages and its wondrous ones. Being careful to avoid anachronisms, they cautiously assert that some aspects of his private life might not be entirely different from contemporary ways of being.[17] The evidence takes many forms, one of the most suggestive being the long lists of names of men he met on the street. For instance, Walt recorded these names in a pocket notebook he carried with him in 1857:

Hank Pierce (4th av
Charley (black hair & eyes—round face) 4th av.
Albert, (Mrs. Jones's son.) Jack (—4th av.—now in a N.Y. Express
   wagon
Frank (Beeswax)
Anson W Turner (oyster Fulton Market)
Charles Brown (Broadway Brownie)
Jakey (James) tall, genteel friend of Brownie)
Jay (5th av.)—19
Bill (Moses) 5th av. . . .
Bill—(big, black round eyes, large coarse . . .).
Playing *ball* Abe (round red pleasant grayish keeping tally
John Campbell, round light complex lymphatic, *good look*
John (light complex—light gray eyes light hair
Tom Gray—smallish (legs)
Edward Smithson (20) full-eyed genteel boy . . .[18]

By the time of this list-making, Walt was the author of two editions of *Leaves of Grass* and the self-declared Poet of Democracy, a celebrator of the sheer profuse humanity to be encountered on the city's boulevards. Most of the names he recorded, though, are of a particular sort of person—the young working-class male, the cart driver, oyster dealer, butcher, omnibus driver, or machinist of a social background much like his own. And within this category of person, Walt had what can only be described as a favorite physical type—tall, bearded, strong featured, with warm eyes.

And sometimes the list entries reveal even more:

Daniel Spencer . . . somewhat feminine . . . told me he had never been in a fight and did not drink at all [enlisted] in 2d N.Y. Lt Artillery deserted, returned to it   slept with me Sept 3d. . . .

Horace Ostrander Oct. 22 '62 24 4th av. from Otsego [County] 60 miles west of Albany was in the hospital to see Chas. Green . . . about 28 yr's of age . . . slept with him Dec. 4th '62[19]

"Slept with me" or "slept with him" did not necessarily mean then what they mean now. But, equally, they might have. On the night of October 11, 1862, Walt brought a nineteen-year-old blacksmith named David Wilson home to his mother's house on Portland Avenue in Brooklyn; they slept together there that night. Wilson might have been a traveler in need of a place to stay, but in fact he lived close by, on Hampden Street, within easy walking distance of the Whitman house.[20]

To use a word like *cruising* seems wrong, but the impressive number of names raises the issue. Walt's poetry of the 1850s contains numerous descriptions of the experience of noticing and becoming attracted to a passing stranger, of locking eyes and exchanging what feels like an understanding:

> as I pass O Manhattan! your frequent and swift flash of eyes
>   offering me love,
> Offering response to my own—those repay me,
> Lovers, continual lovers. . . .[21]

There are scores of names in the notebooks—hundreds, in fact. They raise the question of how Walt went about collecting his information. Did he pull out a notebook in the street, penciling in name and size and type of eye while still speaking to a man? Or did he wait till he got home, trusting to memory? How, for that matter, did he get so many strangers to respond to him so fully? Maybe strangers in Manhattan in the 1850s and '60s were simply more open than now. Although he may have been exaggerating, Walt often alludes to being the object of *others'* attention, thus implying that name collecting was in some ways thrust upon him. In "Poem of the Road" (later named "Song of the Open Road"), he writes, "I and mine do not convince by arguments, similes, rhymes, / We convince by our presence," and here is surely part of the answer, his magnetism, his personal attractiveness.

The sturdy effort undertaken from the end of the Civil War onward, to enshrine Walt as the "Good Gray Poet," a national father-figure and emblem of healing, has substantially erased memory of the earlier presence, of Whitman in his scintillating youth. His poetry, especially the first three editions of *Leaves of Grass* (1855, '56, and '60), brings him before us but, inevitably, in a "poeticized" version, as the performer of a certain self-created role. This version of Walt—"one of the roughs," a poet of "the divine average," also the poet of the body, of sexual delight—must bear some resemblance to the handsome man who in his teens, twenties, thirties, and early forties freely roamed the liveliest, most sybaritic streets in America, looking to make contact. But even he is not really "the man."

Walt knew this, and was troubled by it. He wanted to be remembered for what he actually was. His poems often try to reach beyond the page, to go skin-to-skin with the reader:

> This is no book,
> Who touches this, touches a man
> (Is it night? Are we here alone?),
> It is I you hold, and who holds you,
> I spring from the pages into your arms. . . .[22]

and

> Come closer to me,
> Push close my lovers and take the best I possess,
> Yield closer and closer and give me the best you possess
> . . . .
> I was chilled with the cold types and cylinder and wet paper
> between us.[23]

As far as he can, he gives us tokens of his true self, of the man who roamed, who wanted adventure, who was on the hunt. For in the presence of that man was a powerful attraction. His brother George spoke of Walt "even when he was quite young" being admired by the neighbors, who sought his counsel. His slow-spoken, "forbearing," "conciliating," "gentle till you got him started" intelligence must have been part of that magnetism. He was also, as George insisted, "a muscular young man at that time—very strong—already of striking appearance."[24]

George, speaking for the record, hints at Walt's lifelong modus operandus, of roaming as he wanted, getting beyond the range and oversight of his family. Although he lived with them in Brooklyn from the mid-1840s through 1862, "Walt was a mystery . . . He never counseled with anybody. I do not think he took a word of advice from any one . . . It was in him not to do it—in his head, in his heart."[25] The house on Portland Avenue, stuffed full of Whitmans, was also "a great large house, twenty-five by fifty," with space enough for privacy.* Later, when Walt lived in a house that George built for his young family in Camden, New Jersey, "If we had dinner at one, like as not he would come at three; always late. Just as we were fixing things on the table he would get up and go round the block . . . go where he was of a mind to—and come back in his own time."[26]

"As for dissipation and women," George notes, "I know well enough that his skirts were clean . . . As a young man he was always correct and clean in his conversation." And then—perhaps with a wink at his readers—he adds, "*All those fellows intimate with Walt, at night, anywhere, anytime*, will tell you the same thing [author's italics] . . . I could quote all sorts of things from these men."

"Give me now libidinous joys only!" Walt wrote exultantly in the 1860 *Leaves*,

> Give me the drench of my passions! Give me life coarse and rank!
> To-day, I go consort with nature's darlings—to-night too,
> I am for those who believe in loose delights—I share the midnight
>   orgies of young men. . . .
> I take for my love some prostitute—I pick out some low person
>   for my dearest friend,
> He shall be lawless, rude, illiterate—he shall be one condemned
>   by others for deeds done

Whether he ever did pick out a rude male prostitute, or need to, is difficult to determine. But that he roamed, that he tasted of "libidinous

---

*What qualified as a large house for people of the Whitmans' resources was in fact quite modest—but certainly, grander than a tenement house.

joys," that there was something hungry and forward and prolific in his collecting of male companions, is a truth that through his poems and his carefully preserved papers he ensured that we, those who came after, would surely know.

THE WHITMAN FAMILY returned to Brooklyn from Long Island in August 1844.[1] They had been ten years out of the city. By October, Walter Sr. had acquired a lot on Prince Street, in Brooklyn's Seventh Ward, planning to build a house on it. But the real buyer was his second-eldest son. Aged just twenty-five, Walt made payments to Austin Reeves, the seller of the lot, as well as interest payments to the Long Island Insurance Company, which held a $900 mortgage. In the summer of 1847, Walt took over formal title to the property, assuming sole responsibility for the remaining payments.[2]

Walter Sr. had returned from his family's ten-year sojourn in the country probably with few resources, and probably having sold or lost his wife's property "S. on the Neck of land" in Huntington as well. Walt's assumption of financial responsibility for the family, in whole or in part, needs to be added to the image of the gay blade of Manhattan, the carefree wanderer seeking out nightspots while he edited or wrote freelance for the *Evening Tatler*, the *New York Sun*, the *Aristidean*, *Brother Jonathan*, the *Sunday Times & Noah's Weekly Messenger*, the *New-York Democrat*, *Columbian Magazine*, the *Daily Plebeian*, and the *Brooklyn Evening Star*, among others. In fact, soon Walt moved back in with his family. By December 1846, they were at home in the new house on Prince Street built by the father, possibly with the help of Walt and/or sons Jesse (age twenty-eight), Andrew Jackson (nineteen), George Washington (seventeen), and Thomas Jefferson (thirteen).

Something of the material life they led in that house, and in others they occupied in the next fifteen years, can be gleaned from receipts that Walt carefully kept. In March 1846, he became editor of the *Daily Eagle*, the most successful newspaper in Brooklyn, upon the death of its founding editor, William B. Marsh. With a regular salary in his pocket, Walt was able to step in formally as buyer of the Prince Street property—his signature appears in pencil on the original sales indenture ("Walter Whitman, Jr.—Eagle Office").[3] In the next few years, he paid City of Brooklyn taxes on the property; bought nails, screws, pipes, and other hardware for it; bought a gold ring, a silver watch, a carnelian pin, some thimbles, and a purse (for his mother?); bought eighteen gilt picture frames for $10.06; and paid a mason $56. In late spring of 1847, he paid a local shoemaker $19.16 for six months of services, including boots "Soled & heeled for Brother—62 cents; Boots repaired for Brother—12 cents; [and] New boots brother—3.25."[4]

He paid the interest on the mortgage on time, and in November 1847 he bought a bureau ($5.50) and paid for "hanging a bell with engraved plate, night latch & 2 numbers" ($3.92 plus $3.50 credit for an ad in the *Eagle*). In December, he bought more pipes and hardware for the house, and he paid a tailor named Turner $32 for a frock coat, pants, and a vest.

While running the *Eagle*, Walt played the part, giving an impression of dignity and professionalism, according to a young printer on the paper, Henry Sutton. His beard was short and trim. Like other editors of the time, he wore dark clothing and might almost have passed for a man of the cloth—a daguerreotype of 1848, taken in New Orleans, where he went after leaving the *Eagle* (fired for his strongly anti-expansion-of-slavery politics), suggests as much. Although paying for the Prince Street house, Walt lived on his own sometimes, boarding on Adams Street, Brooklyn, for a while. Henry Sutton remembered going there to pick up copy. The young editor in frock coat and vest would write his editorials in the morning at the office, go for a short walk, return to read the editorials now set up in type, then repair to Gray's Swimming Bath, on Fulton Street near the harbor, for a swim lasting twenty minutes. After the bath, a shower, with the pump manned by young Henry.[5]

He was always setting off for Manhattan—almost daily, he took the ferry (a three- to five-minute trip, costing two cents) then strolled or rode up Broadway in a horse-drawn omnibus, often seated beside the driver.[6] Manhattan was where he went to refresh and enlarge himself, to

Walt Whitman during his three-month tenure as editor of the New Orleans Crescent, *1848. He was twenty-eight years old.*

get story ideas, to visit theaters and concert halls as a member of the press. Walt was just awakening to opera at this same time. He saw his first performances in the early 1840s, and his writing about productions of the mid-'40s is full of mockery, seeing in opera the very epitome of fatuous European artifice.

But something excited him about operatic voices, and in 1847 he wrote that Anna Bishop, an Englishwoman trained in the Italian style, had one that put him happily "in mind of the gyrations of a bird in the air."[7] He began going whenever he could, preparing for performances by reading the libretto in advance, just as he prepared for Shakespeare by reading the play beforehand. For his fellow philistine Americans, who might be encountering opera for the first time, he wrote in the *Eagle* that "during the intervals of the performance [you should] be not afraid of talking, laughing and moving.—You are not having daguerreotypes taken." Hoping to knock the whole thing down a peg or two, he likened operatic voices to "the voices of the native healthy substrata of [New York] young men, especially the drivers of horses . . . all those whose work leads to free loud calling and commanding."[8]

In October 1849, Walt paid another bill to his tailor, this one for repair of a jacket, for new clothes for his brothers, and for a suit for his father. The buying of a suit of clothes for a father is a signal act. This may have been the suit in which Walter Sr. was buried six years later, and very likely it was the suit he wore in September 1850, when he took a three-day trip with Walt to see some relatives in the country.[9] The "old native place," as Walt called the homestead in West Hills, "is a romantic and beautiful spot . . . The old grave yard, on the Hill has some new graves." The Whitmans were "a stalwart, massive . . . long-lived race," he wrote proudly, yet the unpublished sketch about the trip makes many observations about death and memorial monuments, for instance, "The Whitmans appear to have been mostly of the Quaker notion, concerning tomb stones; for on the old hill . . . among all the numerous graves, there is [only] one inscribed grave stone"—Quakers being believers in simple, sober grave markings.

Walter Sr. is a very quiet presence in Walt's sketch—he travels with his son "in the L.IRR. [Long Island Rail Road], and so in the stage to Woodbury," but never acts or speaks in his own person. By 1850, Walt had achieved a milestone for a Whitman of Brooklyn: He had taken on a mortgage, had made the interest payments on schedule, and had assisted in the building of a house where the family lived for a time, then sold that house for a profit ($600).[10] Moreover, half a year before this sale of June 19, 1849, he had acquired another property, a lot seventy-five by twenty feet on Myrtle Avenue, where he built yet another house, where the family would live for three years, and which he would also sell successfully.

He had done what his father had not been able to—no doubt benefiting from his hard experience. The gruff, stern, love-denying fathers of Walt's early stories have been seen as suggesting an Oedipal conflict between Walt and Walter, and that may be so, just as the writing of a long novel about the damage done to families by heavy drinking may express some personal truth. But a father replaced as breadwinner, clothed and sheltered by his own son, presents a different sort of problem. In his youth, if his stories are any reflection of his personal reality, Walt felt some kind of harshness from his father, but the force he identified with fathers—a force tinged with cruelty, but a useful force, maybe even a necessary one for a son growing into capacity—is mostly absent from his later work. The early depictions of fathers may have come to seem to him exaggerated, bogeyman-ish—in a word, fictional.

The house on Myrtle, where the family lived from 1849 until 1852, was Walt's creation top to bottom, roof to basement. His receipts include a bill for forty-three yards of carpet bought in May 1849, another for work that included "the flagging on the sidewalk in front," others for a bathtub and wallpaper.[11] This is the home "on the southerly side of Myrtle . . . about 60 ft from Duffield St.," a dwelling "with brick front and tin roof," as it says in an insurance policy from 1851, the same home where the Whitmans were visited in 1850 by the U.S. census takers for Brooklyn.[12] The census recorders noted that Walter, a carpenter aged sixty-one, was the eldest in the house, and that his wife, fifty-four, plus six of their children were living under the same roof. (A twenty-year-old woman, Mary Farrell, also lived there, as boarder or possibly maid.) Walter Jr., thirty-one, gave his occupation as "editor" and said he owned real estate worth $3,000. (No other Whitman claimed to own real property with a dollar value.)

On the street level of the house, Walt had a shop where he operated a printing press, and where he also sold books and stationery. Some of his bills for this period were paid in kind, by print jobs ("500 cards") or ads in a flier he produced called the *Salesman*. His receipts show purchases of paper supplies and printer's type; of a stove for heat; of two tons of coal; of more boots and clothes for his brothers; of a large old painting of a "colossal human figure"; of a Britannia teapot and a round clock. He paid $22 for an old-fashioned upright hall clock, $10 for a frock coat in black, and $65 plus a plot in Cypress Hills Cemetery for a melodeon (a small reed organ) for his brother Jeff or his sister Hannah to play.[13] That the house was filling up with materials of some value, in the common estimation of the time, is signified by the fire insurance policy that Walt took out for $800, in which he noted "household furniture of every description including pictures printed books family clothing," plus "piano and [other] musical instruments."

Their neighborhood, Brooklyn's Eleventh Ward (formerly Seventh), was not a wealthy one. But it was growing. Of eighteen wards in the city, the Eleventh had the fourth highest total value of dwellings, including a few stone houses, a goodly number of brick houses, and more wood-frame houses than any other ward.[14] That Walt troubled to face

The Myrtle Street house, Brooklyn, built by Walt and occupied by the Whitman family from 1849 until 1852. The brick facing may have been removed when the structure was expanded to include 108 Myrtle.

the house he built at 106 Myrtle in brick shows that he was building not for the very bottom of the market (plain wood dwellings) but for something above, and that he had an awareness of the markers of relative desirability (tin roof, three stories) and the resources to achieve them. The really feverish activity in Brooklyn building was farther south in the city, close to the harbor, where areas of sand dunes and marsh were being drained and graded and built upon for the first time.[15] Walt probably lacked the resources to compete in these development projects, but by local standards he was a player: By borrowing carefully (and always making his payments), designing useful dwellings, and controlling the work of the contractors he hired, he built and sold four more houses in as many years (1852–55).[16]

Myrtle Avenue sold for $3,500 in June 1852—a handsome sum.[17] Walt was already at work on his next, a multihouse project in Cumberland

Street, near Atlantic Avenue. The contracts he wrote in his own hand for his builders to sign—highly detailed yet entirely lucid documents that bound them to perform according to standards left in no way uncertain—have a pugnacious tone. "*Framing, Enclosing, flooring &c. of a small House*, Two stories & Basement—size on the ground 16X26 feet—front elevation 20 feet, (above basement) rear elevation, (including basement,) 26 feet," he wrote to a Mr. M. N. Hedges, carpenter, before getting down to the real specifics: "To be framed complete, according to plan, with good stuff . . . 6 inch beams for roof.—studs of joist 4 inches all round . . . To be enclosed with weatherboards in the same manner as the red houses built by W. Whitman adjoining . . . Cornice in front made complete, with brackets, mouldings &c . . . Roof to be boarded with good hemlock . . . Furnished with box for scuttle, & sash of scuttle all hung & made tight and complete."[18]

His instructions for the masons ("Stone Wall, for Cellar . . . Intersecting Wall of Brick . . . Cistern . . . Privy . . . Cess Pool") are if anything more specific, and peremptory in tone. He concluded his contract with Mr. Hedges: "Flight of stairs to be made . . . so that it can be sealed up.—made substantial & workmanlike . . . Furring for the masons to fill in, to be furnished . . . W. Whitman furnishes all the sashes, and the locks for the front door, and basement doors . . . The work above is to be pushed on so that . . . W. Whitman may occupy it on the 16th of April—this without fail."[19]

While building on Cumberland, Walt rented a storefront there, with a sign over his shop's door that read, "Carpenter & Builder."[20] All the myriad concerns of a busy builder were his, from payments to lawyers for title searches and deed conveyances, to bills for lumber, gas fixtures, bracketing, paints, oil, flagstone, wall moldings, and ads to run in a New York paper about a "Genteel House" being offered for sale.

Walter Sr. had done his own carpentering—that had defined him, as an artisan-builder of an earlier era. Walt was fundamentally an entrepreneur, a man who used the labor of others and exploited access to credit (access he earned by paying his debts, and possibly by dint of personal charm and a reputation for competence). Suppliers advanced him materials he needed and billed him later, and meanwhile he paid his contractors as promised.[21] A certain no-nonsense tone attends the whole enterprise—when a carpenter working for him asked Walt to cover one of his debts, Walt did so, but wrote a note to himself on the back of the memorandum, "This sucker & Liar won't pay this bill. Walter Whitman."[22]

Later, he recalled this time of house building with pride, noting that he had provided homes for working people, and that he might have made a fortune this way, had he only been more interested in making a fortune. He had become the pillar of his family. His older brother, Jesse, had been declining for some years (he would eventually become violently deranged). George, twenty-two years old in June 1852, was working locally as a carpenter, possibly contributing something to the family, and Jeff was also working, although as a poorly paid apprentice. Andrew was carpentering, too, but would soon earn a reputation as a drinker, if he did not already have it.[23] One of Walt's sisters, Mary Elizabeth, had married young and moved to Greenport, the old whaling town on the north shore of Long Island. Hannah, the younger sister, would marry, disastrously, in 1852—there is no record of her ever sending money home to the family, nor of her ever working for wages.

Their father, now in his sixties, was physically a ruin. "DIED in Brooklyn, on the night of July 11th, 1855," read the obituary that Walt himself possibly wrote, "Walter Whitman, sr, after an exhausting illness of nearly 3 years, from paralysis."[24] Their mother always worked hard in the home, cooking and cleaning to exacting Dutch standards, but she looked to her sons now. The period when the burden came mostly onto Walt's shoulders happens to be the very moment of his transformation, his miraculous self-invention, when the writer of doggerel on the order of

> Could I this sacred solace share,
>   'Twould still my struggling bosom's moan;
> And the deep peacefulness of prayer,
>   Might for thy heavy loss atone [1842][25]

became the poet of original ideas, expressed in *Leaves* in an idiom never heard before in the history of the world:

> This hour I tell things in confidence,
> I might not tell everybody but I will tell you.
> Who goes there! hankering, gross, mystical, nude?[26]

and

> This is the meal pleasantly set....this is the meat and drink for
>   natural hunger,
> It is for the wicked just the same as the righteous....I make
>   appointments with all,
> I will not have a single person slighted or left away,
> The keptwoman and sponger and thief are hereby invited....
> . . . .
> This is the press of a bashful hand....this is the float and odor of
>   hair,
> This is the touch of my lips to yours....this is the murmur of
>   yearning [1855][27]

While house building, he continued contributing to the papers (the *Brooklyn Advertizer* and the *New York Post*). He had some long, relaxed visits with his sister Mary and her husband, a shipbuilder named Ansel Van Nostrand, in Greenport, boating and swimming and eating bluefish (his favorite), and when in the city he cultivated a widening circle of artistic acquaintance, including painters and sculptors and writers such as William Cullen Bryant, whose poetry he considered of the first rank. Busy as a builder, busy conducting his rich nightlife, attending opera with an increasingly fanatical devotion, he yet had the time to do the work of self-invention.[28] Surely the press of family, the absence of a regular paycheck, the growing recognition that he was not, after all, cut out to be the next James Gordon Bennett or Horace Greeley (considering that he was always getting fired as an editor) would have produced anxiety in most people, and probably they did in Walt, too—although they did not erode his literary hope.

Without an indoor job, gradually he stopped dressing like an editor. In October 1849, after he resigned from yet another position (at the short-lived *Brooklyn Freeman*), he was the subject of a mocking profile in a competing paper, which called him "a civilized but not a polished" example of "native raw material":

And, by the way, it has been asserted . . . that he is a lineal descendant from some Indian tribe, with what truth we will not venture to say. In dress and gait he apes in some degree the gravity of the student, with inverted shirt collar, of course, after the manner of "Childe Harold." His face, good looking but remarkably indolent in expression, is sometimes "bearded like the pard," and at other times, probably to suit the season, as free from hair as the fair cheek of "Justice."[29]

Only a year before, he had worn a starched collar in the daguerreotype taken in New Orleans. Then he had looked a man older than his years, with furrowed brow, a conventional man of the press; now he wore an open-collared shirt à la Lord Byron, and his demeanor was the more youthful one of a student lost in thought, a little self-serious. The open-throated shirt, made famous by the "mad, bad, and dangerous to know" poetic celebrity of the prior generation, was the sort of thing a working man might also wear, and in these years of tramping over construction sites and through city and country, he said farewell to the frock coats and vests he had earlier favored. As the man who would become "the most photographed and painted poet of modern times," he was in ever more specific control of his image, too, even as his image and style now became more relaxed, more a matter, seemingly, of indifference.[30]

In 1854, he had his most famous picture ever taken, the one for the frontispiece of the first edition of *Leaves*. But by now he was truly "one of the roughs," dressed really like a workman, like someone who might earn a living with a hammer or a pick. The reviewer for Greeley's *New York Tribune*, commenting on the new book of poetry, noted that this fellow Whitman appeared in the frontispiece engraving "in a garb . . . half sailor's, half workingman's, with no superfluous appendage of coat or waistcoat, a 'wideake' [hat] perched jauntily on his head, one hand in his pocket and the other on his hip, with a certain air of mild defiance."*

---

*These may be Walt's own words. He wrote numerous self-reviews, publishing them anonymously or under the name of a writer friendly to his cause. At least three articles by Walt greeted the publication of the 1855 *Leaves*: "Walt Whitman and His Poems," in *United States Review*; "An English and American Poet," in *American Phrenological Journal*; and "Walt Whitman, a Brooklyn Boy," in the *Daily Times*.

Walt Whitman, 1854, a year before the appearance of Leaves of Grass.

He wore high boots now—no more of an office-worker's supple slippers—with his pantlegs tucked in.

The influence of his building work can be read in the poetry he was now writing, poetry that honors hardy workers, the "young mechanic," the "woodman," the "farmboy," "fishermen and seamen," and that takes pleasure in getting the tradesman's lingo right:

> tongs and hammer..the axe and wedge..the square and mitre
>   and jointer and smoothingplane;
> The plumbob and trowel and level. . . .

The ship's compass..the sailor's tarpaulin..the stays and
   lanyards, and the ground-tackle for anchoring. . . .
..the stevedore's hook..the saw and buck of the
   sawyer. . . .
..the handpress..the frisket and tympan..the compositor's
   stick and rule[31]

The contracts he wrote with his builders also, insistently, got the terms
just right: "furring" (strips of wood or brick to make a level surface for
plastering), "weather boards," "nine feet in the clear," "neck" of a cistern, and so forth. His father was speaking through him, and a whole
tradition of artisanal craft, and the diction of his new poetry was similarly more real, more earnest, weight-bearing. He had been a friend of
workingmen and women for a long time now. His politics were strongly
democratic and progressive, as befitted the son of a man born on Bastille
Day, a man who had known Tom Paine. But now his identification with
laboring people was less an ideological inclination than a matter of
worldly tasks, of undertakings.

A host of influences was buzzing around his hungry intelligence in
these years, and their effect on his poetry—the effect of his prodigious
reading and lecture-attending, of Emerson, Carlyle, Shakespeare, the
biblical Thomas, Epictetus, Dickens, Scott, Sand, and Milton; the effect
of great dramatic performances seen and savored in lively theaters and
of opera, especially Italian opera, and its passionate opening of the
heart and throat—is demonstrable and essential to know about, to account for the artist he was becoming. But his efforts as an ordinary
neighborhood housebuilder, efforts that continued for a decade, gave
bottom to it all, and gave him an air of competence and of making-real
in a time that might otherwise have felt untethered. His father was dying in these same years, protractedly, pitiably. Not as a displacement of
him, then, but in fulfillment of who he had been and what he had
taught, Walt built another new house, on Skillman Street near Myrtle,
in the spring of 1854 and moved the family into it for a year. The next
spring, with the proceeds from selling that house and maybe others,
he bought a preexisting place on Ryerson Street, also close to Myrtle,
for $1,840 cash and put it in his mother's name. This property that
was Mrs. Whitman's—the first that the family had been able to buy,

unmortgaged, after thirty years of trying—may have given her a feeling of rootedness and relative security in that turbulent season of her husband's dying, of other changes of domicile, of her second-eldest son's radical poetic bursting-forth.

A SAILOR, JESSE WHITMAN had "the best mind of any of the children," according to family legend.[1] But in 1848, when he was about thirty, Jesse fell from a mast and injured his head. He was hospitalized for six months and released "apparently well," according to a medical history taken sixteen years later, when he was first admitted to the Kings County (Brooklyn) Lunatic Asylum. Prior to this admission, Jesse had been "considered somewhat insane" for four years, the history continued, and in the last year he had become "worse, at times violent, usually in the night or awaking from sleep."[2]

Walt, his younger brother by a year, was the one who committed Jesse—and presumably the one who provided the details of his history. There is no mention of another version of the head-injury story that was passed around the family, that in some sailors' dive or other likely setting Jesse had been beaten by thugs, who cracked his skull with brass knuckles.[3] Maybe both things had happened. That Jesse had been a seafaring man, that he had lived rough in an era when sailors commonly suffered grievous injury onboard ship or were lost at sea, was established, and what was also established was that *something* had happened to him mentally—that his once fine mind was gone.

If he went to sea when other Whitman sons first set forth in life, in his teens, he might have had an experience something like Melville's, which began in service on a packet ship running between New York and Liverpool. Melville, who taught school when and for the same reason that Walt did (financial necessity), who studied surveying and engineering just like Jeff Whitman, hoping thereby to qualify as a ship's officer, who also came from a family of eight children, and whose ancestry, like the Whitmans', was Dutch and British, served on whaling ships in some of the same years when Jesse Whitman was also at sea, the early 1840s.[4] The dangers of a sailor's life are starkly suggested by the experiences of Melville's relatives, several of whom were mariners. Of four of his first cousins, one served for many years in the U.S. Navy, yet failed to qualify as an officer, was court-martialed, and died on a whaleboat; another qualified as an officer but fell into enduring disgrace for his role in the hanging, at sea, of three men accused of mutiny; one died in a ship-wreck early in a promising career; and another, the closest to Melville in age, a man named Hunn Gansevoort, had thrilling adventures in the South Pacific, contracted a "virulent and obstinate" venereal disease, was cured of it after six years of suffering, only to die, with all hands, in an ocean storm.[5]

Jesse may have sailed, off and on, for several years, until his accident in the late 1840s.[6] That he was probably not a whale man or a navy sailor is suggested by the absence of mention of those employments in the family correspondence. As an ordinary seaman on merchant ships, wearing the rough red shirt of a deckhand, he would have benefited to some degree from the booming China trade, the growing traffic with British and other European ports, and the California trade before and after the U.S. victory in the war with Mexico. The ports of New York were wildly busy, forested with the masts of all kinds of ships, as brother Walt noted in his writing ("look on the numberless masts . . . and the thick-stemmed pipes of steamboats"), and the world literally opened out, the whole world, from homely Brooklyn.[7]

The absence of seafaring exploits recounted in the family suggests that Jesse's sailing was possibly less a matter of wild adventures than of sim-ple toil. He may have preferred serving as an ordinary sailor to becom-ing an officer, with the attendant responsibilities, and he may have been for some time a heavy drinker, like the brandy-swilling tars in Walt's short story. Jeff Whitman, fifteen years younger, claims another reason for Jesse's mental decline in a letter written December 15, 1863. There had been an appalling incident nine days before at the Whitman home in Brooklyn. On December 5, Andrew Whitman had died, probably of tu-berculosis of the throat. His body had been laid out in the house where

Mrs. Whitman lived with Jeff and his young wife, Martha, and their two children, Hattie and Jessie Louisa. "The next day after Andrew's death," Jeff wrote Walt,

Hatty was down stairs—and Mat with the baby—Mother and Jess [too] in front of the stove was a chair upon which Mat had hung a dia-per. Hattie commenced shoving the chair slowly toward the stove. Jess told her to stop—she kept on—he all at once jumped up and swore out at her, and said he would break her damn'd neck.—Mat, of course was bound to defend her child and—although trembling like a leaf with fright—she as bold as she could—told Jess to set down and let Hattie be—not to dare to lay his hand on her. Jess then turned from the child to Mat and swore that he would kill her.—said that she had been at him for a long time and now he would finish her.[8]

When Jeff returned later that day, he "felt pretty rathey" when he learned what had happened:

Jess essayed twice to get at her. Swore he would beat her brains out. Called her a damed old bitch—in the same breath added—"not you Mother, not you"   Mother managed to keep Jess away till Mat got out of the room. Mat was over *one hour* in getting from the basement up to her rooms. She had an awful attack of the old complaint in her back and had to set down every few step. When I got home she was not able to set up—there she was with her two children frightened al-most to death.[9]

Mrs. Whitman begged Jeff in his wrath not to attack Jesse. Jeff wanted to move out immediately, to "remove Mat and the babies away" for safety, but Mrs. Whitman "said that it would kill her to part with Mat," her daughter-in-law, "that she couldn't stand it and begged me not. Since [then] we dont allow Jess to come in our rooms."

Calling Jesse "treacherous" and a "hell-drag to his Mother," Jeff added,

He says he dont know any better   he lies—he does know better. I wish to God he was ready to put along side of Andrew   There would be but few tears shed on my part I can tell you . . . I hav'nt written you before because I was afraid to think about it. To think that the wretch should go off and live with an irish whore, get in the condition he is by her act and then come and be a source of shortening his mothers life by years.[10]

The implication is that Jesse, by living with an "irish whore," had begun his mental decline—possibly, by contracting syphilis, which in its last stage can manifest in mental illness (or possibly while living with the woman he suffered the beating with brass knuckles that had become part of family lore). The psychiatric symptoms associated with tertiary syphilis are numerous and may include hostility, confusion, personality changes, impairment of judgment, and full-blown psychosis. Such symptoms can appear years later—in the classic onset, between five and twenty years after first infection.[11]

There are other symptoms—motor paralysis, loss of peripheral reflexes, blindness, hearing loss—not mentioned in Jeff's letter, nor in the medical history that was taken a year later. Indeed, the admitting doctor noted only that Jesse was "temperate" when brought to the Brooklyn asylum: not a drinker, or not a drinker at that time. Jeff, in the December 15 letter, broached the idea of putting Jesse away, and Walt may have agreed, in a return letter now lost, because in a letter of December 28 Jeff noted, "You wrote Mother abt getting Jess in the Asylum—It does not seem to meet with her wishes—when I wrote you my idea was that . . . we could keep him in some one of the hospitals around new York—I think it would be best yet."[12]

"Jess did it to himself and made himself what he is [and] is answerable"—Jeff clearly believed this, but there are other possible explanations for rages such as Jesse's. In the aftermath of the incident, Mrs. Whitman revealed to Jeff that "he has these kind of things quite often with her   calls her everything—and even swears that he will keel her over."[13] Congenital mental illness seems to have been something the Whitman family especially feared, particularly as it might be affecting the male children. Walter Sr. had sometimes brooded darkly for long periods, and George, after the Civil War, when he was back living with his mother and struggling to get started in the building business, was "moody" for two weeks, which caused Mrs. Whitman to write worriedly to Walt,

[George] would hardly speak only when i spoke to him well of course you will say mother put the worst construction on it well walt i did not the first few days i thought perhaps something had gone wrong in his business affairs . . . i felt awful bad and what has made him act so god only knows but i beleive it runs in the Whitman family to have such spells any how i hope they wont come often.[14]

Jesse, once placed in an asylum, lived only a few more years. He died of a cerebral aneurysm, and all that is known of him between his commitment in 1864 and his death in 1870 is that his retarded younger brother, Edward, once met an escaped mental patient on the streets of Brooklyn, a fellow inmate of Jesse's, who when asked why Jesse had not also broken out, said that he preferred to stay were he was.[15]

Jesse may have suffered other strokes before the fatal one. This was another great fear of the family: strokes and paralysis. Walter Sr.'s decline likewise began in his fifties, and his final illness was marked by paralysis and exhaustion. Walt, at fifty-three, suffered a crippling stroke that left him weakened for the rest of his life, and his letters written during the Civil War, when he was in his forties, are full of descriptions of what would now be called hypertensive events, including transient strokes. Jesse died at fifty-two, and his symptoms of mental decline (paranoia, confusion, violent outbursts) can, in fact, be ascribed with about the same degree of likelihood to cerebral arteriosclerosis, a stroke precursor, as to late-stage syphilis. "[O]f course his brain is very weak," Mrs. Whitman noted about her firstborn son, the one who had once had "the best mind" of all, and that marked decline was a puzzlement and a heartbreak for her.

Mrs. Whitman, who looks out at us, in her only known photographs, like some caricature of early American motherhood—bonneted, shapeless, possibly toothless, benign—bore much. That she acted to defend her children, all of them, suggests what must have been the first principle of her existence. Yet, the sheer number of trials, of situations giving rise to fear and distress, that beset her brings her story into the realm of the Job-like. By 1863, the family had moved to North Portland Avenue, on the edge of Fort Greene's hill. They shared a house with a second family, the Browns, and conditions in the multistory dwelling were crowded

Louisa Van Velsor Whitman.

and at times complicated. The Whitman kitchen was in the basement. Here Jesse sat by the stove with his mother, who continued, in her sixty-eighth year, to do her own cooking and light housekeeping.[16] On December 6, the day of the big blowup, Andrew's body was only a few feet above their heads, in a first-floor room.[17]

Andrew, thirty-six when he died, had been living with a woman whom Mrs. Whitman got to know well as his illness progressed, and who had borne him two sons and was pregnant with a third. Her name was Nancy, and as Mrs. Whitman wrote Walt,

[W]hether she was always so or we know more about her i dont know but i think she is about the lazeyest and dirtiest woman i ever want to see she come round here to put a blister on andrews neck i gave her a pair of trowsers [for their son, Jim] i said will you make them for the child is not comfortable with those thin trowsers on i made him a pair myself of woolen but i dont know why she dont let him wear them shes as ugly as she is dirty.[18]

As he weakened, Andrew sought care in his mother's house:

[W]ell walt i will tell how my daily routine without any variations i get up in the morning and not very early between 6 and 7 and make a fire and sweep out and get some coffee and bread and butter butter is 36 cents per lb dear eating aint it well by this time Andrew comes lays down part of the time but stays all day untill dark eats his dinner here and then edd goes round for his medicine . . . to night i sent half loaf fresh bread with a lot of flour to make some more if nancy feels disposed . . . matty sent roast beef baked quinces apple sauce and parsnips Andrew eats better than he has done he looks very thin but he says his throat is a little better.[19]

Andrew lived on a street nearby, according to the 1863 Brooklyn directory. Like his younger brother George, he had enlisted in the Union Army, but he was sent home after only a brief service, probably because of illness. When he died,

he was laid out in A black frock coat of Georges and vest and shirt looked as if he was asleep i never in all my life saw any person look so beautifull with his high forehead mary [his sister] said he looked too pretty to be put in the ground . . . some of nances acquaintences came [to Andrew's house] and made a great time said they would . . . have him laid out . . . so she came round with a great adue so i got Jeffy to go down again and he came up and [Andrew] was brought round and put in mrs browns room and the doors locked only when some one came to see him nancy dident behave as i could have wished her too.[20]

Some of Mrs. Whitman's distaste for Nancy may have been an expression of a mother's anguish, identifying a human cause for some of her son's suffering; but Jeff, too, found Nancy to be "not one of the doing kind, and posessed with rather an ugly high temper." As he

wrote to Walt, "His disease of course makes Andrew fretful and discouraged, and instead of soothing and nursing him Nancy does the reverse."[21] Right after Andrew's death, Nancy was "in the street,"
according to Mrs. Whitman, "going some where or other she says she
cant make any thing by sewing." Three weeks later, on Christmas
Day, Nancy "goes it yet in the street," Mrs. Whitman tells Walt—the
implication is that she had begun, or possibly resumed, working as a
prostitute.

All during Andrew's illness, Mrs. Whitman tended to Edward, her fee-
bleminded youngest child. From his birth in 1835, he had needed special
care, and his mother supplied it for the rest of her life. Thus, when Jesse
Whitman succumbed to mental illness during the Civil War, he was
Mrs. Whitman's second adult son to attach himself to her skirts, to need
to spend his days at home with her. Edward (or Eddy, or Edd) had a
crippled left hand and a paralyzed leg, and he was epileptic.[22] He was
said to resemble Walt uncannily: the same light blue eyes, the same
white hair by the time he was in his forties, the same stocky build. A man
who knew both affirmed that "any of the famous portraits of Walt
would do equally well as a portrait of Eddy."[23] Mrs. Whitman bathed,
dressed, and fed Eddy—if left to himself, he would eat whatever there
was, never stopping.[24]

Then there was Hannah, Mrs. Whitman's second-oldest daughter.
The beautiful, well-educated sister of whom Walt was especially fond,
whom he once described as "a child of light and loveliness," lived in
Vermont after about 1852 with a bullying, drunken, half-talented husband, Charles Heyde, a landscape painter probably born in France.
Heyde scorned her and wrote letters to Mrs. Whitman (letters also
read by Walt, George, and Jeff) threatening to abandon her, and Hannah wrote her own pathetic and distressing letters home, hinting at
Heyde's cruelties. Heyde ended up in an insane asylum, like Jesse, and
although Hannah did not lose her mind, she was a deeply peculiar
woman in a childless and torturing marriage, a figure of pity in the
family.

Mrs. Whitman's fifth-born son, George, was strong and capable,
authentically "one of the roughs." Yet this promising son lived daily
in the very jaws of death, and, more to the point, Mrs. Whitman
knew all about it. A great reader of the papers, she followed the mili-

tary campaigns closely, scanning the lists of casualties after battles.
By late 1863, the nature of the war was plain. Mass armies were having at each other in savage, relentless, lumbering encounters—
tactical brilliance there might have been, on both sides, but too many
of the Union commanders were refighting the wars of fifty years earlier, sending waves of infantry forth in bloody assaults on entrenched
positions.

The weapons trained on them were vastly more deadly—more accurate, capable of rapid firing—than the most lethal infantry weapons
used anywhere to that point in history.[25] On both sides, rifle muskets
had been adopted that were highly accurate at a range of two hundred
yards, and surprisingly so at five hundred or even a thousand. (In the
Napoleonic era, the standard infantry weapon, a smoothbore flint-
lock, was accurate only up to seventy-five yards.) Ninety percent of
battlefield casualties in the Civil War were due to rifle bullets—not to
bombs or artillery shells, or to swords wielded by charging cavalry.[26]
George Whitman wrote more than once of doing "terrible execution"
on enemy soldiers ranged in front of him, solely with rifle-musket
fire. From his letters, an alert reader might well have taken an impression of his unit's skill and pluck but also of an overarching machinery
of death operating at the local level according to the dictates of pure
chance—not an inaccurate impression of the actual combat, as it
happens.

There is no reason to think that Mrs. Whitman suffered more with
anxiety than any other Civil War mother. But the vivid battle accounts
that George provided for her, on top of the newspaper coverage she
routinely looked at, arrived in tandem with Walt's letters about the care
that awaited the wounded soldiers who made it to hospital—there, often, to die of septicemia or pyemia (a systemic bacterial infection producing abscesses in many organs), or of gangrene, or diarrhea, or
shock brought on by amputation or some other kind of surgery. For
better or worse, she was fully, more than fully, informed. She was also
not the kind of woman to take refuge in thoughts of a higher purpose,
of God's protection of her son under fire, of His inscrutable will always
working for the best. Just as Walt, in the letters he wrote on behalf of
dying soldiers, almost never tried to justify personal tragedy by referring to the larger cause of preserving the Union, Mrs. Whitman, in her

letters of the time, completely leaves out religion and the spiritual realm. We cannot know what she wrote to George, since those letters are lost, but to judge from her other writings the war for her had little to do with God or redemption.

Her cleverness in a simple human way can be seen in the details of the worrisome Jesse episode—which might easily have fractured the family permanently. Mrs. Whitman had been living, quietly, with Jesse's rages for some time; now that the secret was out, she appealed to Walt—more or less the family's father figure—with an account of things that spoke the raw truth but urgently enlisted him in a nonalarmist response. After giving the details of Andrew's dying, she noted,

> [W]hat i am going to write i would say nothing only i think Jeffy will last night marthe sent Jess around with nancy tea and seeing his brothers corps seemed to effect him very much he had not ought to been sent he took on very much and looked a little strange when he came back . . . seemed to be very sad but this afternoon marthe and sis and hattie were down here hattie done something he dident like he got up and with a vengeance to whip her . . .

Describing how Hattie's mother rushed to defend her ("i told marthe to go up stairs or not say any thing but she would she began to cry and her back pained her"), she implies that things were never really out of hand: "I said Jesse your brother lies up stairs dead he calmed down immediately and is very good natured I think it was going there last night that affected him."[27]

Nor was Jesse entirely in the wrong. Mrs. Whitman makes plain that Hattie, who was then three years old, is a handful, and that helping take care of her is a heavy burden. Two months earlier she had written,

> Dear Walt here goes another of mothers scientific letters when i get desperate i write commit to paper as you literary folk say well i am rather better of my cold but my cough still hangs on it always does when i get A cold . . . we have jimmy here . . . then add to that i have hatty of coarse and she is very obstropolous and her uncle Andrew says if she was his hed break her neck so you see Walt what we go through every day.

Mrs. Whitman knew what she wanted, and she acted to get it. The situation that December was that one son was dying, another was going mad, a third was living in the top floor rooms with his family, and grandchildren were often underfoot (as was an imbecilic fourth son). "[I] think sometimes I wish I was a hundred miles off," she told Walt, but what she in fact wanted was for the family to remain intact. She wanted this on general principles, probably, but also because caring for a dying son and then mourning him in a fit way was for her an utterly compelling duty. Nothing should interfere with that maternal task. The main threat came from Jeff, who, hotheadedly, wanted to leave just at this fraught moment, when a defection from the family would be most sad.

She controlled Jeff by enlisting Walt's help; by saying soothing things to him; by assuring him that she "couldn't stand" to have Martha, his young wife, leave with the babies. Mrs. Whitman was in fact ambivalent about Martha Whitman's presence in her home—about the presence of any other woman, for that matter. Her letters to Walt during the war are full of complaints about Martha ("Mattie"), whom she resented for not contributing enough to the family kitty, for taking more than her fair share, for having an "obstropolous" older child ("hattie is the worst child i ever had anything to do with   so very ugly with her mischeivousness").[28] As Jeff moved ahead in his profession, as a salaried engineer for the Brooklyn Water Works, Mrs. Whitman displayed frank envy over Mat's ability to afford nice clothes, to cultivate stylish friends. Following a trip that she took to Philadelphia with an acquaintance, leaving one and perhaps both daughters for their grandmother to look after, Mrs. Whitman wrote, "[I] dont think they will ever come such a game over me again . . . the work has been very hard on me . . . they think its all nothing   i dont even get thanked . . . its very cold here to night hattie is sitting one side of me and Edd the other . . . i doo hope when mat comes home she will settle down   they have went it this winter if they never did before."[29]

At the same time, Mrs. Whitman appears to have loved her daughter-in-law dearly—and to have been adored by her in return. Mattie, who was probably an orphan, who may have been a foundling, embraced the Whitman family from the time of her marriage to Jeff (February 1859).[30] She found a secure place among them, a place that meant a great deal to her, by dint of personal warmth and devoted help in the home. Mrs. Whitman complained of her gadding about, but Mattie cooked and cleaned and served the older woman loyally, while also working hard as a piecework seamstress ("martha has very much to doo she has been foolish enoughf to take [on] 2 or 300 dozens of shirt fronts," Mrs. Whitman wrote).[31] Walt came also to love this smart, befriending sister-in-law who "was always there to help," as he noted, whose "nature is to come out a first class girl in times of trouble and sickness, & do any thing."[32]

She was not strong, though—even in her youth. The "old complaint in her back" that Jeff wrote about may have been a minor problem, but it was chronic. Mrs. Whitman notes that Mattie's back "pained" her, and Jeff, probably a more accurate, if overheated, reporter on the Jesse incident, paints a picture of Mat so disabled by pain that a direct threat to herself and her child leaves her sprawled on the basement steps—unable to flee just when she most needs to. Yet her own letters, many written to Walt, do not give an impression of a hypochondriac or a weakling, or of someone whose will would desert her at a moment of danger.

The truth was that she was dying, slowly, probably of tuberculosis. Jeff writes early in 1863 of Mat being "nearly the same as usual   she is not very well and sometimes has to give up for a little while."[33] She had married a promising if poor young man who cherished her, and with whom she quickly had two children; as luck would have it, he was on the verge of a stellar career, one that would make them wonderfully well off by their standards, that would lead them to Saint Louis, which after the Civil War promised to be *the* great new western city. Here they would live in material comfort far beyond anything they had ever known in Brooklyn, and here they would soon be welcomed and valued by local society, which saw in them two attractive people of consequence.

But even as her hopes panned out, she was failing. Her back problem may have been almost anything—a congenital weakness, a damaged disk. But its persistence and the considerable and at last unbearable suffering it led to suggest something grave, probably a tubercular infection manifesting in the spine. John Bunyan, the author of *Pilgrim's Progress*, from the seventeenth century, called tuberculosis "the captain of all these men of death," and what was true in Bunyan's era was still true in Martha Whitman's, that tuberculosis was the most prevalent fatal human infection. So common was death from TB that physicians often failed to mention it in postmortems. It was assumed in all deaths of a certain type—all those involving wasting, weakening, a cough that never went away, pulmonary hemorrhaging—and was considered by many to be tantamount to death, another name for death from nonaccidental causes.[34]

Walt, whose poetry often asserts his fine health ("I dote on myself. . . . there is that lot of me, and all so luscious"), died of tuberculosis in the end, not of a stroke. He may have been infected later in life, in one of the Civil War hospitals, for instance, but just as likely he was infected in his youth, possibly in the family home. Mrs. Whitman complained near the end of her own life of "soreness and distress in my side" and of "bad coughing," possible signs of pulmonary tuberculosis.[35] Laryngeal TB, Andrew's probable form of the disease, is an especially infectious one, the germ passing easily into the air through the mouth, and Mattie Whitman came to live with the family just when Andrew began showing symptoms of serious infection. No one can know who infected whom or if anyone did, but what is known is that tuberculosis shadowed an entire century and culture, and that the Whitmans' slow progress upward as a family, toward material security, toward a footing in a new class of salaried professionals, was also a struggle against that shadow.

Mattie's attentions to Andrew, in the months when he was dying, included bedside sitting through the night.[36] In a letter she wrote Walt on December 21, 1863, she spoke of the hard times that had befallen Nancy and Andrew's sons since his death:

> Jimmy has been very sick   he has had the Gastric fever . . . Mother sent them 50 cts last Thursday and afterwards I thought I would go around and see Jimmy . . . I took him a chicken   he said he thought he would get well now he liked chicken   I asked Nancy if she had things to eat . . . I knew by her manner it was not so and come to question her she had nothing but a crust of bread   I gave her a Dollar.[37]

Unlike Mrs. Whitman, Mattie does not express revulsion against the whore in their midst. But she does say of Nancy that "she will never make out much as she is in the street most all day . . . her case is awful   she is going to have another child and it seems as if the creature cant do much." For Mattie, not to be able to do was unthinkable, unbearable. "We are very lonesome here," she tells Walt:

> Jeff has gone away again   he is now at Albany [moonlighting as a surveyor] I expect him home Friday   Dear Brother I commenced this letter Monday and I am finishing it today Wednesday . . . I have been trying to plan some way to send you a mince pie   I made 17 large ones and they are splendid   if you could get a pass [to come north to Brooklyn] I think it would pay to come home.[38]

Mrs. Whitman, in a letter to Walt about Andrew's last days, makes clear her dependence on Mattie, and also on her daughter Mary:

> [W]endsday morning [Andrew] was very bad and [Mary] sent the children here i went again and marthe went he wanted her to come she was there nearly all day only came home to nurse the baby when she or mary went to come away he would becon for them too him that they would come back.[39]

Andrew asks to be taken out of bed and set up in a chair. "[P]oor soul he [later] died in it," Mrs. Whitman says,

> marthe was there till late then she came home and mary and Jeffy staid all night [The next day] he wanted to see Jeffy marthe went to the office for him . . . they had to fan him all night and bathe him in brandy nance went to bed when she came out in the morning she brought such a smell that Jeffy got sick and had to come home.[40]

In this scene of despair, disorder, and grim dying, Mattie went to be with Andrew when his siblings, Jeff and Mary, could temporarily no longer stand the squalor. Mrs. Whitman sent for a doctor, to see what could be done, but "[M]at went round behind the doctor and staid till he came." After a while, Jeff and Mary recovered their composure. All were there with Andrew when he finally passed on:

> [B]efore i got there mary said he would look around she asked him if it was mother he wanted he mooved his head . . . he died like any one

going to sleep without a struggle sensible to the last just before he died he turned his head and looked at your and georges pictures for some time and then shut his eyes god grant i may never witness another.[41]

MRS. WHITMAN'S LETTERS bring us into the presence of a woman who was personally unassuming, whose critique of other people tended to avoid any suggestion of social or material superiority. She was of humble background, economically distressed—although sometimes less distressed than she pretended—and when she disapproved of someone, her often sharp words skewered them for being dirty, greedy, sluttish, thoughtless, or selfish, but never for being of a lesser class. Nancy Whitman's failings were gross and revolting to her, but Nancy was not an embarrassment. The fear was not that Nancy would bring shame to the Whitman name, but that her children would run ragged, that her dying husband would go unfed, that she would spread disease.

George Whitman made gentle fun of his mother as someone who would go to any sort of church when the spirit moved her. But if she was anything by temperament, she was a Quaker. Her mother had been a Quaker, and along with Walter Sr., Mrs. Whitman favored the radically leveling, anti-institutional form of American Quakerism associated with Elias Hicks. Not that she was observant—George never mentioned her going to a Quaker meeting, and her letters, again, are lacking in the sorts of pious expression that were common at the time, the talk of God's will, of the progress of the soul, of a finer world beyond this vale of suffering.

To judge from her known photos, the head covering she often wore was Quakerish (a Quaker "soft cap" rather than a true Quaker bonnet). There were "no religious exercises or observances in the family," but there was a subtle influence for simplicity, for not "going" it too much. The critique of greed and the firm belief in equality to be found in Walt's writings, even his very early ones, have been rightly traced to his father's radicalism. But his mother's simplicity and the moral intensity of nineteenth-century Quaker social reform movements seem to speak in passages like this one, written when he was twenty-two:

> If we were asked the particular trait of national character from which might be apprehended the greatest evil to the land, we should unhesitatingly point to the strife for gain . . . This unholy spirit seems to have no bound or check. It leads yearly to the commission, among us, of the most abominable actions . . . It imbues the popular mind with a disposition to connive at villainy, if joined with wealth . . . to smile gently at a swindler, if he has only been a swindler of millions.[1]

At the same time, the Whitman household was a locus for ambition. The task of escaping poverty animated those in the family able and willing to shoulder it. As Jeff wrote Walt in late 1863, in the same letter that reported Jesse's outburst, "There are three of us, You George and I"— three competent, moneymaking sons. The loyalty of these three to one another, to their mother, and to their variously troubled siblings was notable and long-lived, and took many forms.

The Whitman household at the time of the Civil War was unusually stable, by the family's standards. In May 1859 they moved into the house on North Portland Avenue, and here they remained till after the war, their longest residence in one locale for their entire history in Brooklyn.[2] In April 1860, Mrs. Whitman rented space to "one of Mr Beecher church members by the uncommon name of John Brown," as she wrote Walt.[3] Beecher was Henry Ward Beecher, the pastor of Brooklyn's Plymouth Church, and the brother of the author of *Uncle Tom's Cabin*, Harriet Beecher Stowe. Brown, a tailor, and his wife had two sons, aged seventeen and nine. Rent for the whole house was thirty dollars per month. Mrs. Whitman told Walt:

> [Mrs. Brown] is a long island woman and very clever they have the back bacement and the next floor through and one bedroom in the

attic for 14 dollars per month we are a little crampt in the basement
we miss the water but well do the best we can they want gazs very
much but I did not promice it when they hired.[4]

Many homes in Brooklyn at this time had gas, for illumination, and
water delivered by pipe inside the house. A list of houses "To Let" in the
Brooklyn Daily Eagle, April 1861, even noted two houses (out of ten) with
hot water in the house.[5] But the house on North Portland either lacked
piped water or, more likely, had but one outlet or a simple well in the
basement, and this in the part of the basement ceded to the Browns.

Brooklyn City was then bringing a modern water supply online, with
reservoirs, pumping stations, and clean water from rural streams. The
first water was let into the new municipal system on December 15, 1858,
and work continued—Jeff Whitman was one of the engineers—until
May 26, 1862.[6] Before that date, and probably for some time after, much
of the water used in the city came from shallow wells dug on street cor-
ners, which fed public cisterns. Walt, for one—and here he gave expression to the deep fear of contagion that underlay his trumpeting of his
"reckless" good health, of being "free from taint from top to toe"—
wrote for the papers about the need for better, purer supplies of water.[7]
"Reader, have you ever thought what this [cistern] stuff really is?" he
asked in an editorial for the *Brooklyn Daily Advertizer*. "Imagine all the
accumulations of filth in a great city, not merely the slops and rottenness
thrown in the streets and by-ways . . . but the numberless privies, cess-
pools, sinks and gulches and abomination . . . the unnameable and
immeasurable dirt . . . daily and hourly taken into our stomachs, our
veins, our blood."[8]

Brooklyn still had outbreaks of cholera in the 1850s. Cholera is spread
through fecal contamination of drinking water, and while the precise
mechanism of the disease—how people pass it one to another, and that a
bacterium causes it—was only beginning to be understood, Walt was
surely right in fearing the water gotten from some street sources, and in
campaigning, in his articles, for betterment. His obsession with pure water showed in an 1849 essay about the Croton Aqueduct, a thirty-eight-
mile-long system delivering clean river water to New York City. Walt
rejoiced that Manhattanites would no longer be drinking water mixed
with the foul seepage from graves.[9] His concern for good water and new,

modern waterworks must surely have caught the attention of his brother Jeff, who was especially attached to Walt and who shared others of his deep enthusiasms, for example, for long rambles over the Long Island countryside, and for opera, which the two often saw together in New York.[10]

By the summer of 1860, Jeff was a young husband and a new father, and a main support of the household on North Portland. His life had found a focus and a motive—now the flow of expertise went in the other direction as well, and Walt's essays about the engineering challenge of building a modern water system show the influence of someone with inside information.[11] Jeff's first jobs had been in a newspaper office and a print shop. Walt got him the first and steered him toward the second, but Jeff had his own interests, as suggested in a letter written when he was fourteen:

Yesterday evening and this morning is the finest weather we have had since we have been [in New Orleans, where Walt was editing a local paper and Jeff was his office boy] . . . We took a very long walk last night, way out Camp street beyond the limits of the city. There are no hills like on old Long Island   the whole state is as level as a race course. In some of the streets they have a kind of canal or drain to let the water run off, and even then in some places there is not enough "down-hill" to make it run off good. Just a little farther up town there is a canal . . . where sloops &c can come up from the lake (about 7 miles westward of the city). Along by this canal . . . there is a road called shell road where we take frequent (and very pleasant) walks, the road is nearly as hard as a brick.[12]

He had already written his father about rates of flow on the Ohio River. Drainage problems were compelling to him, maybe even romantic:

Dear Father, I hope you are getting along good with your work &c. Mother says it is cold so you can't work . . . In building houses here they do not do as they do in New York. Here they dig a hole in the ground some two feet deep . . . and in length as far as the wall is to go, (they can not dig cellars here like in the north, you don't dig in the ground more than two feet before it is filled with water.) This trench they cover the bottom with boards (the ground is mostly made of quick-sand).[13]

Like thousands of other ambitious, practical-minded young men in the seventeenth, eighteenth, and nineteenth centuries—George Washington also comes to mind—Jeff first learned surveying, from which all manner of promising lines of work opened out in North America: mapping, road building, canal designing, land speculation. Jeff found early work with a man who made harbor improvements at New York.[14] Later, in his early twenties, he was sufficiently well trained to satisfy James Kirkwood, one of the great engineers of the nineteenth century and the former chief engineer of the Missouri Pacific Railroad. Kirkwood was building the new Brooklyn waterworks as a coordinated sewer-and-water system, the first scientifically engineered example of such a thing in America.[15] Walt may have known Kirkwood personally, and he wrote an editorial expressing faith in the engineer's skill in a moment of crisis for the project (August 1857).[16] This is roughly when Jeff first went to work for Kirkwood.

If Walt did get his brother hired on at the works, Jeff very much made his own way thereafter. He was bright and hardworking. As George said of his brothers years later, "Walt was not markedly sober or jolly—could be either one way or the other. Jeff was always the jolly one."[17] Acute, sometimes prankish, Jeff showed his own instincts early on, successfully riding the ups and downs of the city government's interfering relationship with the engineers, and learning how to read a sometimes byzantine political environment. As he wrote Walt in April 1863,

I have had quite a disappointment in a small way There was a bill introduced in the Leg[islature] to give the Brooklyn Sewer Com[mission] the power to build a large sewer in Kent Av. . . . quite a large job and we all surely thought it would go through as it is very much needed, and Mr Lane [chief engineer after Kirkwood] had promised me charge of it. Indeed I had commenced making plans, profiles &c when at the last moment the thing got squelched, but yet I don't know a[s] I am *very* sorry for we still expect to get . . . a new line of pipe from the Reservoir down to the city, and even if we dont do that

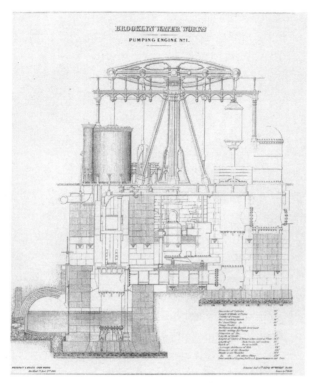

Brooklyn Water Works Pumping Engine # 1, built and brought online during Jeff Whitman's tenure as an engineer in Brooklyn.

why I shall have work enough . . . doing anything and everything that turns up.[18]

Moses Lane, who became a friend and invaluable mentor, promoted Jeff to chief assistant at the waterworks in 1863. Jeff's comfort around experienced, powerful men able to advance him owes something to his great trust in Walt, his elder by fourteen years and his life teacher. "I like to know such men," he wrote frankly, "I can learn from them."[19] His hunger to learn was prodigious. Walt being in Washington, newly launched on his mission to the hospitals, Jeff pestered him with requests for books on engineering, books "that Uncle Sam prints," as Jeff put it. On April 11, 1863, he wrote:

The two books you sent me . . . came all right. I am extremely obliged to you . . . and shall, Oliver Twist like, ask for more. I should dearly love to get together a set of the Pacific R.R. Explorations and

Reports . . . I told you that I had written to Boston for a Report on
the Hoosac Tunnel, that also has come and I have already found it of
great use . . . in solving two or three questions that I was not up
in . . . If you, in looking around the second hand book stalls, see any
Engnring works please write me what they are and the price. I am
very much in want of a copy of "Wisbachs Mechanics" but cannot
meet with it in New York.[20]

Jeff wanted also a copy of Captain John Mullan's *Report on the Construction of a Military Road From Fort Walla-Walla to Fort Benton*
(1863). Mullan was a young army officer who had spent six years out
west, looking for, among other things, a possible route for a transconti-
nental railroad. Walt got to know Mullan in Washington, and talked to
him "intimately, and . . . freely" about his adventures in the Rockies.[21]
Jeff urged Walt to give Mullan a letter of introduction to Moses Lane,
sensing that his boss at the waterworks would enjoy meeting such a man.
Jeff wanted to meet him, too—at this moment of great new works being
undertaken across the breadth of a continent, to gain a sense of the possibilities, the techniques, and the players was altogether exciting.

A certain skill in dealing with other people, especially other men,
marked the careers of all three of the competent Whitman sons. All
were comfortable in situations of personal politicking, winning or ten-
dering allegiance while keeping self-interest comfortably in view. They
were not the lone woodsmen of the American myths becoming established in the same period, suspicious of towns and the affairs of townish
men. Walt, the eldest, probably formed the template, and his brothers
saw him immersed in one thick human context after another, the world
of newspapering, the world of neighborhood home building, the book-
authoring world. They were *urban* men, of the first generation in America that can reasonably be described that way. When required to operate
in groups, or negotiate professional hierarchies, they knew what to do.

If the Browns controlled the basement water spigot, the Whitmans had
to carry their own. Edd, who could be trusted to fetch Andrew's medicine, probably also fetched water, as did Jesse, who was fired from a job
at the Brooklyn Navy Yard in 1861 and thereafter spent many hours in
the home.[22]

Before the blowup, Jesse often babysat for Jeff's wife Mattie, who gave
birth to her second child, Jessie Louisa, on June 17, 1863.* Jesse was especially useful for rocking the cradle—a task suggestive of his state of
mind and also of his fallen status in the family. "I do not have Jess up in
my room any more," Mattie wrote on December 21, giving her version
of the kitchen incident to Walt. "He has such ugly spells that I am affraid
of him   last week he . . . made [more] terrible threats and this conduct
is nothing new only he used to confine it to your mother."[23]

The house on North Portland had three or four stories. The Browns
were more or less sandwiched between floors of Whitmans, a situation
maddening to both camps. Mrs. Brown had won Mrs. Whitman's favor,
temporarily, by being solicitous as Andrew lay dying, but by late 1863
there had been bad blood between the two groups for some time. Probably it was a struggle over who would control the lease. In March 1863,
Jeff wrote Walt,

> That she bitch of Hell, the Brown, is trying her strongest to clear us
> out and I honestly think Walt that I shall just take and belt old Johny
> [Brown] under the eye if he attempts any of his last summers
> games . . . To day the bitch could do nothing better than spend an
> hour or two in getting the lid of the cistern up and has left it in the old
> dangerous style half on and half [off] the hole . . . Brown is continu-
> ally at [Mother] about Mats conduct and keeps her in continued hot
> water. Everything is going on as usual.[24]

To try to imagine the physical house, and the close life lived in it, is to
appreciate the daily exercise of self-control on the part of many people.
Mr. Brown may have been continually at Mrs. Whitman because the

---

*The Whitman family fished in a very shallow pond for names. This new daughter bor-
rowed both her uncle's and her grandmother's Christian names, and there was a third
Louisa in the family as well, George's wife, Louisa Orr Haslam, whom he married after
the war. Walt suggested that the new baby be named California, but the name Jessie is the
one that stuck. The names Hattie—from Mannahatta, another Walt-suggested name—
Mattie, and Hannah seem almost to court confusion, and George and Louisa Whitman
named their two sons, who both died young, Walter and George.

stairs Mat and her children used to clamber up and down echoed throughout the house. If it was a wood-frame house, it would have been of the most plentiful type in Brooklyn; if built of brick, the rent of $360 per year would have put it at the low end of the price range of such multistory dwellings.[25] Yet it must have been well constructed, since it remained standing for many years (George Whitman told an interviewer in 1893, "It is there now," should anyone care to look). The general complaint from the Brown family seems to have been that there was too much going on, too much Whitman chaos. In the midst of this, Mrs. Whitman's anxieties about money added to the stress. At sixty-eight, she had been making do on an uncertain income for forty years, while rearing eight children and now grandchildren. She may have been overreacting to the wartime rise in prices—as Jeff noted in April 1863, "[E]verything is so awful dear that you can hardly get enough to make a happy dinner on for less than 15octs."*

Overcontrol of the family budget may have been a way to seem to be doing something about insoluble problems, just as constant housecleaning may have been a gesture at order. "If mother could be persuaded to let the scrubbing of the lower entry alone for a few days," Jeff wrote that February, "she would recover [from a bad cold], but I believe that she is too much afraid of Mrs Brown, for this morning, and it was one of those cold rainy ones, she went to work and scrubbed as usual."[26] In reality, Mrs. Whitman was no longer dependent solely on the wages of an artisan-husband who was losing economic ground (and on the small earnings of apprenticed sons). In almost every letter Walt wrote her, no matter his own situation in Washington, he sent her a few dollars. Jeff contributed most of the rent owed by the Whitmans per month, and Mattie and he provided many meals in their upstairs apartment. Other costs, for coal or wood or gas, were probably paid out of a communal

---

*In fact, a severe wartime inflation did not take hold in the North as it did in the South. The Federal government issued paper money ("greenbacks") in a controlled and thoughtful manner. New taxes, under the Internal Revenue Act passed July 1, 1862, soaked up much of the inflationary pressure created by the issuing of greenbacks. For an excellent brief discussion of the war economies North and South, see James M. McPherson, *Battle Cry of Freedom*, 444–50.

pot. Although the days were gone when Walt, as a successful local builder, would fill a place up with carpets, clocks, bathtubs, and melodeons, the house was more than adequately furnished, in a style that people like the Whitmans, and the Browns, who wanted it for themselves, found attractive.

But Mrs. Whitman's principal financial support in these years, and a very substantial source, was the army pay of her son George. Beginning as a private, and then as a commissioned officer rising steadily in rank, George earned considerable sums and sent most of it home to Mrs. Whitman. Union privates in 1863 earned $13 per month, but a second lieutenant (George's rank after April 15, 1862) earned $105.50 per month.[27] A captain—his pay grade as of November 1 that year—earned $115.50.[28] George intended his mother to use as much of this money as she needed and to bank the rest. Early in June, he sent her $35, and sometime in August he sent $140 by Adams Express, a private delivery service offering secure transfers.[29] At the end of September, he wrote, "Mother I have three months pay due me to day so dont deprive yourself of anything you need." And in early November, "I have something over 400$ comeing to me besides the $100 bounty which I believe I am entitled to."[30]

Perhaps thinking of her tendency to thrift, George wrote a few days after First Fredericksburg, the battle in which he sustained his only wound of the war,

> Mother . . . I hope you have everything comfortable there at home. I should be mad as blazes if I knew you did not use the money I sent on, for anything you need, whenever you want clothing or anything else   dont be afraid to use the money for there is plenty more where that came from, so go in lemons, and remember that your galliant Son is a Capting, and expects you to keep up the dignity of the family.[31]

Mrs. Whitman did spend out of George's wages, but not overfreely. To judge from her letters to Walt, there was frequent carping back and forth between her and Jeff (and wife Mattie), each side accusing the other of being tight. The month of Andrew's death, Mrs. Whitman worried, "[I] cant put much of Georges money in the bank this time i had a very larg grocery bill to pay." She seems to have assumed that her duty was to spend as little as possible, and to "go in lemons" (buy luxuries) was simply beyond her. "[W]alt they expect to much from me," she complained in a letter in November 1862, speaking of Jeff and Andrew and their wives:

> [I] suppose marthe has told nancy i have got 2 or 3 hundred dollars in the bank [Jeff and Mat] never gave [Andrew] one cents worth . . . not even a shirt when jeff has 18 [shirts] . . . i said to mat the other day in a joke if they had another young one they would be so stingey we wouldent know what to doo but I got the same old retort that it was me that was stingey with my bank book that is such a common thing to hear.[32]

For certain expenses, unavoidable ones, she paid readily enough:

> [I] have got A letter from George to day . . . he sent me 150 dollars . . . i don't think it was one hour after i received it that the undertaker came for his money i was rather surprised at his presenting the bill so soon jeffy told him we wanted A little time but i paid it . . . 52 dollars[33]

Her thrift, edging over into neurotic parsimony, served George well. When the war ended, the nest egg his mother had nurtured for him bought him a start in a familiar Whitman game, speculative house building.[34] Eventually he made a substantial fortune, less as a builder than as a private investor with many income streams. And for all the accusations of cheapness, all the anxious worry over the financial future, the Whitman clan, in the years of the war, lived well. The grocery bill, although large sometimes, did get paid. When short on cash, Mrs. Whitman ran a tab with the local grocer, Amerman—in itself a sign of being thought a person of some resources.[35]

Mother Whitman's comfort included a "new stove"—she referred to it in a letter to Walt about the surprise appearance one morning of George, home from the front on a ten-day furlough. George mentioned there being "Sewing Machines" in the house in a letter of April 1862; these machines, used by Mattie for piecework, were probably new or almost new

Singer sewing machines, because Jeff described Hattie taking "an immensely bad fall" and striking her head on "the frame of the Extension table leaves," and one of the features of Singer's new machine was an attached extension table to support cloth horizontally.*[36]

Other small details of life on North Portland Avenue suggest that it was crowded, bustling, stressed, but not mean. On Christmas Day 1863, the Whitmans gathered together and had a holiday dinner, eating "not turkeys nor geese but pot pie made of mutton," Mrs. Whitman wrote to Walt—mutton being a modest repast, but a repast nonetheless.[37] On Christmas Eve, they had likewise gathered in Mrs. Whitman's kitchen, "matty and hattie and all" joining Edd, Mrs. Whitman, and probably the volcanic Jesse.

Mrs. Whitman's rheumatism found relief in regular visits to private baths near City Hall, where she took "sulphur vapor" treatments for a fee.[38] An avid reader, she felt comfortable ordering Walt to acquire books that sounded good to her, such as James Redpath's 1860 biography of John Brown and something by the author of *Consuelo* (George Sand), a book that both Walt and his mother enjoyed.[39] During that ten-day furlough in Brooklyn, George was feted by family and friends, went to the theater (to see Matilda Heron, an actress famous for her "Camille"), and had the funds to buy a complete new set of clothes from Manhattan tailors, at prices that shocked Mrs. Whitman.[40] His two-and-a-half-year-old niece was fascinated by her dashing uncle "wounded in the cheek," Mrs. Whitman noted, and George was flush enough to bestow on little Hattie "a gold locket cost six dollars and a half," which she mistook for a watch.[41]

Hattie and the baby Jessie brightened things, while also making conditions in the house noisier and more complicated. Letters from Jeff, Martha, and even Mrs. Whitman at her most querulous often resolve in loving descriptions of the girls, of how fat they are, of their antics. Martha, as their mother, can be expected to have thought the new baby

---

*A Singer home sewing machine at the start of the Civil War cost about $75, a considerable sum. Singer reduced the price of the family machine in late 1862 to $50 ($75 for factory machines). An ad offering both machines at the new prices appeared in the *Brooklyn Eagle* on September 5, 1862. Source: author's communication with Amy Isaacs Koplowicz.

"just about cunning enough," and Jeff, as Hattie's father, that his older daughter was a "Harem-scarem . . . joyous little thing."[42] But Mrs. Whitman, with all her worries and her aching arthritic wrists and knees, also rejoiced that Hattie "goes the whole figure" over handsome Uncle George, who returned the affection.[43] The girls wanted for nothing—unlike Andrew's unlucky sons—and their health and clean clothes and strong spirits owed everything to the devotion of their parents and grandmother, while that devotion was in turn buttressed by a quiet ongoing financial breakthrough.

George by 1863 had moved up socially—he was now a member of the officer class. What this would mean after the war, should he survive, was unknown, but American officers in the Revolution had won distinction and, sometimes, social advancement for their meritorious service. In England, to take a culturally close example, to be the son of a workingman and become a commissioned officer was to gain a foothold in the middle classes. George's strong words to his mother about spending the money he sent home were sincere—he wanted her to live well, but he also firmly believed that there was "plenty more where that came from," that he would continue to earn well if he survived. Proud of having won the equivalent of a battlefield commission, he had written home in March 1862, after the Battle of New Bern,

> A day or two after the [earlier] battle of Roanoke Col. Ferero came to me and said he would soon give me a chance, but as there was no vacancies of course he could do nothing . . . My apointment dates from . . . the day of the battle of Newberne. There has been a great deal of figuring for positions in this regt   some of the Leiuts paying as high as 3 or $400 for the place but I never asked for it, and I feel a great deal better satisfied than if I had bought it.[44]

Suggesting to his mother, maybe unintentionally, what becoming an officer might mean for him economically, he added:

> Our Captain is a young man from Buffalo N.Y. named Hazard whose father is very rich and we live in fine style I tell you. Cap has bread made in the Citty and buys lots of eggs, fish Oysters chickens, milk

and everything else he can see. We have three nigger boys to cook and wait on us, but Cap can afford it so I don't care.[45]

Like his brother George, Jeff was accomplishing his own upward move at this same time. Although he earned less, and his pay did not arrive home in impressive lump sums, he was dependably salaried and beginning to realize just how well situated he was professionally. In 1863, when he became chief assistant engineer at the Brooklyn waterworks, he was close to the top of a staff of some fifty men, at only thirty years of age.[46] October 1863, when his salary was temporarily cut, he wrote Walt,

[I]t is not like you think in regard to cutting down my wages. I was working for the two boards of Commissioners, one at $40 and the other at $50 per month, and I have got all the work for one board finished . . . It is not the meanness or anything of that kind of anybody and they would pay me more and will probably in a short time . . . I have every reason to think that the Commissioners (both boards) think well of me, and I know that Mr Lane will ever do everything in his power for me, and I undoubtedly in a short time shall be getting more.[47]

Mat was able to lay off her contract sewing in 1863, as the birth of Jessie approached. Jeff was sanguine enough about money to acquire a local lot on which to build a "small 2 Story house" for his young family; he ordered plans drawn up and put the contract out to bid, but the local carpenters asked more than he thought they should for the work, and he decided that "the best thing I could do would be to hold on to the lot and wait for cheaper times."[48]

That he would seriously consider building a new house probably says more about his growing sense of security than about his actual cash reserves. Following the New York draft riots of July 13–16, 1863, Jeff wrote Walt about his own vulnerability to the draft:

Abt. the $300 [to buy a commutation of service]. I'm a little afraid that I shant be able to raise it through Mr Lane as he has been a little unfortunate lately, but still I keep a bold front   I lately got a position where I am getting $90 per month . . . This will be permanent (as long as

Jeff Whitman in the 1850s, near the start of his career as a water engineer.

Mr Lane is here, perhaps for years.) and with such a certain prospect of paying it back in a few months, I think that George would lend me the money. I, by sailing very close, think I could pay him in five months.[49]

Walt, also worried about Jeff being drafted, had written his mother the day before that if it should so happen that Jeff should be drafted—of course he could not go, without its being the downfall almost of our whole family, as you may say, Mat & his young ones, & a sad blow to you too, mother . . . I have no doubt I shall make a few hundred dollars by the lectures I shall certainly commence soon . . . & I could lend that am't to Jeff to pay it back—May be the draft will not come off after all.[50]

In the end, Jeff did buy his way out of service in 1864. Walt was surely right, that sending a second son to fight would have worked a financial and emotional hardship for the Whitman family, but part of the loss would surely have been of Jeff's promising future. He had won a fairly secure position and could expect further advancement. He was impressively good at what he did, and his prospects were of the sort that the Whitman family had been working toward for two generations, prospects of a kind not easily surrendered.

Other families sent two (and sometimes three and more) sons to the Civil War. But among the Whitmans there appears to have been no anguished debate about the correctness of avoiding service. George, probably most of all, opposed his younger brother's joining him on the battlefield. After the draft riots, he wrote his mother, "I do hope that Jeff has escaped [conscription]," and in another letter he told her about an incident during the Vicksburg campaign that he knew of personally: "One wooman came on there from Michagan after the body of her son, which she said was the seventh she had lost during the war. Six had been killed in battle, and this one . . . had died of fever and was buried near our camp."[51]

George wanted his brother at home, safe. No, he replied to a question Jeff asked, about hiring a substitute from among some recently discharged veterans, "None of the men who have been through this Campaign, will listen to Re-enlisting at present they all think they have had sogering enough and its no use talking to them untill they have been home a month or two."[52] And he admonished, "Jeff if you know any one . . . that is anxious to extinguish themselves, tell them to try and get in Co K [George's company] and if they do right smart, they'l soon get to be Corporels, or something, and get the splendid Salary of $13 a month. Poor devils I fear theyl have rather a hard time."[53]

George had seen and felt much by late summer 1863. Roanoke, New

Bern, Cedar Mountain, Second Manassas; Chantilly, South Mountain, Antietam, Fredericksburg, Vicksburg—this partial list of battles the 51st New York had taken part in suggests why they were regarded as one of the most veteran of veteran units. Although George could not have known that more men were killed or wounded at Antietam than on any other single day in the war—on any other day in American history—he had a very clear idea of what he was living through.

All things considered, he wanted his brother out of it. On August 30, 1864, a month before being taken prisoner along with most of his regiment (of 333 men captured that day, fewer than half survived captivity), George wrote home,

> Dear mother.   Your letter and Walts containing the pictures came all right, and yesterday I received another from Walt, saying that you had received the money [I sent]. We have moved 4 or 5 miles since I wrote you last. We came here [near Petersburg, Virginia] on the 19th and expected to have a right smart fight, but so far, we have been very agreeably disappointed, as our Division has not been engaged to any extent.[54]

Recently, the 51st had fought in the disastrous Battle of the Crater. George's division had come close to taking its objective on that ill-starred day for the North, and George was afterward mentioned in dispatches for gallantry.[55] Allowing himself a quiet exercise of pride, he sent his mother a copy of the official letter praising him, and he noted:

> I am in command of the Regt. as Major Wright is away somewhere sick . . . I am very glad to hear that Jeff is clear of the draft on the 5th of next month, although $400 seems like a pretty large sum to pay for a substitute . . . Mother I hope you take things easy and dont worry and keep a bright look out for [a] little place in the country,   When I get the New York papers I almost always look over the Farms for sale to see if there is anything offered that will suit us.[56]

No longer dreaming only of home-cooked buckwheat cakes, he fantasized retreating to a place of true peace, one beyond even Brooklyn in its powers to heal. Two weeks later, he wrote,

Here we are yet in the same place, and everything goes on . . . I
rather think Lee has about made up his mind that this Rail Road [the
Weldon Railroad] is a gone case, but if he thinks he can drive us away
I wish he would pitch in, as we are all prepared for him . . . Mother I
am Brigade Officer of the day to day, and must take a walk out to the
picket line to see that things are all right. It is very quiet here to day
and there is no picket fireing going on, sometimes the johnies come
out and fire a few shots . . . but it don't amount to much . . . Mother,
give my love to Mattie and the little gals.[57]

Fᴏʀ ᴍʀs. ᴡʜɪᴛᴍᴀɴ's ᴘᴏᴇᴛ sᴏɴ, 1863 was an epochal year. So full of excitement and event was it that in October Walt proposed to James Redpath, the Boston author-publisher, a new book with the working title of "Memoranda of a Year." The book would be a handy volume offering "skeleton memoranda of incidents, persons, places, sights, the past year," relating all that had happened to Walt since he first rushed to his brother's side after Fredericksburg. It would have "much to say of the hospitals, the immense national hospitals," because Walt had spent the ten months since George's wounding as a hospital volunteer in Washington.[1]

Louisa May Alcott had just published her own small book, likewise with Redpath, called *Hospital Sketches*. The future author of *Little Women* and other immensely popular works had hurried to Washington on almost the same schedule as Walt, to take up duties as a nurse, one of the hundreds of slightly trained women being provided by the newly constituted United States Sanitary Commission. A game, droll spinster of thirty, Miss Alcott left Boston on December 12, 1862, and arrived in Washington on the fourteenth, just in time for the first wave of casualties coming north from Fredericksburg. (George, wounded there on the thirteenth, was surprised by the appearance in camp of his brother on December 19.) Louisa wrote descriptive letters home from wartime Washington, letters published the following spring in the *Commonwealth*, an antislavery paper, and reprinted throughout the North. The news that the letters brought of the suffering of the wounded soldiers electrified Union families anxious about their sons at war, and Redpath quickly bundled them into a book that was offered for sale that August.[2]

It was a modest success, and Walt, as a professional writer, took note. He thought he could do better, in much the same vein ("My idea is a book of the time, worthy the time—something considerably beyond mere hospital sketches," he wrote Redpath). Miss Alcott had served as a nurse for only three weeks. She came down with typhoid fever, one of the war's principal epidemic infections (the others were malaria and diarrhea), and nearly died after being dosed with calomel (a compound of mercury), which caused her hair and teeth to fall out.[3] The dangers of serving in pestiferous army hospitals, if not already obvious, would have been borne in upon Walt by her hard fate.

Arriving back in Washington after being at George's side at Fredericksburg, Walt took lodging with a friend and ardent Whitman admirer, William D. O'Connor. But by the time of his letter to Redpath he was

Louisa May Alcott at about age twenty-five.

boarding with an "old & feeble" woman at 456 sixth Street West, close to the Capitol and two blocks north of Pennsylvania Avenue. "[I]t is in 3d story, an addition back, seems to be going to prove a very good winter room," he wrote his mother. "[O]ne thing is I am quite by myself, there is no passage up there except to my room . . . good big bed, I sleep first rate—there is a young wench of 12 or 13, Lucy . . . she comes & goes, gets water &c., she is pretty much the only one I see."[4]

By day he worked part-time as a copyist in the U.S. Army Paymaster's Office, corner Fifteenth and F streets, fifth floor. After a few hours of this drudgery—drudgery that he found enjoyable, for the office camaraderie, the parade of young soldiers passing through, the view of the wooded Potomac from his high window—he went home, dined, bathed, and, in a fortified and sweet-smelling condition, went out to the wards. Part of his strategy for spreading health among the wounded was to be himself an avatar of red-cheeked, manly vigor, and he dressed often in a suit made of burgundy corduroy, over a clean white shirt (the collar, of course, left open).[5]

He was forty-four. A photo taken by Mathew Brady shows him with beard gone fully gray, wearing a light-colored slouch hat (broad of brim, soft to the hand). Nelly O'Connor, William's wife, fell in love with him. She described his "splendid health" in a memoir she wrote, that he had "no ailment but those occasional intense headaches" that had been brought on, Walt told her, by sunstroke suffered one day on Broadway, when he went outdoors with no head cover. "At that time," Nelly wrote,

> Washington had no general system of water supply or drainage, and a pump at the corner of our street was reputed to be of very pure water . . . fed from a spring at Rock Creek. To this pump every morning Walt would go for a pitcher for our table, and he was especially fond of taking a long draught . . . I remember how his warm, strong hands . . . communicated their genial temperature.[6]

Walt "had a pleasant habit of singing in his room while making his morning toilet," she recalled. He was about six feet, two hundred pounds—a mighty specimen. His baggy trousers stayed up without help of suspenders, and his slow walk along Washington's unpaved streets, clogged often with bluecoats and mule-drawn army wagons, not to mention free-ranging

*Walt Whitman in characteristic pose (hands in pockets) and attire,
the Civil War Years.*

hogs, was more of a saunter, his hands buried in deep coat pockets, his wrists turned down. Walt's presence in her home for nine months of 1863 was highly tonic for Nelly, who had recently lost a child. She wrote,

Those of us who . . . saw him day and night, before and after his watches with his sick and maimed soldier[s], feel that a great privilege was ours . . . A man who felt that after all, the world was pretty

good, and men and women not so bad as they were pictured, was up-
lifting and helpful in those awful days, and all other days.[7]

The time with the O'Connors was for Whitman one of his most
deeply stirring encounters with other writer-intellectuals. But to give up
the "werry little bedroom" he had with them for his own place, "quite
by himself" at the top of a private staircase, was probably a relief. In the
ten years he lived in Washington, he moved to seven different resi-
dences, most of the moves coinciding with visits he made to his family
back in Brooklyn. (He would give up one boardinghouse for the time he
was gone to New York and move into another on his return, thus saving
himself some rent.)[8] It was the old Whitman family pattern. Some of his
moves were to better places, with better board. Others were for the
worse. To move this often, despite a severe wartime housing shortage,
suggests either the enjoyment of change for its own sake or a preference
for anonymity, or both.

As a young man, a fresh newspaperman, he had vanished almost daily
into turbulent New York crowds, ever on the hunt, one of the thousands,
the hundreds of thousands, of city strangers. But Washington as recently as two years before his arrival had struck observers as backward,
villagelike, desolate. Henry Adams, who spent the war in London, said
of Washington, "As in 1800 and 1850, so in 1860, the same rude
colony . . . camped in the same forest, with the same unfinished Greek
temples for workrooms, and sloughs for roads."[9]

Anthony Trollope, visiting in 1861, wrote that in Washington "a man
may lose himself in the streets, not as one loses oneself in London between Shoreditch and Russell Square, but as one does . . . in the deserts
of the Holy Land . . . [T]he country is wild, trackless, unbridged . . . If
you are a sportsman, you will desire to shoot snipe within sight of the
President's house."[10]

That house, not yet officially called the White House, was in an unkempt park. It little resembled a presidential mansion and was more like
a Southern plantation house, with straggling kitchen gardens and outly-
ing sheds. Nearby among the trees were modest, old-fashioned
dwellings that contained government offices—the State Department was
in a small brick house along a path. The President's Park had the advantage of shade trees but the disadvantage of being bordered by the City

Canal, a foul channel cut between the Potomac's main and eastern branches. Sewage and dead pack animals produced spectacular smells when the winds and the temperature were right.[11]

Pennsylvania Avenue, the town's main promenade, often had a deserted air. Washington had been laid out according to a grand scheme, but after sixty years the half-dozen major public buildings were still unfinished, including the Capitol, with its absent steps and half-built dome. On the avenue, one of only two stretches of paved street in town (albeit paved with cobblestones, with mud freely oozing out between), the sleepy summer off-season yielded to something slightly more lively come November, when Congress was back in session.

It was a seasonal city, stuffed full of bachelors and married men living like bachelors, many as Walt did, in single rooms heated with wood-stoves. One consequence was rough woodyards scattered all over town, some operating in the public squares. Louisa May Alcott noticed the booming mule and street pig populations during her few weeks' residence. As in Brooklyn many years before, people in Washington still threw their slops in the gutters, and there was a sizable hog wallow in Judiciary Square, where City Hall was located and where a military hospital, which Walt visited, opened in 1862.[12]

So many corpses emerged from this hospital that they were laid out in a nearby vacant lot. In full view of the neighboring houses, the naked bodies were wrapped in shrouds and then carted off by an undertaker under contract to the government, who provided horse cart, coffin, grave digging, and grave filling for $4.99 per body.[13]

The rude town was becoming a rude city. If in 1863 Walt found fewer crowds with which to merge than in Manhattan, he was by no means marooned in the country, nor a solitary figure wandering alone down echoing streets. Just at his moment of arrival, Washington was transforming itself under press of war, filling up with soldiers, speculators, newsmen, contractors, prostitutes, actors, and hotel keepers. A shadow army of clerks, of which Walt was a fair example, was descending to fill the positions in federal offices that were expanding with the war. Traditionally, as a mostly male town, Washington had numbers of prostitutes (an estimated five hundred before the war). Now, more than seven thousand operated out of 450 registered houses of prostitution, according to the

Grand review of the Union Army, Pennsylvania Avenue, Washington, D.C.,
May 1865.

town's provost marshall, Major William Doster, and the *Washington*
Evening Star.[14]

Ford's Theatre, one of two legitimate theaters in town, barred prostitutes at the door. But other venues did not. As in New York thirty years
before, the brothels were colonizing neighborhoods all over town, including entire blocks on the south side of Pennsylvania Avenue and ar-

eas to the west and east of the White House, and others close to Lafayette Square.[15] Respectable people found themselves living next door to busy bawdy houses, and again as in New York in the 1830s, a campaign for suppression of prostitution got under way in the press and the courts, and eventually had some small effect.

Walt's move to Washington, usually represented as a sharp break with his past, is more remarkable for the many points of continuity with his New York life. He was a journalist there and he remained one here—within days, he was mailing articles to editors he knew, for instance, "Our Brooklyn Boys in the War," which appeared in the *Brooklyn Daily Eagle* on January 5, 1863. More of his reportage was on the way—"The Great Army of the Sick," a story about the hospitals, ran in the *New York Times* for February 26, and a long Washington dispatch, covering topics such as "The Army of the Potomac," "A Brooklyn Soldier's Death," and "The Fifty-first New York," was in the *Brooklyn Daily Union* on September 22.[16]

Washington was at the heart of the biggest story of the age, and once he had stumbled on it, there was no way he was going to miss it. His hospital visiting also had deep roots in his New York past, going back, possibly, to the old Dutch Church idea of "comforters of the sick," as well as to the people he had called "God's angels" in his early story about a cholera outbreak. Other elements of his personal story give rise to a sense almost of clairvoyance, as if, just as great poets are supposed to, he had seen deep into his nation's soul, his sense of an impending cataclysm leading him to become a healer, a keeper of spirits. Before he ever set foot in a Washington hospital, he had made himself familiar at the old New York Hospital on lower Broadway, where his omnibus-driving pals were often taken with broken heads and limbs after accidents on Manhattan's surging streets, and where he loyally visited them. He came to admire the nurses and the doctors he met on these visits—the good ones—and assisted at medical procedures when allowed, and he might almost have become a doctor, a reader feels, so detailed and wide ranging is the curiosity he displays in his early writings about health.

In 1855, in the poem later called "Song of Myself," he wrote,

> To anyone dying....thither I speed and twist the knob of the
>   door,
> Turn the bedclothes toward the foot of the bed,

Let the physician and the priest go home.
I seize the descending man....I raise him with resistless will.
O despairer, here is my neck,
By God! you shall not go down! Hang your whole weight upon
   me.[17]

These famous lines, in the most groundbreaking poem of a ground-breaking book, announced his vocation as spirit-nurse nearly a decade before he ever came to Washington. In the same poem, he imagines special kinds of trauma, the kinds of wounds that result when bodies are ferociously assaulted, as in a war:

I am the mashed fireman with breastbone broken....tumbling walls
   buried me in their debris,
Heat and smoke I inspired....I heard the yelling shouts of my
   comrades. . . .
. . . .
I am an old artillerist, and tell of some fort's bombardment....
Again the reveille of drummers....again the attacking cannon and
   mortars and howitzers. . . .
The ambulanza . . . trailing its red drip. . . .
The fall of grenades through the rent roof....
Again gurgles the mouth of my dying general....
He gasps through the clot....
. . . .
Formless stacks of bodies....dabs of flesh upon the masts and
   spars. . . .
The hiss of the surgeon's knife and the gnawing teeth of his saw,
The wheeze, the cluck, the swash of falling blood[18]

That something dreadful was in store he seemed to know, and he tried to prepare himself. Other writers, as well as ordinary citizens, sensed the bloodletting that awaited their country should the sectional conflict over slavery not find a political solution, but Walt seems to have been shaping himself for the role he eventually played. Even his most homoerotic poetry, appearing in the 1860 edition of *Leaves*—the "Calamus" cluster, forty-five poems frankly celebrating "the need of comrades"—sounds notes of alarm, and martial imagery, talk of raw wounds, and thoughts of death leaven the account of an urgent, earthy sexual search. From Calamus 15:

> O Drops of me! trickle, slow drops,
> Candid, from me falling—drip, bleeding drops,
> From wounds made to free you whence you were prisoned. . . .
> Stain every page—stain every song I sing, every word I say,
>   bloody drops.[19]

From 17:

> And I dreamed I wandered, searching among burial-places, to
>   find him,
> And I found that every place was a burial-place,
> The houses full of life were equally full of death. . . .
> The streets, the shipping, the places of amusement. . . .
> And fuller, O vastly fuller, of the dead than of the living[20]

and from 31:

> What place is besieged, and vainly tries to raise the siege?
> Lo! I send to that place a commander, swift, brave, immortal,
> And with him horse and foot—and parks of artillery,
> And artillerymen, the deadliest that ever fired gun.[21]

Maybe he *was* prophetic, as he boisterously claimed. His poem featuring a new American Colossus ("Walt Whitman, a kosmos, of Manhattan the son") hails the new continental democracy in the days of its heady youth, a fabulous race of rawboned, ax-wielding men (and a few women) lighting a light unto the nations, beginning history anew. But that the great new democracy needed a redeemer—needed a Whitman—was a confession right at the start of something amiss, of an ill to be cured.

His idea of "adhesiveness," developed in the first editions of *Leaves*, borrows its name from the then-popular pseudoscience of phrenology, wherein bumps on the skull correspond to inner qualities such as cautiousness, combativeness, hope, and self-esteem. Adhesiveness meant comradely love—a love similar to friendship, but more impassioned. Adhesiveness would be the force to bind the people of These States together, in Walt's view, a natural flowering of passionate friendship being all to the good in every respect. The long lists of young men, mostly working class, found in his notebooks suggest a trying out of this theory in the streets—from some of the entries, we can picture Walt adhering eagerly to some lad met in a noisy bar, or while crossing to Brooklyn on the ferry:

John Sweeten—tall, well-tann'd . . . driver 40 4th av. May 27 '62,—
   was a boy, in Philadelphia riots of '44 . . .
Thos Gray good looking young Scotchman elegantly dress'd,—does
   the tricks, cutting his finger &c—at Pfaff's [a cellar-saloon on
   Broadway at Bleecker] . . .
Wm Miller 8th st (has powder slightly in his face.) . . .
Pell, young man, American, introduced by Chas. Kingsley, at 6th st.
   lager bier house, night July 8th . . . [22]

A straightforward reading of such a list—or a slightly cynical one— may put one in mind of a wily seducer, a homosexual "collector" able to charm young men with a combination of warm patter and middle-aged good looks. And this is not wrong, exactly. Walt in the months just before his Washington move was definitely on the prowl. One entry, for "Theodore M Carr," suggests a liaison of two weeks' duration, with a man met one morning on Fort Greene (a block away from the Whitman house on North Portland, where Walt sometimes took little Hattie for walks). Carr was a military deserter, an escapee from a New York volunteer regiment like the one that George was serving in. On the morning when Walt was meeting Carr, George and his regiment were starting out for Manassas, Virginia, and Second Bull Run. While George fought there and then in a murderous rearguard action at Chantilly, Carr was quite possibly staying overnight with Walt in Mrs. Whitman's house ("came to the house with me . . . left Sept 11th '62").[23]
Union soldiers often bivouacked just across Myrtle Avenue at the fort—Walt mentions meeting others in the park there, and he may have roamed the slopes on a regular basis, with or without his niece. Mrs.

Whitman herself sometimes walked over and struck up conversations with young recruits. He was "adhering" out of a complex of motives. While he found the young men attractive sexually, he may also have been putting his theory of adhesiveness into play in some way, spontaneous bonds of interest and allure between strangers being for him important evidence. Another entry in the notebooks from summer 1862 reads, "Fred Vaughn 1393 Broadway." Here may be a clue to Walt's intense collecting just before his move to Washington, because Fred Vaughan was no inconsequential pickup forgotten the next morning. A young Brooklynite, Vaughan had been a close companion of Walt's for years—in a letter written in 1874, Vaughan mentions living on Atlantic Avenue "one door above Classon" and often passing by "our old home" on Classon Avenue near Myrtle, a home where he stayed with Walt in the 1850s.[24]

The Whitman family lived in the Classon house from May 1, 1856, until May 1, 1859, when they moved to the house on North Portland. That Vaughan referred to it as a "home" he shared with Walt suggests more than casual visits—indeed, he got to know the poet's mother well and used to joke with her about Walt's slow-as-molasses manner. In the spring of 1860, when Walt was in Boston seeing to the printing of the third edition of *Leaves*, Fred wrote him a series of letters from New York that can only be described as love letters, for their intimate joking and passages of yearning (and complaints about getting no letters in return). "In accordance with not only your wishes, but my own," Fred wrote, "I went to Brooklyn yesterday and saw your Mother . . . She did not remember me at first but as soon as she did she was very much pleased."[25]

There were many possible reasons not to recognize a young fellow who showed up suddenly at her door—that the young man and Walt had passed nights together under her own roof might not guarantee recognition if it was her practice, her sensible practice, as the mother of grown sons still living at home to cede them a degree of invisibility, privacy, or the illusion of it being a secret to survival in a family at close quarters.

There may have been numbers of young men—enough of them to make quick recognition unlikely. These friends of Walt need not all have been his lovers, and maybe few were. But in this period when he was writing his best and most original poetry, he was highly conscious of himself as a sexual quantity. He was trying to write the truth of his, or anyone's, bodily life, which to his way of thinking meant speaking of sex in a way that challenged Victorian norms but that also avoided the dirty storytelling that he deplored, the sniggering wit and salacious tale-bearing, mostly among men, that was more common in print in mid-nineteenth-century America than was actual prudery.[26] Still, on the personal level, he was notably ardent, even rampant. We can get a sense of how he appeared in the Fred Vaughan period from an unlikely source, an account that Bronson Alcott, the high-minded transcendentalist educator and father of Louisa May Alcott, wrote of an 1856 visit he made to Classon Avenue.

Alcott had been alerted to Walt as an unusually promising young American poet by Ralph Waldo Emerson, a friend of Alcott's. Visiting New York, Alcott took a special trip over to Brooklyn to meet the young writer, and Walt, after greeting him at the door, led Alcott and two companions up to an attic bedroom he shared with brother Eddy. Alcott immediately noticed "some characteristic pictures . . . upon the rude walls," classical images of roguish male allure, one of Hercules, one of Bacchus, a third of a satyr. There were a few books on the mantelpiece. " 'Which, now, of the three [pictures],' " Alcott asked Walt, " 'is [you] . . . this Hercules, the Bacchus, or the satyr?' " Walt refused to say, but he did so in a way that implied that "the virtues of the three" belonged to him.[27]

One of Alcott's companions that day was Henry David Thoreau. It was a Sunday, and they had come directly from Henry Ward Beecher's church, where the minister had impressed Alcott as being as much actor as man of the cloth. And here was the rude Brooklyn bard taking Alcott, Thoreau, and a woman friend, a Mrs. Tyndall, whom Alcott described as "a solid walrus of a woman," directly upstairs to his private bedchamber. Alcott could not help but notice the imprint of two bodies in the still un-made bed. And half-hidden beneath it was "the vessel"—a chamber pot.

The stairs to the attic were narrow, and Alcott categorized the building as a "tenement," one of three on that block on the eastern edge of Brooklyn. But it was not so modest a house as to lack a parlor, to which the three later repaired. On an earlier visit to get to know Whitman, about a month before, Alcott had found the poet to be "full of brute power," "broad-shouldered, rouge-fleshed, Bacchus-browed, bearded like a satyr, and rank"—the Bacchus and satyr references suggesting that on that occasion, too, Walt took his visitor straight upstairs to his classically illustrated lair, rather than into the parlor. "[H]e wears his man-Bloomer [broad loose pants] in defiance of everybody," Alcott wrote, further noting a "red flannel undershirt, open-breasted, exposing his brawny neck; striped calico [shirt] over this, the collar Byroneal . . . cowhide boots; a heavy round-about [jacket] with huge outside pockets and buttons to match; and a slouched hat, for house and street alike. Eyes gray, unimaginative, cautious yet sagacious; his voice deep, sharp, tender sometimes and almost melting."[28]

Most telling, Walt received his decorous, no doubt very properly attired visitor while reclining at sensuous full length, "pillowing his head upon his bended arm, and informing you naively how lazy he is, and slow."[29] Some ninety years later, the young Truman Capote would assume a similar pose for the sensational Harold Halma photo appearing on the back cover of his first novel, *Other Voices, Other Rooms*. In Capote's case, the lounging, come-hither posture suggested something more effete, but for both writers the pose invited attention to the man, and the body of the man, as well as to the literatus near the start of a large career. "Inquisitive, very," Alcott concluded about Whitman at his first visit, "inviting [comments] on himself, on his poems . . . In fine, an egotist, incapable of omitting, or suffering any one long to omit, noting Walt Whitman."[30]

This same room is probably where Fred Vaughan stayed, on a somewhat frequent basis, beginning in 1857 or '58. Younger than Walt, Fred was a horse driver and, to judge from the letters he wrote, intelligent and humorous but probably not much schooled. His intimate friendship with Whitman coincided with the years when Walt was writing most or all of the "Calamus" poems, along with other essential poems of the 1860 edition, such as "A Word Out of the Sea" (later "Out of the Cradle Endlessly Rocking"). At the time of their publication in book form, the "Calamus" poems caused hardly a whisper of scandal as compared to those in another cluster, "Enfans d'Adam," which was partly about male-female love. Poems concerned with male-male attachment were asexual by their very nature, to the minds of many readers—so suppressed, so coded, were writings about sexualized male love that the implications simply sailed over people's heads.

Now, though, an erotic message is plain. "Not heat flames up and consumes," Walt wrote in Calamus 14,

> Not sea-waves hurry in and out,
>   Not the air, delicious and dry, the air of the ripe summer,
>   bears lightly along white down-balls of myriads of seeds,
>   wafted, sailing gracefully, to drop where they may,
>   Not these—O none of these, more than the flames of me,
>   consuming, burning for his love whom I love![31]

In Calamus 11, a new tone of calm, grateful confession can be heard:

> And when I thought how my dear friend, my lover,
>   was on his way coming, O then I was happy;
> O then each breath tasted sweeter—and all that day my food
>   nourished me more—And the beautiful day passed well,
> And the next came with equal joy—And with the next, at evening,
>   came my friend[32]

Whether Fred Vaughan was the "dear friend" is impossible to know; an author need not be feeling happy to write about happiness, or well fed to write of a good meal. Still, many of the "Calamus" poems sound like a man telling a personal truth, reckoning with his aloneness and acknowledging the only thing that works for him, the sole relief that his nature allows. He has been tortured by a deep longing and now he has found an answer—thank God. Calamus 11 continues:

> And that night, while all was still, I heard the waters roll slowly
>   continually up the shores,
> I heard the hissing rustle of the liquid and sands . . . to congratulate
>   me,
> For the one I love most lay sleeping by me under the same cover
>   in the cool night,
> In the stillness, in the autumn moonbeams, his face was inclined
>   toward me,
> And his arm lay lightly around my breast—And that night I was
>   happy.[33]

Maybe all that can be said for sure is that for a period of time, probably two years or more, Walt had as close companion a certain young man. And that during that period, he wrote a cluster of straight-from-the-heart lyrics, poetry unlike anything he had written before (or would write afterward). Nor are those lyrics all joyful records of romantic smooth sailing. In Calamus 9 he recalls,

Hours continuing long, sore and heavy-hearted,
Hours of the dusk, when I withdraw to a lonesome and
    unfrequented spot, seating myself, leaning my face in
    my hands;
Hours sleepless, deep in the night, when I go forth . . . stifling
    plaintive cries;
Hours discouraged, distracted—for the one I cannot content myself
    without, soon I saw him content himself without me. . . .
Sullen and suffering hours! (I am ashamed—but it is useless—
    I am what I am. . . .)[34]

Then, in the spring of 1862, Walt received a terse, applecart-overturning note from Fred. It was only seven months before Walt would leave New York for good, rushing to his brother's camp in Virginia. (Although he visited his mother several times during and after the war, he never again lived in Brooklyn.) The note, which he kept in his private papers for the rest of his life, guaranteeing that posterity would find it, reads:

Walt,
    I am to be marri'd tomorrow, Saturday at 3 o'cl at 213 W. 43rd St.—
near 8th Ave.
    I shall have no show! I have invited no company.—
    I want you to be there.—
    Do not fail please, as I am very anxious you should come.—
    Truly yours, Fred[35]

Between May 2, when he received this note, and the day of his departure for Virginia, December 16, Walt recorded more than 135 names of men met in the streets: more than one every two days. This was his busiest period of young man collecting, to judge from the evidence of all the notebooks he saved. Whether he did Fred Vaughan the kindness of attending his wedding is hard to know; in a letter written years later, Fred implies that Walt never met his wife, but by then both may have forgotten the day of nuptials.[36]

The many names may signal an intense phase of the "adhesiveness" experiment. Or something simpler, more purely personal, may account for all the activity. When fate organized a summons to Fredericksburg, Walt was more than ready to go. "Breaking up a few weeks since," he wrote Emerson at the end of December 1862, ". . . my New York stagnation . . . I fetch up here [Washington] in harsh and superb plight— wretchedly poor, excellent well . . . realizing at last that it is necessary for me to fall for the time in the wise old way, to push my fortune."[37]

T HE NOTE TO Emerson was for a humble purpose: to request letters of recommendation. Walt was a lowly job seeker in Washington, but he happened to have written a book about which the mighty Emerson, the indispensable man of letters in the American nineteenth century, had expressed admiration. Emerson's deeply kind, perceptive, and magically useful letter of praise for *Leaves of Grass*—Walt had wisely sent him a copy—made the commercial failure of the book beside the point. It was the copy that Walt sent Emerson that Bronson Alcott had read, Alcott being a frequent borrower of Emerson's books.

"I am not blind to the worth of the wonderful gift of 'Leaves of Grass,'" Emerson wrote back:

> I find it the most extraordinary piece of wit & wisdom that America has yet contributed. I am very happy in reading it, as great power makes us happy . . . I give you joy of your free & brave thought. I have great joy in it. I find incomparable things said incomparably well, as they must be . . . I greet you at the beginning of a great career, which yet must have had a long foreground somewhere for such a start.[1]

Walt used Emerson's letter shamelessly, publishing it in the *New York Tribune* (October 10, 1855) and quoting from it on the spine of his next edition (1856), so that along with the book's title and the name of the

author appear the words "I Greet you at the/Beginning of a Great Ca-
reer/R. W. Emerson."[2] A few years later, trying to land a job in Washington, Walt required of the Sage of Concord three letters of
introduction, which he requested using the same commanding tone
found in the contracts he wrote with Brooklyn carpenters:

> Write for me something like the enclosed form of letter . . . I wish
> you to write two copies—put the one in an envelope directed to Mr.
> Seward, Secretary of State—and the other in an envelope directed to
> Mr. Chase, Secretary of the Treasury—and enclose both envelopes
> in the one I send herewith . . . I wish you also to send me a note of
> introduction to Charles Sumner [U.S. senator from New York].[3]

Emerson did as Walt required—but the letters did Walt no good. He
might have known a letter to Chase would not help; the summer before,
he had met a man who knew the secretary, who reported that Chase,
seeing a copy of *Leaves of Grass* on a table, said, "How is it possible you
can have this nasty book here?"[4]

Walt had arrived in Washington from New York penniless. While changing railroad cars in Philadelphia he had his pocket picked, and he roamed
the capital for two days and nights, unable to pay for a ride to the hospitals
but determined to visit each one on the chance that George had already
been evacuated from Fredericksburg. He called this period "three days of
the greatest suffering I ever experienced in my life."[5] His immediate and
emotional concern for his brother, who, for all he knew, had been griev-
ously wounded, suggests something about the nature of their bond—a
bond that Whitman biographers, concerned to depict Walt as a lonely artist
in a family of philistines, have often devalued. Washington in this first passage through was dismaying, overwhelming, and Walt would describe it to
his sister-in-law Mattie as "the greatest place of delays and puttings off, and
no finding the clue to any thing."[6] He tried to get help from "big people"
like Moses Odell, a congressman from New York, but no one had time for
him, or knew anything useful about George.

On Thursday, December 18, he had luck. In the street he met Charles
Eldridge, one of the publishers of the 1860 edition of *Leaves*, whose lit-
tle publishing firm had since gone under. Eldridge led him to William
O'Connor, whom Walt had met in Boston two years before. The two

younger literary men turned clerks gave the poet the few dollars they could spare. They steadied him—his penniless search for a wounded brother must have touched them, and Eldridge got him a pass on a military train heading to Virginia.[7]

The Battle of Fredericksburg, concluded on December 15, had been a great slaughter. It represented in some ways the low point of Northern fortunes in the war—George, writing home to Jeff, observed that "we have been most terribly outgenerald . . . the men fight as well as men can fight, and I firmly believe that all we want, is some one competent to lead."[8] At Fredericksburg, the leading had been done by Major General Ambrose E. Burnside, the newly appointed commander of the Union Army of the Potomac. Burnside had replaced Major General George B. McClellan, who had lost Lincoln's confidence, and he had taken over only because ordered to do so by the president.[9] Burnside had doubts about his own capacity. He was not known for incompetence—the Union campaign against coastal North Carolina, which became known as the "Burnside Expedition," had been one of the few Federal victories in the first two years of war. But to lead the largest army fighting for the Union, the one that must confront Robert E. Lee in Virginia, daunted him.

Lincoln wanted a commander who would take the fight to Lee, pursue and crush him. He cashiered McClellan because he had "the slows," because to use McClellan against Lee was to "bore with an auger too dull to take hold," as the president said.[10] Burnside was a different sort of man, if not a more gifted general. He drove his army of 110,000 men south in cold and often wet weather in the last weeks of November 1862, arriving before Fredericksburg in good time, but not fast enough to prevent Lee, with a force of 75,000, from digging in atop a range of hills behind the city.

A soldier from New York, writing for the *New York Sunday Mercury*, which printed many letters from the field, declared,

If General Burnside had three times as many men, he could not rouse the Rebels out of where they are. The place puts me in mind of Weehawken, the bluffs along the Hudson. We were so close to their batteries that they could not depress their guns low enough to hit us, but they gave us the devil from their rifle-pits.[11]

Another soldier, a Pennsylvanian, described the setup as nothing less than a "slaughter pen."[12] George wrote home to Jeff, "You see we had to advance over a level plane and their batteries being on high ground and they being behind breastworks we had no chance at them, while they could take as deliberate aim as a fellow would at a chicken."[13] The idea of shooting something helpless—and poultrylike—occurred to the enemy, too; a Confederate officer, relishing the fight about to start, observed that "a chicken could not live on that field when we open on it."[14]

Fredericksburg excited even the normally phlegmatic Robert E. Lee, who saw here the opportunity to kill many Federals. Observing the battle from the safety of his command post, he remarked, in a phrase that would become world famous, "It is well that war is so terrible—we should grow too fond of it!"[15] Union losses for the day were thirteen thousand, Confederate five thousand. It astounded Lee that his opponents would attack an obviously impregnable position, but attack they did, via pontoon bridges laid across the Rappahannock, with heavy loss of bridge builders to rebel sharpshooters.[16] Meanwhile, artillery exchanges reduced Fredericksburg, a once-lovely riverside town, to ruins. One Union soldier described the cannonading as "terrific . . . the rebels returned shot for shot, and the earth quaked for miles around as if convulsed by some hidden spasm of nature in the very center of its rotundity."[17]

Once across on the pontoons, Yankee skirmishers fought house to house, driving an advance force of rebel soldiers back and out of the city. All was as Lee had hardly dared hope. Now in control of the ruins, the Yankees might, if they were foolish enough, exit to the rear of Fredericksburg and enter onto the killing field itself. The grid of streets of the town offered a foretaste of conditions there—huddled in the cross streets, the Union troops were protected, but whenever they showed themselves in streets running parallel with the enemy's hillside guns, they felt a withering fire.[18]

All George Whitman had to do was survive this, while leading a company of men. It was his first battle as a commissioned captain, and the men depended on his judgment and luck. "The air seemed to be so full of [bullets]," wrote the soldier from Pennsylvania, "that one would suppose that a finger could not be pointed toward the rebel batteries without being hit on the end."[19] On the morning of December 13, a dense fog temporarily stilled the shooting. George halted his company at the back edge of Fredericksburg. They waited for the cold haze to clear. When it did, he led his unit (Company E, of about fifty-five men) out from the protection of the ruins and into "the most terrific fire of grape, canister, percussion Shell musketry and everything else, that I ever saw," as he wrote in his diary.[20] The open ground they crossed had damp soil of a clayey consistency that balled up on the feet, slowing progress. "Our regiment appeared to melt away," another soldier, who also became mired in the clay field, wrote, "before the leaden storm that was poured into us."[21]

Though a newly minted commander (his captaincy dated from the day before, December 12), George was not without experience. All that fall he had led a company whose captain of record, Henry W. Francis, was sick with a "bowel complaint" whenever it was necessary to lead his men in tense engagements, for example, at South Mountain and at Antietam.[22] "Captain Francis has not come back yet," George wrote his mother in November, "and I am getting almost tired of haveing the whole trouble and responsibility of the Company and someone else getting the pay for it." George's performance as substitute won the notice of his superiors, Colonel Robert Potter, regimental commander, and Brigadier General Edward Ferrero, chief of the 2nd Brigade.* Now George had his own soldiers to lead and better pay, but the prospect was for serious losses in the moments just ahead.

Captain Francis, who did see action at Fredericksburg (he had just returned from two months at home with his wife), recorded that the regiment spent part of December 13 supporting an artillery battery. So many of the artillerymen were hit by return fire that the position, on a low rise,

---

*Brigades varied in size, but were composed of several regiments, usually four to six, each regiment contributing on average a few hundred men. The organizational units of the Union and Confederate forces were (from largest to smallest): armies, corps, divisions, brigades, regiments, companies. Theoretically, company strength was 100 men; regimental, 1,000; brigade, 4,000; divisional, 12,000. A corps was often composed of three divisions, and a division of roughly the same number of brigades. Armies, the largest organizations—for instance, Grant's Army of the Potomac and Lee's Army of Northern Virginia—were elastic in size.

had to be abandoned, and the 51st, emerging from dubious shelter, "knew it would be the last hill that some of us would ever cross for the rebel batteries had a fair sweep of us as we went over . . . it was the best artiliry practice that I ever saw [since] they could drop a shell just where they wanted it . . . it was here that we lost the most of our men."[23] George probably sustained the wound to his face crossing the hill. As he described the situation to Jeff, "[T]he range was so short, that they threw percussion shells into our ranks, that would drop at our feet and explode killing and wounding Three or four every pop. It was a peice of one of that kind of varmints that struck me in the jaw."[24]

Ferrero's brigade moved to the front at three P.M. The clay field consisted by then of some four hundred yards of "dead and mutilated men, half immersed in the mud," one soldier recalled. The carnage of Fredericksburg can be understood by reference to legendary incidents of modern, mechanized war—to the kinds of battle that it anticipated, for example, the Battle of the Somme or Passchendaele, in World War I. The Somme, which lasted thirty-eight days, produced more than a million casualties, but its first day (July 1, 1916) ended with casualties in numbers not far different from those at Fredericksburg, even allowing for Fredericksburg's far smaller geographic compass. The concentrated rifle fire of Confederate infantrymen at Fredericksburg achieved the effect of modern machine guns, as Union brigades poured out of the ruins of the town, wave after wave, and met a steady fusillade.[25] The 51st lost a third of its men in the first five minutes.[26] "The leaden shower was so thick and ceaseless," a soldier remembered, "that it was almost certain death to raise the head," and many accounts refer to soldiers unconsciously hunching up their jackets, as if to protect themselves against a driving hail.[27]

Death came from rifle fire, but the clay fields were perfectly blanketed by rebel cannon as well. Explosive death, mass dismemberment, was thus a keynote of Fredericksburg as it was not at most other Civil War battles. Splattered flesh, men without heads, men with both legs blown off at the thigh; disembowelings, catastrophic face wounds, brain matter showerings; living comrades blown into rags of bloody cloth and fragments of pale bone, or half gone but still able to talk or scream: These are elements encountered over and over in the letters and memoirs that report the experience of those who fought at Fredericksburg.[28] At the Somme, cameramen captured a few such horrors on film, and for the first time the home front saw something of the realities of modern war with the release of *The Battle of the Somme*, a propaganda film that became one of the most-viewed movies in British history. There were no filmed accounts of Fredericksburg, but that a new order of disaster had been achieved, and a new kind of awfulness, is a conclusion many of the firsthand accounts point to.

General Burnside, who observed the battle from a position across the river, on the second floor of a Greek Revival house full of good furniture (and featuring indoor plumbing), was said by one of his aides to have fallen asleep early in the afternoon.[29] He was probably not bored of the battle, only exhausted from overwork in the days leading up to it. His main error was to have kept later brigades pouring out of Fredericksburg when the first ones had been decimated. This error cost thousands of lives for nothing. The rebels, rejoicing in the opportunity to kill that the assaults provided (General Lee, after an artillery shot that mowed down bluecoats like bowling pins, said, "Well done, give them another"), were sometimes also sickened. The valor of the Union troops, marching forward under a rain of doom, crawling over the bodies of their dead comrades, and often using the corpses as cover, inspired awe.[30]

George wrote that his brigade advanced "beautifully" despite the bombardment. He mentioned no particular obstacles on the muddy plain, but soldiers with regiments that fought alongside the 51st shuddered to remember certain fences, too tall to be climbed, that were splattered with flesh and were only gotten past by wrenching boards off and worming through the slots. The openings were "blocked up with heaps of dead . . . who had to be trampled upon" to get to the other side.[31]

Many soldiers did not make it this far. Aside from the wounded and dead, there were those who carried injured soldiers away and never bothered to return; who remained behind the fences or in a few isolated dwellings offering protection; who somehow could not make themselves emerge from the ruins of the city at all, and who mysteriously reappeared only after darkness fell that night, and the fighting tailed off. George led his company to an advanced position on the field, at the near edge of a watercourse with muddy banks that ran, he told his mother, at the very base of the chief rebel redoubt, called Marye's Heights. Here Company E "blazed away untill night," George wrote in a brisk, breathless tone to

Mrs. Whitman on December 16, the same day that she, at home in Brooklyn, read of a "First Lieutenant G. W. Whitmore" having been wounded
at a new battle called Fredericksburg. Unlike most of George's letters,
this one does not jest nor does it assure his mother that he is "hearty" and
eating well. Instead, in careful detail it describes the catastrophe in which
he has just played his part.

When Walt also read his brother's name among the wounded (the notice was in the *New York Herald*; the next day, a more accurate notice appeared in the *New York Times*, "Lieut. Whitman . . . 51st . . . cheek"),
he threw some clothes and probably some writing materials into a carpetbag and was out of the house within two hours. He withdrew fifty
dollars from Mrs. Whitman's Brooklyn bank account (swollen with
George's army earnings) and set out for Washington and the unknown,
in so uncollected a state that he failed to protect his wallet at the
Philadelphia station. Arriving in Falmouth, Virginia, across the river
from Fredericksburg on December 19, after two days of confusion in
Washington, he had no trouble locating the camp of the 2nd Brigade,
and soon he found his brother, too. George was in good spirits—barely
wounded, and glad to be alive. An entirely different reality had asserted
itself, the reality of camp life, a survivors' reality. Soldiers were cooking
and building "shebangs," small shelters they put together out of fresh
pine boughs, scavenged fence rails, and mud. They were washing and
repairing their clothes. A spell of fine weather having followed the storm
of war, they lay about or roamed, enjoying the sun.

"The grub was good," Walt wrote in one of his pocket notebooks,
adding,

> had a tip-top time every way. Capt. [Samuel] Sims, Lieut. Frank But-
> ler, [Sergeant Frederick] McReady and all used me well . . . went
> around among the camps—saw the hard accommodations . . . the
> improvised fireplaces in holes in the ground, with small subterranean
> passages and small mud chimneys, lengthened out by a barrel with
> both ends knocked out . . . The bivouac fired at night, the singing
> and story telling among the crowded crouching groups.[32]

Many of the soldiers were from Brooklyn. Being George's brother,
Walt was welcomed, but his own charm would have won him accep-

tance in any case. From the start Walt was scribbling notes; he must have appeared to the men as a camp follower of a familiar type, another war reporter. Reporters were common at battlefields within easy distance of Washington, and the men generally smiled on their efforts, being avid readers themselves. "I carried sometimes half a dozen [notebooks] in my pocket at one time," Walt told a biographer later, "never was without one . . . took notes as I went along—often as I sat—talking, maybe, as with you here now—I writing while the other fellow told his story."[33]

He witnessed a balloon ascension: "forenoon very pleasant . . . a great huge, slow moving thing, with a curious look to me, as it crawled up, and slanted down again, as if it were alive . . . A beautiful object . . . graceful, pear-shaped."[34] The camp being across from Fredericksburg, he could look over at the ruined city, behind which the rebels still held their position. "The walk along the Rappahannock in front, a pleasant shore, with trees," he wrote. "See that old town over there—how splintered, bursted, crumbled . . . the hospitals—the man with his mouth blown out."

Walt himself was half observation balloon, half budding rescuer. There is no doubt he spent some time in the hospital that had been set up at the Lacy House, a Georgian mansion on the Falmouth side, writing letters home for a few of the wounded, and bringing them such comfort as the presence of a sympathetic stranger afforded. Clara Barton was working here at this time; the future leader of the American Red Cross, a woman of great kindness and remarkable physical courage, she had watched parts of the battle from a second-story balcony, but had crossed a pontoon bridge under fire to get closer to the wounded.[35] Her own vocation as ministering angel resembles Walt's uncannily. Both began with a surge of instinctive feeling, both brought small gifts to the wounded soldiers (in Barton's case, soup, cornmeal mush, tobacco, and shots of whiskey, among other things), both worked as government copyists in Washington (Barton could inscribe sixty-five thousand words in a month and earned eight cents per hundred).[36]

Both were in their early forties, both decidedly unorthodox— disinclined to hand out Bible tracts to dying men, unlike other hospital visitors—and both had a proud faith in their own physical health, believing that they could "out-robust" the threats to themselves, and were too fit to catch infections. On Sunday, December 21, Walt entered the Lacy

House for the first time. The mansion's twelve rooms were probably crowded; on December 15, twelve hundred wounded men had covered every square inch of floor.[37] Another nurse who worked at the hospital wrote, "The poor fellows just arrived had not had their clothes off since they were wounded, and were sleeping in blood and filth, and were swarming with vermin. They lay as close as they could be packed, the contaminated air growing worse every hour . . . The air was so close and nauseating that we often reeled with faintness."[38]

Walt may have seen Miss Barton at work. She was a small, good-looking woman dressed drably. She had been at this sort of thing for some time now, uncovering a deep capacity for organization and raw hard work within herself. At the Battle of Cedar Mountain (August 9, 1862), "she appeared in front of the hospital at twelve o'clock at night," a Union surgeon wrote, "with a four-mule team loaded with everything needed . . . we were entirely out of dressings of every kind . . . shells were bursting in every direction."[39] Earlier she had tried to attach herself to the Burnside expedition, but she had been denied permission because an official felt that the "field is no place for a woman."[40] By late summer 1862, though, she had gained formal license to travel in support of the Army of the Potomac, and she showed up at Fairfax, Virginia, to receive three thousand wounded from Second Bull Run (August 28–30) and at Antietam on the most deadly day (September 17).

Walt's pocket notebooks make no mention of nurses or nursing. In extensive commentary (close to five thousand words) written during his week and a half with George, he mentions only two wounded soldiers ("John Lowerie—Co G . . . arm amputated . . . Amos H. Vliet—feet frozen") and a few corpses seen on the ground in front of hospital tents, awaiting burial. There is also mention of a Brooklyn boy, Charley Parker, who was "shot on the advance at Fredericksburgh, died hard, suffered much, frothed at the mouth," and whose clothes were stolen by the rebels, and, of course, there is the famous description of "a heap of feet, legs, arms, and human fragments, cut, bloody, black and blue" under a tree in front of the Lacy House. But nursing and the soldiers' need of it escape comment. If we could send Walt back, we might ask him to describe for us the precise smell and atmosphere inside the hospital, as the worst cases from among 9,600 men wounded at the battle were cycled through a mere twelve rooms; we might also ask him to observe,

Clara Barton in 1851.

with the same quick understanding that he brought to other phenomena, Clara Barton at her ordinary labors—with his usual acuity, he might well have noticed that she wore simple, unstarched skirts, not too long, and not widened by crinolines, thus not to sweep the gory, teeming floors.[41]

What he was eager to record, in detail, was his brother's life. He bunked with George and with Captain Francis, along with two other men of Company D. These other men were probably First Lieutenant Francis W. Tryon, an aide-de-camp to General Ferrero, and Sam Pooley, the second lieutenant in the company. Pooley was a good friend of George's and became a friend of Walt's, too—on March 6, 1863, he visited Mrs. Whitman at home in Brooklyn, fulfilling a duty that the Whitman sons imposed on selected friends, knowing that their mother would treat them well and enjoy the firsthand reports they brought.[42] Pooley was eight years younger than George. He was a carpenter, on the small side (five feet six inches), dark-haired and dark-complected, with blue eyes.[43] He had fought with George from Roanoke Island through the recent Virginia contretemps, and he would fight alongside him in Mississippi (the Vicksburg campaign) and at the Wilderness, physically close enough at times to be able to tell Walt about George's raw luck in battle—that sometimes his uniform was shredded by bullets or shrapnel, yet he remained untouched.[44]

At the time of Walt's visit, George and Pooley had begun serving in separate units. George would move out of Captain Francis's tent in a few weeks (as a company commander, he had a right to his own, with his junior officers bunking with him if he chose). George was growing less enamored of Captain Francis by late 1862. They had begun as brothers in arms, being of the same age and both house builders. George wrote home in April that "Francis is a first rate fellow," but the strain of leading another man's company got to him, and he reported to his mother after South Mountain, "[T]he Captain was not well although he was on the field."[45] Francis was a man of indifferent education but quick to understand military matters.[46] His letters to his wife suggest a special concern for advancement in rank. Writing when he was still a first lieutenant, he told her, "We are very short of officers so many killed and wounded . . . [Our current captain] will probably be major he being Senior Capt of the regt and that gives me this Captains position in the Company at least I have the promise of it."[47]

Hearing he might be passed over, he wrote, "There is some talk of filling our regt up to one thousand strong if they do they may try to put a Captain into this Company but I will never submit to it . . . Should a Captain be appointed over me God help him if the Company ever go in to action for the men have heard that there is such a thing talked of and they express their opinion pretty freely."[48] Francis had style. He cut his chin whiskers early in the war, preferring a rakish mustache. Posted briefly to Fort Lincoln, in Washington, he hired two slaves as personal servants, their owner in North Carolina billing Francis eight dollars for an unspecified period of service.[49] On February 25, 1862, he wrote his wife at home in Buffalo, "I see the officers of the 8th Conn[ecticut] often they are over to my quarters . . . Yours of the 17th I received yesterday and commenced an answer last night but my head did not feel very good from the night before drinking champaign and I had to give it up and go to bed."

Walt Whitman said of this officer, "While I was there George still lived in Capt. Francis's tent . . . [we] would have got along to perfection, but Capt. Francis is not a man I could like much—I had very little to say to him."[50] That Walt, who openly disliked very few men, whose deepest impulse was to practice comradeship, to find points of "adhesion" wherever possible, should have so disliked his brother's friend is curious. Walt said nothing more, beyond commenting, "George had very good times while Francis was away," which might mean that on Francis's return he quickly asserted rank, and that George was forced in some way to humble himself. Francis may have displayed social markers that repelled Walt. Although he would soon, in his hospital work, prove himself a friend to all soldiers, Walt preferred working-class men, examples of what he liked to call the Divine Average.

Too much of Francis's effort may have gone toward assertions of distinction. Not literary or intellectual, he would have failed to interest Walt in the way that such men as Emerson or William O'Connor did, and his careerism, to the extent that it was put on display, might have been unseemly, especially on a battleground welted with fresh graves. George shared Francis's concern with advancement in rank—he, too, wanted good pay, and his promotions made him proud. But his letters do not show him scheming, as Francis did, to gain a higher rank by resigning from the 51st and joining a newly forming regiment.

That George admired such a man might have disturbed his older brother. That this admiration was waning might, by the same token, have reassured him. To their mother, Walt wrote, "George is very well in health, has a good appetite—I think he is at times more wearied out and homesick than he shows, but stands it upon the whole very well."[51] Indeed, George stood everything well—extraordinarily well. In one of his notebooks, Walt recorded, "Everyone speaks so well of George—they say he is so brave, steady, is good natured, of few words—he is now Captain."[52] The captaincy mattered. It suited the formidable younger brother, and maybe Walt was even a little surprised at how well it did. In the article he wrote for the *Brooklyn Eagle*, he would mention a few of the soldiers in the 51st as having a special distinction—they were ordinary Americans who yet incarnated certain classical virtues, who could be described by use of the ancient word "hero." George was one of these few. With someone as vain and self-promoting as Walt, to mention a younger brother's gallantry can be assumed to be part of the larger mythmaking, but the paragraph about George in "Our Brooklyn Boys in the War" is largely factual and not intended in any obvious way to reflect glory on himself. Walt recorded that George had been promoted three times, each time for observed acts of valor in a battle. George's fellow soldiers valued him for "coolness, courage, and military shrewdness," Walt wrote, and this was significant. "Brooklyn may well keep in memory such samples" as George and Captain Samuel Sims, another officer whom Walt praised highly.[53]

George won notice in Walt's eyes for being soldierly—skillful, professional. Sims, on the other hand, did so because beloved of his men; "All the harshness of war has not changed," Walt said, "his cheerful spirits and native kindness . . . the men all like him, as well probably as any officer was ever liked by his company." George may have been a somewhat sterner officer than Sims, although not by much. The evidence of George's letters suggests someone with a sense of humor and access to his emotions, including sympathy. The letters home to his family, especially to his mother, often strike a tone of rustic foolery, as for example in this one written from rural Virginia:

> [O]ld Stonewall had skedadled back in the mountains [when the 51st arrived on scene], pretty badly licked too, as near as I can find out. This is as handsome a country as I ever saw,   we find plenty of forage in the shape of Beef, Chickens, eggs, potatoes, and the way the cattle and sheep have suffered since we have been here is a caution to secesh farmers . . . some of our boys go to a house where there is a sheep dog, take the dog and make him catch as many sheep as they want, and bring them in and cook them, and you may be sure the Yankees get some tall cussing.[54]

Reflecting on the suffering of the men, George wrote about the Battle of the Crater later in the war,

> It must have been horrible lying in that crowded place [a deep pit caused by an explosion], as there was quite a large number of dead and wounded among them . . . The day was very hot indeed, and they could not get a drop of water . . . quite a number of our wounded lay between the rebel lines and ours, and there the poor

creatures had to lay . . . untill the afternoon of the next day, when the
rebs allowed us to . . . give them some water.[55]

Normally accurate—meticulous, in fact—in his accounts of combat,
George grows less forthcoming when discussing war wounds, suffering,
and the real risks a soldier runs. He aims to tell the truth, but he dreads
its effect:

Poor old Mother   she is hardly ever out of my mind, when we are
going into a fight, and I have often thought when I have been in a
pretty hot place, how glad I was that none of you at home, knew anything about it . . . it makes me feel quite bad to think how worried
you all were, on account of seeing my name in the list of wounded.[56]

That George inspired strong feelings among his men is suggested by
an incident from the spring of 1862. He described it to Mrs. Whitman
this way:

The boys in our company gave me quite a surprise yesterday. I was in
my tent, washing and getting ready to go on parade, when our Orderly Sergeant . . . said some of the men wanted to see me out at their
quarters. I supposed there was some little difficulty they wanted me to
settle but when I got there I found the Company all formed in line
and all hands seemed in mighty good humor by the way they grined,
and one of them went into his tent and brought out a splendid sword
and sash . . . and gave them to me, in behalf of the company. I was
quite taken aback I tell you as it was done so quietly . . . it was the
last thing that I expected.[57]

This impromptu ceremony took place on May 31. George was then a
second lieutenant serving under Francis, and Francis, as the senior officer in Company D, might well have expected such an honor to be paid
him and not someone junior to him in rank. That Captain Francis over-
came any irritated or envious feelings and wrote of this event in a
straightforward and even generous way, not at all underestimating its
significance, speaks well of him. "We had a nice little presentation," he
told his wife,

from the men in the company to 2nd Lieut Whitman yesterday
Just as the Company was [preparing?] to go on Review he was sent
for by one of the men and Presented with a Sword Sash belt and
Shoulder Straps   he was very much surprised for he did not know
anything about it   it was a very handsome present and highly appreciated Coming from the sorce which it did.[58]

Francis explained further that George "had no Sword but a Secesh one"
captured at Roanoke, and that the men "felt their pride a little touched to
see him on parade" with such an inferior item. The men had likely purchased the new sword and kit, since they were Union models—had they
belonged to an officer recently resigned or slain in battle, they would
most probably have been retained or sent home to his family.

Francis added, a little weakly, as if to prove that he, too, was held in
high regard by the troops:

[T]o day one of the men come and brought me nearly a peck of
blackberries which he had geathered nearly two miles from camp . . .
snakes are about as thick as berries in this country one can hardly go
amiss of them one man got one around his leg while in bathing this
morning.[59]

The berries, which Francis says he would like to eat baked in a pie (one
prepared by his own wife), have been gathered with significant effort, he
makes clear, and at risk of injury or even death. Like other objects to be
found in the rude army camp, they are half on their way to becoming
natural symbols—berries of meaning, of distinction.

CHAPTER TWELVE

THE MILITARY CAMP, and the men and the ordinary objects they used, were rich material to Walt. His notebooks are full of rough-draft lines of poetry that would appear eventually in *Drum-Taps*, the little book he published late in 1865. The dead soldiers seen in front of a hospital tent found their way into "A Sight in Camp in the Daybreak Gray and Dim," a poem that reproduces Walt's Fredericksburg notebook scribblings almost verbatim. Thus,

Sight at daybreak (in camp in front of the hospital tent) on a stretcher, three dead men lying, each with a blanket spread over him—I lift up one and look at the young man's face, calm and yellow. 'tis strange![1]

becomes

> A sight in camp in the daybreak gray and dim,
> As from my tent I emerge so early sleepless,
> As slow I walk in the cool fresh air the path near by the hospital
>   tent,
> Three forms I see on stretchers lying, brought out there
>   untended lying,
> Over each the blanket spread. . . .
> Gray and heavy blanket, folding, covering all.[2]

He was visiting his brother, but he was also on the lookout for poetry. And in the encampment he found a wealth of inspiration, or so it seemed at first: talismans of war, death, heroism, fear, comradeship. On Sunday, December 21, the same day he first entered the Lacy House, he witnessed a regimental inspection parade (George quite possibly wearing the sword and sash the men had given him). It was a fine cold morning, "bright & sunshining," and the men looked very good to Walt:

> not in the sense of a march down Broadway, but with the look of men who had long known what real war was, and taken many a hand in—held their own in seven engagements, about a score of skirmishes &c. a regiment that had been sifted by death . . . any one of whom had now an experience, after eighteen months, worth more, and more wonderful, than all the romances ever written— whose story, if written out, would be first class.[3]

We hear the professional writer stirring. If only he can write that story, tell it "first class," he will outdo "all the romances ever written." Walt had long believed that he would find in war a fertile ground for his writing; his early poetry anticipates war, and the labor of hospital visiting that he would soon take up had a long foreground, an active apprenticeship. The pile of "feet, arms, legs, &c." did not overwhelm him or make him sick—as shocking as it was, he was accustomed to seeing, and thinking about, such things.

His notebooks show him taking in the whole war-reality, trying to see it all in a glance:

> I write this standing on high slope between Gen. Sumner's headquarters and the railroad terminus down towards the river . . . below is spread out a picturesque scene. The countless baggage wagons, with their white roofs . . . the railroad locomotive, the broad spread of slopes and hills winding their way . . . making a huge S. towards the river, which is only a few hundred yards distant.[4]

He watches George's regiment going out on picket duty. On Christmas Day, he writes from

> the midst of a large deserted camp ground, with the remains of hundreds of mud-huts, and the debris of an old brigade or division of

soldiers all around me. On a road near at hand successive caravans of army wagons . . . In sight as I sweep my eye over the open ground, (for I can see without obstruction from two to four miles every [direction]) I behold several teamsters' camps. Off outside I see the carcases of dead horses and mules. The wooded parts of the surface have been cleared for fuel, & building purposes, for a hundred thousand soldiers.[5]

From the broad view he zooms in for finer details:

eating the green corn—grated through tin pans with rough holes pierced in them—the troops had to do this repeatedly in Virginia. . . .

Old flag shot through with fragments of shell, bullets . . . its staff shattered . . . full of shreds, fringed as with the sword, the silk stained with blood. . . .

After a march at dusk, in fifteen minutes . . . [the men] will have their camp fires burning in all directions, and grub in process of cooking, coffee, pork, beef, potatoes boiling, chickens, or anything they stole. . . .

One of the men came out of a tent close by with a couple of slices of beef, and some crackers, and commenced cooking the mess in a frying pan, for his breakfast . . . I examined the little shelter tent through the open entrance, the ground strewn with pine twigs, and protected on each side with a pine log for an entrance, the knapsacks piled at one end for pillows.[6]

Captain Francis's tent, where Walt spent some nights, was probably pitched atop a rectangular frame of logs embedded in the ground, with a stove dug in for heat. George was working on his own hut but never finished it while Walt was around. About a month later he wrote,

I . . . should have had it completed long ago, but after I had cut the logs . . . orders came for us to be ready to move the next day so I used the logs for fire wood, and since then, the weather has been so stormy I could not do much . . . I shall finish it this week, and as soon as I get it done, I want you to come down and see me.[7]

Possibly in Captain Francis's tent, possibly somewhere in the open, George sat down with his brother for an interview. George had been keeping a diary since September 1861. In it he recorded in telegraphic style the battles fought, the marches marched, encampments made, and other events and conditions that bespoke his own experience of the war. Walt knew a great source when he found one. He later described George's pocket diaries as "merely a skeleton of dates, voyages, places camped in or marched through," but added, "It does not need calling in play the imagination to see that in such a record as this lies folded a perfect poem of the war."[8]

Biographers of Whitman have emphasized that George's diary writings are sketchy. Gay Wilson Allen, the great twentieth-century Whitman scholar, wrote that "George had no gift for literary detail," but literary detail is in fact exactly what he had a gift for. Probably he wrote every few days, in a free moment in camp or on the march. About his first battle, which resulted in the capture of many enemy, George noted, "The prisoners were mostly North Carolinaons but some, were from Georgia and Virginia   The North Carolinaons and Georgians were regular buternuts, gaunt long haired and long leged chaps   most of them dressed in Butternut clothing [brown or gray homespun], but the Virginians wore a neat, grey uniform."[9]

"Act[ing] Lieut Carrington was badly wounded," he added, "and had his leg Amputated but it did not save his life and after great suffering he was sent home to New York and died the next day after arriving . . . Major LeGendre (rifle ball passed through his cheek and came out of the back of his neck below his coat collar)   Just after the battle I found Major Le-Gendre on the battlefield perfectly unable to move   I took the blankets that I have strapped to my back, laid him on them . . . had him carried to the rear where the Surgeon was at work."[10]

Often George's notations are terse, but give a sense of the definable spirit of a moment: "August 21st   Rebel Cavelry showed themselves on the opposite side of the river in considerable force and seemed to be feeling for a crossing." "Oct 26th   Rained hard all day, marching orders countermanded . . . Oct 27th   Struck tents at 8 AM went through Knoxville Md crossed the canal . . . crossed the Potomac on pontoon Bridge (How are you old Virginia again)."[11]

In the spring of 1863, he noted, "As I was sitting in my tent writing (about 12 O clock at night) I heard one of Gen Ferreros staff ride into camp and give the Col. orders to have his men ready to move, with one days rations and in light marching order [a likely prelude to a skirmish] . . . In five minutes all was bustle in the camp and about 1 A.M. on the morning of the 15th we fell in and started . . . No one knew where we were going, but we all surmised that we were on a hunt after Guerrilas, a kind of animal that we were all curious to see."[12]

When something significant happens—for instance, Fredericksburg—George's account slows down, and, like the grain of a board fence coming into view through binoculars, the sequence of smaller incidents, and their lived tempo, make themselves felt. After the horrors of December 13th, George's regiment was ordered back onto the foul killing field. Under cover of darkness they were fairly safe from enemy fire, but when daylight returned they found themselves marooned:

Dec 15th   Spent a most miserable day   we were laying in a place where the ground just protected us from the enemys shot if we lay down flat . . . they amused themselves by fireing at us with Artillery, first they tried a solid shot, that just skimed the ground in front of us . . . next they tried a percussion shell but they could not depress their guns enough and the shell struck and exploded just to the rear of us   they next fired a fuse shell but they dare not cut the fuse short enough (for fear the shell would explode in the gun) . . . finally they tried a charge of grape but were just as unsuccessful . . . and they gave it up in despair.[13]

The 51st remained pinned down for twenty-seven hours, as the muddy surface froze and thawed and froze. At last, at midnight of the sixteenth, "we fell back across the pontoon bridge and went back to our old camp" on the Falmouth side.[14]

Even the slowing down and speeding up of George's account was valuable to Walt. It showed him how to shape this material, what parts to feature. His five thousand words written during his visit are overwhelmingly a borrowed account of the history of George's regiment, these notes no doubt the main source. The younger brother may have simply handed his diaries over. Or, since the two were passing many hours together, George may have told Walt his story, now and then consulting or reading from his notes. There are many identical expressions. George wrote about troop movements early in July of 1862, "[W]e were ordered to Newport News where we went into camp and stopped until August 2d when we struck camp and . . . sailed down past Fortress Monroe and entered the mouth of the Potomac . . . and landed at Aquia Creek."[15] Walt, condensing while taking notes, recorded, "Landed at Newport News, July 9th, and lay in good quarters, till Aug. 2nd—then struck tents, and went aboard transports to Fort Monroe—from there went up the Potomac to Aquia Creek."[16]

Walt borrowed phrases from, indeed duplicated, George's account of being trapped for twenty-seven hours. Where George said, "[I]t was devilish aggrevating to . . . hear the rebs moving about behind their works talking and whistling," Walt wrote, "[E]very one from the Colonel down was compelled to lie at full length on his back or belly in the mud, which was deep . . . the troops could plainly hear the rebels whistling &c. [but] the latter did not dare to advance upon them."[17]

Walt shaped George's rush of facts into a few larger ideas; for example, he called the sweep of nearly continuous battle and maneuver between midsummer 1862 and late November "a march of about 100 days, which if properly narrated would stand on a par with anything in military movements, ancient or modern."[18] The idea of a "100 days" campaign had a good ring to it, and it may have helped Walt sell the article he sent to the *Eagle* early in January, in which he described "absolutely one of the most remarkable fighting marches and expeditions known in modern history—a fighting march on the bivouac . . . with one or two brief intervals, for one hundred days."[19]

George, too, tried his hand at journalism. In early October he published a letter in the *New York Sunday Mercury* describing his brigade's actions at South Mountain and Antietam. The *Mercury* was the most widely read weekly paper in the country, indispensable for soldiers and their families as a source of up-to-date information from the several theaters of war.[20] George described a particularly brilliant piece of tactical maneuvering on the part of Brigadier General Ferrero, who, in George's telling, spotted a weakness in the position of one of his regiments and rushed the 51st in on the left, "just in time to prevent the Pennsylvania boys from being

General Edward Ferrero. A dancing instructor before the war, Ferrero numbered among the pupils at his New York studio the young Henry James.

flanked." George made no mention of this maneuver ("one of the most masterly pieces of generalship ever displayed," the article adds) in his own diary. Ferrero was not notably brilliant or inspiring in the pages of private notes, but in an article read by hundreds of thousands it was gallant, not to mention politic, to speak well of a superior officer.

George may have had larger ambitions. He is known to history as the brother who, recalling *Leaves of Grass*, said, "I was about twenty-five [when it first appeared]. I saw the book—didn't read it all—didn't think it worth reading—fingered it a little." He also recalled, "Mother thought as I did—did not know what to make of it . . . I remember mother comparing Hiawatha to Walt's, and the one seemed to us pretty much the same muddle as the other. Mother said that if Hiawatha was poetry, perhaps Walt's was."[21]

There was surely a difference—call it a large difference—in literary

sensibility between the brothers.* But just as Walt, in those nine days in
Falmouth, was making an effort to understand George and his fellow
soldiers, going so far as to live in their huts and eat their grub, George
may have been inspired, or furthered in his quiet ambitions, to be a little
like his writer brother. Something large was happening to him—he
knew that. He was afloat on a dreadful current of history, and his letters
to his family and his diary notes show him trying to get the living facts
down and to make some preliminary sense of them. A letter from his sister Hannah, written early in 1864, gives backhanded evidence of some
kind of literary effort on George's part. "Dear brother George," she
wrote on a "Friday night, pretty late,"

> I am glad you are home again [George was in Brooklyn on leave].—
> I cant bear to think of not seeing you this time.   so if you can you
> must come out here [to Vermont]:—if you are well;   I cant tempt
> you with anything, only we want to see you   I expect George you
> would like to rest home.—   I hear of your having work writing. I
> don't want you to overwork to make yourself ill.   but come if you
> can . . . I am tired tonight—our place is pretty plain here George but
> I dont think of that.   I should like to have you come so much.[22]

George had a special feeling for Hannah. His letters home almost always asked after her, and they often expressed a near-frantic concern
over her situation in Vermont, with her mentally abusive, half-
deranged husband (whom George considered a "scoundrell" and a
"contemptible little cuss" and longed to give "a good square kicking").
They shared a birthday, November 28, and Hannah seems both to have
felt a deep fondness for her brother and to have enjoyed teasing him, as
shown when she warned him not to "make yourself ill" by writing too
much.

Walt was the acknowledged man of letters in the family, with Hannah,

---

*It should be remembered that George had a puckish streak and that he made the deflating
comments quoted above to an adoring acolyte of Walt's, someone central to the cult of the
Good Gray Poet that emerged after the Civil War, and that Walt worked in many ways to
encourage.

possibly, considered also someone of artistic temperament. George, in contrast, was a foursquare, get-on-with-it sort of person, no intellectual. When Bronson Alcott, on one of his visits to Brooklyn, asked Mrs. Whitman if it was true that Walt had built houses, she replied that his brother George was the real builder in the family. When he became, after the war, an inspector of sewer pipes, George found an employment that probably accorded well with his perceived character within the family. Walt was moved to comment that his brother believed in "pipes, not poems."[23] To think of him writing something for publication—articles about the war, or a regimental history—was amusing.[24]

George may have read his own diary notes for the first time when Walt asked to see them. Thus, the sweep of things may have occurred as an idea to both brothers at about the same time. Walt, always scribbling, and giving evidence by his demeanor of his great respect for what the soldiers were engaged upon, an enterprise that touched on the greatest of human themes—mortality, courage, the struggle for liberty—may have led George and some of the other soldiers to view their experience in a different light. So much curiosity validated what they were about. Surely *someone* would write their story some day—a great poet, perhaps. Homer had immortalized acts of desperate valor no more solemn than those displayed in the freezing mud at Fredericksburg. So much sacrifice had to bear forth meaning of some kind.

Walt got so much right on his Falmouth visit, gleaned so much, that it surprises to realize he got a few things wrong. He was wrong about Captain Francis, for example. Francis had his eye on the main chance in a professional sense and considered resigning, but he never did abandon the 51st New York as long as his health permitted. As he wrote his wife, Antoinette, "I did not like to [leave] the old Co that I had been with so long," even when moving to another regiment would have brought a good promotion.[25] Francis had a different kind of courage from George's. George was rarely ill, and when he fell ill he recovered quickly. Francis was chronically sick. His illness began to show itself after less than a year of service, when he began feeling tired all the time. After a short march in May 1862, he found that he was "prety well tired out . . . and to day I am officer of the day but my duties are not very hard if they were I fear they would be neglected."[26]

Army doctors identified his problems as rheumatism and diarrhea, both common complaints. He returned after a long medical leave just in time for Fredericksburg, then collapsed anew. "[T]he Doctor says that I shall be [weak] for some time yet I find that I cant do much yet and have to keep quiet," he wrote Antoinette, adding, "it is a hard place in camp to be sick." On December 23, the same day that Walt, from a lookout high above the river, watched George's regiment deploying as pickets, Francis wrote, "The weather is splendid today like spring so warm I should like to go out but no I must remain shut up for a while yet." He had been unable to sit up for a week. He missed his wife's tender care but was doing fairly well, "for I have the last tent in the line and a very comfortable bed but it is not like home after all."[27]

Walt took his impression of Francis when Francis was bed bound, suffering a recurrence of diarrhea or dysentery, from which he had suffered for nine months. That he was strong enough to leave any kind of impression is remarkable. Possibly in a bleak mood, possibly feeling ashamed of himself, Francis may have tried to appear strong or dominant despite the evidence of his helplessness. His sense of hopelessness, about his own situation but also about the Union's, shows in letters he wrote in January, when he admitted that he was finished as a field officer ("I dont think I could ever stand the marching that I did last summer and have no desire to try").

About the conduct of the war, he wrote,

I must say that my patriotism has nearly played the way things are conducted of late . . . if things dont take a change soon *God* save the country for the army *wont*, every man that has any thing to do with goverment his whole study is to rob it and the one that can steal the most is kept in office while an honest man has no show at all.[28]

Turning his attention to the recent engagement on the Rappahannock, he exclaimed,

[S]ome General did not know the . . . ground or did not know that such a battiry was in such a position or that the enemy had so many men what the d——l are Generals for with their *thousand and one*

aids if not to find out those things, this experimenting and killing
eight or ten thousand men at every experiment has about played out
at least with me.[29]

General Burnside, who historians agree had failed to reconnoiter the
battleground well (yet sent brigade after brigade into the killing crossfire), came in for pointed mention:

> Burnside thought by throwing his bridges across in a hurry and ad-
> vancing his whole force . . . he could cut [the enemy] in two but after
> being delayed all day on the bridge and another day laying on the
> bank of the river . . . he still adheres to his original plan and what is
> the consequence look at those *little mounds* all over the battle field
> and . . . your question is answered.[30]

With true bitterness—his empathy perhaps deepened by his own
suffering—Francis noted,

> [T]he blunder is [soon] forgotten by all save those who have cause to
> remember it . . . perhaps a limb amputated there to linger for months
> to go forth a cripple . . . one man of my company who had his arm
> off above the elbow was sent to Washington among the other
> wounded was in the best of spirits when he left here (and a noble fel-
> low) last week I read a notice of his death he leaves a wife and three
> little children and there is thousands of simular but no one is to
> blame.[31]

We hear something almost modern in this frankness—no drawing
back from hard truths. It would not be till after World War I, and
slaughters like the Somme and the Marne, that a sense of the active ab-
surdity of war would become common in published writing about it. But
Francis, writing for his wife's eyes only, was poised on the literary
threshold. By comparison, Walt's contemporaneous comments offer a
very different vision:

> Taking the army as a whole, it is almost certain that never did mortal
> man in an aggregate fight better than . . . at Fredericksburgh. In the

highest sense, it was *no failure*. The main body [of] troops descending the hills . . . to cross the pontoon bridge could plainly see . . . the Secesh batteries, rising in tremendous force and plenty . . . Yet all the brigade . . . advance[d] with unsurpassed gallantry—and would have gone further, if ordered.[32]

George may have commented to Walt that his brigade advanced "beautifully" at Fredericksburg. But that is far different from saying that the effort was not a failure. It was, indeed, a catastrophic failure. After Fredericksburg, the regiment was down to about 160 men, from an active strength of 297 on the day of battle (and over one thousand at the beginning of the war).[33] To speak of going "further, if ordered" in the face of losses on this scale was, at the very least, unkind.

Walt ate their food, slept in a real army tent, and in a hundred ways tried to experience the life of the soldiers. But what he did not— possibly could not—experience was the harrowing of spirit that comes from a true cannon-fodder episode. The exploding bodies and the machine-gun effect from ranks of enemy infantry firing rapidly were data inscribed on the souls of the soldiers who had fought, and these men knew less well, surely, than an accomplished poet how to express their experience. History had outrun conception. A way of talking about the horror had not yet been invented—and less so, a true reckoning with its meaning, or lack thereof. The soldiers when Walt showed up were already four days out from the last hours of battle. Those who had survived and were not badly wounded were gladly immersed in camp domesticity, fitting out their shelters, taking the sun, and their plucky spirit was a delight to see (Walt's notes tell us he was delighted). Reporting back to the folks in Brooklyn, he wrote, "I feel that you . . . are perhaps needlessly unhappy and morbid about our dear brother—to be in the army is a mixture of danger and *security* in this war which few realize—they think exclusively of the danger."[34]

Walt took much of what he saw at face value. The day after Christmas, he walked out into a field, where he found a few soldiers digging graves. "Death is nothing here," he concluded. "No one makes an ado . . . all useless ceremony is omitted." The soldiers who survived

Fredericksburg had a lot of burying to do. Indeed, the work of burying had begun while combat was still ongoing. That they appeared
matter-of-fact may have reflected their exhaustion and disgust—not
necessarily that the "stern realities of the marches . . . make the old
etiquets a cumber and a nuisance."[35] Burial details at Fredericksburg
had to deal with frozen ground. Many men avoided burial detail at all
costs, finding it too horrifically depressing, and at Fredericksburg the
soldiers were sometimes forced to dig shallow graves with bayonets or
pieces of exploded shell, or to make mass graves out of muddy
trenches, or to bury a soup of body parts and bloody tissue spread
over an area of several square yards, where an uncertain number of
soldiers had been turned, as one man described it, into "one complete
jelly."[36]

Walt was seeing the real thing when he saw some bodies, brought out
from a tent, buried on December 26. But he was not seeing the *real* real
thing. For that, he would have needed to be on the battlefield itself, or
intensely curious to know what had happened on that dark ground.
His notes from Fredericksburg show him being curious about many
things, but not especially about the inner experience of the men who
fought. His brother may have been too stoical to speak up, and maybe
Fredericksburg represented no sort of turn in George's thinking. But for
others, the slaughter at Fredericksburg brought an inner crisis. The very
idea of courage, and the related idea of a beneficent God who looks out
for us, who favors those who try to do good, found a brutal challenge at
this battle. The mechanical slaughter was more like something that happens in an abattoir than in a human contest of wills. Courage, gallantry,
honor: These splendid qualities were valued, on both the Confederate
and the Union sides, for their presumed rightfulness, but also because
those who displayed them were believed to enjoy Fate's special protection. Yet at Fredericksburg the brave had died alongside the cowardly—
like cattle.[37]

Walt had an interest in believing the soldiers would go on, that they
would resist despair (all pro-Union citizens of the North had such an
interest). But as a far-seeing and eerily perceptive poet, he might well
have been alert to more than he was, to something other than the light-
heartedness of soldiers after battle, their comradeliness in a crowded
tent. His Fredericksburg notes make mention of the men being "great

growlers" at times, but he hurries to assure himself that "a large portion of men in the world even the good fellows would burst if they couldn't grumble."[38] There is no problem of morale in the Falmouth camp as Walt re-creates it. In fact, desertions were many, and feelings of disgust like the ones that Captain Francis expressed were common, to judge from other soldiers' letters and many news accounts.[39] Walt does gather some notes on the "inside" experience of the battle, but these are aesthetic rather than psychological impressions, oddly distanced. For example, he writes of

> The opening of the fight, when the skirmishes begin, the irregular
>   snap, snap
> The varied sounds of the different missiles—the short s-s-t of the
>   rifled ball
> Of the shells exploding, leaving a small white cloud,
> The hum and buzz of the great shells
> The grape like the rushing whirr of wind hurtled through the
>   trees. . . .
> The shouts and curses of men—the orders from the officers. . . .
> The gaps cut by the enemy's batteries, (quickly fill'd up, no
>   delay,)[40]

Lines similar to these, appearing in *Drum-Taps* three years later, make of one soldier's battle a collection of vivid sound and sight effects— altogether a rousing experience. The soldier recalls them years afterward, lying peacefully in bed at home with his wife. The memory of battle comes to him in a dream and almost makes the war into dangerous fun:

> The chief-gunner ranges and sights his piece and selects a fuse. . . .
> After firing I see him lean aside and look eagerly off to note the
>   effect;
> Elsewhere I hear the cry of a regiment charging. . . .
> Now a strange lull for a few seconds, not a shot fired on either side,
> Then resumed the chaos louder than ever. . . .
> While from some distant part of the field the wind wafts to my
>   ears a shout of applause, (some special success,)

And ever the sound of the cannon far or near, (rousing even in
   dreams a devilish exultation . . .)*

Other poems in *Drum-Taps* are darker, more attuned to the damage
of war. But the aesthetic approach persists. Some of the poems have
easy-reading rhythms, and the poet on occasion strips away his ego-
tism, his fondness for bombast, and his hunt for higher meanings and
simply reports what he sees. Many of the verses are memorable in the
way of good journalism, or scenes in a well-made movie about
the war:

[Mounted cavalry] take a serpentine course, their arms flash in
   the sun—hark to the musical clank,
Behold the silvery river . . . the splashing horses loitering stop to
   drink,
Behold the brown-faced men . . . the negligent rest on the
   saddles,
Some emerge on the opposite bank, others are just entering the
   ford.†

and

The swarming ranks press on . . . the dense brigades press on,
Glittering dimly, toiling under the sun—the dust-cover'd men,
In columns rise and fall to the undulations of the ground,
With artillery interspers'd—the wheels rumble, the horses sweat‡

A number of the *Drum-Taps* poems report the experience of nursing
the soldiers. And an addendum to the book—rushed into print a few
months after the planned publication, in April 1865, and called "Sequel to
Drum-Taps"—contains a great and enduring Whitman poem, "When
Lilacs Last in the Door-Yard Bloom'd," the profound elegy on the death

---

*"The Artilleryman's Vision"

†"Cavalry Crossing a Ford"

‡"An Army Corps on the March"

of Lincoln. But *Drum-Taps*, Walt's main poetic response to the Civil War, is surprisingly thin. Aside from "Lilacs," there are no poems on the order of the complex, mysterious, far-reaching ones from the 1855, '56, and '60 editions of *Leaves*—poems like "Crossing Brooklyn Ferry," "The Sleepers," "Out of the Cradle Endlessly Rocking," "Song of Myself," and "There Was a Child Went Forth," to name a few.[41]

One successful poem from *Drum-Taps*, "Look Down Fair Moon," suggests what had changed about Walt's poetic endeavor by 1865. It reads in its entirety:

> Look down, fair moon, and bathe this scene;
> Pour softly down night's nimbus floods, on faces ghastly, swollen,
>   purple;
> On the dead, on their backs, with their arms toss'd wide,
> Pour down your unstinted nimbus, sacred moon.

The poet presents horrors from the war and asks the moon to bear simple witness, as the poet himself has done. These are not "inner" horrors, though. The soldiers are perfectly mute—they are dead. Being dead, they cannot tell us what they felt, how the end came for them, what the slaughtering felt like. They are similar to the other soldiers in *Drum-Taps* in their speechlessness—even the still-living ones lack speech. To the extent that they are allowed to speak at all, it is the poet who frames their responses.

The wounded soldier in "Vigil Strange I Kept on the Field One Night," for example, says nothing before he dies, although he does exchange one meaningful look with the poem's narrator:

> One look I but gave which your dear eyes return'd with a look I
>   shall never forget,
> One touch of your hand to mine O boy, reach'd up as you lay on
>   the ground,
> Then onward I sped in the battle . . .
> Till late in the night reliev'd to the place at last again I made my
>   way,
> Found you in death so cold dear comrade, found your body son of
>   responding kisses, (never again on earth responding . . .)

The "vigil strange" is also a vigil silent, as the dead soldier's comrade lies beside him through the night, musing. In "Come Up from the Fields Father," another famous *Drum-Taps* poem, a family at home in Ohio receives a letter from their soldier-son, reporting him wounded but on the mend. The irony is that Pete, the son, is already dead when the letter arrives, but a second irony is that this final word from a departed son is not really his own—someone else has written the letter and signed his name.

The poem about bodies encountered before a hospital tent, "A Sight in Camp in the Daybreak Gray and Dim," is, likewise, short on dialogue. The poet asks each of three corpses who he is, and when the poet beholds the face of the third corpse, he himself provides an answer:

> . . . a face nor child nor old, very calm, as of beautiful yellow-
>   white ivory;
> Young man I think I know you—I think this is the face of the
>   Christ himself,
> Dead and divine and brother of all, and here again he lies.

Dead soldiers, silent soldiers, buried soldiers. These make up the army of *Drum-Taps*. Like the all-seeing moon, Walt registered with great dignity the carnage, the mad waste. Part of his originality as a poet was his willingness to let the facts speak for themselves at times, and surely it does the soldiers' corpses a better honor to let them *be* corpses than to enlist them always as metaphors.

Yet their silence—and this poet's qualifications to speak for them—are presumptions, large ones. Among all the dead of *Drum-Taps*, and the much larger number of soldiers whom Walt would know in Washington, when he began his hospital visiting in earnest, not one dies with a cry of outrage in his throat, snarling hatred of the great cheat that has been done to him, the theft of his youth and life. No one curses his luck and execrates God, nor does anyone blather in terror. It may be that the codes of manhood were so iron hard that feelings of fear, or second thoughts, never manifested. Certainly, habits of self-expression were different in the middle of the nineteenth century, and to look for evidence of "traumatic stress" or to expect

Burial of Federal dead, Fredericksburg, Virginia, 1864. Photograph by
Timothy H. O 'Sullivan.

eloquent protests from men dying of battle wounds is to be disappointed. But the complete absence of anything of the sort—and the
way those young soldiers seem almost to be hurried into silence,
buried alive—is odd.

Other writers also presumed to speak for the soldiers. Louisa May
Alcott went so far as to interpret the different snores she heard on
the ward where she worked as a night nurse. Alcott paid attention as
well to the way the faces of the wounded and sick changed as they
slept:

> Some grew stern and grim, the men evidently dreaming of war, as
> they gave orders, groaned over their wounds, or damned the rebels
> vigorously; some grew sad and infinitely pathetic, as if the pain
> borne silently all day, revenged itself by now betraying what the
> man's pride had concealed so well.[42]

One soldier, wounded at Fredericksburg, had been

crazed by the horrors of that dreadful Saturday. A slight wound in the knee brought him [to the hospital]; but his mind had suffered more than his body . . . for days he had been reliving . . . the scenes he could not forget, till his distress broke out in incoherent ravings, pitiful to hear. As I sat by him . . . he lay cheering his comrades on, hurrying them back, then counting them as they fell around him, often clutching my arm, to drag me from the vicinity of a bursting shell . . . his eyes restless; his head never still; every muscle strained and rigid; while an incessant stream of defiant shouts, whispered warnings, and broken laments, poured from his lips.[43]

This soldier lacks the calm demeanor of the grateful dead. Alcott, although she nursed soldiers for only three weeks, seems to have understood the awfulness, and a large part of her nursing was an effort to bring that into expression.[44]

Captain Francis, writing home to his Antoinette, told a story that, while not directly about combat, or any inner wounds, hinted at the all-around degradation of serving in an army that was fighting desperate battles under sometimes thoughtless leaders. The chaplain attached to the 51st New York was a drunkard, and by January 1863 he had embarrassed himself repeatedly. Yet he was not allowed to retire, to remove himself from the scenes of his deep shaming:

[O]ur old chaplain sent in his resignation . . . but it was sent back again and he continues to drink whiskey at uncle Sams expense he got drunk the other night and fell down and tore his pants half of himself and covered himself with mud from head to foot . . . got the nigger to scrape of the mud and had his pants sewed up so that [next morning] when he got about 3 drinks he was all right . . . the colonel makes him preach now every Sunday it is rather rough on him but he has to comply there is generaly about a dozen to hear him.[45]

The officer who would tell such a story to his wife—who would seem almost to relish it, as a token of larger absurdities—is someone who, revealingly, Walt had "very little to say to, " who was "not a man I could like much." His truth was a complicated truth, ugly and despairing at times, bracingly bitter—above all, it was a soldier's truth, one that only *he* could tell.

WALT RETURNED TO Washington on December 28, traveling up from Falmouth by railcar and Potomac River steamer. He went straight to William O'Connor's apartment to retrieve a carpetbag he had left, and the reception from William and Nelly and their daughter Jeannie must have been warm, because he stayed with them for the next six months. His plan was to remain in Washington for only about a week, he told them, visiting Brooklyn soldiers in the hospitals. But from the start he must have been contemplating a sojourn of some length, because the next morning he wrote his urgent letter to Emerson, requesting notes of introduction to three of the most powerful men in Washington.[1]

That same Monday morning, he wrote his mother to report on George's status after Fredericksburg ("very well . . . good appetite"). He added,

> And now that I have lived for eight or nine days amid such scenes as the camps furnish, and had a practical part in it all, and realize the way that hundreds of thousands of good men are now living . . . not only without any of the comforts, but with death and sickness and hard marching and hard fighting . . . really nothing we call trouble seems worth talking about.[2]

He had nursed soldiers on the steamer coming up from Fredericksburg. He had also lent a hand near the battleground, in a small way. A program for the future, for Walt Whitman, poet and healer, must already have been taking shape in his mind as he polished the first of several articles he would send to the New York papers. He would write more articles, supporting himself by "hacking on the press," as he put it; meanwhile, he would visit more of the wounded, joining himself to the exciting war effort. "I will stay here for the present," he told his mother, "at any rate long enough to see if I can get any employment at any thing, and shall write what luck I have. Of course I am unsettled at present."[3]

In fact, he was remarkably well settled. The O'Connors had made it clear that they would accept his company on almost any terms. William O'Connor was a fervent lover of *Leaves of Grass*, a talented professional writer himself, author of *Harrington* (1860), an antislavery novel, and of a number of stories published in mainstream journals such as *Harper's Weekly* and *Putnam's*.[4] He was an eloquent and sometimes ferocious journalistic crusader, who rode odd hobbyhorses on occasion (such as anti-Shakespearism) but mostly lent his talents to high moral reforms, for example, for abolition and temperance. Asked to comment on a bust of Shakespeare, he called its subject "a chuck headed, loblolly, burly, bloated and beef-eating specimen of humanity."[5] Above all else, he was good intellectual company—excitable, voluble, well read, like Walt a product of a poor childhood on a northern city's streets (in his case, Boston's).

Some years later O'Connor said of an essay of too-tepid praise of Walt in *Harper's Weekly*, that it "resembles excellent mutton-broth made by boiling, without condiment, the shadow of a sheep's trotter."[6] Of Walt himself he told a friend, after first meeting him in 1860, "The great Walt is very grand & it is health & happiness to be near him . . . He is so large & strong—so pure, proud, & tender, with such an ineffable *bonhommie* & wholesome sweetness of presence [that] all the young men & women are in love with him."[7] Walt returned the favor, describing O'Connor as "personally and intellectually the most attractive man I . . . ever met . . . a gallant, handsome, fine-voiced, glowing-eyed man . . . of healthy magnetic atmosphere and presence, and the most welcome company in the world."[8]

They were a bit of a love affair, but in the mode of Walt's other friendships with intellectuals—that is, completely platonic. Even with men as

William O'Connor in about 1865.

close to him as O'Connor or, later, John Burroughs, the young naturalist and future author of *Wake-Robin, Locusts and Wild Honey*, and the
first short biography, *Notes on Walt Whitman as Poet and Person* (1867),
Walt was carefully unphysical. His letters to these loyal and entertaining
writer-friends, even to the good-looking ones, were impersonal in the
extreme, emptied entirely of the currents of sexual suggestion to be
found in some of his letters to working-class men. O'Connor was about
the same age as George (and Burroughs close to Jeff's). Their sincere
devotion achieved that very high level denoted by one of the rarest kinds
of literary product, a book of praise written by one author about another while he is still alive. O'Connor's book (more a long pamphlet)
was *The Good Gray Poet*. Released early in 1866, it began the work of
praising, not to say sanctifying, Walt as faithful hospital visitor, Walt as
poetic immortal. O'Connor marveled at Whitman's astonishing physical
beauty, declaring him classically proportioned. Amazed to find himself in

the *presence* of such a fellow, he declared Walt "irreproachable in his relations to the other sex" and claimed that he exhibited "the largest and
truest manliness," and that his literary equals were only the very greatest, titans on the order of Aeschylus, Dante, Cervantes, and Shakespeare (maybe some small slight intended with that last comparison).[9]

The Good Gray Poet was written in answer to an outrage. Walt had
been fired from a government job after being identified as the author of
Leaves of Grass, supposedly a dirty book. O'Connor seized on the dismissal in the way of able literary infighters before and since, exposing
the small-mindedness of a self-appointed moral arbiter—James Harlan,
the incoming secretary of the interior, who had been shocked to find a
"high degree of . . . moral decadence" among the clerks working in his
department. With the brouhaha that O'Connor stirred up over Walt's
firing, Walt's fame as an American author began its season of true increase. No longer was there a need to defend himself—indeed, it was
seemlier to maintain a humble silence, to let another accomplished
writer compare him to Homer and Christ, to anoint him the Great
American Bard.[10]

This wonderful bit of good luck, from a career-building point of view,
was still three years down the road in January 1863, when Walt took up
residence in Washington. On that New Year's Day, the two friends
strolled up Pennsylvania Avenue under sunny skies, encountering, in
front of Willard's Hotel, John James Piatt, a minor poet from Ohio, who
wrote afterward that O'Connor's companion was "a large, gray-haired,
gray-bearded man, dressed rather shabbily, in . . . 'country clothes.' "[11]
Piatt and his wife were on their way to the White House, where President
Lincoln was to hold a New Year's Day reception for dignitaries (morning
hours) and the general public (afternoon, with coverings placed over the
White House carpets to protect them from dirt). That same day, Lincoln
would sign the final order enacting the Emancipation Proclamation. His
demeanor on that day of great moment, only two weeks since the disaster
at Fredericksburg, was serene but remote, people who attended said—he
stood erect, but with his gaze often fixed over the heads of the crowd.[12]

Walt and William did not go to Lincoln's levee, but instead headed up
Fifteenth Street to Charles Eldridge's fifth-floor office. By the next
morning, this was Walt's office, too, or at any rate, a place he was given
the freedom of; he wrote his sister-in-law Mattie a breezy letter noting

that he was "way up in the top of a big high house," and that "the weather is perfect . . . bright, and plenty warm enough."[13] Within days of arriving he had found both a decent place to write and a good place to sleep, surely two of the essential requirements of a wandering poet. Eldridge had been instrumental in getting him permission to visit Fredericksburg, too, in his search for George; his devotion to the Whitman cause was as strong as O'Connor's and at this early stage, probably more crucial, for he soon got Walt paying work under his own boss, Major Lyman S. Hapgood, the U.S. Army paymaster of volunteer regiments.

Like George receiving an honorary sword—or Jeff, at the Brooklyn Water Works, attracting helpful mentors—Walt had a way of winning the devotion of men. The three knew how to be good brothers, too. During the war, when each was much involved in his own affairs, they remained alertly concerned about one another. Jeff, at home in Brooklyn, became highly anxious about George after Fredericksburg and urged him strongly, through Walt and also in letters, now lost, that he sent directly, to quit the service. "I think that it is the duty of all of us to urge this upon him," he wrote Walt:

> I honestly think that he has done enough and run risk enough for any one man. And too there is no judgement used in putting the old regiments [like the 51st] in battle, they just keep throwing them in as long as there is a man left . . . Walt do see him and talk this matter over with him   Speak with him of Mother, who is getting old very old, and if anything should happen [to] him I am quite sure she could not survive it.[14]

Earlier, on the very day when Walt arrived in Falmouth, Jeff was writing,

> We are all very much worried at not hearing anything from you. I have been over to the headquarters of the 51st three or four times but could get no information about brother George. The Times of day before yesterday gave his name among the wounded . . . We certainly expected to hear from you before this . . . I *know* you will spare neither pains nor anything else to find him.[15]

Jeff was not notably stoic, and when the family did receive Walt's detailed, and reassuring, letter about George, he wrote,

> Dear Walt, what hours of trouble you must of past till you found
> George   Mother and Mat each had a "good cry" yesterday in read-
> ing of how you had to get along, and I myself could hardly keep the
> water from my face   If you had only been coming home they say,
> and lost your money, twould have been no matter   but to loose it
> when you did not know how much you would need it on Georges ac-
> count must have made you feel miserable . . . the most trying scene
> of all must have been your sight [of severed limbs in front of the
> Lacy House], not knowing how severely George was wounded. I
> should think that it would almost have been too much.[16]

Jeff began writing George regularly, at Walt's urging. He sent clothing
that found its way to George, and to help Walt in his hospital work, he
recruited a number of charitable donors, people who subscribed a dollar
or two or five on a fairly regular basis. These sums, forwarded to Washington, were put to use to buy the gifts that Walt brought the soldiers on
the wards. Many of the donors were Jeff's fellow waterworks men, and
others were businessmen he met through his outside contracting. He
wisely urged Walt to write thank-you letters describing the great good
that was being done with the donors' money, thus encouraging them to
keep giving. "You must write oftener, home," he advised at one point,

> particulay [to] Mr Lane. He likes much to hear from [you], every let-
> ter is productive of good, of course I mean those speaking of the
> manner of your visits to the Hospitals. Walt, you must be doing more
> *real good* than the whole sanitary Commission put to-gether*   Mr
> Lane, in conversation with a gentleman in the office, said yesterday
> that we ought [to] raise money enough to keep a 100 Walt Whitmans,
> support them and pay them . . . and by that means take the rough
> edge off the War.[17]

---

*The U.S. Sanitary Commission, chartered in 1861, provided medical and other supplies to
the Union soldiers. See chapter 20.

Jeff mailed Walt copies of his newspaper articles as they appeared. At Walt's request, Jeff mailed several copies of the frontispiece engraving from the 1860 edition of *Leaves*, along with photos of George taken during his 1863 Brooklyn furlough. Walt kept one of these photos above his desk for the duration of the war. Walt also accepted job-seeking advice from his brother in Brooklyn; Jeff, exploiting such connections as he had there, got his boss to write on Walt's behalf to a political acquaintance in Secretary of State William H. Seward's office, and he also suggested other possible strings that Walt might pull in the capital.[18]

Pulling strings the other way, Walt, at Jeff's request, inquired at the paymaster's office to learn if George could collect $500 in wages while on that 1863 furlough. The answer was no; but a few months later, Walt used his insider's position to learn that George's regiment would soon be paid—an employee of the paymaster's office, who normally paid the 51st, had been sent out west, where it was then stationed, to settle accounts.[19]

Probably the Whitmans were like many other sets of brothers in the Civil War, but the frequency and frankness of their letter writing create a strong impression of unusual loyalty. Walt began saving his letters around 1860, believing that posterity might show an interest, and these documents give evidence of the brothers' ongoing mutual concern. But the actual correspondence among them was much, much larger than what remains in archival collections today. George, for instance, saved none of the many letters that Walt, Jeff, his mother, or anyone else wrote him while he was actively soldiering (probably because it would have been a nuisance to do so), and Walt by himself wrote him scores of letters now lost. (On February 9, 1863, Walt told his mother, "I have written [George] I should think four letters since the 27th Jan," suggesting a rate of about two a week; on May 13 he wrote her, "I send papers to George almost every day.")[20]

In a letter to his mother, Walt gives a sense of the dense epistolary web that the family spun:

Jeff must have got a letter from me yesterday, containing George's last letter. The news of your sickness, and the strange silence of Han made me feel somewhat gloomy. I wrote to George yesterday, conveying the news—and to-day I have sent him another letter, with much more comfortable news, for I was so glad to hear from Han, (her letter, enclosed in Jeff's, received this morning) that I wrote him right away, and sent Han's letter.[21]

Seven letters are here mentioned, involving five separate correspondents. The letter offering this summary is number eight, and the writer mentions a ninth he intends to write soon (thanking Moses Lane for ten dollars sent to help the soldiers). This was not an unusual exchange among the Whitmans, and it suggests how the mails allowed them to constitute their family despite geographic separations and other obstacles, such as Hannah's strange marriage. In 1863—the year of Andrew's death, Jesse's violent outburst, George's hard campaigning, and Walt's encounter with the hospitals—the letters created a shared family space, a sort of virtual kitchen table around which matters could be chewed over at length.

On the day after his stroll up Pennsylvania Avenue, Walt visited a Washington hospital for the first time as caregiver. The two wounded soldiers mentioned in his Fredericksburg notebook were now at Campbell Hospital, a converted army barracks on Boundary Street (later, Florida Avenue NW) between Fifth and Sixth, a distance of about two miles from downtown. He wrote Mattie,

> O my dear sister, how your heart would ache to go through the rows of wounded young men, as I did—and stopt to speak a comforting word to them. There were about 100 in one long room, just a long shed neatly whitewashed inside. One young man was . . . groaning with pain . . . I found he had not had any medical attention since he was brought there—among so many he had been overlooked.[22]

Walt sent for a doctor, who performed a quick exam, pronouncing the soldier, a private from Massachusetts, "pretty low with diarroeha, and now . . . bronchitis." Walt continued,

> I talked to him some time—he seemed to have entirely give up, and lost heart—he had not a cent of money—not a friend or acquaintance—I wrote a letter from him to his sister . . . I gave him a

little change I had—he said he would like to buy a drink of milk, when the woman came through with milk. Trifling as this was, he was overcome and began to cry.[23]

A few weeks later, the story of this visit, much elaborated, appeared in an article Walt wrote for the *New York Times*. Describing how the Massachusetts soldier had fallen sick at Fredericksburg and had been left out on the freezing ground, then evacuated in an open railcar "such as hogs are transported upon," Walt recounted their meeting in Campbell Hospital:

He now lay, at times out of his head but quite silent, asking nothing of anyone for some days, with death getting a closer and surer grip upon him . . . His heart was broken . . . As luck would have it, at this time I found him. I was passing down Ward No. 6 one day about dusk . . . and noticed his glassy eyes, with a look of despair . . . One learns to divine quickly in the hospital, and as I stopped by him and spoke some commonplace remark . . . I saw as I looked that it was a case for ministering to the affection first and other nourishment and medicines afterward.[24]

Walt sat down beside the youth (John A. Holmes, of Plymouth County, Massachusetts, a farmer's son—Walt identified him only as "H.," to spare him embarrassment). He said a casual hello; got him to talk a little. Seeing how weak the boy was, Walt calmed him when he grew "a little too much agitated [with] tears in his eyes." He gave him some money, wrote a letter home for him, and promised to come back soon.

This first meeting was followed by other visits. "Of course I did not forget him, for he was a young fellow to interest anyone," Walt wrote:

He remained very sick—vomiting much every day . . . For a while, I visited him almost every day, cheered him up, took him some little gifts, and gave him small sums . . . For a couple of weeks his condition was uncertain; sometimes I thought there was no chance for him at all, but of late he is doing better—is up and dressed and goes around more and more.[25]

The visits continued at least until February 21. As of that date, Walt was able to declare,

> He will not die but will recover . . . The other evening, passing through the ward, he called me—he wanted to say a few words, particular. I sat down by his side on the cot in the dimness of the long ward, with the wounded soldiers there in their beds . . . He told me I had saved his life. He was in the deepest earnest about it.[26]

Walt was moved—as well he might be. "It was one of those things that repay a . . . hospital missionary a thousandfold," he wrote in the *Times*, adding,

> A benevolent person . . . cannot, perhaps, make a better investment of himself at present . . . than in these military hospitals, among such thousands of most interesting young men. The army is very young—

Hospital tents in the rear of Douglas Hospital, Washington, D.C., May 1864.

and so much more American than I supposed [i.e., not composed of recent immigrants].[27]

This early visit shows Walt's hospital method already well thought through. He is walking down a crowded ward with useful materials in his pockets (spare change, writing paper, pen or pencil), on the lookout for suffering. A young man arrests his attention. Powerful emotions—and powerful realities, life or death—attend the decision to stop. Walt makes simple contact—probably real physical contact. Unlike many hospital visitors, Whitman believed in the magic of touch, and he became known for embracing, touching the knee of, holding hands with, and even kissing soldiers—kissing them warmly.

One visit was the promise of others, as many as it took. When he said, "I saw . . . that it was a case for administering to the affections first," he betrayed his belief in compassionate contact or, as he put it in the *Times* article, "friendship has literally cured a fever, and the medicine of daily affection, a bad wound." Given the available medical options, holding hands with a patient about to die from days of vomiting and weeks of diarrhea made sense. Potable water (for replenishing fluids) was often unavailable, and the practice of boiling water or treating it with an antibacterial unknown. Civil War physicians were mostly trained in "heroic" medicine—also called allopathic or regular medicine—with its strong preference for bleeding and purging, and they were likely to throw almost anything at a case of chronic diarrhea. John Holmes does not appear to have been treated with the most destructive of Civil War medicines, the mercury-based ones, and the indifference of the medical staff before Walt came along had spared him doses of ipecac, strychnine, turpentine, castor oil, belladonna, lead acetate, and silver nitrate, to name some common nostrums.[28] All things considered, the few sips of (unpasteurized) milk he aimed to buy with the pennies Walt gave him were unlikely to make him much sicker, which was saying something.

The hospitals, even the newly whitewashed ones, were somber places, zones of waiting and wasting. By January 1863, some of the more squalid facilities were on their way to being shut down, and the reforms undertaken by Dr. Jonathan Letterman, the medical director of the Army of the Potomac, had made a positive change in the kind of care a Yankee soldier had a chance of encountering after a battle. At Fredericksburg, for instance, field surgeries had been established in advance of the fight, and a trained ambulance corps was poised to haul bodies in for treatment, in whatever numbers. Walt's pile of amputated limbs, that icon of Civil War barbarity, was itself a sign of progress. At least it *was* a pile, rather than a scattering. The Lacy House had been well stocked with medical supplies beforehand and was manned by experienced surgeons. They dropped the limbs they amputated out of two windows convenient to the operating tables in a room fitted out as a surgery; the limbs piled up at the base of a catalpa tree just below the windows, and were later taken away for burial.[29]

To sit beside a soldier and chat quietly was thus no error, nor was it a mere sentimental gesture. Walt's long practice of meeting men on the streets of New York and striking a spark of friendship—and often recording the strike—has here an echo, although his notebook jottings now are less about attractive shapes and more about wounds, illnesses, and simple needs:

> Thos Butterworth, bed no. 2—something to read. . . .
> Henry Thurer bed 62 Ward 6 wants to see a German Lutheran
>   clergyman. . . .
> Llewllyn Woodin (bed 14) sore throat . . . wants some candy. . . .
> bed 15—wants an orange. . . .
> bed 59. (Janns) wants some liquorice. . . .
> [bed] 27 wants some figs and a book. . . .
> John W. Gaskell . . . weak and prostrated . . . bring him some *nice*
>   cake sponge cake.[30]

These are medical cases, not pickups. That Walt had not turned entirely into an angel of mercy, however, is suggested by a prose fantasy he wrote at about the same time:

> Fatigued by their journey they sat down on Nature's divan whence they regarded the sky. Pressing one another's hands, shoulder to shoulder neither knowing why both became oppressed, their mouths opened, without uttering a word they kissed one another. Near them the hyacinths & the violet marrying their perfume; on raising their heads they both saw God who smiled at them from his azure balcony:

Love one another said he it is for that I have clothed your path with velvet; kiss one another, I am not looking. Love one another, love one another & if you are happy, instead of a prayer to thank me kiss again.[31]

This connoisseur of kisses would bring all of himself into the army hospitals, not just the side of him predicted by early poems and stories about saintly healers. Whether he would have been in the hospitals at all without his attraction to young men is a question impossible to answer, but that he was there in full regalia, feeling fully and engendering strong feelings in others, from the very start is not.

CHAPTER FOURTEEN

PRIVATE HOLMES, WHO returned to action and survived the war, had many of the characteristics that Walt favored in young soldiers. He was of humble background and had probably grown up doing hard physical work. He was also nearly mute ("quite silent, asking nothing of anyone for some days"). Walt got him to talk, but we never hear his actual speech, and we have to trust Walt for a summary of what he reported—that he had been callously neglected, that he wanted a bit of milk, that he credited Walt with saving his life.

"Reader!" Walt exclaims, after telling us Holmes's story:

How can I describe to you the mute appealing look that rolls and moves from many a manly eye, from many a sick cot, following you as you walk slowly down one of these wards? To see these and to be incapable of responding to them, except in a few cases . . . is enough to make one's heart crack.[1]

Probably Walt preferred, for his own personal enjoyment, more talkative soldiers: men with a gift of gab, easygoing raconteurs. In a letter to a young friend in New York, he wrote, "[D]o you not know how much more agreeable to me is the conversation . . . that does not take hard paved tracks, the usual & stereotyped, but has little peculiarities & even kinks of its own?"[2] But for his purposes as a hospital visitor—and, more to the point, as a writer—he preferred the nearly silent ones. These men he could presume to speak for, rendering their character as he understood it.

Two weeks after first meeting Holmes, Walt wrote a second letter to Emerson, explaining what he was up to. "I go a great deal into the Hospitals," he declared:

Washington is full of them—both in town and out around the outskirts. Some of the larger ones are towns in themselves. In small and large, all forty to fifty thousand inmates are ministered to . . . Being sent for by a particular soldier, three weeks since, in the Campbell Hospital, I soon fell to going there and elsewhere . . . The first shudder has long passed over, and I must say I find deep things, unreckoned by current print or speech.[3]

Walt planned to write "a little book" about the hospitals, he told Emerson, a book about "this phase of America, her masculine young manhood, its conduct under most trying of and highest of all exigency." He contrasted the usual crop of Americans that found its way to Washington—gabby politicians—with the stoic soldiers, representatives of America "in her fair youth . . . genuine of the soil . . . the first unquestioned and convincing western crop . . . of perfect beauty, tenderness and pluck."[4]

Walt's idea of a book thus predated by half a year Louisa May Alcott's *Hospital Sketches.* He was in the grip of an inspiration, and he explained to Emerson, "A new world here I find . . . a world full of its separate action, play, suggestiveness—surely a medium world, advanced between our well-known practised one of body and of mind, and one there maybe somewhere on beyond, we dream of, of the soul."[5] By "medium world" he meant a world of the spirit—maybe not exactly the world of mediums and séances, but definitely a metaphysical realm, and he intended to use the wounded soldiers to penetrate its mysteries. Their mute nobility and long lingering, many of them, between life and death made them spirit guides—a phalanx with which to conquer heaven. Walt wanted Emerson to understand how things looked from the common soldier's point of view, too:

[O]ne of the Wards, for sample, a long stretch, a hundred and sixty feet long, with aisle down the middle, with cots, fifty or more on each side—and Death there up and down the aisle, tapping lightly by night or day here and there some poor young man, with relieving touch—that is one Ward . . . wherein this moment lie languishing, burning with fever or down with diarrhea, the imperial blood and rarest marrow of the North.[6]

Having been at his work for two weeks, he could instruct Emerson on the character of young Americans:

I find the masses . . . never vulgar, ever calm, without greediness, no flummery, no frivolity—responding electric and without fail to affection, yet no whining—not the first unmanly whimper have I yet seen or heard . . . In the Patent Office Hospital, Dr. [Horatio] Stone . . . told me last evening that he had not in memory one single case of a man's meeting the approach of death, whether sudden or slow, with fear or trembling—but always of these young men meeting their death with steady composure, and often with curious readiness.[7]

For Emerson, these bulletins of the spirit may or may not have been interesting. But they were surely comprehensible. Walt took the trouble to explain his visiting in transcendentalist terms—in some of the same terms Emerson had used in his great essays of the 1830s and '40s, such as *Nature* and "The Poet." The authentic poet, to Emerson's way of thinking, was the man who could see "the double meaning . . . of every sensuous fact."[8] "It is nature the symbol, nature certifying the supernatural," that the poet has a gift for putting into words—unlike the rest of us, upon whom "too feeble fall the impressions of nature."[9]

Walt's understanding of himself as poet, to an extent that can hardly be overstated, was Emersonian. He had first encountered the New England notable in 1842, when, working for the *New York Aurora*, he attended a lecture that Emerson gave on "Poetry of the Times." Walt made fun of the audience at that event ("a few beautiful maids—but more ugly women, mostly blue stockings; several interesting young men with Byron collars") but concluded about Emerson's performance, "The lecture was one of the richest and most beautiful compositions, both for its matter and style, we have ever heard anywhere, at any time."[10] Emerson's vision of a native American poetry, based on truly

Ralph Waldo Emerson.

American materials, can only have seemed prophetic to the older man when later he read the copy of *Leaves of Grass* that Walt carefully sent him. Walt had followed through on the Emersonian prescription in every particular—for instance, by treating himself as a representative figure, one who "will tell us how it was with him, and all men will be the richer in his fortune."[11]

Emerson had further advised hopeful poets to cherish their American experience; unlike Europe, where the natural world came overlaid with a dense poetic past, America had no indigenous cultural history worth speaking of. An Indian wigwam was hardly equivalent to the Roman Colosseum, but nature in the New World was different in that it gave direct access to higher truths—unencrusted with culture, American reality bespoke metaphysical perfections, a realm of grandeur. "Crossing a bare common, in snow puddles . . . I have enjoyed a perfect exhilaration, I am glad to the brink of fear," Emerson wrote in *Nature*.[12] The humble materials of the American scene brought him to the verge of ecstatic visions, and Walt—studying his Emerson closely—likewise awoke to the majesties of Long Island shorelines, of Manhattan's streaming streets, of his own male body.

The soldiers were poems waiting to happen, he believed. Meeting death with "curious readiness," they were talismans of mystic revelation, of the weighty if familiar idea that death need hold no fear, that the end is not the end. Walt found other meanings, too, in their mute manly looks—here was adhesiveness in the flesh, an urgent need for touch and consolation. His second letter to Emerson is thus the announcement of a new poetic subject, the suffering of the soldiers, but the meaning of that subject is already known in advance. American men are worth writing about—nothing could be worth more—but their trials point mainly to a conventional religious insight.

This may be why Walt never mailed his second letter. The draft that survives bears a scrawled note added years later ("Jan 17 '63 to Emerson—was it sent? I think not").[13] To write to Emerson on a literary topic was a serious matter, and all aspects of the communication needed to be considered carefully. Walt's only previous such communication with the man he acknowledged as his "Master" was an open letter appended to the 1856 *Leaves*, in which he spelled out his entire poetic program over several pages and thousands of words. Emerson might well have dissented from Walt's newest project, on the simple grounds that he was setting out to discover what Emerson already knew: that there is a higher realm; that we do not die when our bodies die. Indeed, Emerson spoke in dismissive tones about Whitman's poetry after 1860—the first three editions of *Leaves* were one thing, but the later work was no longer "oracular," he believed. To an English friend he described Whitman as played out by 1870, as someone "from whom [Emerson] evidently does not expect much more now."[14]

Of the poet of 1860, almost anything might have been expected. By no means conventional in thought, nor in the emotional colorations he introduced into poetry, the Whitman of 1860 was a wonder, an astonishment. He had made good on Emerson's prescriptions and predictions; he had also conjured a style and ventured into areas of feeling far beyond the borders of the rigidly Emersonian. *Leaves of Grass* startled American readers who had been waiting—without knowing they were—for a bomb to be thrown into the wan tea party of mid-Victorian

Walt Whitman, early 1860s.

literary culture. The 1855 and '56 editions had done good work in this regard, but the third edition represented a prodigious expansion, an overtopping. The "Calamus" poems, along with the daring new entries in the "Enfans d'Adam" group, were sexual and deeply personal, so frank as often to be misread, but more captivating than these flagrant items were a few longer, more ambiguous poems—formally adventurous verse that gave evidence of a doubled, skeptical, half-despairing cast of thought.

The great mystery of Walt's poetry is that this new turn, this potent beginning to a process of promising change, finally came to little. Emerson's judgment of 1870, that it was wrong to "expect much more" of Whitman now, was correct. Emerson himself had had a short creative prime. His great innovative phase, during which he wrote the essays that established him as the presiding genius of the American Renaissance, was finished by age forty.[15] Walt, forty-one with the publication of the

1860 *Leaves*, was about to engage with a great subject (the war, the suffering), but without the energies he had formerly summoned.

How he responded, meanwhile, to the soldiers and to their needs was, in purely human terms, immense. He would display during the war remarkable courage and tenacity, showing himself, in the work he undertook in the hospitals, to be a man at the very top of his form. But as a poet he was stymied, if to be a poet is to be a voyager simultaneously at great heights and to deep depths. He may simply have been exhausted—in 1861, he said as much, in an unprinted introduction to *Leaves of Grass*:

> The paths to the house are made—but where is the house itself? At most only indicated or touched . . . I keep it in my plan of work ahead to yet fill up these *Whisperings* (if I live & have luck) . . . If it should turn out otherwise (which is most likely, dear Reader), I hereby bequeath it to you . . . to form and breathe Whisperings for yourself.[16]

There is a subtle threat here: He may not "live & have luck," in which case, others will have to finish his great book. He had intended it to be

> the Chant, the Book of Universal Life, and of the Body,—and then, just as much, to be the Chant of Universal Death, and of the Soul . . . [Its purpose is] to suggest the substance and form of a large, sane, perfect Human Being or character for an American man and for woman . . . I have not done the work and cannot do it. But you must do the work . . . And now . . . we would pourtray, at least in pale reflection . . . one that, having offered salutation & join'd and journeyed on a while in close companionship, has now to resign you, Dearest Reader, and, with mingled cheer and sadness, bid farewell.[17]

He sounds depleted—maybe disappointed. By 1861 the evidence was in that his masterpiece, the richest, most ambitious edition of *Leaves* so far—containing poems such as "A Word out of the Sea" and "As I Ebb'd with the Ocean of Life," among his greatest, and among the greatest poems of the century—had enjoyed a small success only. The two earlier editions had sold even less well, gaining notice within only a select circle of readers. Maybe Walt was not so much disappointed as resentful. He had gone deep and written things he knew were extraordinary, yet as a writer who hoped to live by his pen, and a poet who longed to be embraced by his age, he had earned mostly obscurity.

He may also have sensed some physical or cognitive change within himself. In a letter to Charles Eldridge he said, "I feel to devote myself more to the work of my life, which is making poems . . . I *must* be continually bringing out poems—now is the hey day. I shall range along the high plateau of my life & capacity for a few years now, & then swiftly descend."[18] Entirely prophetic, these words now seem. By November 1863, when he wrote Eldridge, he had composed most of the new *Drum-Taps* verses, poems in a very different mode from his best, and almost all that remained to him to write of a high order was "When Lilacs Last in the Door-Yard Bloom'd," composed in the summer of 1865. To forecast a swift descent, and to forecast it so accurately, suggests that he had felt something already, that he was aware of new limits.

In 1858 he had had the "sunstroke" he told Nelly O'Connor about. Ever after he carried an umbrella in hot weather, and he sometimes also carried a fan, joking to his mother that he looked like "quite a Japanee."[19] Also to his mother he mentioned being often red in the face:

> I believe I weigh about 200 and as to my face, (so scarlet,) and my beard and neck, they are terrible to behold—I fancy the reason I am able to do some good in the hospitals, among the poor languishing & wounded boys, is that I am so large and well—indeed like a great wild buffalo.[20]

He complained about an annoying pressure in his head, and many of his letters home begin with either a report of having this trouble again or grateful mention of not having it for once. Because he would suffer a cerebral hemorrhage in 1873, it seems likely that some of these symptoms indicate the onset of cerebral artery disease, and some of the feelings of oppression may have been what would now be called hypertensive episodes. One possible reading of the Eldridge letter is that he had been trying, and in his own eyes sometimes succeeding, to range still along a "high plateau." But another possible reading is that he had been doing little real poetic work and felt a need to remind himself that poetry was his life's labor, and that he needed to get on with it.

Then again, the war may have baffled him. Other gifted writers were entirely at a loss; Henry James, Mark Twain, and William Dean Howells, to name three, never engaged with it as a subject, and Herman Melville, whose instinct for epic adventure would seem to have made the war a natural subject, wrote a book of poetic sketches and then concluded, "The glory of the war falls short of its pathos."[21] It may be that the war was just too awful in its reality and its implications for an American writer of the time to feel comfortable making hay with it, although many writers of a lesser rank than the four just mentioned did write Civil War stories. *Miss Ravenel's Conversion from Secession to Loyalty* (1867), by John W. De Forest, a Union officer, contains brilliantly written battle scenes that anticipate Tolstoy's in *War and Peace* (1869), and *The Red Badge of Courage* (1895), Stephen Crane's short novel, is surely one of the strongest accounts of common soldiering ever written.*

Apparently a grand subject, full of heroism and historical significance, the war was hard to grasp for contemporary Americans, and even harder to render in a way that appealed to a commercial audience. The experience of the common soldiers, if honestly told, was too raw for polite literature, and a national narrative of brother slaughtering brother only *sounds* like a good idea for a book—in the reading and writing of it, a quality of unredeemed horror would make itself felt. Tolstoy, when he came to write *War and Peace* forty years after the end of the Napoleonic wars, had the benefit of distance in time, but even more he had a story to tell that was likely to warm Russian hearts, since it described a society full of spoiled aristocrats and other feckless types that eventually summoned itself to repel a tyrannous foreign foe.

The American war, furthermore, had been about something—as Lincoln proposed at his second inaugural, "One eighth of the whole population were colored slaves . . . These slaves constituted a peculiar and powerful interest. All knew that this interest was, somehow, the cause of

---

*Born after the war, Crane had not seen combat before he wrote his novella.

the war." An epic novel or poem of the war would have to reckon with slavery and its effects, and more to the point, with the reality of black people, who as convincing and articulate characters are almost entirely missing from the literature that did get written.[22] Nor was the story of Reconstruction something that Americans were eager to tell each other, or knew how to speak of. The rapid retreat from postwar reform by the Federal authorities, and the return almost to the status quo ante for Southern blacks, threw an odd light on the recent vast bloodletting—if not for this, then, good God, for what?

Whitman, unlike other major writers at the time of the war, engaged with the dire reality. Yet it daunted him. A short poem in *Drum-Taps* suggests his unease:

> Year that trembled and reel'd beneath me!
> Your summer wind was warm enough—yet the air I breathed froze me;
> A thick gloom fell through the sunshine and darken'd me;
> Must I change my triumphant songs? said I to myself;
> Must I indeed learn to chant the cold dirges of the baffled?
> And sullen hymns of defeat?[23]

Another, similar poem, not published until 1871, but roughed out during his visit to George at Fredericksburg, finds a similar mood:

> Quicksand years that whirl me I know not whither,
> Your schemes, arrangements politics, fail—your laws, lives [give] way—all is shaken, eluding,
> Only the scheme I sing, the great, possess'd Soul, eludes not,
> One's-Self, need never be shaken—that stands firm. . . .
> Out of politics, wars, death—what at last but One's-Self is sure?[24]

He is one of the "baffled," yet, quickly, he reaches for what has served him in the past, intimations of a great "Soul" that overrides all, and to which all of us belong. The terrible year reels beneath him, but he stands firm. The rhetorical question, "Must I change?" is left hanging in the first poem; the second offers an answer—the Soul and One's-Self, as

bastions—but possibly it comes too easily. Walt soon added a third reason not to fear the chaos into which America had descended. The suffering of the soldiers gave evidence of a superb national character that
would preserve American democracy in the end—the silent, suffering
boys, for whom Walt presumed to speak, were the solidest guarantee.

Someone who follows Walt's path through the war and who reads his
poetry and prose of the time is faced with a paradox—a writer profoundly immersed in the human material, intimate with thousands of
wounded men and their personal stories, who yet appears not really to
be listening. He sifts mountains of firsthand testimony and arrives always at the same meaning. Surely he told a kind of truth when he spoke
of the nobility of the soldiers, but if some of the men had complicated
things to say about their experience—as human nature, and the intensity
of their suffering, give grounds to suspect—either they did not reveal
that complexity or he chose not to report it.

The poet he had worked hard to become by 1860—a poet of contrari-
eties and complications, of rich subtleties, who reported on his inner life
in brave and exhaustive detail—seems unlikely to have settled for only a
partial truth. Henry James was not the man to do the work, to get down
in the trenches with the soldiers to ferret out their true story, and neither
was Twain or Howells, to judge from their shunning of the conflict. But
Walt's embrace of the war likewise only went so far. Of war in its military aspect he remained largely ignorant; he never saw a fight in
progress, although his presence in Washington put him in proximity to
many great battles, which other civilians took the trouble to observe.
After Fredericksburg he visited the front only once, to see a promised
engagement that failed to transpire; after that, he quickly returned to the
capital.

George often invited him to the front, but after the Fredericksburg interlude Walt was too taken up with his Washington life. In February
1863, while George was still camped near Falmouth, he wrote, "I want
you to come down and see me"; about a month later, from a new camp
he again wrote Walt, "I have a bran new tent and when I get it fixed up
to suit me, it will just be gay I tell you . . . you must come down here and
see a feller, and if I do go home [on furlough] you must come as soon as
I get back."[25] From a camp in Kentucky he wrote his mother, "When
you write to Walt . . . tell him if we stay here this winter I shall certainly

expect him to come down here and stay a month or two," and he repeated the invitation when the regiment returned to the eastern theater
later in the war.[26]

Walt, who thought about George every day, who loved him in an enduring and useful way, and who depended on him for firsthand reports
of war's reality, was probably too busy. He had seen something like real
combat—Fredericksburg's aftermath—and that plus the bodies of the
young soldiers brought to hospital added up to enough for his purposes.

Henry James, who wrote a scathing review of *Drum-Taps* in 1865, calling it "an offense against art," railed against Whitman not because of
any failure to report the complex truth of war but because the poet in his
opinion was someone exhibiting "an essentially prosaic mind [that tries]
to lift itself, by a prolonged muscular strain, into poetry."[27] "Every
tragic event," James went on, "collects about it a number of persons
who delight to dwell upon its superficial points . . . The temper of such
minds seems to us to be the reverse of the poetic temper; for the poet, although he incidentally masters . . . the superficial traits of his theme, is
really a poet only insofar as he extracts" what escapes a glancing study.
There was something lacking in *Drum-Taps*—some failure to go deep,
to transmute the war into art. "*Of course* the tumult of battle is grand, the
results of a battle tragic, and the untimely deaths of young men a theme
for elegies," James wrote. But the real poet "must be *possessed*, and . . .
must strive to possess his possession. If in your striving you break into
divine eloquence, then you are a poet."

James came to regret this cruel review. Later in life he read Whitman
with deep feeling and made his emotional response to poems such as
"Out of the Cradle Endlessly Rocking" and "When Lilacs Last in the
Door-Yard Bloom'd" known to Edith Wharton, among other close
friends.[28] But in 1865 he faced Walt across a cultural divide. Walt was too
grossly self-promoting, and just plain too gross, for the future novelist
of sensibility, who had escaped military service by suffering a mysterious wound (probably a hernia or a back strain, incurred when he tried to
help some people at a fire). James's amusing slur against Walt—a "prosaic mind [that tries] to lift itself, by a prolonged muscular strain"—is
suggestive in light of the convenient injury that sent the younger man to
his bed of rest just as others were volunteering, but in any case, his critique of *Drum-Taps* still illumines, still half-persuades. What it mainly

shows us is Walt attempting an impossible thing: to write great poetry that allows itself to go only so far. That already knows the destination it intends to arrive at. That the men were noble and their sacrifice immensely poignant, was a truth acknowledged practically by all; but a poetry of inarguable general opinions, no matter how skillfully deployed, is limited. It may need to be written, or may seem as if it does, in the light of a national calamity, but in the end it visits its hesitations on the writer's craft.

SOMETIME IN THE fall of 1863, John Burroughs was taking a ramble through the woods near Washington when "I plumply encountered [Walt Whitman] traveling along a foot-path between the trees, with a well-stuffed haversack over his shoulder, and the pockets of his overcoat also filled." The poet was on his way "to some army hospital barracks in the vicinity." Burroughs decided to tag along.[1]

With the sack over his shoulder, Walt may have looked like Saint Nicholas, an impression furthered by his whitening beard and solid girth. Burroughs was already an adoring Whitmanian. He had read the 1860 edition of *Leaves of Grass* and been stirred, and his recent move to Washington had grown out of a desire to be "nearer the war," to have some part in it, but perhaps equally out of a desire to meet the great Walt in the flesh.[2]

Burroughs had tried to run into him before. He had visited Pfaff's beer cellar in Manhattan, where Walt was known to idle away hours in the late 1850s through early '60s. After Walt's move to Washington, Burroughs received news about the great man's doings from a friend who ran a Washington army supply store. "Between Walt Whitman and me has passed the bond of beer," Elijah M. Allen wrote Burroughs in May 1863, "and we are friends." Walt liked to sit in the back of the store and muse, Allen said; he reported to Burroughs of one warm afternoon, "Walt just passed [in the street] with his arms full of bottles and lemons, going to some hospitals . . . to give the boys a good time. He was sweating finely; his collar and shirt were thrown open, showing his great hairy throat and breast."[3]

Eventually Burroughs ventured to Washington himself, and he began to frequent Allen's store, in hopes of meeting his idol. The poet showed up one magical evening. "[H]e reached out to me a large, warm, soft hand, and regarded me with a look of infinite good nature and contentment," Burroughs recorded. "I was struck with the strange new beauty of him as he sat there in the gaslight . . . and the curious blending of youth and age in his expression."[4]

The Sunday meeting in the woods followed this one in the store by a few days. Burroughs, twenty-six, has left us one of the more vivid reports of what it felt like to fall within range of the seductive poet's crosshair gaze. Although they were never lovers, there was a period of infatuated courtship about which Burroughs wrote, "I love him very much. The more I see and talk with him, the greater he becomes to me . . . He is much handsomer than his picture represents him . . . He kisses me as if I were a girl."[5]

John Burroughs in the 1860s.

He added, "Notwithstanding the beauty and expressiveness of his eyes, I occasionally see something in them as he bends upon me, that almost makes me draw back. I cannot explain it—whether it is more, or less, than human. It is as if the earth looked at me—dumb, yearning, relentless, immodest."[6]

Here was the useful vagueness of adhesiveness. It licensed looks of all kinds, communicating many meanings. In the debate over Walt's sexuality, it has sometimes been possible to lose sight of his own confusion, his long attempt to make sense of himself, to puzzle out the unusual nature that he felt to be his own. In a way of which he may have been mostly unconscious, he was in a race to define himself before someone else did, before his man-loving propensities were categorized, negatively, as would happen over the next half century, with same-sex behavior defined as sin and psychopathology.

"His magnetism," Burroughs wrote, "was incredible and exhaustless." In the hospitals, "the lusterless eye brightened up at his approach . . . a bracing air seemed to fill the ward, and neutralize the bad smells."[7] Burroughs marveled at how certain lines from *Leaves* were proving prophetic, for instance, from "Song of Myself": "To anyone dying—thither I speed" and "Lovers of me, bafflers of graves." He noted also Walt's simplicity, how his method boiled down to the plainest of brotherly gestures: being present, giving gifts, writing letters. A verbal description of such ministrations would always prove inadequate, Burroughs believed—something was going on that words could not capture.

At about the time of their first meeting, Walt was moving to his second address in Washington, 456 Sixth Street, the back apartment with a private entrance. On the night of October 9, a week before he moved, he entertained a soldier in his old room on L Street, in the house that he had shared for six months with the O'Connors, who had moved out in June. In his pocket diary he noted,

October 9. Jerry Taylor (N.J.) of 2d dist. reg't slept with me last night—weather soft, cool enough, warm enough, heavenly.—rec'd letter from Jeff with $10 from Mr. Kirkwood.[8]

Mr. Kirkwood, Jeff's former boss, was contributing to Walt's hospital fund. Jerry Taylor may have been a soldier recently released from a hospital and on his way back to his regiment, or he may have been someone seen by chance in a crowd on the street, a soldier who answered Walt's vagrant gaze with one of his own. Walt had just cut his hair and beard. The weather had been superb lately, and Walt's use of the word "heavenly" to describe his night with a soldier may refer only to the clean breezes that found their way to his "werry little" L Street room. Or, it may have meant just what it seems to. Colorful words suggesting pleasure and happiness are rare in Walt's diaries, which are terse and impersonal, unlike some of his pocket notebooks. The entries for a few days before and after October 9 give the flavor, or rather, the lack of flavor of the diaries:

> October 4. Letter in N.Y. *Times* celebrating Washington.
> October 5. Sent letter to Thuly Smith either this day or yesterday.
> October 6. Receiving now the letter from L.B. Russell—Margaret Curtis & Hannah E. Stevenson, Boston.
> October 9. Jerry Taylor . . .
> October 10. Rec'd letter from Jeff—with $5 from Moses Lane—$2 from J.D. Martin—$1 from Henry Carlow—wrote to Caleb Babbitt.
> October 12. Rec'd letter from J. Redpath, Boston—wrote to him.
> October 13. Photographs from Brady's, Washington. Sent letter to dear mother.[9]

In this context, "heavenly" is like a Roman candle, its uncertain reference—to the weather, to lovemaking, possibly to something else—drawing more attention to itself, while leaving an impression of sweet discretion, as of an admirer whose lips are sealed.

The soldier mentioned for October 5, Thuly (Bethuel) Smith, had been wounded earlier that year and treated at Armory Square, where Walt first met him. Smith went to a convalescent camp in Pennsylvania after Armory Square, and Walt wrote him there on September 16, inaugurating a correspondence that lasted more than ten years. Walt addressed Smith as "Dear Comrade":

> I was very much disappointed when I went to Armory that evening to find [you] gone so sudden & unexpected . . . What kind of accom-

modations have you at Carlisle, Thu, & how is the foot? I want to
hear all about it—If you get this you must write to me, Thu, you
need not mind ceremony—there is no need of *ceremony* between
dear friends for that I hope we are, my loving boy . . . I am very well
in health & spirits, & only need some employment . . . no, there is
one thing more I need & that is Thuey, for I believe I am quite a fool,
I miss you so.[10]

Smith was not put off by Walt's ardent confession, to judge by the letter he wrote in response, on September 17, and by the several he wrote
after that. About a year later, he told Walt, "I would like to see you verry
much, I have drempt of you often and thought of you oftener still."[11]

Walt was awash in promising friendships. This was a happy side effect
of his work as a "Soldier's Missionary," as his formal appointment, on
January 20, 1863, as an affiliate of the Young Men's Christian Commission named him.* For intellectual companionship he had O'Connor,
Burroughs, Eldridge, Count Adam Gurowski (a Polish abolitionist),
William Swinton (a war correspondent for the *New York Times*), John
Piatt (the minor poet from Ohio), and other writers and literary enthu-
siasts.[12] Meanwhile, each plunge into the streets crowded with soldiers,
each session at his desk in the army paymaster's office, which saw a
daily parade-through of young men, many on crutches, was a foray full
of possibility.

On September 23, wandering the grounds of the Capitol, he met a soldier from Brooklyn, William Van Pelt, and brought him back to his bedroom. The young cavalryman responded to Walt's warm gesture by
bursting into tears. "[W]ent up to my room," Walt noted, but "very
down hearted" the soldier soon proved himself to be, crying "about
home" and needing to be reassured.[13]

Caleb Babbitt, mentioned in the diary for October 10, was a soldier
with whom Walt formed a bond in some ways typical of his involve-
ments for this very busy year. Babbitt had suffered some kind of brain

---

*Walt had little to do with the Christian Commission over time, but admired the work of
its unpaid volunteers, which he considered more truly compassionate than the work of the
U.S. Sanitary Commission.

trauma, identified as sunstroke, in July and been taken to Armory Square Hospital. Walt visited him there often, and when he was sent home to Massachusetts, Walt stayed in touch and at a distance was persistent about getting help for this "young man whom I love very much, who has fallen into deepest affliction," as he wrote to one of his hospital-fund contributors in Boston.

On August 18, Caleb's sister Mary wrote Walt:

My brother wishes me to inform you of the state of his health . . . he arrived home last week Wednesday very much exhausted, and he was obliged to take to his bed from which he has not yet got up . . . He often speaks of you telling of your kindness during his sickness there, and wishes he could see you and tries to gratify himself by looking at your portraits which he has out 5 or 6 times during the day.[14]

On September 18, Caleb was himself able to write, although he cautioned that

I am very weak and my mind is not as it was before I was *sun stroke*. Walt, this is the first letter I have written since I came home, but it is by no means the first one I would like to have written you . . . your letters have been of more value to me than you can imagine. it was not only the words that was written that don me the good . . . It does not seem as though I could ever repay you for your kindness towards me . . . I am just about the same as I was when I saw you at Armory Hospital. I have . . . been with kind friend who have been friends sure, but then Walt I would have dismissed them all for a few days if you could have been with me, how often think of the many fine chat we have had all alone by ourselvs in a loving and peaceful manner.[15]

Caleb had a setback in October and again was hospitalized. Walt heard that he was being treated at Pemberton Square, Boston, and he quickly wrote Margaret Curtis, of that city, asking her to visit the young man. He also wrote to John T. Trowbridge, a Boston author, and to Benjamin Shillaber, a well-known journalist and humorist, about Caleb. They dutifully paid him visits and reported back to Walt on how he was, and

Trowbridge troubled himself further on Babbitt's behalf, when red tape delayed the soldier's release that December.

In the period when he was corresponding with Thuey Smith, and worrying about Caleb, and bringing William Van Pelt up to his room, Walt became friendly with another soldier at Armory Square, Elijah Douglass Fox, of the 2nd Wisconsin Volunteers. In November, Walt wrote Fox about the "suppers, drinking, & what is called *pleasure*" that he was enjoying in Manhattan during a month's rest back home. This high life was all very good, but "[I] have had enough of going around New York," he claimed:

Dearest son, it would be more pleasure if we could be together just in quiet, in some plain way of living, with some good employment & reasonable income, where I could have you often with me, than all the dissipations & amusements of this great city—O I hope things may work so that we can yet have each other's society—for I cannot bear the thought of being separated from you—I know I am a great fool about such things, but I tell you the truth, dear son.[16]

Fox had written Walt a few days before, addressing Walt as "Dear Father." "I have never before met with a man that I could love as I do you," he told Walt. "Still there is nothing strange about it for . . . how any person could know you and not love you is a wonder to me."[17]

Walt replied,

I do not think one night has passed in New York or Brooklyn when I have been at the theatre or opera or afterward to some supper party or carouse . . . but what amid the play or the singing, I would perhaps suddenly think of you . . . see your face before me in my thought as I have seen it so often there in Ward G, & my amusement or drink would be all turned to nothing, & I would realize how happy it would be if I could leave all the fun & noise & the crowd & be with you.[18]

Another letter from Brooklyn, addressed to yet another soldier, gives a sense of how prodigiously broad was the net of contacts that Walt had worked about himself. To Lewis K. Brown, a Maryland infantryman, he

wrote about carousing and operagoing, and about the curious prosperity
of the North in this ruinous war ("every thing going with a big rush &
so gay . . . almost everybody well-drest, & appearing to have enough").
Walt enjoined Brown to show the letter to all the lads there at Armory
Square, to have someone read it aloud some evening, and he ventured a
catalog of soldiers whom he was specially thinking of, including

> my dear comrade Elijah Fox in Ward G [who I wish] was here with
> me—but perhaps he is on his way to Wisconsin . . . Oscar Cunning-
> ham in your ward . . . he must try to keep up good courage while he
> is confined there with his wound. Lewy, I want you to give my love
> to Charley Cate and all the boys in Ward K, & to Benton if he is [still
> there]—I wish you would go in Ward C and see James S Stilwell, &
> also Thomas Carson . . . & Chambers that lays next to him . . . in
> Ward B . . . tell a young cavalry man, his first name is Edwin, he is
> wounded in the right arm, that I sent him my love, & on the opposite
> side a young man named Charley . . . [and] Pleasant Borley, if he is
> still there . . . I hope it will be God's will that he will live & get
> strong . . . [and] little Billy, the Ohio boy in Ward A.[19]

Some of these soldiers were dying. Pleasant Borley, with a gangrenous
leg, would soon die of tuberculosis.[20] Oscar Cunningham, who came
from Ohio, had been wounded at Chancellorsville (May 3, 1863).
"[W]hen he was brought here," Walt wrote in a notebook, "I thought he
ought to have been taken to a sculptor to model for an emblematical figure of the west, he was such a handsome young giant over 6 feet high,
with a great head of brown yellow shining hair thick & longish." Over
the course of a year, Cunningham's leg wound festered, and by the end,
when an amputation at the thigh led to his exhaustion and death, he had
been horribly transformed. "I have just left Oscar Cunningham," the
poet wrote his mother in June 1864, "he is in a dying condition . . . it
would draw tears from the hardest heart to look at him . . . you remember I told you a year ago, when he was first brought in, I thought him the
noblest specimen of a young western man I had seen . . . O what a
change."[21]

The net of caring was immensely wider than suggested even by the letter to Lewy Brown, for Armory Square was only one of the hospitals

Walt visited, and in each he cultivated highly personal connections. From his days as a novice journalist he had sought to merge with the teeming crowd, and he identified with all the human types thrown up by American democracy in its first generations. In the thousands of wounded and sick soldiers, he had found at last a crowd that he could examine, caress, love, and heal in his own good time. As he wrote to Emerson, in the letter that probably never got mailed, he was fascinated by "this phase of America, her masculine young manhood, its conduct under most trying of and highest of all exigency." It was America "brought to Hospital in her fair youth—brought and deposited here in this great, whited sepulchre of Washington."[22]

After but ten months in town, Walt was a well-known character on the city streets. Although he dressed modestly, he was distinctive, like other nineteenth- and early-twentieth-century literary figures who found it useful to publish a personal image along with their written works.* In May, Walt wrote his mother about some adjustments recently made to his costume:

> I had to discard my old clothes, somewhat because they were too [heavy for the weather] & more still because they were worse gone in than any I yet wore . . . I have a nice plain suit, of a dark wine color, looks very well, & feels good . . . & vest & pants same as what I always wear, (pants pretty full,) so upon the whole all looks unusually good for me, my hat is very good yet, boots ditto, have a new necktie, nice shirts, you can imagine I cut quite a swell.[23]

The necktie was something different, and maybe not worn every day, but encounters with hospital officials and other gatekeepers may have gone better when Walt was demurely dressed. John Trowbridge noted that Walt "was more trimly attired [than when they had first met three

---

*There was Byron with his famous collars; Longfellow with his prim professor's garb augmented by a full beard, a likely precursor to Walt's; Mark Twain, often seen publicly in a white suit; Oscar Wilde with a velvet coat, knee breeches, black silk stockings, and a lily in his buttonhole; and Count Leo Tolstoy in a peasant smock.

years before], wearing a loosely fitting but quite elegant suit of black—
yes, black at last!" Black was the color of respectability as well as
mourning. Trowbridge may have missed the dark wine tint of Walt's
new suit, although he caught the move toward presentability.

Washington was becoming a glamorous city—its carpe diem atmosphere intensified by the threat of rebel attack, its boomtown energies
complicated by a sense of historical moment. As Walt wrote his mother in
June 1863, "We are generally anticipating a lively time here or in the
neighborhood, as it is probable Lee is feeling about to strike a blow
[following his victories at Chancellorsville and elsewhere] . . . I fancy I
should take it very quietly if I found myself in the midst of a desperate
conflict . . . in Washington."[24]

He admired the capital city. As noted in a diary entry for October 4, he
felt like "celebrating" it (and did so in his *New York Times* article that
month). Wartime Washington had something of the hurly-burly spirit
of New York, and now something like its population density. Walt had
lived in a wartime city before. While a newspaper editor in 1848, he had
gotten to know New Orleans in the immediate aftermath of the
Mexican-American War, when it was the principal staging area for the
U.S. side of the conflict. A wartime city often licensed indecent excess,
and although Walt avoided vulgar display himself, he had a sneaking
fondness for it, as he showed in letters he wrote his brother Jeff, in which
he described the gaudy interior furnishings of the Capitol, where he had
gone to see Congress at work ("the incredible gorgeousness of some of
the rooms . . . Costly frescoes in the style of Taylor's Saloon in Broadway . . . indeed by far the richest and gayest, and most un-American . . .
interior workmanship . . . possible").[25]

Washington was growing rich, even as tens of thousands of diseased
and wounded soldiers crowded in. Investors in real estate and construction made fortunes as rents and property values boomed; northern capital flowed in as local businesses supplied mattresses, iron bedsteads,
stoves, copperplate, howitzers, cartridges, mortar shells, saddlery, military clothing, and frigates and other shipping to the war effort.[26] A
youth spent in New York to the constant sound and sight of housing
construction and commercial expansion was good preparation for what
was happening in Washington in the 1860s. Also in the New York style
was the superabundance of goods available in the market on Capitol

Hill, where Walt often shopped early in the morning in a clientele composed mostly of women. As large army encampments near the city were closed down, farmers returned to plow the land now fabulously enriched by the manure left by thousands of army mules and horses. Walt enthused about the fresh strawberries and other produce he found for sale; the fall of 1863 was a banner season also for grouse, venison, oysters, quail, swans, reedbirds, and turkey.[27]

The notes Walt kept about the soldiers' needs suggest that he was often in the local shops, supplying them. A sample passage from a notebook from early 1863 gives a hint of the varied shopping he must have undertaken:

> I buy [tobacco] by the pound, and do it up in little bits of parcels,— of course cakes &c. I always find [requests] for—also plenty of note-paper, envelopes . . . through any new ward a heap of loose reading matter, novels, old magazines . . . many want apples—one young man wanted a rice pudding which I carried him next day—two or three some liquorish—one poor fellow in the Patent Office Hospital, with his leg amputated . . . I made . . . a small jar of very nice spiced and pickled cherries . . . some of the young fellows are quite crotchetty—one lad in bed 23 . . . had set his heart on a pair of suspenders . . . I gave him 30 cts and the next time I came, I took him a pair of suspenders.[28]

Someone had to hunt down these goods or prepare them. Even with occasional help from others, Walt would have been walking the streets, going to the shops, on a regular basis, and he also undertook to fulfill many other kinds of requests: "Of course there are plenty of little commissions . . . to go to Adams's Express office, and see about a box . . . to find out a brother or some special comrade, somewhere in Washington, but they know not where, &c. &c."[29] His willingness to do almost anything requested of him by a soldier—to fetch a visiting relative from the train station; to pour some juicy relish on a slice of bread—did not diminish as the months and the years went by. In 1865 he was as amenable, as biddable, as in 1863, and as likely to take a moment to write down the specifics of a particularly sad, heroic, or bizarre case he happened to come across on the wards.

The sight of him at the foot of your bed, if you were an ailing soldier, pulling out a handmade notebook and starting to write as you told him your story, his ability to jot as he spoke and went on looking you in the eye, remarkable in itself; his whole demeanor of attending, of caring enough to get the details down right, making a quiet answer to the impersonality of the ward, and to the squalor of the numberless other men sweating, groaning, stinking, and dying in nearby beds; his focus on what *you* wanted, as whimsical as that might be, implying that it was reasonable to hope for the day after tomorrow, when he promised to return, and by extension for a more distant future, a time when the open wound might heal or the fever pass or the dysentery miraculously cure itself—the simple sight of him there, scribbling, writing against the mass of unacknowledged, otherwise never-to-be-recorded misery, must have been good medicine.

In the many letters Walt received from soldiers, further responsibilities were laid on him. Some asked for his personal photo, for advice about business affairs, for help getting a furlough extended; one wanted help redeeming a pawned watch, the receipt for which had been lost when the soldier's wallet was stolen; some wanted help landing a Washington job when the war ended; one wanted Walt to send him a nice selection of flower seeds.[30] Few ever learned that he was a poet, let alone a noted and controversial one. One soldier, writing to him ten years after the war, expressed astonishment on that score:

> Early in the year 1863 . . . I lay on a cot . . . at Judiciary Sqre . . . sick "Nigh unto death" when there came in one day, with charitable intent, a stalwart man of genial appearance . . . Although I have never since heard a word from my quondam friend, still the name Walt Whitman is a household one in our family & the picture . . . with the autograph, Walt Whitman 1863 . . . is lying here on the table having been brought downstairs a little while ago to be compared with one which appears in [Frank] Leslie's [*Illustrated Weekly*] for April 8th [1876] . . . The question that naturally comes to us now is this, Is *this* Walt Whitman,— "The Poet of health& strength," *our* Walt Whitman of old?[31]

He came to them not in the guise of author—even less so as celebrity. To have presented himself thus would have worked against the main goal, that of making a quick and intimate connection, with the focus on the soldier's needs. Some of them were very young, only fifteen or sixteen.[32] His warm assurance around boys had many sources, but probably his loving identification with a number of brothers had something to do with it, his distance in age from his youngest four (twelve years on average) having encouraged in him a semipaternal style. No doubt as he met new men brought in in the wake of great and small battles, he thought of George and his condition of peril in the field; the letters he wrote to Mrs. Whitman often toggle back and forth between talk of the war-wounded and immediate talk of George, as well as of Jeff (at risk of being drafted) and Andrew (who enlisted but was soon invalided out).

A letter sent October 13 mentioned George, Jeff, and particularly Andrew, whom Walt said "I desire much to see," then got on to the human debris of battle:

> There is a new lot of wounded . . . long strings of ambulances . . . I thought I was cooler & more used to it, but the sight of some of them brought tears to my eyes—Mother, I had the good luck yesterday to do quite a great deal of good . . . these new wounded as they came in were faint & hungry, and fagged out with a long rough journey, all dirty & torn, & many pale as ashes . . . as many as I could I fed myself—Then besides I found a lot of oyster soup handy, & I procured it . . . Mother, it is the most pitiful sight I think when first the men are brought in—I have to bustle round, to keep from crying.[33]

Walt wrote again two weeks later, saying,

> [I]f any of my soldier boys should ever call upon you, (as they are often anxious to have my address in Brooklyn,) you just use them as you know how to without ceremony, & if you happen to have pot luck & feel to ask them to take a bite, dont be afraid to do so . . . possibly a Mr. Haskell . . . from western New York, may call—he had a son died here, a very fine boy . . . Mother, when I come home I will show you some of the letters I get from mothers, sisters, fathers &c. They will make you cry.[34]

Mrs. Whitman, for her part, caught the linkage between home and battleground, between worry about Whitman sons and worry about the nation's. By the fall of 1863 she had been put through a stark education
about war as a bringer of sorrows, via Walt's unvarnished letters. To his
mother more than anyone else, Walt expressed his anguish. To her he
could show how close he came to being overwhelmed, how sickened he
was by the carnage, how fretful and mournful it made him. In late October, shortly before his break at home, he received a long letter from Mrs.
Whitman, six closely written double pages that detailed the mounting
crisis in the house on Portland Avenue, with Andrew fast wasting and
money problems and crowded living driving everyone half mad, a letter
that displayed in passing a sound grasp of the psychosexual sources of
Walt's devotion to the broken bodies of young men:

> [I] pity Andrew very much but i think sometimes how much more
> those poor wounded and sick soldiers suffer with so much patience
> poor souls i think much about them and always glad to hear you speak
> of them i dont think walt after you being amongst them so long you
> could content yourself from them it becomes a kind of fasination.[35]

"Always glad to hear you speak of them," she assured him, sensing the
role he wanted her to play, as a sort of confessor. Then—as if anxious
not to burden him with too much news of family woe—she turned her
attention to a hopeful thing, to Jeff and Mattie's new child, their darling,
still unnamed second daughter:

> [W]ell the little baby is well and fat and prettyer than [her sister]
> She grows tall and not so fat as she was   she goes to [Jamaica,
> Queens] with her father [on buggy rides]   O walt don't you never
> hear from hann it is so strange she never writes I got your letter yes-
> terday money and all [arrived safely]   walt you might almost write
> a book from this letter.

O MOTHER, HOW WELCOME the shirts were," Walt wrote home on May 19, 1863. "[M]y old ones . . . when they come back from the wash I had to laugh, they were a lot of rags held together with starch—I have a very nice old black aunty for a washwoman, but she bears down pretty hard."[1]

The "O Mother" form of address appears over and over in Walt's letters. It answers Mrs. Whitman's own "O Walt," the correspondents falling naturally into an intimate register, one that accommodates almost anything either needs to say. Walt seems to echo Mrs. Whitman's style sometimes, salting his sentences with "ain't"s and other homey bits of bad grammar, as for example, while thanking her for a cake she sent,

> [D]ear mother, I am almost like the boy that put it under his pillow— & woke up in the night & eat some—I carried a good chunk to a young man wounded, I think a good deal of, & it did him so much good—it is dry, but all the better, as he eat it with tea & it relished—I eat a piece with him & drinked some tea, out of his cup.[2]

If Walt seemed to be writing down when he addressed his mother, that impression disappeared as he ventured to deal with a wider range of topics, with fully as much intellectual complexity as he would summon for the most educated of his correspondents. On June 30 he told her the story of a cavalryman dying of typhoid fever, whom Walt had rescued by, among other things, lying to him about how serious his case was.[3] The psychological effect of believing one was about to die—an effect Walt saw demonstrated over and over—was an important part of his early hospital experience, and it was something he thought his mother could appreciate. He had been ministering to this fever patient for fifteen days, leaning over the bed, hand-feeding him, despite having a sore throat himself and having been warned by the doctors not to get too close. Walt further showed his wartime Washington sangfroid in this letter:

> I suppose you folks think we are in a somewhat dubious position here . . . with Lee in strong force almost between us & you northerners—well it does look ticklish, if the rebs cut the connection, then there will be fun—The reb cavalry come quite near us, dash in & steal wagon trains, &c—It would be funny if they should come some night to the President's country house . . . where he goes out to sleep every night—it is in the same direction as their saucy raid last Sunday.[4]

For his mother's benefit—and for Jeff's, Mattie's, and that of anybody else who might read it—Walt's letter offered a vivid portrait of the president, whom Walt found the more fascinating the longer he observed him under the press of national crisis:

> Mr. Lincoln passes here (14th st) every evening on his way out [to the Soldier's Home northeast of the White House, where he often slept in hot weather]—I noticed him last evening about 1/2 past 6, he was in his barouche, two horses, guarded by about thirty cavalry . . . he looks more careworn even than usual—his face with deep cut lines, seams, & his *complexion gray*, through very dark skin, a curious looking man, very sad—I said to a lady who was looking with me, "Who can see that man without losing all wish to be sharp upon him personally? Who can say that he has not a good soul?" . . . As he came up, he first drove over to the house of the Sec of War, on K st about 300 feet from here, sat in his carriage while Stanton came out & had a 15 minutes interview with him . . . then wheeled around, &

President Abraham Lincoln, shortly after Antietam, October 3, 1862. To his right, Allan Pinkerton, head of the Union Intelligence Service; to his left, Major General John A. McClernand.

slowly trotted around the corner & up Fourteenth st . . . I really think it would be safer for him just now to stop at the White House, but I expect he is too proud to abandon the former custom.[5]

This letter was a rough draft—but not very rough—of the well-known passage in *Memoranda During the War* that describes the poet's encounters with Lincoln. First published in 1875, and later incorporated into *Specimen Days & Collect* (1882), this passage in *Memoranda* retained the tone and most of the detail of Walt's letter to his untutored mother:

Sometimes the President goes and comes in an open barouche. The cavalry always accompany him, with drawn sabers. Often I notice . . . he turns off and halts at the large and handsome residence of the Secretary of War, on K street, and holds conference there. If in his barouche . . . he does not alight, but . . . Stanton comes out to attend him.[6]

Walt saw the president going the other way, too, back into town after a night at the Soldier's Home:

> The party makes no great show in uniforms or horses. Mr. Lincoln . . . is dress'd in plain black, somewhat rusty and dusty; wears a black stiff hat . . . I see very plainly [his] dark brown face, with the deep cut lines, the eyes . . . always to me with a deep latent sadness in the expression. We have got so that we always exchange bows, and very cordial ones.[7]

Another encounter on a city street—another exchange of meaning looks.[8] For the most part, Walt spared his mother descriptions of his ardent searching for men, but he spared her not much else. Mrs. Whitman's powers of understanding have been discounted by some historians, and her own letters display qualities that make her seem unsophisticated. Walt himself said of her that she "stood before *Leaves of Grass* mystified, defeated," but the strong evidence is that he counted on her as on nobody else for comprehension.[9] To his mother he could explain his attraction to bedridden boys. On June 9, he wrote her about yet another young soldier, John Barker, who had been captured and tortured for his Union sympathies. "[H]e suffered every thing but death . . . they hung [him] up by the heels . . . a real manly fellow, I saw much of him & heard much" from him about East Tennessee, where his home was.[10]

In a few of his letters, Walt conveyed a feeling of distraction, almost of frenzy. Writing near the end of May, he apologized to his mother for speaking so much about wounds and suffering, but added, "O the sad, sad things I see, the noble young men with legs & arms taken off—the deaths—the sick weakness . . . after amputations."[11] Late in June he wrote, "I get more and more wound round," and on July 7, three days after the Battle of Gettysburg, as casualties flooded in, "Mother, one's heart grows sick of war, after all, when you see what it really is . . . I feel so horrified & disgusted—it seems to me like a great slaughter-house and the men mutually butchering each other."[12]

He had been to a nearby contraband camp, where escaped slaves lived in horrid squalor. About the foul hospital there, he wrote, "I could not bring myself to go again—when I meet black men or boys among my own hospitals, I use them kindly . . . but . . . there is a limit to one's sinews & endurance."[13] In mid-July, after the murderous draft riots in New York, he confessed to her,

We are in the midst of strange & terrible times—one is pulled a dozen different ways in his mind, & hardly knows what to think or do . . . I was in Armory all day yesterday & day & night before— they have the men wounded in the railroad accident at Laurel [Maryland] station . . . poor, poor, poor men . . . I see so much of butcher sights, so much sickness & suffering I must get away a while I believe for self preservation.[14]

The notes of torment are obscured in letters not written to his mother; one reason may be that he wrote preliminary drafts of those letters, correcting, shading, and shaping how he came across. Writing to Jeff, or to his sister-in-law Mattie, but especially to his mother, he worried less about seeming overwhelmed.

Mrs. Whitman, the locus and lodestone of the family correspondence, was "illiterate, in the formal sense," Walt told a biographer near the end of his life. But the "reality, the simplicity, the transparency of my dear, dear mother's life [were] responsible for the main things in the letters, as in *Leaves of Grass* itself. How much I owe her! It could not be put in a scale . . . measured . . . it can only be apprehended through the intuitions. *Leaves of Grass* is the flower of her temperament active in me. My mother was . . . strangely knowing; she excelled in narrative—had great mimetic power; she could tell stories, impersonate; she was very eloquent in the utterance of noble moral axioms—was very original in her manner, her style."[15]

Although illiterate to his way of thinking—by which he meant, probably, that she was no grammarian—and although "defeated" by the poetic originalities of *Leaves of Grass*, she was a discerning sampler of belles lettres when it came to anything that touched on his own career. Two years after the war ended, hearing that Walt's friend, William O'Connor, was looking for a new place to rent, she wrote,

[I] feel to sympathise with mr Oconor in his getting a house   i think its about the worst and most disagreable fix any one can be in   Walt do

you know i like his writings the good gray poet better than I doo
[John Burroughs's]   Oconors shows [much by] the spirit its wrote
in i should form an idea of the man if i had never seen him by reading his writings   i suppose you see that peice in the sunday times as
you dident say any thing about it i will send it.[16]

She was comparing the first two extended works of literary analysis
ever written about her son, the newly published pamphlet by O'Connor,
The Good Gray Poet, and the even more recently published book by Burroughs, *Notes on Walt Whitman as Poet and Person*. O'Connor's essay, in
particular, was a dense, allusion-studded polemic of great power and
stylistic brilliance, nigh unto an American rhetorical tour de force.

Burroughs's book, full of subtle touches and conveying a sense of
Walt's human presence—the poet himself dictated parts of it, strongly
influencing its overall tendency—was, just as Mrs. Whitman said, less
forceful and impressive. Walt writing on Walt (through Burroughs) resulted in a colorful, meandering text full of perceptive lines that somehow grow tiresome; maybe because its authorship was shared, *Notes on
Walt Whitman* comes across as gentlemanly, not fiery and convulsively
overtopping like O'Connor's screed (which, true to Mrs. Whitman's
observation, gives a vivid idea of the author's actual temperament).

The "peice in the sunday times" she mentioned was a review of Burroughs's book, written by his good friend O'Connor, who was at that
time being considered for an editorial position at the paper. The review
appeared on June 30, 1867, and it showed the literary handwashing
growing incestuous, O'Connor putting his connections at the *Times* in
service to Burroughs's book, which was partly written by Walt himself,
entirely in praise of Walt, and partly by O'Connor (who had helped
Burroughs with the literary passages while Walt helped with the biogra-
phical material).[17]

Mrs. Whitman's own literary products, if they may be called that, her
letters, have a stamp of originality. Describing George's visit to Brooklyn on a furlough in March 1863, she wrote,

[H]e come at last quite unexpected although i had looked for him
every day for A week . . . he went up stairs and went to bed and said
nothing and [I] was busy fixing the fire [next morning] . . . as he

opened the door i says Edd get your thick boots [on] without looking around you may depend i was so glad to see him i did not know how to get breakfast.[18]

George, now a captain, and a hero of Fredericksburg, was lionized by his local friends. As Mrs. Whitman put it, "The folks do as if they would eat him up he has invitation from all quarters." Writing about a week later, after George had left again, she said, "[W]e all eat dinner up stairs the night he went away not so very solem as you would suppose but when he came to go I felt bad enough."[19] Mrs. Whitman notified Walt when she got a letter from George, and she expressed to him how much she longed to hear from her soldier son; the letters told her that George had survived this or that battle, but, as she admitted, "I like to get letters [even] if there aint any thing so very particular in them."[20]

Like many Americans, Mrs. Whitman never wrote so much as she did during the war. The whole country was communicating at a mad pace; in the North alone, 180,000 letters passed every day between the soldiers and their correspondents back home.[21] Mrs. Whitman was aware of writing a great deal. "Dear Walter i write quite often dont i," she noted in the fall of 1863, having observed earlier, "[T]his 12 sheets of writing paper for 4 cents is awful stuff to write on it want better writer than mammy i dont think i shall invest in it again."[22] Writing to and hearing from her sons in the service (George officially, Walt less so), she offered such solace and support as a mother could, meanwhile participating in her era's great events. She might not have said, as Walt did after the war, that these were the years of being most fully alive, but they were momentous times, and through her sons she was brought very close to the heart of the struggle.

A few of her letters, longer ones, have an appealing shapeliness that arises from what must have been an innate sense of proportion, household problems claiming her and dictating what she writes about, but only up to a point. Walt asks over and over for ground-level reports out of her homely kitchen, and she supplies them:

[I] think Andrew is better he was here yesterday and i think his throat is somewhat better he says it is not but i know it is nancy was here last night . . . he took home some pie and she said he eat that and 3 eggs so his throat couldent hurt him so bad . . . he wanted some roast lamb i said get a small piece and have it cooked . . . but to be saving of what he had . . . but Walt it is no use to talk they just get the very most expensive things lamb is 20 cents per lb.[23]

She seems to know, even as she says his throat is better, that Andrew is dying; in early September, she told Walt, "[I] hope he will be better but am afraid it has gone to long." To discuss Andrew was to open the door on the vexing issues of money, the crowded house, Jeff's noisy children, Nancy's shiftlessness, Jesse's decline, and her own aching knees and shoulders. In letter after letter, she revisited these complexly braided realities, updating Walt while enlisting him on her side in unresolved family disputes. She asked after his health (advising him, for instance, to put "a very little sweet oil" in his ear to help relieve the pressure in his head) and reported on her own, usually in pitiful terms. She made fun of her own stream-of-complaints narrative style ("here goes another of mothers scientific letters") but knew when to pull back, to undercut it.

"[Y]ou are my whole depandance," she wrote Walt in the fall of 1863, finding him to be the most faithful correspondent among her many children, the one who always sent money or other useful gifts. "[I] think every morning if I could give you a cup of coffee i should be glad i am pretty lonesome."[24] Writing to Walt was a way to remain engaged, to think out loud about the problems that never resolved, and for Walt there must have been instruction and courage to be taken from the example of her humble enduringness. The similarities of their positions may have been obvious to both of them. Both were nurses of a kind to numbers of helpless people. Their duties were never at an end. Both subsisted on the gifts of others, Walt's hospital fund requiring the same sorts of effort (letters of solicitation, notes of thank-you, a self-presentation that verged sometimes on the pathetic) as Mrs. Whitman's poverty imposed on her.

Both practiced abstinence, bordering on mortification, during the war. Walt lived in humble rooms that seemed to him fitting, given the way the fighting men were forced to live. John Trowbridge recalled Walt's apartment at 456 Sixth Street as nothing but a "bare and desolate back room" in an "old wooden tenement" after a visit there in late 1863, comparing its rudeness to the splendor of a mansion across the street that was occupied by Salmon P. Chase, Lincoln's secretary of the treasury. Mrs. Whitman, for her part, managed to convince herself that she was nearly penniless, despite having George's wages to draw on; her self-denials alarmed Jeff and Mattie and led to this affectionate lecture from Walt:

> Mother, I hope you will live better—Jeff tells me you & Jess & Ed live on poor stuff, you are so economical—Mother, you mustn't do so . . . I hope you will at least four or five times a week have a steak of beef or mutton . . . I have one good meal of that kind every day, or at least five or six days out of the seven . . . as to using George's money for your & Jess & Ed's needful living . . . I know George would be mad & hurt in his feelings, if he thought you was afraid to.[25]

Mrs. Whitman performed tasks within her family that resembled those Walt performed among the soldiers. She had less occasion to attend the dying, but Andrew's feckless wife and children provided occasions for feeding and clothing and giving small gifts to people in need under sometimes repellent circumstances. There was the time when Georgy, Nancy's oldest son, was "besmeard head to foot" and had to be cleaned up at his grandmother's house, and the time when Andrew, nearly dead, went off on a drunken spree with a friend, and, as Mrs. Whitman reported to Walt,

> [N]ancy came here the night after he first went with very great complaints she said george was sick and Andrew had gone and left her without any money i gave her one dollar and one of my gowns and a quilt petticoat little jim was here yesterday and nancy . . . had got a letter from Andrew he wrote he was not so well as when he went away i gave her some paper and envelopes and told her to write to him.[26]

Walt was always writing for, or giving paper and envelopes to, his soldier boys—so many letters did he write or promote that he might almost be called the attending spirit of Civil War correspondence. Mrs. Whitman's effort, in Andrew's last days, to encourage a civil exchange between her dying son and his unkempt wife speaks of a faith in pen and page not so different from Walt's, albeit in this case poorly placed.

Walt not only needed to write to his mother—he needed to see her. He spent November 1863 in Brooklyn, brought there by his own exhaustion and by the need to see Andrew now if he was to see him ever again alive. But visiting his mother—sitting in her kitchen, passing some normal-seeming hours in her presence—was another compelling requirement. "Dear mother," he wrote on September 1,

> how are you nowadays—I do hope you feel well & in good spirits—I think about you every day of my life out here—sometimes I see women in the hospitals, mothers come to see their sons, & occasionally one that makes me think of my dear mother—one did very much, a lady about 60, from Pennsylvania, come to see her son, a Captain, very badly wounded, and his wound gangrened.[27]

After a century of suspicion of close mother-son attachments, Walt's devotion seems a little exaggerated. But George, too, yearned to be with his mother—to shelter again in that simple kitchen. Not at all abashed, Walt took steps to ensure that ample evidence of his mother-adoration would survive—that his biographers would find it, and through them generations of readers.

"The letters to my mother are all here," he declared in his last years, "—I have them—I got them after she died . . . all scrupulously kept together."[28] He preserved as well the letters she wrote him, with their talk of bunions and bad smells and their inventive spelling. Motherhood as a subject plays only a minor role in *Leaves of Grass* and his other books; but healing, one of his profound concerns, is always bound up in the behavior of mothers, and his novel ideas of masculinity are accented always with maternal traits and ways. John Burroughs described him as "a great tender mother-man," and Walt, writing at a time when nurses were usually men, held that it was a womanly, indeed a motherly, touch that succeeded in the hospitals:

> Middle-aged or healthy and good condition'd elderly women, mothers of children, are always best [because younger women were some-

times prudish]. Many of the wounded must be handled . . . a good middle-aged or elderly woman, the magnetic touch of hands, the expressive features of the mother, the silent soothing of her presence, her words, her knowledge and privileges arrived at only through having children, are precious and final qualifications . . . One of the finest nurses I met was a red-faced illiterate old Irish woman; I have seen her take the poor wasted naked boys so tenderly up in her arms.[29]

"[T]he institution of the father," by contrast, was "a failure," Walt wrote, adding that "mothers were loving, affectionate, indulgent . . . in many cases . . . undue severity [from fathers] had driven the boys to enlist in the army, when not of age."[30]

During that month of rest in Brooklyn, he wrote Nelly O'Connor

from my room at my mother's house. It is Sunday afternoon, dripping & rainy, the air thick & warm, & the sky lowering. My poor brother Andrew is very ill. It is not likely he can live . . . Still he moves about & is here all the time during the day . . . Mother is very well & active & cheerful—she still does her own . . . housework, & keeps up handsomely under her surroundings of domestic pressure— one case of sickness & its accompanying irritability—two of grown helplessness—& the two little children, very much with her, & one of them unsurpassed in volatility and restlessness—Nelly, I have thought before that the real & best bravery is to be discovered somewhere else than in the bravery of war, & beyond the heroisms of men.[31]

He seems to have spent much of November not actually at his mother's side, or even Andrew's, but in Manhattan attending parties and musical entertainments. But he had seen what he needed to, his mother "so well, & so bravely sailing on amid many troubles & discouragements," he wrote Charles Eldridge, "like a noble old ship."[32] She was bearing up, and he would also bear up.

TWO BLUE SHIRTS made of wool flannel followed Walt to Washington. Jeff mailed them soon after Walt rushed off to find George at Fredericksburg, and they were waiting for him when he returned from Virginia. Walt wrote his sister-in-law Mat, "I have not heard anything from dear brother George since I left the camp last Sunday . . . I wrote to him on Tuesday last—I wish to get him the two . . . woolen shirts . . . as they would come very acceptable to him."[1] Walt kept the shirts temporarily—and probably wore them. They had been made to fit Jeff, but Jeff thought they would fit Walt well enough, and they eventually fit George, too—from which we can conclude that the brothers were roughly of a size.

George wrote his mother in late February, "Another thing I want to come home for is to get a suit of Clothes as the ones I have are getting pretty seedy and if I dont get home soon I have been thinking of getting measured here and sending on to Walt or Jeff to have me a suit made. Mother how are the bank funds[?]"[2] On the same day, he wrote Walt about his attempts to get a furlough; none was being "alowed except in case of sickness or in a case of life and death or something of that sort," and again he mentioned needing new clothes.[3]

On March 12—George having gotten his furlough—Jeff again wrote about the two blue shirts, asking Walt to mail them to Brooklyn:

[I]f you *possibly* can get them to me by or before Tuesday morning next . . . George . . . wants them very much indeed   Nothing that he can buy will make him half as comfortable. The thought just strikes me that perhaps you are using them yourself, if so all right, or if you want one and can send him one why do so . . . I think it would be a "big thing" for George to get them as they would be very useful both winter and summer.[4]

The saga of the blue shirts was not over yet. Mrs. Whitman urged Walt to "send those flannel shirts" by express courier before George returned to his regiment. On March 18, Walt wrote Jeff,

I suppose George must be about leaving you to-day . . . and I can realize how gloomy you will all be . . . I suppose the bundle of George's shirts, drawers, &c came safe by Adams express. I sent it last Saturday, and it ought to have been delivered Monday in Brooklyn. I did not pay the freight.[5]

The shirts, plus some underwear Walt probably bought new, arrived just in time. Mrs. Whitman wrote on the nineteenth,

[T]hose things you sent George all came safe he thinks he wont want any more cloths in some time he had just gone when the express came he said he gesst they would not come that he must get some shirts he was going down to Harrisons [photographers] to have his likeness taken so marthe got ready quick and [ran after him] and told him they had come.[6]

Mattie, a skilled seamstress, probably made the shirts herself, cutting them to fit her young husband. The intimacy of this exchange among the brothers had nothing sentimental about it, but the hopeful offering of yet another blue shirt—by Walt to one of his wounded boys—was the most passionate, most seductive gesture he made during the war of which there remains evidence. Very soon after he began in the hospitals, probably in February, he met a young sergeant by the now-iconic name of Tom Sawyer, a Massachusetts boy who had been wounded at Second Bull Run (August 28–30, 1862). Tom was nearly healed and soon to return to his regiment when Walt got to know him at Armory Square, in the company of Lewy Brown, who was also a patient there.

"Dear comrade," Walt wrote Tom on April 26,

> I have not heard from you for some time [Sawyer had now rejoined his unit], Lewy Brown has received two letters from you, & Walter in Ward E has received one three weeks ago . . . I was sorry you did not come up to my room to get the shirt & other things you promised to accept from me and take when you went away. I got them all ready, a good strong blue shirt, a pair of drawers & socks, and it would have been a satisfaction to me if you had accepted them.[7]

Walt had prepared a bundle that was an exact duplicate of the one for his brother George—its very sameness may have convinced him that the gesture could not be taken amiss. Had Sawyer come up to his room, "I should have often thought now Tom may be wearing around his body something from *me*," Walt added, "& that it might contribute to your comfort, down there in camp on picket, or sleeping in your tent."[8]

Sawyer had dark hair and gray eyes.[9] He could read and write, and a nature both sociable and appealing is suggested by his postwar course in life, as a father of eight who sometimes worked as a traveling salesman.[10] Whether it was his physical beauty, his warmth, his workman's hands, or a combination of these and other factors unknown, Walt went for him in a big way. The first letter to Sawyer is unmistakably romantic:

> Tom, I wish you was here. Somehow I don't find the comrade that suits me to a dot—and I won't have any other, not for good . . .
>
> Dear comrade, you must not forget me, for I never shall you. My love you have in life or death forever. I don't know how you feel about it, but it is the wish of my heart to have your friendship, and also that if you should come safe out of this war, we should come together again in some place where we could make our living, and be true comrades and never be separated while life lasts.[11]

Walt added Lewy Brown to the proposal ("and take Lew Brown too, and never separate from him"); "Lew is so good, so affectionate—when I came away [last evening from Armory Square], he reached up his face, I put my arm around him, and we gave each other a long kiss, half a minute long."[12]

Walt may have been hoping to make his proposal of a life lived together less shocking by including another man. Or he may have hoped to kindle jealousy. The letters written to Tom Sawyer, although pitched always in a loving key, with endearing and intentional grammatical slips here and there, were composed most carefully—again, we know of their existence only because Walt saved his first drafts, which show many corrections, and corrections of corrections.[13]

On May 27 he wrote,

> I sit down to rattle off in haste a few lines to you. I do not know what is the reason I have been favored with nary a word from you, to let me know whether you are alive & well . . . My thoughts are with you often enough, & I make reckoning when we shall one day be together again—yet how useless it is to make calculations for the future.[14]

This letter written in haste shows much reworking—especially when he tried to describe his emotions, Walt grew cautious, and at the same time entirely bold:

> I cannot, though I attempt it, put in a letter the feelings of my heart—I suppose my letters ~~look~~ sound strange ~~and unaccustomed~~ & unusual to you as it is, ~~and perhaps unaccountable, but I shall not~~—but as I am and have been only expressing the truth in them, I ~~must~~ do not trouble myself on that account.[15]

He added, "Lewy Brown seems to be getting along pretty well . . . he is a good boy, & has my love, & when he is discharged, I should feel it a comfort to share with [him] whatever I might have—& indeed if I ever have the means, he shall never want."[16]

This seems to be an offer of financial support, to Sawyer as to Brown, should either decide to throw in their lot with a certain older man.[17] The vagueness of the proposal offered a degree of protection, but only a degree—to promise money for intimate favors was to flirt with serious trouble, or at least with serious embarrassment. Walt skated right up to and over a line with Tom. The "feelings of his heart" overwhelmed him. This is the same man who, in *Leaves of Grass*, contrived in a

Walt Whitman's draft of a letter to Tom Sawyer, May 27, 1863.

masterful way to say "everything" but never quite to define himself; the poet who always took back with one hand what he gave with the other, singing the pleasures of man-to-man kisses while posing also as a lover of women, a potential husband, a nature worshipper and nothing more.

The mad chaos of war, with beautiful young men being torn apart, pushed feelings further than they might have gone in calmer times. This is one conclusion to draw from Walt's passion for Sawyer, and one measure of its seriousness is that he kept on writing to the elusive soldier. But by November, the dangerous proposals had lost their heedlessness, becoming more what they had half-pretended to be all along—simple offers of friendship. "I wrote to you six or seven weeks ago," Walt reminded Tom on the twentieth:

I am well & fat, eat my rations regular . . . [In Brooklyn] I have so many friends, I believe, now I am here they will kill me with kindness, I go around too much, & I think it would be policy for me to put back to Washington . . . Well, comrade, I must close. I do not know why you do not write to me . . . Anyhow I go on my own gait, & wherever I am in this world . . . if I should have some shanty of my own, no living man will ever be more welcome there than Tom Sawyer. So good by, dear comrade, & God bless you, & if fortune should keep you from me here, in this world, it must not hereafter.[18]

Following the Sawyer infatuation, Walt became more guarded. His work in the hospitals required control: If he was to accomplish the sober tasks he had taken upon himself, he needed to preserve himself, to avoid vulnerabilities of a certain kind. What he saw in the hospitals in his first weeks in Washington was trying enough. On February 4, a soldier met at Armory Square had "a fearful wound in a fearful condition, was having some loose splinters of bone taken from the neighborhood of the wound. The operation was long, and one of great pain . . . He sat up, propp'd—was much wasted—had lain a long time quiet in one position . . . a bloodless, brown-skinn'd face—"[19]

Another soldier nearby was dying. A female nurse tended him, and Walt watched:

I noticed how she sat a long time by [the] poor fellow who just had, that morning, in addition to his other sickness, [had a] bad hemmorhage—she gently . . . reliev'd him of the blood, holding a cloth to his mouth, as he cough'd it up . . . so weak he could only just turn his head over on the pillow.[20]

About a soldier named William Thomas, Walt wrote in a hurry:

[W]e are there as—the dresser bed sores great hole in which you can stick—round edges rotted away / flies— / two men hold him / the smell is awful great sores—the flies act as if they were mad / he has one horrible wound three bad ones / a fracture— / & several shocking bed sores—three men besides the dresser.[21]

The phrase "three men besides the dresser" suggests that the soldier was fighting his treatment. Walt may have been one of those who held him; certainly, he was close enough to smell and see everything that went on.

Another young soldier, a "New York man with a bright, handsome face," had been "lying several months from a most disagreeable wound . . . A bullet had shot him right through the bladder, hitting him front, low in the belly, and coming out back. He had suffer'd much—the water came out of the wound, by slow but steady quantities, for many weeks—so that he lay almost constantly in a sort of puddle."[22]

Walt came to know this soldier well; his name was John Mahay, and, there being only a slim chance of repairing such a lesion, Mahay's task was to await the end with as much composure as he could summon. Walt saw such things if not every day then often enough. He came to prefer Armory Square to the other hospitals in Washington at the time—it routinely accepted the worst cases, and it was commanded by a competent surgeon, D. Willard Bliss, who was friendly to Walt and welcomed his presence on the wards.*

President Lincoln sometimes showed up at Armory Square, moving gravely from bed to bed and clasping the hand of each soldier.[23] The hospital was located close to a steamboat landing at the foot of Seventh Street, SW, and near the tracks of the Washington and Alexandria Railroad. Soldiers wounded in battles in northern Virginia were often left there as a matter of convenience or for fear of carrying them any farther. Over the course of the war, it recorded more deaths than any other hospital in Washington, although it was not the largest.[24]

Walt had visited in hospitals before. In New York he had been well

---

*Walt cycled through most, if not all, of the fifty-plus military hospitals operating in or near Washington during the war and immediately after.

known at the general hospital on Broadway, which he sometimes wrote about in the papers. He described an operation he attended there on

> an United States soldier, who had been badly wounded in the foot . . . Under the old dispensations, the operation would have taken off the leg nearly up to the knee . . . but in this case it was done . . . after what is known as the Symes' [method]. The bones of the foot forward were all amputated, and then the flap of the heel brought around and left to make a cushion to walk upon, so that the crippled leg will only be a trifle shorter.[25]

His detached tone—scientific, doctorly—hinted at a degree of pride in his own cool head. But what began in January 1863 was different, an immersion to the very end. This was not just "the tragic interest of mortal reality," as he described, in an article, what had drawn him to hospitals in the first place; no, it *was* reality, a flood of it.

On January 21, he "went pretty thoroughly through Wards F, G, H, and

Ward K, Armory Square Hospital, a few months after the end of the war.

I" of Armory Square, giving away apples, oranges, tobacco plugs, and stationery to some two hundred men. Following this initial run-through, he sat
with a few "interesting cases in Ward I," distributing further gifts of money
as needed.[26] That evening he returned for more, this time visiting Campbell
Hospital, the converted army barracks at Boundary Street between Fifth
and Sixth. He distributed more writing paper, then sat with D. F. Russell, a
farmer's son who was recovering from typhoid fever.[27]

Armory Hospital, unlike Campbell, represented the most up-to-date
thinking about hospital design. It had long wooden ward buildings
raised up on cedar posts for all-around circulation of air, and there
were many windows in the whitewashed walls. The morgue and stables
were kept separate, for hygienic reasons, but the sewage and water-
delivery systems were primitive, and something harum-scarum about
the plumbing can be gathered from an account that Walt gave about a
strange incident:

> [T]here has been a man in ward I, named Lane, with two fingers ampu-
> tated, very bad with gangrene . . . last Thursday his wife came to see
> him, she seemed a nice woman but very poor, she stopt at the
> chaplain's—about 3 o'clock in the morning she got up & went to the
> sink, & there she gave birth to a child, which fell down the sink into
> the sewer runs beneath, fortunately the water was not turned on.[28]

> The chaplain, Eliphalet W. Jackson, grabbed some men who

> with spades &c. dug a trench . . . and got into the sink, & took out
> the poor little child, it lay there on its back, in about two inches of
> water . . . strange as it may seem, the child was alive, (it fell about
> five feet through the sink)—& is now living and likely to live, is
> quite bright, has a head of thick black hair.[29]

The latrines were only wooden commodes over holes in the ground; the
wards were often foul smelling, no matter how scrupulously swept and
whitewashed.[30]

Writing to Margaret Curtis, his hospital-fund donor, Walt communicated the feeling of peace that sometimes obtained at Armory Square—
or that he wished her to believe did:

As it happens I find myself rapidly making acknowledgment of your welcome letter [and recent thirty dollar donation] from the midst of those it was sent to aid . . . As I write I sit in a large pretty well-fill'd ward by the cot of a lad of 18 belonging to Company M, 2d N Y cavalry, wounded three weeks ago to-day . . . a large part of the calf of the leg is torn away . . . I have been writing to his mother . . . Although so young he has been in many fights & tells me shrewdly about them, but only when I ask him—He is a cheerful good-natured child—has to lie in bed constantly, his leg in a box—I bring him things—he says little or nothing in the way of thanks . . . smiles & brightens much when I appear—looks straight in my face & never at what I may have in my hand for him.[31]

Armory Square has twenty-five to thirty wards, he tells Mrs. Curtis:

[W]ard C, has beds for 60 patients, they are mostly full . . . the principal here, Dr Bliss, is a very fine operating surgeon—sometimes he performs several amputations or other operations of importance in a day . . . you will see a group absorbed playing cards up at the other end of the room [as the amputations are done] . . . one must be calm & cheerful, & not let on how their case really is . . . brace them up, kiss them, discard all ceremony, & fight for them, as it were, with all weapons . . . It is now between 8 & 9, evening—the atmosphere is rather solemn here to-night—there are some very sick men here . . . all is quite still—an occasional sigh or groan—up in the middle of the ward the lady nurse sits at a little table with a shaded lamp, reading . . . the light up & down the ward from a few gas-burners about half turned down—It is Sunday evening—to-day I have been in the hospital, one part or another, since 3 o'clock.[32] *

---

*Walt's hospital visiting was an ample vocation. He divided his time on the wards into two shifts, from twelve to four in the afternoon and again for a few hours after dinner. When he felt the need of it, he sat up all night with a patient; if not up all night, he might exhaust himself to the point of needing to sleep over at a hospital in a spare room. Except for the months when he was home in Brooklyn recuperating, he was in the hospitals for six or seven days a week.

Very early on, probably in January, Walt scrawled in one of his pocket notebooks, "My opinion is *to stop the war now*."[33] He had just returned from seeing George at Fredericksburg, and his first hospital visits in Washington produced this unequivocal response.

He supported the Union war effort—supported it firmly. Short of enlisting in the army himself, he would do everything he could to bring that cause success, yet hatred of war was his deepest feeling. The savaging of young men's bodies was not to be borne. Nothing was worth that.

Still, it would have to be borne. If he was to continue on in Washington, doing needful work, then he had to find a way forward emotionally, a way to persist and not be sickened by what he saw. He made careful accommodations to his psychological situation—living with the O'Connors, he was daily among people who supported and admired him, who fed him well (Nelly O'Connor was an excellent cook), and who helped him limit his fixed expenses to not much more than the seven dollars per month he paid for an upstairs room.

The intellectual circle around William O'Connor was also sustaining, and for further diversion from the grimness he did what he had always done—he roamed, immersing himself in the crowd. Washington, which at first he disliked, soon showed itself to be his kind of place, a rough city within walking distance of remnant wilderness, with a great river nearby. In early 1863, as the horrors of the wounds sank in, the weather was temptingly fine, inviting him outdoors. February 16 was "soft and balmy, the atmosphere velvet of clearness"; he joined a crowd on Pennsylvania Avenue made up of people hurrying toward the Capitol in one direction, toward Willard's Hotel in the other. Army wagons pulled by mule teams filled the avenue, "the teamster astride of the wheel-horse, or walking along by the side, drest in blue overcoat with whip over shoulder."[34]

In a pocket journal he noted many ex-slaves, some with brutal faces, others looking "as dandified and handsome as any body," and also "a long train of wood wagons twenty, thirty forty of them passing up the avenue, slowly, heavily rumbling, driven by black drivers, the mules straining with their tails out, as it is up hill here."[35]

As always, he paid special attention to public conveyances, noting "the tinkling bells of the cars, plying toward Georgetown one way, or the

Capitol, the other," adding that "the city cars [are] all driven by tidy handsome young American men—the drivers of the wagons of the Express lines ditto."[36] A fancy carriage with liveried attendants passed by, bearing a diplomat "or one of the great Secretaries," possibly Seward or Stanton. "Occasionaly some ladies, very richly drest, with children, in furs and feathers," and then the

ambulances—not so frequently just here [on Pennsylvania Avenue], though there are plenty of them . . . hundreds, I don't know but thousands, constantly on the move—but they generally take the [sidestreets]. The ambulance . . . at last arrived here, in our land, domiciliated, a common word [a French borrowing], used and understood at last every where in These States—that unknown term three years ago.[37]

That night, winter arrived. At noon on February 17 he wrote,

Now there is thick snow falling,—it commenced before day-light, and is quite deep—no wind so it covers the trees, every limb and twig—the trees in the streets, and in the [Presidential Forest], are thickly powdered—a coverlid of white snow, everywhere . . . falling fine and thick, the air full of it.[38]

Snow was not usually of much interest to him. Unlike Emerson ("The Snowstorm," 1835), John Greenleaf Whittier ("Snow-bound," 1865), and countless lesser poets of the day, he almost never mentioned snow nor did he have much poetic use for its conventional association, of sweet peace beneath the white blanket. But the lovely metamorphosis may have meant something to him after six weeks of immersion in the hospitals. His description of the storm continues at length; on February 22, a second storm, an enormous one, dropped several feet over the city, moving him to write again, rapturously,

Washington has the deepest and most driving snow-storm of the season—would be considered a pretty big storm even in the north—I write this at noon . . . nobody is out—the expanse looks very, very white—every thing is so ample and open here, it makes a very different appearance, under a snowstorm, than from the closely crowded [Northern] cities—being Sunday, no business, no army wagons, nor other vehicles, no pedestrians—a city housed, still, muffled in snow.[39]

He may only have been casting about for a usable scene—something for an article in a New York paper, perhaps, to be called "Washington in White" or the like. "[H]ardly a sound breaks the repressed city . . . there I see one sleigh, hear the merry tinkle of the collars of bells on the horses—a first-class old-fashioned yellow sleigh for four persons . . . trotting cheerfully . . . up the avenue."[40]

Before the cleansing storms, he visited Armory Square one Saturday and found John Mahay enduring "one of his spasms of pain."[41] "[E]xcruciating agony for about half an hour," Walt recorded in a notebook, "the water ran out of his eyes—the muscles of his face distorted, but he bore it all groanless."[42] Mahay was in bed 30 of Ward E. Walt stopped with a young Pennsylvania soldier, Thomas H. B. Geiger, in bed 47 of Ward H, finding him to be "silent and rather weak" until he saw Walt approaching. Then Geiger became animated; it was not Walt's first visit to the "young bright handsome" boy, and he began talking about how "for some time after his [right forearm was amputated] he could yet feel it—could feel the fingers open and shut."[43]

This same day, Walt met Lewy K. Brown for the first time, in a bed in Ward K. Lewy caught his attention with lurid tales about the punishments being meted out to the soldiers, how they were "bucked and gagged" (tied up, with a stick in the mouth like a horse's bit) or forced to stand on a barrel with a knapsack full of bricks for hours, often for trivial offenses. Lewy was engaging; Walt's record of their conversation is colored by the young man's outrage but also by his humor and by his hints of misbehavior among the troops (heavy drinking and consorting with camp followers, probably prostitutes).[44]

Returning to the O'Connors' house, Walt had Saturday dinner with them and with one of the men from Armory Square, Justus F. Boyd, a corporal. Boyd was recovering from pleurisy and a "sick affection of the kidneys" after five months of treatment.[45] He returned to the hospital at around six P.M. that day, which would not have left much time for a visit to Walt's upstairs room, since dinner was at four thirty.[46] That Walt felt something special for Justus can be inferred from a notation made eleven days later, with joyful punctuation: "When I came to L. street, to dinner [on a second occasion, February 25], found Justus Boyd, waiting for me! His papers are through—he is DISCHARGED—and expects to leave . . . for home."[47]

The day after the first Saturday dinner—after meeting Lewy Brown for the first time, and seeing John Mahay in agony, and passing time with numberless other patients at Armory Square—Walt did not go visiting, although it was a Sunday and Sunday was normally his most faithful day in the hospitals. Instead he went to the office of the army paymaster, where he worked part-time during the week, and sat by himself for a few hours and wrote. His writings on this Sabbath day did not include any personal letters now known to scholars—this prolific correspondent who wrote scores or hundreds of letters per week for the soldiers, in addition to his own letters to his mother, brothers, and numerous others, probably needed a rest.[48]

WALT'S NOTEBOOKS CONTAIN only a single poem written during his first Washington winter (an early draft of "A Noise-less, Patient Spider," a short poem not about war or soldiers). The previous December, while visiting George, he had made notes for new poetry and had often recorded his impressions in lines more poetic than prosaic; but for the next nine months, until the fall of 1863, his papers include no drafts of poems or even a single verselike line.

He advanced two reasons for this drought: first, that he was fascinated by the suffering soldiers, therefore too busy to write; and second, that what he saw on the wards "probed deepest . . . bursting the petty bonds of art," in other words, was unsuitable for literary treatment.[1] To some friends in New York he explained, "To these [sufferings], what are your dramas and poems, even the oldest and the tearfulest? Not old Greek mighty ones, where man contends with fate . . . not Virgil showing Dante on and on among the agonized & damned, approach what here I see and take a part in."[2] The "body's tragedies" went beyond art, beyond even the kind of say-anything, go-anywhere poetic art that Walt had pioneered. The raw severity of it all, also the noble way the soldiers bore their hardships, moved him so deeply that he was struck dumb. And yet, "these Hospitals, so different from all others—these thousands . . . of American young men . . . pallid . . . languishing . . . open a new world somehow to me, giving closer insights, new things, exploring deeper mines than any yet, showing our humanity."[3]

Struck dumb but, he hoped, not permanently so. Those deeper mines were to be worked for their poetic riches, and Walt nowhere implies that he is not the man to do it. Though not writing poetry, he was thinking about it; in late March he wrote home, "Mother, when you or Jeff writes again, tell me if my papers & MSS are all right—I should be very sorry indeed if they got scattered . . . *especially* the copy of Leaves of Grass covered in blue paper, and the little MS book 'Drum Taps,' & the MS tied up in . . . loose covers—"[4] The copy of *Leaves* was Walt's personal copy of the 1860 edition, in which he had for some time been penciling in changes for a fourth edition. *Drum-Taps* was also under way—he had written several contributions to the book before ever coming to Washington. Walt hoped his manuscripts would not get used for scrap or lost in Mrs. Whitman's house—his letter tells us that he was full of poetic ambition, even if not actively working.

On February 18, he returned to Armory Square, to visit a soldier recovering from a fever. Snow covered the city, but the airy pavilions were heated by large stoves.[5] The next day Walt toured Wards D and E, stopping again with Lewy K. Brown. Their friendship had quickly become special—Lewy was "a most affectionate fellow very fond of having me come and sit by him," Walt noted.*

Some months later, Walt received a letter from a former ward-mate of Brown's, a man named Alonzo Bush. "I am glad to know that you are once more in the hotbed City of Washington," Bush wrote,

> so that you can go often and see that Friend of ours at Armory Square, LK.B. The fellow that went down on your BK, both so often with me. I wished that I could see him this evening and go in the Ward Master's Room and have some fun for he is a gay boy.[6]

"LK.B" doubtless refers to Brown (who sometimes referred to himself the same way, as "LKB"). "BK" is anyone's guess, although scholars of

---

*Lewy served faithfully as go-between during Walt's attraction to Tom Sawyer. His social nature made him a kind of facilitator of Walt's contacts overall with the men at Armory Square. On July 27, 1863, he wrote Walt, "I got a letter from Tom. Sawyer on Saturday he is well and sens his love to you. he has bin in that Gettysburg Battle. he said that it was awful, and that he never wants to see the like of it again."

nineteenth-century American parlance note that "buck" was common slang for penis.[7] To refer to Lewy as "a gay boy" did not mean then what it would today—*gay* in the nineteenth century more often described someone willing to perform oral sex, commonly a female prostitute.[8]

Bush continued, "Johny Strain my companion wishes to be remembered to all I am sorry to inform you that he met with another misfortune after he got here he was thrown from his Horse and had his arm broken but is getting along very well at presant."[9] In a letter written a few weeks later, Bush added,

> Everything is lovely down here [at his regiment's winter encampment] . . . the goose hangs high the weather has been pretty cold cince I came back and therefor we have had no hunt as yet . . . Walter I told that friend of mine about you and he thinks he will like you very much I showed him your Photograph. he liked it . . . We are all waiting for the 8th June so that we can go home and see our Sweet hearts. I supose you know what they are. If you don't I do and I long for to see mine very much and I think she will want to see me.[10]

Bush had been coy before—using initials for names, using cryptic expressions. He seems to be encouraging here a tongue-in-cheek or leering interpretation of what he writes. "I supose you know *what* they are," rather than *who* they are, directs attention to the gender of the "Sweet hearts," and "Johny Strain my companion" draws further attention to attachments between men.

The "Ward Master's Room" that Alonzo spoke of was probably on Ward K, not E.* Ward K was supervised by Charles Cate, a man with whom Walt and several soldiers were friendly. After the war, Walt wrote about Cate that he was "home in New Hampshire—he has been committing matrimony—& is now supposed to be suffering the consequences— poor reckless young man."[11]

---

*The wardmaster's room, the only private room in a ward pavilion hospital, would have been the likely place to sleep. The other small rooms attached to a ward pavilion were a mess room, a scullery, a bathroom, a water closet, and an ablution room.

These seeming glimpses into a secret arena—a realm of half-furtive sexual carryings-on—are few in Walt's papers. But they are there. Their existence is a part of Walt's authorship in the largest sense. He preserved the notebooks that speak admiringly of certain men, sometimes noting that they had slept with him; he preserved the occasional half-salacious letter from someone like Alonzo Bush.

The glimpses may be few because the behavior was rare. Or, the steps taken to hide what was going on were effective—men having sex with men needed to be somewhat cautious, and were. Walt seems to want us to know that they were not all *that* cautious, however. The kiss he shared with Lewy Brown—the one that lasted thirty seconds—took place at the soldier's bedside, on an open ward.

Another reason why the glimpses are few may be that those involved considered such acts not notable, that is, both so commonplace as not to warrant much comment and more piquant, more fun, for escaping notice. The hospitals were places of compassionate and sometimes passionate friendship; there was occasional handholding, occasional kissing, gift giving, and heartfelt talk. For those who were so inclined, there may also have been a touch or a sexual embrace on occasion, in a private room, a latrine, or under a blanket.

Ward E, like others at Armory Square, was supervised by nurses as well as by a wardmaster. Charles Cate may have imposed a lax regime in some areas he supervised, but the nurses had their own character and standards—about one nurse, Lewy Brown wrote, "We still have Miss Lowell . . . & she is worse than ever since we have got these [officers occupying several of the beds]   she does not allow me to walk over the floor nor to speak nor nothing else.   she even has a guard to set at each door to keep out the visitors that comes."[12] Lewy implied that Walt, despite his excellent relations with the chief surgeon, might be denied entrance the next time he showed up.

Nurse Lowell seems not the type likely to have tolerated much irregularity. In general, the atmosphere on the ward must have been one of propriety and respect for rules—these were rooms where men were dying, after all. Private Hiram Sholes, who slept in the bed next to Lewy Brown's, was at Armory Square for more than a year, in an excellent position to gauge the temper of Walt's interactions with Brown (among other soldiers). Sholes wrote to Walt after the war, and his account of their time of knowing each other has nothing insinuating or off-color about it. "My kind friend," he wrote,

> I have thought of you many times since I left Washington and how well can I remember you as you came into the Wards with the Haversack under your arm, giving some little necessary here, a kind word there, and when you came to Louis bed and mine how cordialy you grasped our hands and anxiously enquired into our condition. I thank you for all this and you in your lonely moments must be happy in thinking of the good you have done to the many suffering ones during the war.[13]

If there were frequent visits to a wardmaster's room for exotic purposes—if sex were "in the air," a large part of ongoing life on the ward—then someone like Sholes is unlikely to have written to Walt with such manifest respect.

Those who did find fault with Walt's bedside manner were few, and they were women. Another nurse of Ward E, Amanda Akin, detested the poet and reacted to his presence with physical loathing. Miss Akin was very fond of young John Mahay and deeply saddened by his death on October 24, 1863; after a leave of absence, she returned to the hospital to find "my bright-eyed Johnny—the 'Pet,' so young and winning, when the spasms of suffering were over—was not there to greet me, but I pray God is awaiting me in heaven."[14]

Akin may have resented Walt's ministrations to Mahay. In August 1863 she wrote her sisters that a "noted author, Walt Whitman, visits our hospital almost daily":

> He took a fancy to [Erastus Haskell, another of her favorites], and would watch with him sometimes half the night. He is a poet, and I believe has written some very queer books about "Free Love," etc. He is an odd-looking genius, with a heavy frame, tall, with a turned-down Byronic collar, high head with straggling hair, and very *pink* rims to his eyes. When he stalks down the ward I feel the "prickings of my thumbs," and never speak to him, if not obliged to.[15]

After the war, Akin collected her diaries and published them as *The Lady Nurse of Ward E.** She declared that Walt had had a "peculiar interest" in the young men. Something about him did not add up—the absence of precise terms of categorical disdain ("fairy," "pervert," "queer") haunts her writings about him, giving her dislike of him a frustrated quality.

Forced by her own good manners to read an open letter that Walt sent the boys from Brooklyn, she afterward confided to her diary,

> A very ludicrous and characteristic letter . . . to his "fellow comrades," as he called the soldiers . . . He was spending a vacation with his mother . . . and his love for them was repeated in many incoherent sentences. I could only imagine it was written very late at night and he had taken "a drop too much."[16]

She distrusted, precisely, his casting of himself as just one of the boys. If they were all "comrades" together—with the nurses, of course, consigned to a different category—then any kind of indiscipline might result. A spirit of revolt seemed to attend the poet, and who knew what nastiness he might someday pull from that haversack.[†]

Walt brought the men tobacco, brandy, and the funny papers, among other gifts. These were already questionable offerings—hospital visitors more commonly brought Bible tracts. His presence was the more troubling as he was often around till late at night, while the nurses retired promptly at eight thirty, leaving night watchers to keep the wards, possibly with relaxed vigilance.[17]

Nurse Akin responded to certain soldiers with a frankly romantic feeling,

---

*The many nursing memoirs published during and after the war constitute a compelling subgenre of Civil War book. Notable among them are L. M. Alcott's *Hospital Sketches*, Georgeanna Woolsey's *Three Weeks at Gettysburg*, *Notes of Hospital Life* (anonymous), Sarah Emma Edmonds's *Nurse and Spy in the Union Army*, Elvira Powers's *Hospital Pencillings*, and Jane Stuart Woolsey's *Hospital Days*.

†Another nurse who worked at Armory Square, the wife of a general, wrote, "There comes that odious Walt Whitman to talk evil and unbelief to my boys. I think I would rather see the evil one himself . . . in my ward. I shall get him out as soon as possible."

and one of the signal traits of the nursing genre is the centrality of scenes
of undisguised physical attraction, the passionate sympathies of the
women edging over into sensuality at times.[18] Sophronia Bucklin, author
of *In Hospital and Camp: A Woman's Record of Thrilling Incidents Among
the Wounded in the Late War*, reported that the "groans of suffering men
echoing on all sides, aroused me to the highest pitch of excitement." Startled by the good looks of one wounded soldier, Bucklin admitted that she
"could hardly turn my fascinated eyes from this feast of beauty."[19]

Walt nowhere mentions Nurse Akin by name. He can hardly have
been unaware of her distaste for him—hers was the ward where he
spent more hours than on any other. He does mention other nurses he
knew, both in his journals and in *Memoranda During the War*, the richest, soberest, and most profound of the Civil War nursing narratives,
which finally saw publication in 1876. Students of the genre have
marked how Walt, even as he toned down the sexual element in his
own poetry, grew bolder in some of the prose accounts he wrote.[20]
Memoranda is shot through with evidence of his intimate responses to
certain of the men—by 1876, although anointed the Good Gray Poet
by William O'Connor, and personally more than willing to be declared a model of saintly sympathy, he was unable or unwilling to dis-
guise his attractions.

His work as a nurse has often been represented as a case of a troubled
sexual impulse finding a higher purpose—becoming "sublimated,"
put to better use.* This commonsensical, not altogether incorrect, understanding of what he was doing in the hospitals has to reckon with
the evidence that the war offered Walt a vastly expanded field of play
for his homoerotism, and that he rejoiced in that expansion.[21] Young
men of just the kind he found most attractive passed in the thousands
before him, reduced to a condition of desperate emotional openness.
Conveniently, the genre of nursing memoir had conferred understanding and a degree of acceptance on romantic responses to the young

---

*Whitman scholars in the half-century after his death in 1892 for the most part denied his
homosexuality. Later scholars sometimes admitted it as a possibility, while downplaying
its significance, but by the last decades of the twentieth century more or less all authorities
on Whitman agreed that he was entirely homosexual.

men, including responses that daringly paired physical arousal with death.[22]

Walt's prewar agenda suited the times uncannily well, and his work on the wards shows his ideology of adhesiveness coming strongly into play. The unspoken assumption of many scholars has been that helping those who suffered, putting his erotic energies to a nobler purpose, should have been a sufficient satisfaction. But on the whole, the signs are that those energies were more protean than suspected. Although channeled into acts of loving kindness beyond counting, they did not exhaust themselves. Probably they were evoked in him more thoroughly, and more deeply, than before by his work with the damaged men. The idea that such feelings could be purified through hospital work rests, finally, on the idea that there was something impure about them—and that Walt hoped to be cleansed.

A reader of his Civil War writings finds no evidence of this self-reforming attitude. While dedicating himself to the grave matters of war wounds and measureless suffering, he found physical arousal almost everywhere, at the bedside of dying boys and in crowded streetcars; in negotiations over gifts of clean underwear; on city streets when columns of handsome cavalrymen rode past, their gallant glamour producing in him a feeling that "quite set me up for hours."[23] In the presence of so much stimulation, there was also the constant need for good sense, for an exercise of precise self-control. He was an older man, one who was inviting younger men to see him as a father or a brother. As they responded to him with full hearts of their own, he faced countless situations in which he must not go too far.

His writings show him struggling with the occasional unbearable impulse, but on the whole, he governed himself with stringent discipline, meeting with near universal gratitude from the soldiers. Nor would his presence in so many different hospitals, for so many years, have been tolerated by physicians, nurses, Sanitary Commission officials, and the men themselves if his purposes had not been on the whole perfectly transparent.

His relations with female nurses other than Amanda Akin are suggested by a letter he wrote to a Miss Gregg, who worked on Armory Square's Ward A. Miss Gregg was about to leave on a vacation when he heard her complaining, half in jest, that the men did not show her what they felt about her efforts. "Dear friend," he wrote,

You spoke the other day . . . about the men being so undemonstrative. I thought I would write you a line, as I hear you leave the hospital tomorrow for a few weeks. Your labor of love & disinterestedness
here in Hospital is appreciated. I have invariably heard the Ward A
patients speak of you with gratitude . . . They have their own ways
(not outside éclat, but in manly American hearts, however rude,
however undemonstrative to you). I thought it would be sweet to
your tender & womanly heart, to know what I have so often heard
from the soldiers about you, as I sat by their sick cots. I too have
learnt to love you.[24]

Impossible to know what this meant to Miss Gregg—but easy to imagine. Miss Gregg figures in other of his letters, his mentions of her always
marked by trust and simple affection. Mrs. Helen Wright, another nurse
at Armory Square, also impressed Walt as being deeply kind and entirely competent. In *Memoranda* he described her as "excellent," a
woman "I like very much," and "a perfect nurse."[25]
     Yet, to give Miss Akin her due—Walt did stand for a certain kind of
male camaraderie, even male mischief. He was proudly a toucher and a
kisser, already therefore a disturbing element by strict standards of Victorian restraint. His shaggy head and high boots marked him, he hoped, as
a specimen out of that same wellspring of authentic American manhood
that was filling up two armies. He was not a gleeful rule breaker nor quite
a Falstaff figure, but he stood on the side of small outrages against decorum. His poetry had brilliantly channeled an American impatience with
tea-party manners in life as in literature, and with the thin-lipped cancel-
lation of sex. On a ward full of ailing soldiers in need of diversion and
hope, he might well have countenanced this or that ripe prank.
     Before Miss Akin appeared on the ward, it was the excellent Mrs.
Wright who presided; who, her other duties done, usually sat at a special
table reserved for the nurse in charge. Alongside this strategically located middle table was a medicine chest kept rigorously under lock and
key. The medicine chest "also contains the stimulants, our especial
charge," Miss Akin noted in her memoir.[26] Walt's description of this
arrangement of central table occupied by supervising nurse, in his letter
to Margaret Curtis, noted the air of deep peace on a ward full of "very
sick men," the head nurse reading quietly by her shaded gas lamp, the

white mosquito nettings suspended over the soldiers' beds adding to the somber play of shadow on whitewashed walls and ceiling.

Imagining this to be Ward E and not some other ward—the very ward on which Walt visited with Lewy Brown, John Mahay, Hiram Sholes, Alonzo Bush, and possibly Tom Sawyer as well—and imagining, further, Miss Akin to be the nurse who was seated at the central table, we can possibly picture Walt on a night not of the most somber repose, a few of the younger soldiers spoiling for fun. Out of Walt's pocket or the famous haversack comes a bottle of fruit brandy, and medicinal swallows are shared all around.* One of the patients now gets carefully out of bed. Miss Akin, engrossed, perhaps, in a book—she enjoyed reading Alcott's *Hospital Sketches* to the patients, she noted in her memoir—looks up, then, seeing nothing about which to be too concerned, looks down at her book again.[27]

Ambulatory soldiers might use the latrines as needed, and they generally had the freedom of the wards. On this evening we are imagining, one soldier moves off quietly, followed a moment later by another, followed, at the right interval, by Walt himself. He takes care not to walk too heavily down the ward, as Miss Akin, who disliked him even for his size, accused him of doing in her diary. Instead, he goes as glidingly as a large man can, with possibly one quick look back at the presiding nurse. She—too proud to acknowledge the men moving away one by one—continues to read, or to pretend to.

By different routes, in the dusk of the wards just now settling down for the night, the three end up eventually at the door of a spare back room. It is a room that belongs to a friendly wardmaster. They go inside. One of them strikes a match. Walt puts his arms around the shoulders of his young friends. They are on their own now. For the time being, they have gotten away.

---

*In a pocket notebook, Walt recorded supplying at least one such bottle to a nurse, Mrs. Reynolds, of Ward F, Armory Square, for administration to the soldiers. This nurse impressed Walt as being a "very good and competent girl."

Fairly early in his hospital work, a radical idea came to Whitman. The battles were insignificant, and the suffering after the battles was everything. He cannot have subscribed entirely to this idea, since he followed the military news as closely as anyone and rejoiced at all Union victories, no matter how slight. Despite his desire to "*stop the war now*," he never developed a pacifist critique of it, and, as he wrote brother Jeff, "To see what I see so much of, puts one entirely out of conceit of war—still for all that I am not so sure but I go in for fighting on—the choice is hard on either part, but to *cave* in the worst."[1]

The soldiers, the wounded soldiers, had a terrific significance in his eyes:

> As we go around, day and night . . . pass down these long wards, with hat for the first time taken involuntarily and reverently off, from an effect upon us of humility that all the Presidents, princes, Congresses and Generals of the world would never begin to produce, we find each and every one of the . . . States plentifully represented. New York and Pennsylvania have their offspring here by hundreds, by thousands. Ohio and Illinois and Indiana and Michigan [and] Massachusetts and Maine.[2]

War is all very well for those who care about campaigns and battles and the details of force dispositions and so on. But what really matters is the human damage, the catastrophe.

To some extent, he was doing what Whitman, the poet, had always done: finding his immediate circumstances and employments important, both representative and instructive to the masses. His notebook jottings about hospitals are early run-throughs of passages in books and articles he would publish, arguing for *his* Civil War as the most dramatic, the most meaningful. Even twelve years later, in the eloquent first pages of *Memoranda*, he struck the same note:

> During the Union War I commenced at the close of 1862 . . . to visit the sick and wounded of the Army, both on the field and in the Hospitals . . . I have perhaps forty . . . little note-books left, forming a special history of those years . . . I wish I could convey to the reader the associations that attach to these soil'd and creas'd little livraisons, each composed of a sheet or two of paper, folded small to carry in the pocket, and fastened with a pin. I leave them just as I threw them by during the War, blotch'd here and there with more than one blood-stain.[3]

His hospital jottings somehow get to the very heart of the war:

> To me the main interest of the War [is] in those specimens, and in the ambulance, the Hospital, and even the dead on the field . . . in the two or three millions of American young and middle-aged men . . . embodied in the armies—and especially the one-third or one-fourth of their number, stricken by wounds or disease.[4]

He was not a pacifist, but neither was he a martial enthusiast. What Walt called the "Political interests involved" in the war were likewise unimportant compared to these bloody revelations of national character:

> [T]he Hospital part of the drama . . . deserves indeed to be recorded . . . over the whole land . . . an unending, universal mourning-wail of women, parents, orphans—the marrow of the tragedy concentrated in those Hospitals—(it seem'd sometimes as if the whole interest of the land, North and South, was one vast central Hospital, and all the rest of the affair but flanges).[5]

The war was about valor, but the valor of suffering—not of men firing rifles. The valor of an ill-fed American lad lying friendless in a hospital dying of shock following an amputation, or of diarrhea. Dying without anger or complaint. "The expression of American personality . . . is not to be looked for in the great campaigns," Walt noted early in 1863. "The looks, manner, & forditude of the men, with their decorum, religious nature, affection . . . The incredible docility & obedience of the American soldier . . ."[6]

The essence of the catastrophe consisted of the invalids' courage, plus their affection. This idea amounted to a radical rereading of the whole American conflict. It rejected not only battlefield heroics but also the political significance that Lincoln, in his second inaugural address, cautiously but firmly descried in the great struggle:

> Both parties deprecated war, but one of them would *make* war rather than let the nation survive . . . One-eighth of the whole population were colored slaves, not distributed generally over the Union, but localized in the southern part of it. These slaves constituted a peculiar and powerful interest. All knew that this interest was somehow the cause of the war. To strengthen, perpetuate, and extend this interest was the object for which the insurgents would rend the Union.

Leaving aside the important question of the president's strict accuracy—of the depth of his own commitment to black emancipation, let alone that of the citizen-soldiers who filled his army—Walt's doctrine of hospital valor is radically simplifying. It suits well his other famous pronouncement from *Memoranda*, "Such was the War. It was not a quadrille in a ball-room. Its interior history will not only never be written, its practicality, minutia of deeds and passions, will never be even suggested."[7] Or as he said in *Specimen Days*, "The real war will never get in the books."[8]

The real war would never be written because it was too awful; because it consisted of suffering, maiming, and dying, it "perhaps must not and should not be" described.[9] This may only have been a trope, an attitude fancifully adopted for writerly purposes—Walt devoted years of his life, after all, to describing exactly what went on in the hospitals, on the theory that "it is the spirit of our democratic age to blink nothing."[10] And he described the soldiers he met—they would not be forgotten, not if he had anything to do with it.

His intention was to honor every one of them by extension, and he succeeded admirably at that rightful task. But his habit of rounding the edges off the young soldiers—rendering them, in the books he eventually published, as silent or near-silent figures, in need of someone to speak for them—had the effect of driving them back into the obscurity from which he otherwise worked to save them. This may be another meaning of the pronouncement, "The real war will never get in the books." It would never get in because he would not permit it. Much of what went on was unspeakable because too distressing for words, and much that was remarkable in a military sense escaped recording because it happened too fast or in too obscure a setting. But more, the soldiers' experience needed damping down. It was too raw, too savage. "Future years," he wrote, "will never know the seething hell and the black infernal background of countless minor scenes . . . In the mushy influences of current times . . . the fervid atmosphere and typical events of those years" have become too strange.[11] The war, the real war, would soon be impossible to imagine.

John Burroughs, Walt's early biographer, gives us access to what Walt himself thought he was doing in his war writing; as mentioned earlier, *Notes on Walt Whitman*, published under Burroughs's name, was closely supervised, if not in large part dictated, by the poet. "Out of that experience in camp and hospital," Burroughs-*cum*-Whitman wrote,

> the pieces called *Drum-Taps* were produced. Their descriptions and pictures, therefore, come from life. The vivid incidents . . . are but daguerreotypes of the poet's own actual movements among the bad cases of the wounded . . . The reader of *Drum-Taps* soon discovers that it is not the purpose of the poet to portray battles and campaigns, or to celebrate special leaders or military prowess, but rather to chant the human aspects of anguish that follow in the train of war . . . War can never be to us what it has been to the nations of all ages down to the present; never the main fact—the paramount condition, tyrannizing over all the affairs of national and individual life; but only an episode, a passing interruption.[12]

War, modern war, has become an anomaly. The natural condition of society is one of peace, and "the poet who in our day would be as true to his nation and times as Homer was to his, must treat of it from the standpoint of peace and progress, and even benevolence."[13]

Partly this is true because war has become so terrible. But partly, Burroughs and Walt tell us, war has simply been outgrown. It will never again play the role that manly combat did in the Greco-Trojan world of *The Iliad*. Hence the focus on "the human aspects of anguish." In a world grown benevolent and progressive, Burroughs urged readers to speak henceforth only of useful things.

Given Walt's uncanny propheticness before, the way he got things *exactly* wrong about the war is notable. The urge to make war was not safely back in the sandal-wearing past. The world was on the threshold of a great and enduring boom in war, with the American Civil War marking the way. A new kind of mechanical conflict, fought with better rifles, ironclads, railroads, the telegraph, and other technological enhancers, and with brilliant innovators like Sherman and Stonewall Jackson making breakthroughs that later tacticians would borrow wholesale, secured a central place in the activities of nations for war on a mass scale.

"I venture to predict," Burroughs wrote, "that what is here contributed in *Drum-Taps* will gradually . . . come to be accepted as the vital and distinguishing memento through literature of the late war . . . the ages to come . . . will leave the volumes of the historian and . . . all the details of military tactics and manoeuvres, and will dwell with emotion amid what this man . . . has sung of that terrible contest."[14]

Drum-Taps has, largely for lack of competition, come to be acknowledged as a masterwork. There is no comparable response to the war by a writer of similar stature, but accounts of "military tactics and manoeuvres" so far outnumber meditations on the meaningful suffering as to produce a comic disproportion. Of some fifty thousand books published to date about the Civil War, *Drum-Taps* may be the only one to hold that the way the soldiers suffered and died trumps all else—and even *Drum-Taps* includes stirring martial poetry among its offerings, plus poems of romantic self-analysis, metaphysical speculation, and "Song of Myself"–type personal proclamation.[15]

Almost every other approach to the war, it seems, has been explored; every material detail figures in some study or other, from the incidence of venereal disease among the troops to their coffee-drinking habits to the frequency with which officers North and South mentioned concepts like duty, honor, and gallantry in their letters home. But overwhelmingly, the strictly military details of battles fought and strategies devised figure in the literature. It seems that there will never be an end to the fascination with military virtue and the way that American soldiers responded to this test at arms. The suffering is part of this fascination, but not in the way Walt forecast—rather than superseding the battlefield accounts, the wounding and dying provide a dark background against which the strictly military "minutia" play out endlessly. Abstracted slightly, the wounds and epidemics and amputations conjure an atmosphere of maximum pathos that deepens, but in no way supplants, the "deeds and passions."

According to Burroughs, Walt broke new ground in *Drum-Taps* by going beyond the strictly military details; by sparing us the glories of man slaughtering man, he pointed to "a capacity that had lain slumbering . . . within us . . . moods of the absolute, the universal, the ecstatic."[16] No doubt Walt's approach was more progressive than that of the old, battle-ax-chanting poets. But it was not therefore more innovative or more modern. The cult of tender feeling was familiar from American poetry of the day—Walt's own early poems of sex and earthly existence had been a potent rejection, precisely, of the blissful-drops-of-anguish school.

If Walt had, instead, identified a readiness to engage in ruinous total war as "a capacity that had lain slumbering," *that* would have been a breakthrough. The war was tragic, according to our national mythology, because brother slaughtered brother; in reality, it was tragic because so many brothers took to the killing and did it so well, for so long. In contemporary terms, the deaths of Civil War soldiers (620,000: 360,000 from the North and 260,000 from the South) represent a mortality of about six million people.[17] That historically resonant number, again speaking in contemporary terms, begins to suggest something almost spreelike about the killing. The wounded whom Walt met in the hospitals had fired rifles, most of them, if not in anger then surely with intent to kill. They were not just debris left by the whirlwind, they *were* the whirlwind, in part.

Although helpless invalids by the time Walt came to know them, they were not just passive victims of larger war-making forces (governments, draft laws, commanding officers, sectional hatred). Many had taken up arms willingly and fought aggressively, relishing the opportunity to do "terrible execution," as George Whitman described the decimating of the enemy in situations of tactical advantage. George's reports of his combat experiences hinted at strong pleasures taken. Not a homicidal monster—by all accounts, a thoughtful man, one who inspired love among his troops—George found many aspects of war congenial. After the Battle of New Bern, he wrote to his mother,

We have given the Secesshers another thundering thrashing, and have gained a splendid victory. I went through the fight and did not get a scratch although the balls fairly rained around me . . . We had skirmishers extending about a quarter of a mile on each side of the railroad and we had not gone more than 3 or 4 miles before they came upon the rebels in strong force . . . We marched right up under a terible fire, formed in line of battle and . . . fought them in Splendid style for about 3 hours, when our boys drove them from their entrenchments and the day was ours.[18]

When Walt reread this letter, he marked the last sentence with parentheses.[19] He often marked passages in letters that George sent home; a number of these passages express soldierly pride or fulfillment in combat. George's entire correspondence is dedicated to lessening his mother's anxiety on his account, but surely he did not conjure feelings of intense satisfaction out of thin air, just to show her he was having a good time.

If there is something like an ideal response to war service, then George Whitman had it. He never testified to enjoying the killing of men— rather, triumphing over the dangerous foe by force of arms, and in the process, capturing or killing some of them, was what he found fulfilling. Remembering the height of the furious fighting at the Lower Bridge, Antietam, he wrote,

Burnside who was looking on ordered Sturgis to send our Brigade there saying . . . that he knew we would take it. As soon as we were ordered to forward we started on a double quick and [reached the bridge] . . . We were then ordered to halt and commence fireing, and the way we showered the lead across that creek was noboddys buisness. I had command of our Company again and as soon as the men got steadily settled down to their work I took a rifle from one of the wounded men and went in, loading and fireing.[20]

Hoping to inspire his men, or maybe just wanting more action, George did not merely guide them but instead picked up a weapon. He had done the same at Chantilly two weeks before, taking a rifle from a fallen comrade and having "a few shots on my own which seemed to encourage the men very much."[21] The Battle of Chantilly, usually reckoned a Union failure, had trappings of moderate success in George's description. His sector of the battle was not a zone of confusion nor of backing down:

[W]e soon drove the rebels but they rallied and came on again but we were ready for them this time and they gave way and fell back   we stayed there . . . until about 9 Oclock but they had enough and did not make another attempt and . . . our Regt left the field marching company front   we being the last Regt engaged in the terrible fight of Saturday and the last to leave the field.[22]

Other signs of George's ready accommodation to soldiering are his steady good health, his many strong friendships, battlefield promotions, and the simple sensual pleasure he took in eating, drinking, and sleeping well in camp. After four years of very active campaigning, including five months in rebel prisons, he was so little disenchanted with the practice of war as to hope to make a permanent career of soldiering. Walt had this evidence before him when he formed his very different opinion of war—that it was pointless and outmoded. His verdict on war seems hasty, to say the least. Even after the dreadful carnage at Fredericksburg, the Union troops were mostly of good cheer and committed to the cause, he found during his visit to the front; and during his only other known visit to a combat zone, in February 1864, he found the soldiers undaunted and eager:

I talked with some of the men [returning from a nighttime march near Culpepper, Virginia]. As usual I found them full of gayety,

Captain George W. Whitman, Company K.

endurance, and many fine little outshows, the signs of the most excellent good manliness . . . The mud was very deep. The men had
their usual burdens, overcoats, knapsacks, guns and blankets. Along
and along they filed by me, with often a laugh, a song, a cheerful
word, but never once a murmur. It may have been odd, but I never
before realized the majesty and reality of the American people *en
masse*. It fell upon me like a great awe.[23]

Walt had this evidence, and that of George's own experiences, yet still
insisted that war was anomalous, atavistic. Nor was his judgment on the

future of warfare based on a more general ignorance. He knew how obsessed the soldiers were with fighting, with the seared-in details of their own passages of combat. In his many thousands of bedside visits, listening to the sick and wounded men tell their stories, it was the memory of combat that they most rushed to communicate.

No doubt he hoped to reform mankind when he consigned war to the premodern darkness—let us pretend it is so, he seems to say, and the world will be better. The ease with which some men adapted to soldiering, and the way it fascinated them, were dreadful recognitions for him. These were not the glorious truths that he had labored so long in the hospitals to discover.

To salvage something from the squalor; to restore America to its sane, exemplary course through history—these purposes color most of what he wrote about the war. They help account for why his poetry of the war years often seems conventional and old-fashioned. The poet who wrote, in the early 1850s, in the poem later called "Song of Myself,"

> Coming home with the bearded and dark-cheeked bush-boy....
>   riding behind him at the drape of the day;
> Far from the settlements studying the print of the animals' feet, or
>   the moccasin print;
> By the cot in the hospital reaching lemonade to a feverish patient,
> By the coffined corpse when all is still, examining with a candle;
> Voyaging to every port to dicker and adventure;
> Hurrying with the modern crowd, as eager and fickle as any,
> Hot toward one I hate, ready in my madness to knife
>   him[24]

by 1865 was writing, in *Drum-Taps*,

> . . . I am affection—I am the cheer-bringing God, with hope, and
>   all-enclosing Charity
> (Conqueror yet—for before me all the armies and soldiers of the
>   earth shall yet bow—and all the weapons of war become
>   impotent);
> With indulgent words, as to children. . . .
> Young and strong I pass, knowing well I am destin'd myself to an
>   early death;

But my charity has no death. . . .
And my sweet Love[25]

In the first passage, he swiftly and convincingly assumes poses recognizable from modern life. He hurries with a mob of sensation-hungry people; he seethes with murderous hatred. In the second, he takes on the persona of Christ, but a Christ made sweet, a swooning sort of savior, no threat to the money changers nor to anyone else. "The Dresser," one of the few great poems in *Drum-Taps*, develops the idea of a tender, salvific older man who is so Christ-like that the parallel need never be made explicit:

I onward go, I stop,
With hinged knees and steady hand, to dress wounds;
I am firm with each—the pangs are sharp, yet unavoidable;
One turns to me his appealing eyes—(poor boy! I never knew
    you,
Yet I think I could not refuse this moment to die for
    you . . .).[26]

The Christ parallel was an idea that Burroughs and, even more, William O'Connor took and ran with. O'Connor's long pamphlet *The Good Gray Poet* described a man so compassionate as to be almost holy; in a short story he published in 1868, "The Carpenter," O'Connor even showed Walt performing a miracle on Christmas Eve, in case there was any doubt.[27] To what extent Walt believed these character depictions written by his close friends is hard to tell. But in "The Dresser," we get a rough idea of his sturdy self-concept. Taking on the guise of an old soldier, one who has lived through hard battles, he explains to some "young men and maidens that love me" what the war was like, downplaying the "hard-fought engagements" and "sieges tremendous" and instead, focusing on his duties as a nurse.

The thrills of combat soon fade, he tells his listeners; what counts instead are the acts of selfless caring. George's vivid combat accounts—and Walt's subtle downplaying of the significance of such martial talk—perhaps influenced the second stanza:

Soldier alert I arrive, after a long march. . . .
In the nick of time I come, plunge in the fight, loudly shout in the
     rush of successful charge;
Enter the captur'd works . . . . yet lo! like a swift-running river, [the
     memories] fade,
Pass and are gone . . . I dwell not on soldiers' perils or soldiers'
     joys
(Both I remember well—many the hardships, few the joys, yet I was
     content).[28]

Warning the young folk to "be of strong heart," he reveals what war
nursing was like:

On, on I go. . . .
The crush'd head I dress (poor crazed hand, tear not the bandage
     away);
The neck of the cavalry-man, with the bullet through and
     through, I examine;
Hard the breathing rattles, quite glazed already the eye. . . .
(Come, sweet death! be persuaded, O beautiful death!
In mercy come quickly.)[29]

He describes other gory wounds, some of which recall the wounds of
men he knew at Armory Square. There is "The fractur'd thigh"
(William C. Thomas), "the wound in the abdomen" (possibly John Mahay), and "the stump of the arm, the amputated hand" (Thomas H. B.
Geiger or many, many others). A soldier with a "wound in the side,
deep, deep / But a day or two more—for see, the frame all wasted and
sinking," recalls a beautiful Irish soldier, Thomas Haley, who died with
Walt in attendance.
   A lesion with "gnawing and putrid gangrene, so sickening, so offensive,"
may refer to any one of many of his cases, but the narrator's revulsion
recalls Walt's deep upset at the foul infection that cost the life of the Ohio
soldier, Oscar Cunningham. There can be no doubt that Walt, himself,
was suffering. By June 1864 he was on the verge, if not in the actual
throes, of an emotional breakdown due to his hospital work. On the seventh of that month, he told Mrs. Whitman,

I was quite blue from the deaths of several of the poor young men . . . things are going pretty badly with the wounded—They are crowded here in Washington in immense numbers . . . The papers are full of puffs . . . but the truth is, the largest proportion of worst cases got little or no attention—we receive them here with their wounds full of worms—some all swelled & inflamed, many of the amputations have to be done over . . . one new feature is that many of the poor afflicted young men are crazy, every ward has some in it that are wandering—they have suffered too much, & it is perhaps a privilege that they are out of their senses—Mother, it is most too much for a fellow, & I sometimes wish I was out of it.[30]

He was soon to be out of it. In late June he took himself home to Brooklyn, where he stayed for the next six months, often bedridden with a "heavy aching head" and a persistent sore throat that may have put the family in mind of Andrew's recent fatal illness. One measure of Walt's dedication is that he worked until he collapsed; another, that he went back to Washington when he recovered. He was loyal to the soldiers and to his vocation among them. The note in his war writings that strikes a modern reader slightly askance—his vaunting of himself as a Christ figure in this situation of vast pathos, and his related determination to find something sublime in the torments of the men—does not detract from the years of faithful attending, the unnumbered mercies. But the practice of modern war has made talk of the sad sweetness of tending to damaged soldiers sound theatrical:

> The hurt and the wounded I pacify with soothing hand,
> I sit by the restless all the dark night—some are so young;
> Some suffer so much—I recall the experience sweet and sad.
> (Many a soldier's loving arms about this neck have cross'd and rested,
> Many a soldier's kiss dwells on these bearded lips.)[31]

It may be that there have simply been too many victims. The great pileup of corpses, including the millions of civilians killed collaterally in modern wars, makes Walt's idea of combat as a theater of tender connectedness seem odd. Worse, this instinctive enemy of the maiming of the young seems to be working for those who promote it at times. Never one to tell the bereaved parents of soldiers that their sons had died in a noble cause—he found other ways to console them, less conventional ways—he enlisted, finally, on the side of those who found meaning and nobility in the slaughter.

It was not the meaning that Southern fire-eaters or Northern diehards found, nor was it the meaning that President Lincoln attached to it. But in lines like these, again from the poem that was later named "The Wound-Dresser," Walt discovered the grounds for a selective forgetting, even as he offered himself as an enemy of forgetting:

> An old man bending, I come, among new faces,
> Years looking backward, resuming, in answer to children,
> Come tell us old man . . .
> . . . of these scenes, of these furious passions, these chances,
> Of unsurpass'd heroes (was one side so brave? the other was
>   equally brave);
> Now be a witness again—paint the mightiest armies of
>   earth[32]

They were mighty, both of the armies: American mighty. And each side was unsurpassed in bravery. Written while the war was still under way, this passage is an early expression of what would come to be the mainstream position on the war—that it was a wash as to heroism and suffering, and that the issues involved no longer needed to be discussed.

The year before Walt's emotional collapse, George and the 51st New York were sent out west, in support of Grant's campaign against Vicksburg. "I feel so anxious to hear from George," Walt wrote their mother at the time, "one cannot help feeling uneasy, although these days sometimes it cannot help being long intervals without one's hearing."[33]

A remarkable letter from George had not yet reached Washington. It detailed what Walt would one day describe as a "tough little campaign"—the retaking of Jackson, Mississippi, following the fall of Vicksburg. The 51st, part of the 9th Army Corps, under General Burnside (later under General John Parke), had occupied a position to the rear of Vicksburg, to prevent Confederate reinforcements from coming to its relief. After the surrender on July 4, 1863, the 9th Corps took off on a rapid march to engage rebel forces under General Joseph E. Johnston. George's regiment was now attached to Sherman's Expeditionary Army, and growing familiar with a highly active style of maneuver.[34]

"I take the first oppertunity," George wrote his mother,

> to let you know that I am well and hearty. I fear . . . that you have been somewhat worried about not hearing from me in so long, but we have been so situated that there was no chance to send letters away, even if we had a chance to write them . . . We returned to camp this morning after about as hard a campaign of 19 days as I want to see . . . We are between the Yazoo and Black rivers and about 7 miles directly in the rear of Vicksburg.[35]

The nineteen days under Sherman had included marches in killing heat, down Southern roads with "the dust laying . . . like flour, 4 or 5 inches thick, and . . . considerable suffering from the scarscity of water and we were forced to drink, from any little pond that could be found . . . Grub to was mighty scarce, and green corn was the chief article of food."[36]

Arriving at Jackson, Union forces found the rebels entrenched:

> There was no general engagement but during the day, and sometimes during the night, quite a brisk fire was kept by sharpshooters on each side . . . the enemy behind their earthworks, and our side behind trees, and . . . the moment anyone showed themselves there was two or three rifles pointed at them. I expected Gen. Sherman . . . intended to skirmish with them, and keep them buisy on this side of the river, while someone crossed . . . and made an attack on the rear . . . but for some probably good reason (that I know nothing about) nothing of the kind was attempted, as far as I can hear.[37]

He was only the commander of a company, the smallest military unit, his view of things largely obscured. Yet, as with his first battles in North Carolina, George assembled the largest possible picture of what he found himself a part of:

[A]bout daylight on the morning of the 17th . . . a white flag was run
up, by some citazens on one of the rebel works and we soon found
that the whole rebel force had skedaddled during the night . . . we
went in and occupied the place. Our Brigade was the first troops inside the town, and the 51st was the second Regt. We found the place
very much damaged by our Artillery, and nearly deserted . . . what
few citazens we found had dug holes or burrows in the ground and
there they had staid.[38]

The taking of Vicksburg, Jackson following, was crucial to the Union
cause. It assured Federal control of the Mississippi, cut the Confederacy
in two, and opened the Deep South to further Yankee depredations.
George, a close reader of the papers as well as an amateur strategist,
sensed the military import in these events in which he was a participant,
but more remarkable may be his sensing of a change in the character and
style of the Union prosecution of the war. Grant's maneuvering behind
Vicksburg, with part of his forces severed from ordinary lines of supply,
represented the dawn of the sort of tactical boldness afterward to be associated with both Grant and Sherman. The two commanders had arrived at an attitude of near-conviction about the likelihood of Northern
victory—should the North embrace a total-war approach, success was
inevitable. The qualms about pillage, the wanton destruction of enemy
property, and casualties among noncombatants evinced by many Union
commanders during the first year or two of war, were now to be decisively overcome.[39]

George, not privy to the deliberations of the great leaders, nevertheless
captured the moment of change, while registering some remnant
qualms:

Soon after we entered [Jackson] . . . the western troops began to
come in, and they ransacked and plundered . . . completely. The
western armies burn and destroy . . . and the same number of men,
marching through the country, will do three times the damage of the
army of the Potomac . . . The planters had generaly left their
houses . . . leaving darkies in charge, and the troops often burn the
houses, and the darkies would run away . . . We traveled through
thousands of acres of corn, and sometimes 4 or 5,000 men with two

or three hundred horses and mules would bivouac in a corn field . . .
two or three times I have went to a pond and took off my clothes and
washed them myself, and two or three times I have been completely
soaked with the rain, and laid down at night on the ground . . . and
slept soundly.[40]

George sensed that something new was afoot. An army with nothing
but the clothes on its back had campaigned for nineteen straight days,
seizing whatever it needed and destroying the rest. Walt read this letter
closely when it caught up with him. The passage on the destructiveness
of the western troops seemed to him especially notable, and he marked it
with parentheses.[41]

While George was campaigning in the west, a young soldier lay dying
in Washington. Erastus Haskell, one of Nurse Akin's pets, had been ill
for the better part of a year. His current diagnosis was of typhoid, but
Walt suspected that some underlying condition was contributing to his
sorry decline.[42]

On July 27, he wrote a worried note to the boy's parents, saying that
Erastus seemed terribly sick. The boy's father hurried to Washington,
only to find his son "dead three days," as Walt reported sorrowfully to
Mrs. Whitman. "[P]oor old man, he had the body embalmed & took
home—they are poor folks but very respectable."[43]

Erastus was a musician, a fifer. He was a "silent dark-skinn'd Spanish-
looking youth, with large very dark blue eyes, peculiar looking."[44] Walt
had been devoted to him and was moved now to write a second letter to
the parents, a letter in some ways representative of all his letters, to all
the families of the dead. "I write in haste," he began,

> & nothing of importance—only I thought any thing about Erastus
> would be welcome. From the time he came to Armory Square Hospi-
> tal till he died, there was hardly a day but I was with him a portion of
> the time—if not during the day, then at night. I had no opportunity
> to do much . . . only to wait the progress of his malady.[45]

Erastus was a good patient. He made no complaints, and he gained
attention only when Walt spoke up for him: "[H]e . . . behaved always

correct & decent . . . I used to sit on the side of his bed—I said once, You don't talk any, Erastus, you leave me to do all the talking—he only answered quietly, I was never much of a talker."[46]

Breathing soon became hard for him. He was "opprest for breath, & with the heat, & I would fan him—occasionally he would want a drink . . . sometimes when I would come in . . . I would lean down & kiss him, he would reach out his hand & pat my hair & beard a little, very friendly, as I sat on the bed & leaned over him."[47]

Walt emphasized the young man's difficulty giving voice. His "throat & chest seemed stopped"—here was a soldier definitely in need of a defender, a mouthpiece. His stopped voice extended even to his fife, which lay on a little stand by his bed, "[and] he once told me that if he got well he would play me a tune on it—but, he says, I am not much of a player yet."[48]

The letter went far in saying, frankly, that there had been physical attraction in the older man's devotion, and possibly also in the dying boy's beard-patting fondness. This being a letter of condolence written to bereaved parents, the sheer inappropriateness of sexual confession provided some cover for it, as did a mother and father's hunger for any physical details of a lost child:

> I was very anxious he should be saved, & so were [all the hospital personnel] . . . poor boy, I can see him as I write—he was tanned & had a fine head of hair, & looked good in the face when he first came, and was in pretty good flesh, too . . . had his hair cut close about ten or twelve days before he died . . . large clear eyes, they seemed to talk better than words—I assure you I was attracted to him much.[49]

The Haskells had a more restricted understanding, no doubt, of the term "attracted" than did Walt. Yet there was probably little miscommunication. The immediate connection of touch, the deep flow of kindness, Walt's awareness of every hard-fought breath—all this added up to an intimacy comprehensible to anyone. The poet was careful not to fall too quickly into the poses of conventional consolation. He had more to say about this one particular soldier, Erastus Haskell:

Many nights I sat in the hospital by his bedside till far in the night . . .
I shall never forget those nights . . . the sick & wounded lying around
in their cots, just visible in the darkness, & this dear young man close
at hand lying on what proved to be his death bed—I do not know his
past life, but . . . what I saw of him, he was a noble boy . . . I think
you have reason to be proud of such a son, & all his relatives have
cause to treasure his memory.[50]

Here, at last, is a conventional phrase or two. Walt avoided, however,
words that would have placed the dead boy in the context of his time and
struggle, words, say, to the effect of, "Though his death was tragic, it
was in a noble and historic cause." There was nobility in the situation,
but it attached to the soldier himself, not his cause. Nor did he assure
Erastus's relatives that they had good *reason* to treasure his memory.
There was reason to be proud, but mere cause for treasuring—in a situation of such waste, to invoke reasons and reasonability too freely was
to go too far.

The effect was not of overly careful, ungenerous laying on of thin
praise. On the contrary, the simple words ring true. Restored to their
weighty original meanings, terms such as "noble," "proud," "treasure,"
and "memory" come as gifts. These were words that the grieving parents of a nineteen-year-old might have read over and over, year after
year, without growing alienated from them or feeling too keenly the disproportion between words and sacrifice. Then, as though he were an actual member of this humble American family—and reluctant, so
reluctant, to say a final farewell—Walt addressed the boy directly, in the
presence of those who so deeply grieved:

Poor dear son, though you were not my son, I felt to love you as a
son, what short time I saw you sick & dying here—it is as well as it
is, perhaps better—for who knows whether he is not better off, that
patient & sweet young soul, to go, than we are to stay? So farewell,
dear boy—it was my opportunity to be with you in your last rapid
days of death—no chance, as I have said, to do any thing particular,
for nothing could be done—only you did not lay here & die among
strangers without having one at hand who loved you dearly, & to
whom you gave your dying kiss.[51]

Erastus, he concluded, was only "one of the thousands," those "about whom there is no record or fame, no fuss made . . . but I find in them the real precious & royal ones of this land." To have known such a boy was an honor—not an honor in the common sense, a conferring of esteem, a social negotiation of a kind, but a simple movement in the heart.

AROUND THE TIME of Erastus Haskell's death, Walt wrote to a prospective hospital donor, "I am at present curiously almost alone here, as visitor & consolatory . . . the work of the different Reliefs & Commissions is nearly all off in the field—& as to private visitors, *there are few or none.*"[1]

That was in the fierce heat of summer 1863, when the roofs of the ward-pavilions "burnt like fire," as Walt wrote Lewy Brown.[2] But he had noticed a scarcity of visitors months earlier, too, when the thousands of wounded from the Battle of Chancellorsville began arriving at the steamer landing behind Armory Square. "The attendants are few, and at night few outsiders also . . . The wounded are getting to be common, and people grow callous."[3]

He said almost the same thing in October, "I come here pretty regularly because this hospital . . . is one of the least visited—there is not much hospital visiting here now—it has become an old story."[4] Ordinary citizens had stopped caring so much; perhaps they had seen too many of the sick and wounded. Moreover, what with major Union victories that July, the war seemed to many in the North to be heading for a satisfying conclusion. There would be trainloads and boatloads of suffering men arriving for a while yet, from the last battles, but not forever—and they could be thought less of.

Walt captured another possible reason for a falloff in volunteerism, when he described Armory Square as "25 or 30 wards . . . beds for 60 patients [per ward] . . . you see a U S general hospital here is quite an establishment . . . has a regular police . . . a great staff of surgeons, cadets, women & men nurses &c &c."[5] The hospitals may have begun to give an impression of being adequate to the health crisis, finally. Although Walt was critical of the rigid, hierarchical U.S. Sanitary Commission, and though he knew well the inadequacies of care visited on many soldiers, by 1863 something was being done and done on a mass scale.

It was part of larger movements in society and the war effort; of transformations as the requirements of prosecuting a conflict of such size and complexity made themselves felt. The powerful men in charge of the commission conceived of their organization as a model structure to discipline the many ad hoc relief groups, mostly staffed by women, that had arisen in the first weeks of war. Their institutional approach amounted to a kind of antihumanitarianism—suspicious of mere pity, of compassion as a serviceable impulse, they proposed to answer the desperate needs of the Union wounded with efficiency, bureaucracy, and order.*

Sanitation in the army camps and medical care before and after battles were main concerns. The commission advised the slow-moving, often recalcitrant Army Medical Bureau—headed, early in the war, by a holdover surgeon general described as a "self-satisfied, supercilious, bigoted blockhead"—while amassing supplies of clothing, medicine, and other relief goods for the troops.[6] Sanitary representatives staged inspections at camps, and under the day-by-day direction of Frederick Law Olmsted, the journalist and cocreator of New York's Central Park, it began compiling an exhaustive list of the soldiers then in Northern hospitals, so that families could find their missing sons.[7] Olmsted was the author of *Report on the Demoralization of the Volunteers,* a scathing account of the unmet needs of the Union forces as of September 1861. He was himself acquainted with the terrors of contemporary surgery—in 1860, after a carriage accident in which he broke his thigh, he was slated

---

*Fearing medical horrors like those seen in the recent Crimean War, when eighteen thousand of twenty-five thousand British troops in the field died within twelve months, the organizers lobbied the Lincoln administration to create what the president called, a little dubiously, a "fifth wheel on the coach," a civilian agency with broad powers to intervene in affairs affecting the war effort.

Sanitary Commission workers in Washington, D.C., June 1863.

for an emergency amputation at the hip, an experience many soldiers did not survive (and which he was spared only because he was deemed too weak for it). Nine months later, limping on a shortened leg, he witnessed the chaotic aftermath of First Bull Run and wrote his wife, "We are in a frightful condition [in Washington, where the wounded were being evacuated], ten times as bad as anyone dare say publicly."[8]

Olmsted served at the pleasure of Henry Whitney Bellows, the commission's president. Pastor of the First Congregational Church of New York, a leader of the Unitarian Fellowship in America, Bellows was a molder of national opinion through the weekly papers he edited, the *Christian Inquirer* and the *Christian Examiner*, and the lyceum lecture series he presented.* Bellows helped define an arch-Unionist position early

---

*One of Bellows's lectures in 1857 was a stern disquisition on "The Treatment of Social Diseases."

in the war, as suggested by the title of his much-reprinted pamphlet-essay, "Unconditional Loyalty." His authoritarian tendencies led him to argue that a national leader, although popularly chosen, was answerable only to God for his actions, and he saw the responsibilities of the ordinary citizen as lying in the direction of unquestioning submission.[9] Walt's strong Unionism, of a more democratic stripe, put him at odds with the further reaches of Sanitary Commission ideology—with the idea, for instance, that war would prove a useful corrective to excessive American idealism and individualism. He tended to be displeased, if not disgusted, with the commission's agents he met in the hospitals, calling them "*hirelings*"—men and women who ministered to the wounded for wages, often in a scolding way.

But Walt also shared many goals and methods with the commission. His approach to hospital work shows him serving as a dutiful one-man relief force, supplying whatever the soldiers said they needed; he raised funds to the extent that he was able (the commission, operating on a different scale, raised $4,400,000 at public sanitary fairs in 1863 to 1865, and collected and spent more than $7,000,000 in the course of the war); and while exemplifying values that the commissioners deplored (individuality, compassion, soulfulness), Walt *was* in the exemplification business—just as the commission was. For him, war meant performance as himself, as the embodiment of qualities he believed were threatened by the times—for example, personal connection and loving kindness. For the commission, meanwhile, a raft of lessons and values attached to its own rescue enterprise, including submission to the stern discipline of suffering, an experience some commissioners believed was too little known from the American past.

Among other rich benefits bestowed by the commission was the selection of William A. Hammond as the new surgeon general. Hammond was an energetic, intelligent young physician; from the time of his appointment in April 1862, the friction between the Army Medical Bureau and the Sanitary Commission ceased, and reforms brought markedly better care to the troops.[10] His most controversial departure was to ban the use of calomel and another mercury-based medicine, tartar emetic, from use in army hospitals.[11] Hammond promoted the hiring of women nurses, mandating that one third or more of the hospital corps be female. The wretched failure of the old methods for evacuating the

Surgeon General William A. Hammond.

wounded led him to appoint another young innovator, Jonathan Letterman, medical director of the Army of the Potomac. Before Letterman's
ascent, no corps of specially trained medics had existed to bear the
wounded from the field with dispatch; civilian teamsters often drove the
jolting carts that served for ambulances, and regimental musicians sometimes served as stretcher bearers—and sometimes ran under fire. In the
lead-up to First Fredericksburg, while Burnside took weeks to arrive at a
position of dire disadvantage before the rebel gun emplacements, Letterman drilled and redrilled his new medics, skillfully deployed his
many field hospitals, and worked with the commission to secure boun-
teous supplies of instruments, anesthetics, dressings, stimulants, and
food, clothing, and bedding for the troops, so that when the terrible fight
began at last, a dependable system was in place.[12]

The ambulance corps worked so well that European armies studied its
composition and fielded their own versions of it for the next half century,

down to the First World War.[13] A soldier wounded at Fredericksburg thus had a generally better experience than one wounded at Bull Run or the Seven Days in the summer of 1862. Walt's shocking encounter with a pile of severed limbs after Fredericksburg represented the best that could be hoped for in the situation—and it signaled, as well, an auspicious hard-fought-for turning in the history of medical care.[14]

His overall estimation of the treatment the men received, aside from the occasional complaint about hospital hirelings, was generous. "[T]he doctor behaved very well—seemed to be anxious to do right," Walt wrote home in one of his first letters from Washington, reporting on one of his early days on the wards; he had found a soldier who had been overlooked, but a quick word to the surgeon brought a good response.[15] About John Elliott, who died following a leg operation, Walt commented, "I think all was done for him that could be . . . they tried their best . . . three long hours were spent" trying to restore him to consciousness (after a dosing with chloroform), by every possible means.[16] The "surgeons & nurses were good to him," Walt assured Mrs. Whitman—and this attitude, of appreciation for hard work on the part of medical staff, no matter the outcome, became standard with him.

It was a time of woeful ignorance but of strenuous attempts to improve. In many ways, the soldiers faced the same sort of care as those who had fought with Washington at Yorktown or with Henry V at Agincourt. In the absence of an understanding of the basics of microbiology, epidemic infections almost always attended the concentration of thousands of sick and wounded men in open wards. But some changes, arrived at almost by accident, had begun to open a door on modern medical practice. Surgeons noticed that soldiers in need of amputations fared better if put under the knife quickly—waits longer than forty-eight hours often led to blood poisoning, which usually proved fatal.* Hospital gangrene, one of the most dread Civil War infections, with a mortality of 50 percent, raged during the second and third years of the war, but became rare by the fourth, as surgeons began bathing wounds in solutions of bromine, a close chemical relative of chlorine.[17] Other

---

*Bacterial infections, becoming established at the wound site, were transmitted to the bloodstream via surgical incision.

surgeons had luck when they quarantined gangrenous or other seriously diseased patients—overall rates of infection went down, they noticed. Some also hit on the practice of washing their surgical instruments of blood and other infectious matter between operations; and some insisted that their nurses wash their hands in chlorinated soda.[18]

Thousands of amputations performed at high speed (to minimize suffering), often in irregular locations (a tent, a barn, or an open field during battle), produced a cadre of skilled surgeons north and south, men who knew, at the least, how to ligate major arteries quickly.[19] Surgeons unfortunately also often explored open wounds with dirty fingers; they wore pus-stained smocks while treating patient after patient; to thread surgical needles, they moistened the silk with their own saliva; and when instruments or sponges fell to the floor, they put them back to use without disinfection.[20] The eagerness to amputate, which left battlegrounds like Fredericksburg littered with body parts, was on the whole probably justified. "The minie ball striking a bone does not permit much debate about amputation," declared Union surgeon Theodore Dimon, who served at Antietam and other battles.[21] The heavy, slow-moving minié fractured bone into hundreds of sharp splinters, which, driven through muscle and skin, created savage wounds requiring surgery far beyond the skills of any emergency medical corps of the 1860s. Dr. William W. Keen, the future author of standard texts on antiseptic surgery, served during the war as an assistant surgeon, and although retrospectively aware of all the damage done, especially through ignorance of germs, wrote, "[T]aking the army as a whole, I have no hesitation in saying that far more lives were lost from refusal to amputate than by amputation."[22]

In January 1864, at Armory Square, Walt witnessed another amputation—one of the many thousands performed on Union soldiers over the course of the war. The patient this time was Lewy Brown, Walt's close friend and probable lover. The wound to Lewy's left leg had failed to heal despite sixteen months of treatment. Dr. Willard Bliss, chief surgeon at Armory Square, determined that the limb was a greater danger on than an inconvenience off, and Walt watched from the doorway as it was severed below the knee. He wrote in a notebook,

The surgeon . . . did not finish the operation being called away . . . Lewy came out of the influence of the ether. It bled & they thought an artery had opened. They were [ready] to cut the stitches again & make a search but after some time concluded it was only surface bleeding . . . stitched it up again & Lew felt every one of those stitches.[23]

The young man, who survived and lived until 1926, was mostly incoherent afterward:

They did not think it safe to give him any more [ether] as he had already taken it excessively. I could hear his cries sometimes quite loud . . . and caught glimpses of him through the open door. At length they . . . brought the boy in on his cot . . . I sat down by him. The . . . ether & exaustion . . . had their effect upon [him] for some time. He talked, quite a good deal. His face was very pale, his eyes dull. He asked often about me . . . could feel the lost foot & leg very plainly. The toes would get twisted, & not possible to disentangle them.[24]

Walt remained by Lewy's side all night. And the next night, too, snatching some sleep on an adjoining cot. Lewy, although "very sick, opprest for breath, with deathly feeling," had experienced the very best of Civil War surgery—performed indoors, under sufficient anesthetic, with no deadly sequelae. In August he was mustered out of the army.[25]

THE SIGNAL UNION victories of the summer of 1863 did not cause the rebels to sue for peace, as many in the North had hoped they would. The South, although suffering from shortages and inflation, was not yet at the end of its reserves of stoic resistance—not nearly. Robert E. Lee's valiant fighting force, the Army of Northern Virginia, had been damaged but not destroyed. Morale remained high. The soldiers fought on for honor and for love of Lee, and out of devotion to the men alongside them in the ranks.[1]

North and South, many who had enlisted for three-year terms were soon to complete them. The Confederate Congress forestalled a manpower crisis by denying its soldiers the right to resign, and by stretching the age limits of the Southern draft to seventeen and fifty.[2] In the North, soldiers might still leave the service, but Congress made reenlistment attractive by offering a four-hundred-dollar bounty plus a thirty-day furlough to all who had served at least two years. Older volunteer regiments, such as George Whitman's 51st, were not split apart and submerged in new-forming regiments if half the men "veteranized."*

The 51st had an original strength of about a thousand. It had formed after the shock-to-the-system of First Bull Run, and, like other three-

---

*In 1864, George Whitman's regiment became known as the 51st New York Veteran Volunteers, assuming an honorific of which the men were justly proud.

year regiments, it superseded the state militias organized at the war's start. Soldiers in militias enlisted mostly for ninety-day terms. Some hint of George's eagerness to serve can be found in the date of his first enrollment—April 23, only ten days after the fall of Fort Sumter—but this eagerness may have disadvantaged him professionally.

Other men of about the same age and education did not enlist during the militia period; they waited until the three-year regiments were being created, later in 1861, and entered when captaincies and other commissions were being handed out. Henry Francis, George's friend and the man whom Walt said he "could not like much," joined a three-year regiment in Buffalo in July 1861. By the time George was completing his militia service and enlisting in the 51st, in September, Francis had been made a lieutenant.[3] Another young man from Buffalo, Morris Hazard, enlisted with Francis and became the first captain of Company D, which later was to become Francis's company (and later still, George's).*

A great number of men passed through the 51st. The original thousand, winnowed by battle and skirmish, were replaced by new recruits, gathered here and there but mostly from New York. In "Fifty-First New-York City Veterans," an article of October 1864, Walt stressed the process of depletion and replacement in the regiment, noting that the 51st had "always lost heavily in officers":

[T]hey were first under fire at Roanoke . . . fought with spirit and coolness from the first, and the next month . . . in the battle of Newbern; in these engagements losing, in killed and wounded, some twenty officers and one hundred and fifty men . . . [T]he regiment . . . took active part in the second Bull Run . . . [and] lost ninety-two men in this fight.[4]

Drawing on his notes from Fredericksburg, which in turn drew on George's diary, Walt described this "sanguinary engagement" under Burnside, in which the 51st again lost many men. "By this time . . . their

---

*Those men who were able to bring numbers of live bodies to a newly forming regiment often became its principal officers. This was true for the 51st, where Edward Ferrero, who headed a group called the Shepard Rifles, became its first colonel, and Charles LeGendre, who headed the New York Rifles, became its major.

1,100 to 1,200 men, (counting recruits since they came out,) had been pretty well exhausted; only about 150 to 200 remaining for duty."[5]

Depleted, the regiment filled up by sending officers to hunt for more men. More than two times the original enrollment eventually served in the regiment (or enrolled, accepted bounties, and disappeared).[6] In just less than four years, the 51st took part in more than fifty battles, sieges, or other notable engagements—a tally not unique for the war, but well on the high side.[7] * The ratio of men who died from wounds to those dying of disease was also unusually high, 1.44 to 1 before deaths due to captivity are factored in.[8] Overall, both North and South, men died more than twice as often of disease as from wounds in the war, which suggests that the 51st was an unusually active, hard-campaigning outfit.[9]

Walt underscored just how hard by emphasizing how often the 51st had engaged in fight after fight, with little pause for recuperation:

> They were on the march [last half of 1862] for nearly four months . . . with battle or pursuit every week, and often men falling by the road from utter exhaustion . . . Following [Vicksburg] they were in active service in Kentucky and Tennessee . . . till the regiment, what there was left of it . . . returned to New York on thirty days' furlough . . . now filled up with new men to about their original complement, they again saw the Southwest as far as Nashville, Chattanooga, Knoxville; &c., whence they were rapidly returned to join the rest of the Ninth Corps, and make junction . . . with the Army of the Potomac.[10]

With apologies for all he had to leave out of his account—because the *complete* story of this one regiment's war would be impossible to write, "space forbids" it—Walt described the Union push from the Rapidan to the James in 1864, the 51st being "active participants" in this crucial late movement of the war:

> [T]hey lost heavily [at the Wilderness and at Spotsylvania] . . . Col. Le Gendre was wounded . . . an eye destroyed . . . At Cold Harbor

---

*Of the 194 volunteer and regular-army regiments from New York State, the 51st suffered the fifth-highest number of casualties.

they came near being flanked and taken, but got off by bold movements and fighting . . . Not an original officer remains . . . The regiment has, indeed, had some three or four crops of officers.[11]

Not all the original officers had died or been captured. Some had resigned, others had been offered staff positions, and still others transferred
to other units. Colonel Robert Brown Potter, leader of the 51st at Antietam, had been promoted to brigadier general in March 1863. Potter was
a thin, balding lawyer from Manhattan, the son and nephew of Anglican
bishops.[12] Wounded in the North Carolina campaign, he seems never to
have overcome an urge to precede the men before the enemy's guns. At
the chaotic, defeat-snatched-from-the-jaws-of-victory Battle of the
Crater, on July 30, 1864, for example, Potter was the only commander of
a division known to be personally on the field with his troops.*

George served under Potter in several hot fights. After the Battle of
New Bern, he wrote,

> I saw our Leiut Col. [Potter] sitting on a log, thinking he was
> wounded, I went up to him and asked if he was struck, he said only
> with a spent ball . . . and he got up and went into the thickest of it
> again and did not give up untill the fighting was over . . . when he
> found a ball had struck him just above the hip and passed through his
> side.[13]

At Antietam, Potter put himself in a position of maximum jeopardy as
the 51st and its brother regiment, the 51st Pennsylvania, tried to take the
soon-to-be-fabled Lower Bridge. On the other side of Antietam Creek,
two regiments of Georgia riflemen held a powerful position on a hillside. Trees and rifle pits gave the Georgians protection as they poured
heavy, accurate fire down onto anyone who tried to cross. After two
failed attempts by another Union brigade, Ferrero, astride a horse, and
sheltering well downstream from the contested crossing, prepared the
two 51sts (and two reserve regiments also under his command) to do the

---

*General Ferrero, also commanding a division, was found negligent in "being in a bomb-
proof habitually," that is, hiding out the whole time in a bunker. He was also drunk.

nigh-unto-impossible. His first orders to Potter and to Colonel John Hartranft, leader of the Pennsylvanians, to "forward" toward the bridge were met with sarcastic looks and backchat.

"Why in the hell don't you forward?" Ferrero yelled some minutes later, riding back in front of the men on his horse.

Hartranft, later a governor of Pennsylvania, replied, "Who do you want to forward?" meaning, which regiment, since both were called the 51st.

"The Fifty-first *Pennsylvania*," Ferrero roared.

"Why don't you say what you mean when you want me to move?" Hartranft replied with cheeky nonchalance.[14]

Ferrero—displaying appropriate behavior for a brigade commander, though behavior much different from that of his regimental leaders— passed the crisis of the battle several hundred yards away, on the safe side of a knoll. Having sent the two 51sts down to the foot of the bridge, where enemy rifle fire forced them to hide behind a stone wall and a fence (and below the crest of the crowning bridge roadway), Ferrero sent a message, ordering the men to take the bridge by crossing it. Hartranft argued with the messenger, incredulous that such a thing was being asked of his troops. Potter did not argue when the message reached him; he shouted to his men to leave such cover as they enjoyed and to swarm the bridge, and he did this shouting from the top of a parapet, which he had mounted despite a squall of enemy fire.[15]

An eyewitness noted that the New York colonel had the demeanor of a madman—he was standing on his parapet entirely exposed to deadly fire, cursing and swearing, and in this way trying to get his men to move. This was a style of leadership effective in extreme situations, assuming it did not get the leader killed (and in those unfortunate circumstances, some- times even more effective). George may well have been instructed by Potter's example. His references to the lawyer-soldier in his letters and diary are not many, but they are quietly telling; in the days leading up to Second Bull Run, for instance, about three weeks before Antietam, the depleted regiment found itself defending a ford on the Rappahannock, anticipating an attempted crossing by a large rebel force. George com- mented in his diary, "Col Potters orders were to hold the Ford while we had a man left. and well we knew he would obey the order."[16]

Potter displayed many of the qualities admired in field officers. Most important was a willingness to face the same risks his men faced. Offi-

General Robert B. Potter.

cers who won the loyalty of veteran soldiers had a quality of self-possession—an ability to arrive at sound decisions under great stress, and then to enforce those decisions. A degree of youth was also almost indispensable. "It was a very rare thing," wrote Union general Jacob Dolson Cox, author of *Military Reminiscences of the Civil War*, "for a man of middle age to make a good company officer . . . Some men retain flexibility of mind and body longer than others, and could more easily adapt . . . such [men] would succeed best."[17]

Potter was the same age as George. He came from a privileged background yet took to soldiering with the same verve, as if savoring the dirt and blood and mortal risk. They, and a few other officers in the 51st (notably Captain Samuel Sims and Major LeGendre) displayed unusual indifference to danger, and they suffered for their gallantry—Sims, a friend of Walt's as well as of George's, died at the Crater, and LeGendre was twice wounded in the face from direct rifle shots. The 51st supplied five generals to the Union, serving as "a kind of West Point" in the opinion of one of its admirers, who claimed that the regiment had also "given about one thousand lives of martyrs" to the cause.[18]

A gifted officer, Andrew L. Fowler, died at Antietam, aged twenty-two. He had been a protégé of Robert Potter's; like Potter, he was well educated and of a religious family. Fowler's death and the manner of his service give a sense of the regiment's esprit de corps. As part of "Burnside's Brigade," the 51st had been brought into condition early in the war with seven to eight hours of drill per day plus cross-country marches. Burnside, whose name would become a byword for dunderheaded incompetence, devised a brilliant, thrillingly successful first campaign for the 51st against Confederate strongholds on the coast of North Carolina. This early experience shaped the unit as a force and went far toward planting an idea among its members of the 51st as something special, as George showed in letters written after New Bern and as Lieutenant Fowler, in letters to his father, also displayed, including one written after Roanoke:

> We remained in the swamp, firing and advancing, for about three hours and over, when . . . a grand charge was . . . made . . . I feel proud of the 51st, as they conducted themselves bravely, and . . . it has been conceded that our flag was the first placed on the Island— first on the masked battery in the wood, and the first on the upper fort on the coast, now . . . named after our brave [General Reno].[19]

At the island battle, Fowler distinguished himself with a gesture that might have proved fatal. The 51st coming under friendly fire, he rose up and waved his sword and then a handkerchief at a nearby regiment, to alert it of the 51st's place of hiding. This act of self-endangerment was reported in the *Brooklyn Daily Eagle* as an example of homegrown heroics.

Fowler was made first lieutenant after New Bern and chosen adjutant as well, for his "remarkable courage and soldierly bearing," an admirer wrote after his death.[20] By dint of his genteel upbringing and probably personal qualities of rectitude and plain friendliness, he belonged to the circle of top officers in the regiment (Ferrero, Potter, LeGendre), and their casual socializing gave rise to this description, from another letter to his father:

I believe that we have attached to our regiment officers, as a whole, who may consistently be ranked among the bravest of the brave . . . Besides most of them are well educated, some of them superlatively so . . . when time affords opportunity, our officers mingle together and are mostly interested in [discussing] the passing events of the war . . . I cannot but prophesy for my regiment that you will yet hear more gloriously of her.[21]

Fowler belonged to the Thirteenth Street Presbyterian Church, of Manhattan. He had "united with" it during "the last great revival," according to his pastor, the Rev. Dr. S. D. Burchard.[22] The secret of his coolness under fire, according to the minister, was his "unshaken confidence in Him who doeth all things well." Within the regiment he was known as " 'the Pious Adjutant,' " and Fowler "mingled with the soldiers for their spiritual good, counseled and prayed with the wounded, the sick and the dying."[23] After his death, one of the officers who wrote letters of condolence noted, "One treasure he prominently possessed . . . and that is, I believe him to have been a Christian. He invariably devoted a portion of his time to the reading of his pocket Bible, [every day] appending notes."

A fellow officer, John Stuart, shipped Fowler's body back home after Antietam. By consulting the marginal notes that the young man had written in his Bible, his parents determined that on the morning of September 17, only minutes before taking a bullet through the chest, Fowler had been reading the Forty-sixth and Forty-seventh Psalms. He "died in a few moments," Captain Stuart assured the senior Fowlers. "My heart was almost broken. I loved him as a brother." The bullet came in the general downpour of lead at the taking of the bridge. Stuart regretted that "I was not with him when he was shot—I was passing onward" in the crush of bodies, and the other lieutenant in their company was also hit at about the same time. "The bullet that struck [the other lieutenant] passed through my coat, and its striking his shoulder probably saved my life," said Stuart, adding that he was hit several other times lower on his uniform as well, but miraculously not hurt.[24]

Company F, Fowler's company, fought just to the side of George Whitman's Company D. A letter that George wrote his mother soon after Antietam notes, "The loss of our regt in the Sunday and Wednesday's fight was from 120 to 125 killed wounded and missing. Our Adjutant

Burnside's Bridge, from the elevated position occupied by
the Confederate forces.

who lived in Brooklyn and was named Fowler, was killed at the
bridge . . . Both lieutenants in Co F which is on the right of [us] and
both in Co K who was next to us on the left, was hit."[25] Mrs. Whitman
cannot have taken much solace from this report—her son, a lieutenant,
was telling her that all the other officers of his rank had been killed or
wounded in a matter of minutes. One further hint of the dense accuracy

of enemy fire over the bridge can be gleaned from the mention of multiple bullet holes in the lower parts of Captain Stuart's uniform. Marksmen firing from above at oncoming targets will ordinarily shoot high, unless given sufficient time and practice to perfect their aim.

Following the fight at the bridge, the 51st was down to 150 men in shape for battle, from an estimated 500 in May.[26] The horror of Antietam had come as a shock. Twenty-three thousand dead and wounded lay upon the field after the one day of fighting—four times as many American casualties as would cover Normandy's beaches after D-Day. It had been a thoughtful battle, a purposeful one. Generals on both sides had been able to pick out their positions and plan their tactics well in advance, and the result had been a notable slaughter.[27]

Antietam was the first battle to be photographed before the bodies were all buried.[28] Mathew Brady's staff took a series of images, about a third of which showed corpses, many of them grotesquely disfigured. Before

Dead soldiers at Antietam.

Antietam, the Brady men had recorded some real scenes of war, including a few shots of wounded men at field hospitals; although truthful, these photos had not quite communicated an essential fact, that war was a butchery, a wallow in death. Here were corpses blown up like comical balloons, with gaping mouths in blackened faces.* The Brady photographs contradicted the general tendency of depictions of war previously by Americans, in woodcuts, lithographs, and paintings, which had shown it to be a serious matter but decorous and in large part an adventure.[29]

The 51st limped on from Antietam. George, a member of a different officers' circle from Andrew Fowler's—his was composed of less well-educated men, of lesser rank—continued in charge of Henry Francis's company, displaying skills often encountered among the competent commanders. One of these was a facility with clerical work. "Accounts are to be kept, rations, clothing, arms, accoutrements, and ammunition are to be receipted," General Cox explained in his book on the war, and "a man wholly without business training would always be an embarrassment, though his other qualifications . . . were good."[30] †

George's coterie roughly duplicated the original officers' roster of Company D. There were Captain Francis himself; First Lieutenant Francis Tryon, wounded in North Carolina and seconded to Ferrero's staff after Antietam; Second Lieutenant Thomas Marsh, whom George followed up the ladder of rank, becoming second lieutenant and later a major when Marsh became first lieutenant and lieutenant colonel, respectively; and Samuel Pooley, a close friend of George's who followed *him* up the hierarchy.[31]

Another close friend was Frank Butler. A lieutenant of Company G, Butler would die of wounds on September 30, 1864, in the same battle in which George and hundreds of other men of the regiment were taken

---

*Despite the chilly nights, the daytime temperatures were in the seventies and promoted rapid decompositon.

†George probably discovered his facility for paper shuffling here, in the midst of war. The records he kept were proper and orderly but not copious—other company commanders wrote richer "Record of Events" cards after battles and sieges, and the two companies George was mostly associated with (D and K) are notable for their sparing "Events" narratives.

Sam Pooley.

prisoner. A sergeant, Bob Smith, was a friend from Brooklyn who also died in battle; George described Smith as a "young fellow . . . that . . . lived in Portland Ave (in one of the brick houses below the vacant lots I think) . . . a good fellow and an intimate friend of mine."[32]

Close to George in age and a kind of equivalent to him in rank and career was another Brooklyn man, Samuel Sims. Walt compared George and Sims in an article he wrote in 1863, suggesting similarities of character but also a difference in command style—Sims, a little more fatherly, perhaps; George, a bit more soldierly. Both commanded the entire regiment at times, and both won mention for gallantry in a formal report written by a superior officer.[33] Both served on courts-martial when so detailed, a typical duty for officers of their grade but one that recognized, ideally, probity and fairness.

Sims left the regiment often to go on recruiting trips in New York. Writing from a camp near Hickam's Bridge, Kentucky, in October 1863, George told Jeff, "Capt. Sims of our regt is now in Brooklyn, after conscripts, have you seen him, If you would like to see him, I think you would be likely to hear from him, at Tom Deans Billiard Saloon, at Montague Hall."[34] Sims had been a glass stainer before the war. He was widowed and had three small children, whom a sister in Brooklyn was raising. A tall man for the era—close to five foot ten— Sims had "Sterling Abilities & . . . fine social qualities," according to one colleague, desirable attributes in a busy recruiter.[35]

George was almost never sent on such trips. He may have been less able to charm and cajole; or, there may have been too much an odor of gunpowder about him. One of Sims's hunts for recruits lasted a full seven months. He had a fiancée in Brooklyn, but it was also true that Sims was of more delicate health than George.[36] Other than a flulike infection just after he joined the 51st, George had no illnesses that required him to seek medical leave until, half starved, he nearly died of what his mother called "lung fever" in the Confederate prison at Danville, Virginia, three years later.[37] Sims was sick for two months in the middle of his seven-month trip, and some of his other frequent missions of recruitment may have had partly a medical basis.[38]

George may have simply been too useful as a field officer. A company commander able to perform every day, one whose letters home during four years of war make no mention of the most debilitating common complaint, diarrhea, was invaluable as an officer, assuming that he was also competent. George's robustness may have been an instance of the generally better health of the men who came from big cities. Although disdained by the rugged frontiersmen as a bunch of pale-faced clerks, the city soldiers proved more resistant to diarrhea and other camp infections, and they were far more likely to die of battle wounds, and less likely to die of disease, than were the woodsmen of the Old Northwest.[39]

Walt's idea of the war—of the human cost of it, of the odds of survival—came to him in many ways, but most pointedly by way of inside knowledge of the fortunes of his brother's coterie. These officers whom George befriended and loved and who loved him in return became Walt's friends, too, in some cases, and he followed their often tragic paths closely.

It was at his first visit, Fredericksburg, that he came to know and like Captain Sims, who offered him a bed in his own tent. Fred McReady, another of George's group, "used me well" on the Fredericksburg visit, Walt remembered; for the rest of the war, Walt stayed in touch with McReady and sometimes relied on him for information about George's whereabouts and safety.[40]

Fred McReady survived the war, although not entirely intact. On May 6, 1864, he was wounded in the left hip, the minié ball "entering . . . near [the] great trochanter [a bony process of the femur and] passing down and lodging in the thigh," according to his official service record. The 51st as a whole lost severely on this day, at what was later to be known as the Battle of the Wilderness. George, not sure yet what the fight was called, told his mother that half his company had been wounded or killed, but that he himself was "all right so far."[41] In Washington, Walt saw firsthand the new harvest of wounded coming in from Virginia and, knowing that George's regiment had been in the thick of the battle, he sought out men who could tell him of his brother's fate.

On May 12, he located a corporal, Fred Sanders, who had served under George, and Sanders told him that as of May 10, when Sanders himself had been evacuated, George had been well. Another wounded man of the 51st, James C. Brown, shot in the shoulder, had more news of George and the casualties in the regiment, and then on May 13—a day after George and his men had again gone into battle, this time at Spotsylvania, near the famously bloody salient known to military history as the Muleshoe—Walt found Colonel Charles LeGendre, commander of the entire regiment, who had been gravely wounded but was able to tell Walt that " 'your brother is well,' " and that the colonel personally felt "very kindly" toward George.[42] *

"[P]oor man, I felt . . . sorry" for him, Walt immediately wrote his mother. "[LeGendre] is . . . disfigured . . . shot through the bridge of

---

*Col. LeGendre may have owed his life to George. Two years before the Wilderness, George had found him severely wounded at the Battle of New Bern and had carried him from the field on a rubberized blanket. LeGendre's French origins and poor English earned him the disdain of Henry Francis and some other officers, but George wrote of him always with respect, possibly in view of his valor in continuing to serve despite a disabling wound.

Colonel Charles W. LeGendre, before his woundings.

the nose, & left eye probably lost—I spent a little time with him this forenoon—he is suffering very much."[43] LeGendre's war was over. Twenty-two years later, when he applied for a disability pension, his official "Declaration for Original Invalid Pension" described the wounds that gave rise to a compassionate response in both George and Walt:

On or about the 14th day of March, 1862, he received a gun shot wound the ball striking the lower jaw on the right side just in front of the first molar, shattered the jaw on the horizontal portion and . . . passed on through the muscles of the neck, Knocked off the spinal process of the Seventh cervical vertebra, and passed out . . . [O]n or about the 4th of May, 1864, while he was in the service of the United States . . . and in the line of his duty as Colonel commanding the 51st Regt. New York Vols . . . he received a wound caused by a musket-ball coming from the right and slightly descending and which struck him in the forehead just above the inner angle of the right eye, carried away the crest of the nasal bone, and destroyed the [other] eye.[44]

In this same letter to his mother, Walt mentioned that Fred McReady had been wounded in the current fight in Virginia. "I cannot hear of his arrival here [in Washington, but] if he comes I shall find him immediately & take care of him myself."[45] Two weeks later, Walt wrote again, "I see Fred McReady about every other day, I have to go down to Alexandria, about six miles from here—he is doing quite well, but very tired of confinement."[46] McReady's wound baffled the doctors at the First Division General Hospital, where he arrived on May 12. Ten years later, McReady declared in his official pension application that the bullet that crippled him had "entered the left hip, a little to the rear . . . and is still lodged in there, the various surgeons having failed entirely to find it."[47] Like thousands of other septic war wounds, McReady's refused to close up. The damaged bone became necrotic and, in 1874, an examining physician declared that there were "two sinuses [open cavities] about 3 inches from each other" that continued to drain the damaged tissue.[48]

McReady's leg was weak ever after; his locomotion was limited. At the end of the war, he went home to Brooklyn and worked there as a weigher; beginning in 1874 he received federal pension benefits of $8.50 per month. The wound that would change his life had not led him to separate from the service at his earliest possible opportunity, however— after a few weeks of treatment at Alexandria, he rejoined the 51st on the battleground in Virginia and served with it for the remainder of the war, despite his pain and his trouble getting around. When most of his brother officers were captured at the Battle of Poplar Springs Church, he assumed regimental responsibilities for which his command experience heretofore had little prepared him, serving as acting colonel and brigade officer of the day.[49] He never married; in 1877, a further surgery succeeded at last in removing the bullet from his left hip, although a "Surgeon's Certificate of Examination" written afterward noted stubbornly, "Scar of entrance inflamed, discharging, connected with dead bone."[50]

WALT HAD BEGUN 1864 with a field trip: his second visit to the front, this time to Culpepper, Virginia, the winter encampment of the Army of the Potomac. He had "a great desire to be present at a first class battle," he wrote his mother, and a "pretty high" officer had hinted to him that something big was in the offing, possibly a major new offensive.[1] Lyman Hapgood, of the army paymaster's office, and his assistant Charles Eldridge were on their way to Culpepper, thirty-five miles west of Fredericksburg, to pay out reenlistment bounties to the veterans, and Walt decided to tag along.[2] He may have rendered some assistance to the paymasters, but basically he was along for the ride—with, as always, a notebook in hand.

On Sunday, February 7, he slept at the home of Mrs. Ashby, a Confederate widow upon whom Union officers were being billeted. Rumors were afoot of an imminent attack by Lee on the Union position, but Walt "cast my eyes at the mud, which was then at its deepest and palmiest condition," and retired to bed.[3] He was roused in the middle of the night by the shouts of soldiers returning from a hard march—this was the same force of Union troops that he would write about in *Specimen Days*, the one that impressed him with "the majesty and reality of the American people *en masse*."

His letters and other jottings from Culpepper show him awed to be gazing upon crowds of soldiers going about their ordinary work. Retreating from the intense intimacy of his sickbed visiting, he put himself at a comfortable middle distance, from where the spectacle of camp life showed itself as in a panorama. He liked the many log-hut villages he could see from a distance; "Some of the camps are quite large," he wrote. "I amuse myself by examining one of them a mile or so off through a strong glass. Some of the men are cooking, others washing cleaning their clothes—others playing ball, smoking lazily, lounging about. I watch the varied performance long. It is better than any play."[4]

Although there were field hospitals to visit, they were nearly empty. The wounded would not reappear in large numbers until spring brought new battles; he saw some men weak with diarrhea ("the great disease of the army," Walt noted), but even the sick were scarce now, the worst cases having been sent to Washington.[5] It was a moment when war seemed almost an idyll. The men of Brooklyn's 14th Regiment, in their distinctive red uniform pants, were guarding the town, and "they have a theatre of their own here. They give musical performances, nearly everything done capitally. Of course the audience is a jam. It is good sport to attend one of these entertainments . . . I like to look around at the soldiers, and the general collection in front of the curtain, more than the scene on the stage."[6]

While Walt was admiring the troops, George was home in Brooklyn on his reenlistment furlough. At Uris's Dance Academy, the evening of February 11, he was the guest of honor at a gala celebrating the veterans of the 51st, the *Eagle* reported. Captain Whitman had recently received his second gift of a sword in recognition of his military exploits. He was the "observed of all observers," the *Eagle* said, noting that the "tables were spread in artistic style by Messrs. Johnson & Merritt, of the 'City Oyster House,'" and that a number of ladies were among the guests. The 9th Corps, of which the 51st was one of about fifty regiments, was trying to replenish itself through recruitment. A major offensive was soon to come, although not until the weather improved—spring would be when to strike at a weakened, sometimes despairing Confederacy, its ragged soldiers made to winter over on short rations, its leadership now conscious of long-term disadvantages vis-à-vis the richer, more populous North. With what Mark Twain, in a different context, described as "the calm confidence of a pilgrim with four aces," Ulysses Grant, newly appointed general in chief of all Union forces, had assembled a leadership group he believed could at last win the war. Sherman would be Grant's successor in charge of the western armies, which would march south from Tennessee into Georgia; Phil Sheridan would assume command of cavalry in the Army of the Potomac, bringing his bold marauding style to the fight in the East.[7]

Walt gave a sense of Grant's purposeful mien and of overall Northern aims in a letter he wrote his mother on April 19:

> Well . . . we have commenced . . . & what [the new season] will bring forth who can tell?—the campaign . . . is expected here to be more active & severe than any yet . . . Grant is determined to bend every thing to take Richmond & break up the banditti of scoundrels that have stuck themselves up there as a "government"—he is earnest about it, his whole soul & all his thoughts night & day are upon it—he is probably the most in earnest of any man in command or in the government either—that's something, ain't it, Mother—[8]

Following his Culpepper idyll, Walt plunged again into the hospitals, but his spirits proved less resilient than before. "Mother, it is serious times," he wrote his main correspondent. "I do not feel to fret or whimper, but . . . I dare say, Mother, I feel the reality more than some because I [am] in the midst of its saddest results so much."[9] On March 31 he wrote, "I have been in the midst of suffering & death for two months worse than ever," and a week later, "O it is terrible, and getting worse, worse, worse."[10] Whether it was seeing a particular suffering soldier that pushed him over some inner limit is hard to tell. His letters of 1864 are often querulous, and he confessed, "I feel lately as though I must have some intermission."[11] He had recently been with a boy "very sick of brain fever . . . only 19, & . . . so good," who raved for eight days and then died. "[I]t was very sad . . . his talk was so affecting it kept the tears in my eyes."[12]

George Whitman, in his active soldiering, had probably seen as much of the butchery. Yet, for all his campaigning, George did not become downhearted in the spring of 1864, as he, like Walt, sensed the gathering of forces for a new and yet more terrible mass effort. As a company commander he might well have thought over "the sights I have myself seen," as his poet brother often did, but his different role required of him another demeanor. Walt, in his hospital work, was developing and deepening an idea about death that had been present in his poetry since the 1850s, an attitude of mystic acceptance, soon to find classic expression in his last great poem, on the death of Lincoln. For that very reason, his hand-wringing letters in the spring of 1864 are puzzling. And they were significant—by the end of June, he had talked himself into an emotional collapse, one that required him to retreat to Brooklyn for the better part of a year.

George, his reenlistment holiday over in late February, returned to the field, his regiment now moderately strengthened. The 51st traveled to Kentucky and Tennessee, then returned east as the 9th Army Corps rejoined the Army of the Potomac. On April 25, the two brothers met in the middle of an enormous crowd of bluecoats passing in review down Fourteenth Street, Washington. Walt described it to "Dearest Mother":

> Burnside's army passed through here yesterday—I saw George & walked with him in the regiment for some distance & had quite a talk—he is very well, he is very much tanned & looks hardy, I told him all the latest news from home—George stands it very well, & looks & behaves the same good & noble fellow he always was & . . . will be.[13]

With John Burroughs, Walt had been scanning the mass of soldiers for three hours before the 51st came along:

> I joined [George] just before they came to where the President & Gen Burnside were standing with others on a [hotel] balcony, & the interest of seeing me &c. made George forget to notice the President & salute him—he was a little annoyed at forgetting it—I called his attention to it, but we had passed a little too far on, & George wouldn't turn round even ever so little.[14]

On that afternoon, the regiment was ten days out from the Battle of the Wilderness. "Mother, it is very different to see a real army of fighting men, from one of those shows . . . on fort Greene," Walt told her:

> ranks after ranks of our own dearest blood of men, mostly young . . . worn & sunburnt & sweaty, with well worn clothes & their bundles & knapsacks, tin cups & some with frying pans . . . nothing real neat about them except their muskets [which are] clean & bright as silver . . . I saw Fred McReady & Capt Sims, & Col LeGendre &c—I

don't know exactly where Burnside's army is going . . . only that there is without doubt to be a terrible campaign.[15]

As much as any civilian of the era, Walt knew the ordinary soldier's lot; sympathized with him; conjoined a poet's insight with pertinent information gathered from newspapers and from thousands of intimate encounters with servicemen. To his customary feeling for rough American lads, his identification with a younger brother needs to be added when toting up the reasons to declare him the war's most knowledgeable noncombatant. And yet, as he marched alongside George as if a member of the regiment himself on that fair, late-April day, he was not truly of them.

It was less because he wore no uniform and had never seen combat, even "through a strong glass," than because the enterprise of war remained for him anomalous, even nonsensical. The mysterious way in which the foul reality of war sometimes, for some men, calls to them the way nothing else can—yields moments of weighty definition in which they act in ways that they can never forget—was a subject that Walt occasionally studied at, but that finally he wished to know little of. The "real war" that would never get in the books included a warrior's ordinary psychology. John W. De Forest, the author of *Miss Ravenel's Conversion* and a veteran of Vicksburg and other engagements, published sketches in *Harper's Weekly* that described his defining experiences of leading men in combat. About his own first taste of battle he wrote, "The terror . . . is not an abiding impression, but comes and goes like throbs of pain . . . this is especially the case with veterans who have learned to know when there is pressing danger and when not; the moment a peril is past they are as tranquil as if it had never come near."[16]

To keep the men advancing, De Forest joked with them; yelled at them; on occasion, hit one with the flat of his sword. His men felt a special tension when under fire yet prevented from firing back; once able to fire their weapons, they had joyous relief.

De Forest claimed, "Nothing is more confounding, fragmentary, incomprehensible, than a battle as one sees it." Yet moment by moment there is sharp clarity, as in a series of stop-action photos, and his descriptions of battles highlight special moments that seared themselves into his awareness and memory—for instance,

[A Confederate colonel] stood gazing at us, while his men thronged by him, and so standing received a bullet through the head. When our men reached him he was lying on his back and facing us, his head supported by a thorn bush, his handsome face grey with death, and one eye lying on his cheek. He seemed to be about thirty years old, a man of noble height.[17]

De Forest, in the sketches, made combat sound doable. Figuring that he had at least a fair chance of surviving, he simply got on with it, as did most soldiers.*

Also part of a soldier's ordinary psychology were moods of extreme fury and something like group psychosis. Union major R. R. Dawes, who led men of the 6th Wisconsin at Antietam, wrote an account in which a mad intensity seems to have touched everyone, from the highest officer on down:

Colonel Bragg . . . with his usual battle ardor, ordered the regiment forward. We climbed the fence, moved across the open space, and pushed on into the corn-field . . . the companies of the right wing received a deadly fire from the woods . . . Meanwhile, I halted the left wing . . . As we appeared . . . a long line of men in butternut and gray rose up from the ground. Simultaneously, the hostile battle lines opened a tremendous fire upon each other. Men, I cannot say fell; they were knocked out of the ranks by dozens. But we . . . pushed on, loading, firing, and shouting . . . There was . . . great hysterical excitement, eagerness to go forward, and a reckless disregard . . . Every body tears cartridges, loads, passes guns . . . The soldier who is shooting is furious in his energy. The soldier who is shot looks around for help with an imploring agony of death on his face . . . The men are loading and firing with demoniacal fury and shouting and laughing hysterically, and the whole field before us is covered with rebels fleeing for life.[18]

---

*De Forest, a company commander just like George Whitman, did not have as extensive an experience of combat, nor did he ever deal with slaughter traps such as those George encountered at Fredericksburg and at Burnside's Bridge, Antietam.

Other participant-witnesses also recalled the onset of this functional madness. David Thompson, a private with the 9th New York, fought near Burnside's Bridge; just as the savage encounter at the Cornfield was dying down at around one P.M. on September 17, Thompson's unit came into play. Following the taking of the soon-to-be-famous stone bridge, Thompson and his comrades crossed Antietam Creek and fought their way uphill, traveling several hundred yards toward an enemy battery. Ordered to take it, Thompson and comrades came under sharp enfilading fire from their left, then hugged the ground in an upward-sloping field, the "shallow undulation[s]" of furrows affording them some cover.[19] The "firing became more rapid," Thompson recalled,

the situation desperate and exasperating to the last degree. Human nature was on the rack, and there burst forth from it the most vehement, terrible swearing I have ever heard . . . the order to charge came just after . . . as we rose and started all the fire that had been held back so long was loosed . . . The mental strain was so great that I saw at that moment the singular effect mentioned . . . in the life of Goethe on a similar occasion—the whole landscape for an instant turned slightly red.[20]

Of 600 healthy men who crossed the creek at three o'clock that afternoon, the 9th lost 211. Thompson ended the day under a locust tree, hearing bullets snip the leaves, and speculating on

the impatience with which men clamor, in dull times, to be led into a fight . . . The truth is, when bullets are whacking against tree-trunks and solid shot are cracking skulls like egg-shells, the consuming passion . . . is to get out of the way. Between the physical fear of going forward and the moral fear of turning back, there is a predicament of exceptional awkwardness.[21]

Although emotionally stretched to the limits that spring, Walt was feeling poetically ambitious. The time had come to see a new book into print, he told his mother. In early April he wrote, "I want to come on in a month, & try to print my 'Drum Taps'—I think it may be a success pecuniarily," and he announced the same plan to George in a letter, as if to commit himself by telling the whole family of his goal.[22]

The previous fall, after months of no poetry, he had composed the elegy now known as "Vigil Strange I Kept on the Field One Night," recording two separate drafts in a four-inch homemade notebook.[23] It was an exercise in getting just the right tone. The poem, about an older soldier burying a boyish comrade, could not be too intimate (Walt deleted terms such as "my sweetest" and "dearest" in his second draft) but neither could it be too distanced (he added terms of direct address, such as "you" and "your," several times in his revisions).[24] The phrases "*your* dear eyes" and "One touch of *your* hand to mine, O boy" appear in the poem as published in 1865, but "When you my darling fell in the battle" became "When you, my son and my comrade, dropt at my side." The poem is packed with dignified feeling. The old soldier stops with his wounded friend, then speeds away as the battle sweeps him up, returning to find his "son of responding kisses" cold and dead. Wrapping him in an army blanket, he buries him in a "rude-dug" grave.

The inspiration for the poem may have come from an incident that Walt had heard about before he ever came to Washington, and that he recorded in another notebook. "William Giggee," the entry reads, "Sept 18th, '62. I heard of poor Bill's death . . . shot on Pope's retreat—Arthur took him in his arms, and he died . . . Arthur buried him himself—he dug his grave."[25] This burial was similar to many thousands of other impromptu burials, North and South, over the course of the war. Soldiers had a horror of dying anonymously, and the war's battlefields showed sometimes appalling evidence of well-meaning if hurried efforts to accord fallen comrades some final decency. At the Wilderness, soldiers going into action on May 6, 1864, realized that the Battle of Chancellorsville had been fought on virtually the same ground just the year before: "The men who had fallen in that fierce fight had apparently been buried where they fell, and buried hastily," according to a Union artilleryman named Frank Wilkeson. "Many polished skulls lay on the ground. Leg bones, arm bones, and ribs could be found . . . Toes of shoes . . . bits of faded, weather-worn uniforms, and occasionally a grinning, bony, fleshless face peered through" the earth where Wilkeson and his comrades rested, before being called to the front lines themselves.[26]

If Walt had served as an ordinary soldier, he might have thought twice about basing a poem on so dubious an interment. Yet it is not the rude grave digging but the "vigil strange" that forms the actual subject of his poem. Having returned to find his comrade now dead, the narrator describes a

> Vigil wondrous and vigil sweet, there in the fragrant silent night;
> But not a tear fell, not even a long-drawn sigh—Long, long I
>   gazed;
> Then on the earth partially reclining, sat by your side, leaning my
>   chin in my hands;
> Passing sweet hours, immortal and mystic hours with you,
>   dearest comrade—Not a tear, not a word;
> Vigil of silence, love and death[27]

The narrator's thoughts as he reclines, chin propped, are suggested in the poem but not directly described. Presumably they concern recent events ("I could not save you, swift was your death") and the men's friendship ("I faithfully loved you and cared for you living—I think we shall surely meet again"), but the silent vigil, the act of communing with a corpse, is asserted to be meaningful in itself.

Walt had been sitting, if not reclining, beside many men as they passed over. The death in New York of a young friend, Charles Chauncey, in August 1863 had caused him to pause and meditate in a way that he described at some length, as if to make a record of its specialness:

Dear friend [he wrote to Hugo Fritsch, another Manhattan intimate], the same evening I received your letter, I saw in the New York papers . . . the announcement of . . . Chauncey's death. When I went up to my room that night towards 11 I took a seat by the open window in the splendid soft moonlit night, and . . . devoted to the dead boy the silent cheerful tribute of an hour or so of floating thought about him, & whatever rose up from the thought of him . . . [recalling] his looks, his handsome face, his hilarious fresh ways . . . his voice, his blonde hair . . . his caprices . . . how we spoke together impromptu, no introduction . . . he with his affectionate heart thought so well of me, & I loved him then, & love him now.[28]

Clearly, "floating" thought could go almost anywhere—it was not necessarily pious, or mournful. It could lead to memories of drinking bouts and boisterous dinners

at Pfaff's [Tavern] . . . O how charming those early times, adjusting our friendship . . . for I believe we all loved each other more than we supposed—Chauncey was frequently the life & soul of these gatherings . . . full of sparkle, & . . . really witty—then for an exception he would have a mood come upon him & right after the outset of our party, he would grow still & cloudy & up & unaccountably depart—but these were seldom.[29]

"Hugo, that's the way I sat there Wednesday night," Walt concluded, ". . . the pleasant Virginia breeze coming up the Potomac . . . and certainly without what they call mourning thought of the boy."

Thought of him at length, but without grieving or praying. As in "Vigil Strange," the session of warmhearted free association was conducted without tears; it was "cheerful" and, depending on the nature of the intimacies that Walt had shared with Chauncey, possibly erotic. Walt drew on his era's fascination with the corpses of loved ones, and with threshold experiences at the moment of death, to posit a way of mourning that was familiar but novel, ritualistic but open to discovery. He hesitated even to call it "mourning," since mourning usually smacks of some degree of falsity and physical constraint. Instead, he simply followed the thought of young Chauncey wherever it went, seated, like some maiden in a love-poem, by a window in the moonlight, caressed by a river breeze.

Two years later, when it was time to mourn Lincoln, his poetic register would be vastly deeper, more resonant and darker, but still it would be informed by the same impulse of freedom, his thoughts floating as they sought images strong enough to bring comprehension and solace. But that was the final loss, the loss of an adored national father, his remains laid alongside those of a generation of slaughtered sons, and to begin to reckon it would require something other than the ordinary way with death.

G ENERAL GRANT'S STRATEGY, the plan behind the spring 1864 offensive, grew out of his experiences in the west, at Vicksburg and earlier. Grant's bravery and coolheadedness, and his willingness to press the fight, had won Lincoln's notice. He was a main author of victories in Tennessee (Fort Henry, Fort Donelson) in early 1862 and the leading Union general at the Battle of Shiloh (April 6–7), where his preference for playing offense almost led to catastrophe. Disinclined to consider possible rebel attacks when he could plan attacks of his own, he allowed his five forward divisions to be taken more or less by surprise by a rebel assault; the Federals spent the first day of Shiloh, consequently, fighting holding actions and retreating, sometimes orderly, sometimes in panic, along a front five miles long.[1]

Grant soon put himself personally in harm's way, visiting each of his divisional commanders in the course of the bloody first day, to see how their sections of the line were faring. Grant's opposite number, Confederate general Albert Sidney Johnston, died of a bullet wound to his leg in midafternoon; fatal wounds to generals on either side of the struggle were common, indeed, Civil War generals suffered more casualties, on a percentage basis, than did any other rank of officer.[2]

George Whitman's regiment did not fight at Shiloh. But the war the 51st fought for the next three years was born at Shiloh, the first mass slaughter (twenty thousand killed and wounded) and a titanic, prolonged tussle between vast armies able and in a mood to devastate each other. Nearly one hundred thousand men took part, and the thousands seriously wounded on the first day mostly lay out, in a torrential rain, until dawn on April 7 brought fresh assaults in the other direction, Union troops forcing Confederates back the way they had come.

No important geographic or logistical objective was taken. Instead, heavy punishment was meted out by each side to the young men of the other. The scale and intensity of the battle were what mattered. Each side proved that it would kill and die to the utmost. General Grant was not the hero of the day in the Northern press, although his words, after the near-disastrous first twelve hours ("Retreat? *No.* I propose to attack at daylight and whip them"), became famous, and he was ceded some respect for having refused to collapse.

Sherman was the day's particular hero. Grant, forced to retire from the prewar army because of his drinking, given a second chance in life with the arrival of the sectional conflict and the need for trained professionals to organize masses of green recruits, saw in Sherman a kindred personality, someone stiffened in his resolve in moments of crisis. He credited Sherman with holding the line on Shiloh's first day. In his *Memoirs*, Grant recalled that he had visited his divisional commanders to offer advice, and he remarked, "I never deemed it important to stay long with Sherman."[3] Sherman had three horses shot out from under him and was wounded in the hand. He withstood concentrated enemy fire without becoming rattled—some observers said he looked calmer than usual at such times. A general senior to Sherman, John A. McLernand, also in charge of a division, clung to Sherman all day and allowed him to direct McLernand's division as well as his own, in unconscious tribute to Sherman's greater presence of mind.[4]

Sherman found himself at this battle, both as field commander and as thinker about the war. He had warned about the immense resources and resistant spirit of the South, foreseeing a vicious struggle if the North were to try to subdue it; called insane for his worries in 1861, he had the pleasure of seeing his critics confounded by the gross fact of a battle like Shiloh, which convinced Grant, too, that the only way to victory lay through total war. The enemy's means of resistance had to be crushed. No single victory, no matter how ringing, would convince the South that rebellion was a false idea. Grant's strategy of 1864 to '65, in consequence—a combination of marauding on the grand scale with trench warfare and other attritional tactics—aimed to disable an entire society.

The remorselessness of the Union approach had echoes in a Southern bloody-mindedness that dated from before the war, and in the idealization of Lee's most effective subordinate commander, Thomas J. "Stonewall" Jackson, whose fondness for destruction was legendary.[5] Jackson's preference was for taking no prisoners—even unarmed captives should be executed, he sometimes said, to show the North the cost of real war.[6] As a commanding officer, Jackson punished deserters with death and put his men in irons for minor infractions; he was at least as hungry to seize the offensive as Grant, arguing for invasions of the North that would lay waste to its cities and see the Southern forces "subsist[ing] on the country we traverse [while] making unrelenting war amidst their homes, [to] force the people of the North to understand what it will cost them to hold the South in the Union at bayonet's point."[7]

Jackson's tactical brilliance, displayed in the Shenandoah Valley campaign, in the Seven Days Battles, at Antietam, and at Chancellorsville, where he was fatally wounded, was the heart of his resonant reputation. But his uncommon zeal for destructive war won him admiration in the North as well as at home, with some Union opinion makers claiming to recognize in his wrathful efficiency a distinctly American ability to get the job done.[8]

Abraham Lincoln, as the months wore on, became a firm convert to the idea of total war. From the time of the victory at Fort Donelson, the president knew he had an unusually vigorous commander in Grant, whom he promoted to major general; and after Shiloh, when some said that Grant had been drinking or accused him of incompetence for having allowed his divisions to be surprised, Lincoln commented, "I can't spare this man; he fights."[9]

For George Whitman, the drama of high strategy expressed itself in specific orders; in removal to particular pieces of contested terrain; in the deaths of many comrades. The army corps of which the 51st was a very small part (1.4 percent of a fighting force of over twenty-five thousand) remained under the command of General Burnside, whose position in the service was anomalous. By spring 1864, Burnside had a reputation for tardy and misconceived responses to the challenges of battle. Grant, in the *Memoirs*, speaks of him as a man who enjoyed the respect of his peers but who was unsuited to head an army. Given the right assignment, though, he was useful. As commander of the Department of the Ohio in 1863, he defended Knoxville ably against a siege directed by James Longstreet, Lee's most capable corps commander after Jackson. An awkward situation developed from the fact of Burnside's seniority to General George Gordon Meade; Meade, in nominal charge of the Army of the Potomac, had control of three army corps (the 2nd, 5th, and 6th, each with about twenty-five thousand men), but Burnside's 9th was an independent unit, directly answerable only to Grant.

In practice, this nicety of lines of command made for confusion and error. Burnside's corps functioned sometimes as a fifth wheel, sometimes as a resented secondary force not trusted to take the lead in the early stages of battle, but expected to respond nimbly to assignments requiring the men to die in large numbers. The opening of what came to be known as the Overland Campaign, the first week of May 1864, was the Battle of the Wilderness. Burnside's forces came to the fight late— while Meade's fourteen divisions were crossing the Rapidan River on May 4, Burnside's four were still mostly north of the Rappahannock, a day's march away.[10] The 9th thus played no appreciable role on May 5.* Horace Porter, an aide to Grant, wrote that he was awakened at four A.M. on May 6 "by the sound of Burnside's forces moving along the Germanna Road [a wood-plank road running southeast from a nearby ford on the Rapidan]. They had been marching since one A.M., hurrying on" to take up a support position near the battle's forward lines.[11]

George, a company commander of the 1st Brigade, 2nd Division, was traveling light—knowing that he was headed for a big fight, he had taken the precaution of storing his trunk in Washington, and he wrote Walt a note with an address on F Street, in case he should be unable to reclaim it later himself.[12] Following the memorable tramp through the capital, the 51st camped in northern Virginia for several days—hopes that they were headed to North Carolina, to join a campaign on Richmond from the south ("by way of Goldsborough while the Potomac Army makes another push for Richmond by the front door," as George put it), had faded. They were about to knock on that front door themselves. George had recently laid eyes on the fabled Grant, lately given

---

*This was as much because of command confusions as because of Burnside's tardiness.

the rank of lieutenant general—a distinction accorded only one other American soldier to that date, George Washington. Grant "paid us a visit [in Annapolis]," George wrote his mother. "There was no grand Review as is generally the case, but the Regiments just fell in line and Grant rode along and looked . . . and then went on about his business."[13]

On the morning of the sixth, George's brigade entered the low, furiously dense, newly leafed pine-and-oak Wilderness forest. The battle was already fully joined.* Burnside had been traveling with Robert Potter that morning, and he passed along Grant's direct order—that Potter's division and two others should deploy in the scrub forest, heading southwesterly until they engaged the enemy. Burnside's corps had been expected to come into play at dawn, as part of a general attack against Lee's forward position, along an east–west route called the Orange Plank Road.[14] Burnside's slowness had disappointed that expectation, but now Potter sent his brigades down a forest path known as Parker's Store Road. A squad of Yankee scouts led the division across a creek and into closely grown, bramble-choked oak woods, down into a ravine, and up a ridge, in places engaging with Confederate skirmishers, who gave way before them. Arriving at the edge of an upward sloping farm field with a whitewashed cabin on a rise, the scouts saw a column of infantry emerging from woods to the southeast, the sun's position (in their eyes) not allowing easy identification of it as either rebel or Federal.[15]

It was rebel—South Carolina troops supported by artillery, which unlimbered and sent canister crashing into the trees surrounding Potter's position, which had formed up behind the scouts. Potter's formal report, submitted several weeks later, made specific mention of Whitman's 1st Brigade in this first sharp passage of battle. "The enemy opened a brisk fire from their battery and from small-arms fire," he wrote. "I moved the line forward to the edge of the wood and formed the First Brigade to cover the left." A few hours later, in a more prolonged encounter a mile away, Potter again used his old regiment in much the same fashion, in a forward position to counter possible flanking attacks.[16]

That more prolonged, bloodier passage of battle, close to another farmstead nearer the Plank Road, involved the 51st in a controversial

---

*One hundred seventy-five thousand men fought at the Wilderness, both sides considered.

maneuver. Brigadier General Potter, at the first farm, had been on the point of charging the enemy when he received an order to withdraw; his division began to move in an easterly direction through "a dense wood and an almost impenetrable undergrowth," he wrote, so dense and so impenetrable that it took his force of 5,500 three hours to cover less than a mile.[17] The woods were not only closely grown, they were on fire. Dry leaves and pine branches on the forest floor had ignited from muzzle flashes, and whole trees were being consumed, filling ravines and hollows with sweetish, roiling, obscuring smoke. "On arriving near the new position," Potter reported, "I reformed as quickly as possible and moved to the attack, being entirely unable to see anything."[18] By some instinct he had halted his men only a few hundred feet from the enemy's concealed trenches.[19]

Potter deployed for attack. The 51st took up a position near the head of the most forward column, adjacent to a bulge in the enemy's lines. The combat that ensued had a phantasmal quality. The rebel forces were close, but largely unseen; there was abundant cover, but lead flew so thickly as to be almost inescapable. It tore the leaf canopy off trees, stripped bark in sheets, and scythed whole trunks in half. "The musketry . . . was one solid, savage crash, crash," one Union artilleryman recalled of the fighting in a neighboring sector, "extending along a line over two miles in length."[20] A color sergeant recalled, "Both sides stand and take the fearful fire, and the whole line seems to be one vast sheet of flame."[21] Frank Wilkeson, the soldier who had rested the night before on grinning skulls from the Battle of Chancellorsville, described the company commanders, men like George Whitman, whose job it was to stiffen the resolve of men convinced that they were about to die: "We could hear them close behind us, or in line with us, saying, 'Steady, men, steady, steady, steady!' as one speaks to frightened and excited horses."[22]

Headlong charges into point-blank fire sometimes succeeded. Then, overrunning an enemy position, the briefly victorious force would seize captives and send them quickly to the rear, before being countercharged and, sometimes, captured themselves. To find oneself flanked or uncovered and exposed to fire from an unexpected direction, given the restricted visibility, was common. Potter seized the offensive. The enemy "were posted on the opposite side of a swampy ravine," he wrote, "and were intrenched. After sharp firing at pretty close range we charged . . .

and got into their rifle-pits in some places, but were unable to maintain our footing and fell back. The charge was twice renewed, but . . . we did not succeed in getting possession of the enemy's line."[23]

This terse account, part of a five-page report on three sequential major battles (the Wilderness, Spotsylvania Court House, Cold Harbor), was much elaborated, in the decades to come, by soldiers claiming to know what had *really* happened on the field. Potter's forward brigade near the second farmstead consisted of the 36th Massachusetts, the 45th Pennsylvania, and the 51st New York, with a fourth regiment in reserve. A veteran of the 36th Massachusetts, Henry S. Burrage, wrote a history of his regiment that was published in 1884; it shows his unit taking a lead role and covering itself with glory.*

No doubt the 36th did display unusual courage that day. But according to a recent history of the Wilderness—published in 1996, and relying substantially on reports written by men of the 36th and the 45th, but not on any by men of the 51st—the 51st did not perform at all well at the second farm. This history observes, "The 51st New York streamed to the rear in panic," leaving its account pretty much at that.[24] From its position hard by the enemy salient, the 51st had responded to sharp fire from its left by pulling back to face in that direction. After an assault by a different Union brigade, Potter's 1st rushed boldly ahead (at least, the 36th Massachusetts and the 45th Pennsylvania regiments did), scattering the enemy and spilling over his works.[25]

There is no reason to doubt this account, although the absence of sources from within the 51st may not be irrelevant to its general tenor. The 51st lacked a historian of its own. In the coming decades, no one would step forward to write a regimental history such as were written by loyal members of many other units—accounts that modern historians, trying to get the real war into the books, often rely on, albeit with careful cross-referencing of other kinds of sources. It is possible that the 51st did stream to the rear in panic; some situations call for nothing so much as a run-like-hell response. Whether true panic characterized the

---

*Another source for what may have happened on May 6 near the second farm is an article published in 1925 by a former member of the 45th Pennsylvania, Ephraim E. Myers. It vaunts the 45th.

streaming—or whether there was a mix of running and walking, with the carrying of wounded comrades and occasional pauses to turn and fire on the foe, to discourage pursuit—is a question of interpretation.*

In a letter written six weeks after this battle, George seemed to anticipate the 51st's lack of a historical advocate. "[N]ow as I write there is a very savage fight going on in our front," he told his mother:

> I think by the fireing that our boys are pushing the enemy back and unless the rebs can make a firmer stand than they have made here yet it will not be long before the long coveted City of Petersburg will be in our possession   I notice by the papers that our Corps is very little spoken of, but for all that they have done some splendid fighting, although we seem to be, rather outsiders here in the Army of the Potomac, and Genl Burnside is one of these kind of men that does the work they give him to doo and finds no fault.[26]

George added, generously, "I am sure I dont object to the noble Potomac Army's getting their full share of praise." But Burnside's reputation was disabling. Even should part of his corps manage to achieve something noteworthy, it was likely to be scanted in the press.

Why no one emerged to celebrate the 51st in a regimental history, as happened for hundreds of other units, may have to do with the sheer extent of its service—it had fought almost everywhere, and to write an adequate account would be to write a history of almost the entire war.[27] Banished to the west following 1st Fredericksburg, Burnside's corps

---

*Readers of regimental histories often find that the unit featured in a given book is remarkably effective. Panicked retreats, collapses of line, capture by the enemy due to being flanked, and other bad outcomes tend to be ascribed to other groups. By the same token, triumphant outcomes tend to be credited to the unit whose name appears in a book's title, even when other regiments contributed to the result. The question of who took Burnside's Bridge, for example—whether it was the 51st New York under Robert Potter, or the 51st Pennsylvania under John Hartranft, that was first onto and across the span—was hotly debated at the time and for many years afterward. George Whitman wrote a newspaper article taking credit for his own regiment; the author of an able history of the Pennsylvania regiment, Thomas H. Parker, as categorically took credit for his.

campaigned widely there; other banished Union Army corps (the 11th and the 12th, for example) were not brought back east after having once lost favor. Why no one in the 51st put pen to paper to record the regiment's contributions may also have to do with an unusual circumstance— that there was already an able chronicler attached to the 51st, someone who had published well-researched versions of parts of the unit's stellar history. These versions, written by Captain Whitman's poet brother, had been read widely in camp when they appeared in the New York papers, and they may have created an impression of Walt as the regiment's special friend, which he certainly was. Moreover, Walt had assembled extensive notes, with a view to writing a full unit history some day, and he had often interviewed and corresponded with officers of the 51st other than his younger brother.

The diary that George kept—a sketch of events, hardly more—ended in 1863. George may have stopped writing because he stopped feeling the novelty of what he was going through, like many other well-traveled soldiers. The accounts of the battles of 1864 that soldiers in the field wrote are less vivid than those of earlier fights; in letters home they reported less on their feelings and more on military maneuvers, and the carnage was by then taken for granted.[28] George's letters remained remarkably consistent over the course of the war, however—they had never dwelt much in raw carnage, possibly out of respect for Mrs. Whitman's anxieties, and the reports of clever maneuvers, a regular feature of even the first letters, continued. He was close mouthed in his account of what had happened on May 6. It may be that there was no way to make a rout look attractive, but the 51st had in fact suffered the highest number (and highest percentage) of soldiers killed of the four regiments of Potter's 1st Brigade.[29] His own company lost half its men. That was damage in the grim Fredericksburg range.

Now the soldiering took on a different character. On assuming a position on a battleground, troops on either side immediately entrenched, using bayonets and tin cups to dig with if they had no better tools. Lieutenant Colonel Theodore Lyman, an aide to General Meade, described this general change in a letter written after the Wilderness: "It is a rule that, when the rebels halt, the first day gives them a good rifle-pit; the second, a regular infantry parapet with artillery . . . the third a parapet with [an abatis] in front and entrenched batteries behind."[30]

After the Wilderness, Grant did not pull back across the Rapidan to allow his forces to lick their wounds. Instead, he pressed on to Spotsylvania
Court House, seven miles farther south, in a race with elements of Lee's
army, which won the race by a nose and threw up strong breastworks
northwest of the little crossroads town. As before, Burnside's forces came
into position more slowly or, as it seemed to some observers, reluctantly,
than other units. Burnside was unsure of his role in the campaign's next
act, or he may have been pouting, since Meade conveyed his instructions
to his own corps commanders but often left Burnside out of the loop.[31] On
May 11, a day when cold, pounding rain arrived after two weeks of hot
weather, the 9th Corps occupied trenches along the east flank of the
Muleshoe, a thumb-shaped, thousand-yard rebel salient. Potter's division,
rain-drenched and exhausted, moved out of its trenches at four A.M. By
five "the engagement had become very hot," Potter recorded in his official
report. Burnside's divisions were acting in support of the main attack on
the salient, aimed at its northern end. His orders, direct from Grant, declared, "You will move against the enemy with your entire force promptly
and with all possible vigor at precisely four o'clock." To enforce his
orders—ostensibly, to explain them better—Grant had sent two of his
staff to Burnside; although they rode herd on him in the coming hours,
and although he mostly submitted to them, Grant was never satisfied with
the 9th Corps' performance at Spotsylvania.[32]

"We [took] two lines of detached rifle-pits and some prisoners," Potter
recorded, "and assaulted their main line, a portion of which, we carried."[33] But Confederate reinforcements counterattacked, and George
and the other men under Potter fell back, fighting in mud and through
pine thickets, to establish a defensive line. Potter wrote, "Severe fire was
kept up all day from both sides," adding that the armies were only yards
apart in places.[34] They fired on each other implacably, achieving wall-of-
flame effects that caused one soldier to declare, "It is impossible to tell
how any man lived through that hour." Another Union soldier recalled,
"It was here we piled dead bodies one on top the other to lie behind for
protection."[35] Potter's brigades yielded ground slowly and bitterly, their
situation compromised by the length of the line that Burnside had been
ordered to maintain (over a mile, with three divisions to cover this
length; in the attack on the north of the salient, Union commanders had
six divisions with which to cover a front a quarter mile long).[36]

One of the Confederate dead, Spotsylvania Court House.

The stretched-out 9th Corps was vulnerable to flanking attacks, but still there was no catastrophic breakthrough. Burnside, ordered, in no uncertain terms, to send a division north, to connect with the main attack force, declined to. The infamous savagery of the fighting on the north of the salient, one of the several "Bloody Angles" of the war, tended to overshadow the fighting in Burnside's sector. Still, casualties were equivalent. The 9th Corps lost 2,534 men (killed, wounded, and

missing) on May 12. The 2nd Army Corps, under Major General Win-
field Scott Hancock, in action mostly at the Bloody Angle, lost 2,537.[37]

George estimated that the 51st had lost twenty men. Spotsylvania was
not yet over—there would be more fighting, sometimes with heavy
losses, for another week. One measure of the decimation that the regiment suffered is to be found in a letter that George wrote his mother on
May 20. On the eighteenth, the 51st had had a "brush" with destruction,
he allowed, when pinned down for eleven hours by a large force of entrenched enemy; George's company, which he had been commanding
now for a year and a half, on average a force of around forty men, was
afterward down to eight.[38]

A N AILING WALT waited in Washington in a boardinghouse on Pennsylvania Avenue, where he had moved May 21. His old place on Sixth Street had been sold out from under him, and he felt oppressed by the "very bad air" at his new digs, close to the foul city canal.[1] What he was waiting for was news of his brother, or—the worst sort of news— George himself, brought to Washington with a wound, like Colonel Le- Gendre or Fred McReady. "I shall certainly remain here while the thing remains undecided," Walt wrote Mrs. Whitman, the thing being Grant's campaign against Richmond.[2] In four weeks, forty-four thousand Union troops fell.[3] Seven thousand were lost in eight minutes at the Battle of Cold Harbor.[4] Walt was mentally already back home in Brooklyn—he warned the family that "I am going to put up a lot of my old things in a box & send them . . . by express"—but concern for George kept him in the capital.

Doctors he knew now strongly advised him to stay clear of the hospi- tals, after he described to them his symptoms of weakness and constant pressures in the head. He may have needed this official warning to begin to draw back. On June 3 he wrote, "It is impossible for me to abstain from going to see & minister to certain cases, & that draws me into others, & so on," but by the fourteenth he was announcing, "I send there by a friend every day, I send things & aid to some cases I know . . . but I do not go myself."[5] George wrote home June 1, a letter that Jeff forwarded to Walt on the tenth. This letter, now lost, seems to have given Walt fur- ther permission to withdraw—"It was so good to see his handwriting once more," he told his mother, and within a couple of weeks he had left Washington.

George, although prone to write reassuringly—"We have plenty to eat and get along very well," he reported just after Spotsylvania, adding, "The Army is in first rate spirits and everyone seems confident and hopefull"—was in jeopardy.[6] Beginning on about May 18, he was acting major of the regiment, probably in consequence of Colonel LeGendre's wounding. The curious incidents of the combat he saw at the Wilderness and Spotsylvania—a canteen shot from his hip; his uniform coat shredded, probably by an exploding shell, although he could never say afterward what hit him, or how he escaped death; three comrades shot down by his side—were unknown to the family until a year later.[7] As a good friend said of George, he was "very little of [a] talker," and "never talking of himself."[8] Beginning in mid-June, he was officially commander of the 51st New York.[9] This brought with it the dubious perk of a horse to ride, from whose back it was easy to imagine getting shot; an acquaintance of Walt's, an officer named McKibben, had recently been wounded while riding in sight of the enemy trenches, and George assured the family that "I dont get much chance" to cut a gallant horseback figure.[10]

Cold Harbor, in late May and early June, brought more personal experience of Grantian combat. Rapid mass marches, often through the night; feints and misdirections, as the Federals sidled steadily southeast, trying to get around Lee's flank and closer to Richmond; brutal, high-casualty combat events, premised on entrenchment and mass attack. Union casualties exceeded Confederate by 75 percent for the four weeks beginning at the Wilderness, but Lee would sooner run out of possible recruits with which to make up his losses, and Sherman meanwhile was advancing in Georgia.[11] This summer of titanic military encounters was also the summer of do-or-die political struggle for Lincoln, who faced a serious electoral challenge from his cashiered former general in chief, McClellan, a Democratic contender accurately seen as a friend to the South. A McClellan victory in November would mean an armistice and possibly Southern independence. The Confederacy, therefore, wished ardently for McClellan's success, and Lee saw his task as one largely of buying time, preventing major Northern victories that might swing votes for Lincoln.

At Cold Harbor, two massive armies again faced each other from entrenched positions. "The entire line of this part of the Union army [has been] transformed to diggers," one soldier wrote before the battle, and Potter's division, with the 1st Brigade playing a forward role, dug in and advanced, dug in and skirmished, dug in and attacked, pick and shovel playing as essential a role as rifled musket.[12] Potter, the ablest general in the 9th Corps, used George's brigade as something like shock troops.[13] On May 21, to prepare for a crossing of the Po River on the way south, he sent the 1st ahead to seize a ford and, upon arriving later with the rest of the division, found the rebel forces driven smartly back across the river, the 1st Brigade engaging "very briskly" in a firefight with remnant elements.[14]

At this point, Potter received orders not to cross the Po. Instead, the entire 9th Corps (plus another whole corps, the 6th) slipped past during the night, while the 1st, with a single battery of artillery, provided cover for the column.[15] At Cold Harbor proper, Potter again used the 51st and other units of the 1st Brigade in a forward way, to lead an advance through a swamp. Potter's report makes clear that he relied on this body of men especially:

> I attacked the enemy vigorously with my First Brigade . . . drove their skirmish line across the creek, taking a few prisoners; crossed the creek, drove the enemy from a house and outbuildings and some breast-works within a few yards of the road running to . . . Cold Harbor, on which was their main line. [The 1st] immediately occupied and held this advanced position, from which we . . . completely silenced the enemy's battery.[16]

He concluded, "My losses during the day were quite severe." The fighting in the swamp, beginning around seven A.M., was nightmarish; the marshy ground and undergrowth slowed the 1st just as it came under severe fire, soldiers "going to the knees in mud nearly ever step . . . men falling . . . the dead sinking and the wounded dragged back," as one infantryman recalled.[17]

Breaching the swamp, George's brigade found better footing and advanced on some enemy rifle pits. But they were subject to intense fire from high ground across the Cold Harbor road. To their right, more earthworks and artillery prevented much movement; to their left, the main entrenched line of the rebels, less than two hundred feet away in places, brought them under a killing crossfire. The field that ran up to the road became a slaughter pen.[18] Still, as one Confederate soldier observed, the bluecoats retained extraordinary discipline; "One line would fire and fall down, another step over, fire and fall down, each line getting nearer us, until they got within sixty or seventy-five yards," when they were "cut to pieces so badly, they fell back in a little disorder."[19] This report by an enemy observer—not a Yankee writing his own regiment's history—may perhaps be trusted as an indication of the temper of the 51st and the other units of the 1st Brigade, at least on this day and in this place.

Falling back, George's regiment dug fast with tin dippers, throwing up small mounds of earth for cover. Digging soon became the principal activity of the 51st New York. A few days after Cold Harbor, the depleted regiment was "detached from the Brigade and [began] doing duty as an Engineer Regt," George wrote his mother with relief. Officially, the 51st was now the acting engineers of Potter's 2nd Division. "The most of our work has to be done at night," George explained, "and we often surprise the enemy in the morning, with works that we have made . . . within 4 or 500 yards of their line of battle."[20] Brigadier Potter may have wanted to reward his old regiment for their recent service. Or, he may only have been in need of good earth movers, recognizing in the New York veterans unusually qualified candidates.

Now Grant's forces swung farther south, all the way past Richmond, with its insuperable defenses, to the busy railroad hub twenty miles farther on, Petersburg. The slaughter seen so far in the spring-to-summer campaign—sixty-five thousand killed, wounded, and missing on the Union side; thirty-five thousand on the Southern—induced an understandable horror of further entrenched combat.[21] The works built at Cold Harbor had been ingeniously complex, with "zig-zagged lines within lines, lines protecting . . . lines, [and] lines built to enfilade opposing lines," as one reporter described them.[22] But at Petersburg, both sides had even longer, months, in which to perfect their defenses. George's men may not have enjoyed themselves as much as he seemed to. "Last night I took the Regt up on the line," he wrote Mrs. Whitman, "and worked all night":

We were in a large open plain,   our Batteries were just behind us and the rebel Batteries were just in front . . . and Three or four times during the night the Batteries opened on each other and kept up a pretty sharp fire for 10 or 15 minutes and then they would quiet down again. It was splendid where we was, both parties fired over our heads, but so high that we were in no danger, and . . . could watch the shells bursting in front and rear . . . we could plainly see both lines of skirmishers blazing . . . and could eaisily tell by the direction of the flame . . . which was our line and which the rebs.[23]

In attacks on well-designed, redundant earthworks, the soldiers of 1864 experienced the kind of war that would characterize the twentieth century. Understandably, they came to loathe massed infantry attacks; those who had undertaken such attacks on the orders of superiors who were themselves often absent from the field often displayed far less energy—less of an eagerness to rise up from a prone position on the ground, to run or walk into the enemy's guns—the second or third or tenth time they found themselves in the situation. Grant, in a war of attrition half against his will—his hope had been to draw Lee into the open for one great, enemy-destroying clash—grew more shy of straight-ahead tactics after Cold Harbor, about which he commented, "I regret this assault more than any one I have ever ordered."[24] Still, he ordered more assaults.

Petersburg became a siege that lasted nearly a year. The trenches stretched for ten miles and featured breastworks twenty feet thick, plus walled batteries, forts, moats, bomb-proofs, abatis, and other defensive contrivances.[25] George's letters home suggest emerging routines; on July 26 he wrote, "All quiet in front of Petersburg, and everything going on just the same . . . We came out from the front line, last night and are now at our camp, in the woods about half a mile from the enemy's works."[26] After two days at the front, the regiment returned to camp for forty-eight hours, where "we live very well . . . and are a great deal more comfortable than one would think," he told the family.[27]

Earlier, he had described how "both parties are working away at night, strengthening their lines and as they are so close togather . . . the least unusual noise at night will frequently start the fire along the whole line." The firing was "commenced by the pickets, and soon . . . the Batteries . . . open pretty savage, and the Mortars join in and altogather they manage to kick up a terrible noise but as both parties are behind earthworks the execution done is very slight."[28] The massed stasis at this late stage of war—after three years of an encompassing struggle, a half-million corpses buried and still lying unburied upon the bloodied American field, and anxious leaders in Washington and Richmond ever more eager for a telling stroke—began to generate its own events. In front of Petersburg, George's regiment returned from engineering service to service in the line. They found themselves on a part of the front assigned to Burnside, opposite high ground on which the enemy had built a fortification. Another regiment in the 1st Brigade, the 48th Pennsylvania, from coal-mining Schuylkill County, had worked since late June to dig a tunnel under the rebel redoubt some five hundred feet away. General Burnside's enthusiasm for the project was mild to begin with, but increased as the miners proceeded with great daring, shoring up the long tunnel with timbers scavenged from a nearby bridge, and using surveyor's tools to triangulate precisely under the fort. Here they packed two underground chambers with 320 kegs (four tons) of gunpowder, to be ignited by a long fuse.[29]

Near dawn on July 30, the explosion buried an entire rebel regiment and opened a crater 350,000 cubic feet in volume. Into this breach in the enemy line, a division of 9th Corps troops dawdled rather than rushed, awed by the destruction they had just witnessed and uncertain what to do next. Under the nominal leadership of Brigadier James H. Ledlie, who was absent from the field, the soldiers walked into the crater rather than alongside it, falling victim to intense fire from rebel units forming up along the rim. The "turkey shoot," as a Confederate general later described it, turned a tactical masterstroke into a disaster. Colored troops under General Ferrero (also not on the field) were slaughtered wholesale. George's rapt description of the affair, in a letter to his mother, is the record of a direct participant, but above all it is the work of a veteran officer. His personal losses were large—forty men killed or wounded of his hard-pressed regiment, among them his closest brother-officer, Captain Sims—yet the emotional notes are muted. He says of Sims that he was "acting Lieut Col. and had charge of the right wing, and I was acting Major and had charge of the left," echoing Walt's description of the two officers as doubles of a kind, different in temperament but closely matched as to capacity for command. George wrote, "Poor Cap Sims led the right wing in fine style," allowing himself but a single word of sympathy to suggest what was especially lamentable

Captain Samuel Sims.

about the day—although he did add, in an account of how the wounded were treated, "During the ceesession of hostilities some of our boys went out and brought in the boddy of Capt. Sims and it is now on the way to Brooklyn."[30]

George knew why the assault had failed. "[M]y own opinion is that if some of the men with stars on their shoulders, had led the way the men wouldent have been backward in following them."[31] As usual, Brigadier Potter was on the field, unlike others of his rank, and the 2nd Division fared better than others. Potter sent units in support of the men pinned down in the crater. The 51st, held back at first, went forward around nine A.M. "As soon as the order was given," George wrote, "I jumped up on the breastworks and sung out for the men to follow me, and the way they tumbled over them breastworks wasent slow." The regiment seized some rifle pits directly to its front. It held these entrenchments for two hours, then, "the rebs massed a heavy force, in a ravine just in front of us, but out of our sight, and came down on us like a whirlwind," forcing the regiment back. This was the moment of Sims's death. At about the same time, the regimental commander of the day, Captain John G. Wright, was temporarily paralyzed by an artillery shell. "The Command . . . then devolved upon Captain George W. Whitman," Wright wrote later in his report, "the next senior officer." Wright took note of the gallantry of Whitman's conduct, also reporting the death of Captain Sims, "who fell fighting nobly while endeavoring to check the retreat of a Regiment on our right."[32]

A scene of turmoil and "terrible execution," to borrow George's phrase, the crater was to be avoided, if it were possible to do so with honor. Union losses were more than 4,000 for the day, with 500 prisoners taken, among them 150 U.S. Colored Troops, sure to be accorded especially brutal treatment by their captors. George and the 51st did not so much avoid it, as dance just slightly out of range of the worst. The crater itself "must have been horrible," he wrote Mrs. Whitman. Potter, ordered to bring his division into play, but not in the first wave, may have had time enough to recognize how things were shaping up, and assigning the 51st to take some rifle pits looks in retrospect like a favor to it, whether or not it was so intended.

Grant said of the battle, "It was the saddest affair I have witnessed in the war." His sadness, though, was mostly for reasons of military advantage: "Such opportunity for carrying fortifications," he added, "I have never seen and do not expect again to have."[33] George may have felt a more ordinary sadness. Sparing in the words he used to describe Samuel Sims's death, he was fulsome, relatively speaking, in his description of the suffering of the many wounded. Twice in his letter he imagined conditions inside the crater, where "there was quite a large number of the dead and wounded," and "the day was very hot indeed, and they could not get a drop of water." After the fighting tailed off in the afternoon, the wounded "lay between the rebel lines and ours, and there the poor creatures had to lay . . . untill the afternoon of the next day, when the rebs allowed us to send out a flag of truce to give them . . . water, but they wouldent allow any of them to be removed untill the second day after the fight." To speak of the anonymous wounded in their suffering may have been easier to do than to memorialize a fallen friend; the wounded, as Walt's poetry shows us, were worthy and convenient emblems of all that was being lost, not quite faceless but silent enough to serve all purposes.

WALT'S SOJOURN IN Brooklyn, while George fought at the Crater and elsewhere south of Richmond, was increasingly a comfortable one. At first too sick with "deathly faintness" to get out of bed, he had mostly recovered by July 8, when he went on a carriage ride with brother Jeff. It was his first move outside his mother's house since June 23. "This is the first sickness I have ever had," he wrote Lewy Brown in Washington, "& I find upon trial such things as faintness . . . & trembling & tossing all night, & all day too, are not proper companions for a good union man like myself."[1]

His letters from home show him making light of his illness of headaches and sore throat, but his condition was bothersome enough to lead him to consult a local physician, Dr. Edward Ruggles, a family friend and a voice of sanity during Andrew's final illness the year before.[2] "But I am making too long a story of it," Walt tells Lewy, then goes on to make the story even longer. He is at pains not to be taken for a shirker. He has abandoned the hospitals at the height of the battles, at the very crest of the flood of war wounded, and he wants people to understand that he is not funking it. To William O'Connor he writes, "[M]y physician thinks that time, with the change of locality . . . will make me well, but says my system is probably saturated with the virus of the hospitals &c which eludes ordinary treatment."[3]

He had a poetic purpose, and he wanted to serve it. No doubt his quick recovery was a boon and, in a small way, an embarrassment, as news of the slaughter at Cold Harbor filled the papers. George was in as much danger as ever, but Walt did not hurry to Washington to look out for him—in a letter dated June 25, he explained to his brother that he was sick and had had to come home, and George responded with no hint of reproval, in a note to Mrs. Whitman, "I received a letter from Walt a few days ago . . . I am very sorry to hear [he] is sick but I am glad he is home and I hope by this time he is all right again."[4]

Walt wrote O'Connor, "I intend to move heaven & earth to publish my 'Drum-Taps' as soon as I am able to go around." In late July he added, "I am trying to make arrangements . . . I shall probably try to bring [the book] out myself, stereotype it, & print an edition of 500— I could sell that number by my own exertions in Brooklyn & New York in three weeks."[5] Yet little evidence survives that he worked on the poems or took useful steps to find a publisher. Eight months later, he was still looking for a stereotypist, and an actual contract with a printer, Peter Eckler, was finally signed only on April 1, 1865.[6]

The impediments to writing poetry that he had noted in 1863 were gone now. He was no longer exhausted by constant bedside visiting, nor did the realities of war necessarily burst "the petty bonds of art." He had written well about some aspects of war ("Vigil Strange") and in some moments even imagined that he could harness war's savage power to strike a blow against the "silly little tinkling & tepid" popular poetry of his era, with its "sentimental warm water."[7] He felt the new book inside him—had already written most of it, had left Washington to get on with it—but now he dropped the thread. His round of enjoyable activities may have diverted him. As soon as he was feeling better, he began keeping "old-fashioned hours," he wrote O'Connor, "rise early, dine at 1, & go to bed before 10," although by late summer he was kicking up his heels: "Last night I was with some of my friends" of the circle of men that had included Charles Chauncey, "till late wandering the east side of the City." They had enjoyed themselves in "the lager bier saloons & . . . elsewhere," including "one crowded, low, most degraded place [where] a poor blear-eyed girl [was] bringing beer." This "sad sad" ruin of a girl was wearing a McClellan button. It was "one of those places where the air is full of the scent of low thievery, druggies . . . & prostitution gangrened," he told O'Connor.[8]

His pocket notebooks again record enigmatic meetings with young men, for example, "John Lefferts 11, 23d st stout, Long Island born . . .

Thos Sutherland Oct '64 31 4th av/ . . . Jim brother died in Troy Madison av . . . Frank Henry Waters, 3 23rd st—from Pittsburgh . . ."[9] Among the many reasons for taking a recess in New York may have been a desire to change his luck, and the teeming and remarkably un-war-disturbed city was a place he knew intimately, and where he had had many adventures. In the fall, "the political meetings in New York & Brooklyn are immense," he wrote Eldridge. "I go to them as to shows, fireworks, cannon, clusters of gaslights . . . 15, 20, 50,000 people." He was also tending to his brawny outdoorsman side: going fishing, and occasionally "riding off in the country . . . or [for] a sail on the water, & many times to the sea shore at Coney Island."[10]

As he had done before the war, he vacationed with his sister Mary Elizabeth in Greenport, where he liked to angle for bluefish, and he thought about visiting his other sister, Hannah, in Vermont. The death of Captain Sims caught his attention. The body sent north from the battleground at Petersburg, after lying out for two days, arrived in Brooklyn and occasioned a funeral that both Walt and Mrs. Whitman attended. "We felt pretty gloomy," he wrote Nelly O'Connor, ". . . as two young [officers] of the 51st N Y, friends of my brother George . . . were killed in battle within ten days of each other." The other slain officer, Charles Bunker, was also accorded a Brooklyn funeral, and Walt and his mother again attended. His thoughts were riveted on the war, in fact, no matter his fishing trips and occasional visits to bars. In September, he recorded that the time was passing and yet " 'Drum Taps' is not yet begun to be printed," or as he put it in letters to some friends, in a tone of mild surprise, "The book is still unprinted" and "My book is not yet being printed," as if the process were something that might happen on its own. He felt the war directly, felt powerfully the urge to write it, in lasting poems, but somehow the moment remained unripe.

That the war itself was hanging in the balance probably added to his inertia. "All the signs are that Grant is going to strike forthwith," he told Eldridge, "perhaps risk all—One feels solemn who sees what depends. The military success, though first-class . . . is the least that depends."[11] Walt's book on the war, with its demurral from excitement over mere military "minutia," needed to be informed by knowing how the clash of arms turned out. And there were other aspects of the war that he had not quite gotten into focus. What it would mean for the great American ex-

periment if the South were to succeed, for example. And what of use
could be said about the vast cascade of death—the orgy of it that the
young, healthful nation had visited on itself.[12]

George's wound at Fredericksburg awoke Walt from his early turn from
the war, and something worse than a simple war wound—the worst sort
of thing, almost, that could befall a soldier—brought him rushing to
George's defense a second time. In combat southwest of Petersburg, as
part of an offensive on September 30 aimed at severing a Southern rail-
way link, George and most of the 51st fell captive. Walt and Mrs. Whitman learned about this dark turn on October 3 and 4, from Brooklyn
newspaper accounts.[13] In "Fifty-first New York City Veterans," published four weeks later, Walt tried above all to demonstrate that the regiment had not surrendered out of weakness or cowardice—the
engagement, near Poplar Springs Church, had put the regiment in an
untenable position, he asserted:

> Our men . . . met with some success at first at PEEBLE'S farm, but
> about five o'clock in the afternoon the Second Division, Ninth
> Corps, in advance, encountered strong rebel works on an acclivity,
> up which they attempted to press, but were repulsed. The secesh
> troops, being reinforced and sallying down, in turn attacked us.
> Their charge was vehement, and caused that part of our force on the
> right of the Fifty-first to give way.[14]

Not the 51st, but some unnamed force to its right, broke ranks, "whereupon
the enemy rapidly throwing a powerful . . . column through the gap . . .
completed the disaster by cutting off the Fifty-first . . . and after a sharp
tussel capturing them, under circumstances honorable to the regiment."
  The fighting was fierce, although losses were what would be called
slight: five soldiers killed or mortally wounded, six with lesser wounds.[15]
One of the dead was George's friend and tent mate, Frank Butler, who
wore a long brown beard; hearing that a lieutenant with a beard had
been mortally wounded, George hoped that this was another officer of
the brigade who also wore a long beard, but he later saw that man alive.[16]
  That the regiment had surrendered in "circumstances honorable" was
important because, as Walt guessed, the fate of the men might depend on

Frank Butler.

popular estimates of its loyalty and worthiness. It would be useful, he saw, to suggest that the 51st was among the most distinguished of Union regiments, its battle flag torn and bloodstained beyond almost any other's. In December, in an angry letter printed in both the *Eagle* and the *Times*, he claimed,

> The public mind is deeply excited, and . . . righteously so, at the starvation of the United States prisoners of war in the hands of the Secessionists. The dogged sullenness and scoundrelism prevailing everywhere among the prison guards and officials . . . the measure-

less torments of the forty or fifty thousand helpless young men, with all their humiliations, hunger, cold, filth . . . I have myself seen the proofs of.[17]

He had seen the proofs in Washington, when groups of prisoners were occasionally brought north. They were starving and diseased, having been made to live "in large open stockades, [with] no shelter, no cooking, no clothes," as he wrote in one of his notebooks.[18] Confinement in concentrations of upward of thirty thousand men was tantamount to a death sentence for many. By fall 1864, the Confederate prison at Andersonville, Georgia, had become foully notorious; in the summer campaign, Sherman had sent a division of cavalry specifically to liberate the camp, only to have six hundred of his horsemen captured and taken in as prisoners.[19]

Walt indicted the Secessionists, but he also asked the uncomfortable question, "Whose fault is it . . . that our men have not been exchanged?" His public letter is a most rare example of Whitmanesque ad hominem vituperation, the poet's fears for his brother no doubt fueling his anger. The exchange of prisoners had foundered on the issue of the black soldiers. When captured, as at the Crater, U.S. Colored Troops were often tortured and murdered; some were returned to their masters or sold to new slave owners, or put to work shoring up rebel fortifications during combat; what was not done with them was to treat them as prisoners of war, for, as Robert G. H. Kean, chief of the Confederate War Bureau, declared, "No people . . . could tolerate . . . the use of savages [as soldiers against them] . . . We cannot . . . allow that *our property* can acquire . . . rights by virtue of a theft of it."[20]

Prisoner exchanges, common early in the war, had halted as a Southern policy of reenslaving or executing captured black troops and their officers came into force. The Lincoln government responded with a firm, not to say obdurate, policy of no further exchanges until black and white captives were treated alike. "[T]he control of exchange," Walt wrote seethingly,

has remained with the Secretary of War . . . also with such personages as Major General [Benjamin] Butler and Major General [Ethan Allen] Hitchcock. In my opinion the Secretary has taken and obstinately held a position of cold-blooded policy . . . more cruel than anything done by

> the Secessionists . . . the Secretary has . . . said (and this is the basis of
> his course and policy,) that it is not for the benefit of the Government of
> the United States that the power of the Secessionists should be repleted
> by some 50,000 men in good condition . . . besides getting relieved of
> the support of nearly the same number of human wrecks . . . of no ad-
> vantage to us, now in [their hands].[21]

He raged at Stanton for cynically claiming to care for the rights of
blacks, while really caring only for how to weaken the Southern war effort. At the cost of thousands of Union deaths from starvation, the enemy was denied a reinfusion of needed manpower. Walt was careful not
to make this damning charge against Lincoln, whose "humane, conscientious and fatherly heart, I have abiding faith in," but rather against
lesser figures such as Hitchcock, a Stanton crony and the chief commissioner for exchange. Of "Major General Hitchcock," Walt fumed, "the
public may judge what a valuable contribution he brings to this matter . . . from a remark he has made not long since, that 'none but cow-
ards are ever taken prisoners in war.' "

Beginning with news of the capture, Walt's thoughts were with George
and his regiment; they were not thoughts about wounded lads languishing in the Washington hospitals, many of them his "darlings," but about
a real fighting unit threatened with extinction. His notebooks mention
several meetings with people who could tell him what had happened at
Poplar Springs Church. On November 17, he spent "most of the day"
with Lieutenant William Babcock, who eluded capture on September
30.[22] Babcock said that the 51st was down to 106 men, from a force of 400
effectives on the unlucky day.[23] Captain Thomas B. Marsh, officially a
member of the regiment, but on detached service since summer of 1862,
had been brought back and put in command, even though, as Walt disap-
provingly noted, he "has not been with the [51st] in a single battle."[24]

On December 12, he saw Captain John Stuart, of Smith Street, Brooklyn, but Stuart had only secondhand reports to give him, having been separated from the regiment since August. Late in December, he met with a
number of men of the 51st at a gathering of the regiment's friends at
Robert Potter's house, 16 Gramercy Park. In an atmosphere of candid
reminiscence, Walt learned about the unit's struggles at Spotsylvania,
where the troops had dug in with spoons and the officers with swords,

everyone desperate to throw up some cover; late in the afternoon, the be-
sieged regiment had "had to skidaddle by crawling off, flat on their bellies,
dog fashion."[25]

Someone at the party told him that Colonel LeGendre, disfigured at
the Wilderness, "was an incompetent officer in every respect." Captain
David F. Wright talked about Samuel Sims—he was "an exemplary
Christian in action," according to Wright, who never did "an unworthy
or mean" thing. A few weeks before, Walt had heard from another officer that Elliot Shepard, the regiment's influential friend and protector, a
New York businessman with political connections, upon hearing
George's name spoken in a meeting in his offices, commented, "That is a
man as modest as he is brave, and in both I don't think he is surpassed by
any soldier in the army." The officer answered, "I think the same as you
do, Colonel, and we all do in the regiment."[26]

There was already a valedictory tone in the way that George was being
spoken of. All knew of the conditions in the prisons. Walt had heard
nothing from George since mid-October, when a note arrived at the
house on Portland Avenue: "Here I am perfectly well and unhurt, but a
prisoner. I was captured day before yesterday with . . . nearly the entire
regiment . . . I am in tip top health and Spirits, and . . . as tough as a
mule and shall get along first rate."[27] The note had been sent from Libby
Prison, Petersburg. From there, George and the other captive officers
were eventually taken to Danville, on the North Carolina border, where
a prison had been established in six tobacco warehouses, the multistory,
brick and wooden buildings emptied of all furnishings. A Confederate
prison inspector, A. S. Cunningham, reported to Richmond, "The prisons at this post are in very bad condition, dirty, filled with vermin . . .
there is an insufficiency of fireplaces . . . It is a matter of surprise that
the prisoners can exist in the close and crowded rooms, the gas from the
coal rendering the air fetid and impure."[28]

Cunningham continued, "The prisoners have almost no clothing, no
blankets . . . The mortality . . . about five per day, is caused, no doubt,
by the insufficiency of food." Cunningham concluded that Danville was
"truly horrible." The floors in the old warehouses were encrusted with
excrement. Prisoners cut slivers of wood from the rafters, boiling them
to make a sort of coffee, weakening the rafters to the breaking point.
The staple food was corn and corncob ground together, then lightly

*Drawing of tobacco warehouses converted into a Confederate
prison, Danville, Virginia.*

baked. A Connecticut officer, Henry Sprague, held captive for about as
long as George, recalled eating bits of potato as well as corn during his
confinement, plus thin soup, salt fish, sorghum syrup, and "nameless
portions of the animal economy."[29]

Those nameless portions included a lot of rat, eaten boiled in soup or
stewed entire. One prisoner padded his diet with lice he collected from his
blanket and body. Drinking water came out of the nearby Dan River; diarrhea was epidemic.[30] A prisoner from a Maine regiment recalled suffering
more from the crowding than from starvation: "[N]one of us had more
space to himself than he actually occupied," he wrote. "We lay in long
rows [on the bare floor], two rows of men with their heads to the side
walls and two . . . along the center of the room, leaving narrow aisles
between the rows of feet."[31]

George wrote home on October 23, announcing his removal to
Danville. Probably his letter eventually arrived in Brooklyn, although

Walt told Nelly O'Connor on December 4, "My brother George still remains a prisoner—as near as we can judge he is at Columbia, S C—we
have had no word from him."[32] Later in December, a Mrs. Lester called
at the Whitman home, bringing news that her son, Frank, also a prisoner, had seen Captain Whitman, and that he was alive.[33] Although
Walt and the other Whitmans did not know it, George was in a failing
condition that month, and he would come close to dying. At first, as
"tough as a mule, and about as ugly," he had organized extra rations for
himself and for at least one other officer, Sam Pooley (who "would fared
poorly," Mrs. Whitman wrote Walt, "if it hadent been for [George]").[34]
Pooley cooked the beans that George scrounged up—afterward, George
was of the opinion that "beans [had] kept them alive," his mother said.

A trooper of the 4th New York Cavalry, also a prisoner at Danville,
weighed 173 pounds upon arrival and 78 when released. His period of
incarceration was almost identical to George's, and he ascribed his suf-
ferings to "the scurvy," which like diarrhea was epidemic.[35] George may
have warded off vitamin C deficiency by occasionally providing beans
for his meals with Pooley—they are a modest but not insignificant
source of the vitamin. Still, he sickened as winter came on. A fellow officer found him delirious one day, and a Confederate doctor put him in
the infirmary. Mrs. Whitman, writing after his safe return on March 7,
filled Walt in on the drama:

> George has come home this morning   he looks quite thin and shows
> his prison life . . . he was six weeks in the [prison] hospital . . . diliri-
> ous and lay in A stupor till the nigth the fever turned   he says he felt
> A thrill run through him and thought he was dying . . . cald to one of
> the nurses to bring A light and to raise him up and give him A piece
> of paper.[36]

George wrote down what he figured was owed him by the government
in a note to be sent to his mother. Then,

> he shut his eyes and never expected to open them again and went to
> sleep and when he awoke he was all in a sweat . . . just at daylight one
> of the officials of the place came very softly to take all he had in his
> pockets . . . when the doctor came . . . he says you are better he said

it was his constitution that saved him . . . he had no drawers and only
A thin pair of flanne[l] trousers and no shirt part of the time   they
stole his things.[37]

Prisoners at Danville died of pneumonia, pleurisy, smallpox, and
scurvy, among other recorded causes.[38] Disease was so prevalent that the
citizens of Danville petitioned Richmond to shut the encampment
down, as smallpox and "fever" were spreading among them, too. Walt
later calculated that 325 enlisted men of the 51st fell captive at Poplar
Springs Church; of these, 125 died in prison (most at Salisbury, North
Carolina), 90 returned, and 110 were never heard from again. Walt assumed these also had died.[39]

Of the thirteen officers captured at Poplar Springs, none died; officers
may have been in better condition to begin with, they were mostly
housed indoors (unlike at Salisbury, where thousands of men spent the
winter under the open sky), and sometimes officers had resources beyond those of ordinary troops, with which to buy food or other necessi-
ties.[40] Indeed, Mrs. Whitman told Walt that George "when he was
captured he had 100 dl   they searched him 3 times and he saved his
money   he cut A place in his neck tie and put 50d bill in and put some
in his tobacco and some silver in his mouth   one next to him they took
600dl from   they took all sam pooleys."[41]

George survived, Mrs. Whitman believed, because the infirmary doctor took a liking to him. The doctor, who was named Wilson, "did what
he could for him . . . blistered him and gave him mercury," questionable
favors, but signs at least of someone's being concerned. George's disease
was probably pneumonia. His habits of modesty and of refusing to
complain nearly doomed him—he lay on the prison floor for days,
denying there was anything wrong with him, before falling into an out-
right delirium that others could not overlook.[42]

Walt became quietly frantic as the winter progressed, with no word from
George and a sense, possibly, that something was amiss. Notes about his
brother, about the other captives of the 51st (including a detailed portrait
of Pooley, a Cornwall-born ship's joiner with two children in Buffalo),
and about the fighting career of the veteran regiment crowd out all other
considerations from his pocket diaries for a period of weeks. On Decem-

ber 12, Lieutenant Babcock wrote from Virginia promising to send
George's belongings home to Brooklyn.[43] A large trunk arrived the day
after Christmas. Walt wrote in a notebook,

> We have had a wet day with fog, mud, slush, & the yet unmelted
> hard-polished ice . . . George's trunk came by express to-day early
> in the forenoon . . . It stood some hours before we felt inclined to
> open it. Towards evening mother & Eddy looked over the things.
> One could not help feeling depressed. There were his uniform coat,
> pants, sash, &c . . . books, nick-nacks, a revolver, a small diary, roll
> of his company, a case of photographs of his comrades (several of
> them I knew as killed in battle,) with other stuff such as a soldier ac-
> cumulates.[44]

Mrs. Whitman looked everything over, and then

> laid out the shirts to be washed, the coats & pants to hang up, & all the
> rest were carefully put back. It made us feel pretty solemn. We have
> not heard from him since October 3d; whether living or dead we know
> not . . . To night I have been looking over Georges diary . . . It is
> merely a skeleton of dates, voyages, places camped in or marched
> through . . . But I can realize clearly that by calling upon even a tithe
> of the myriads of living & actual facts . . . [in] this dry list of times &
> places, it would outvie all the romances in the world . . . in such a
> record as this lies folded a perfect poem of the war.[45]

That same day, December 26, Walt sent his angry letter to the *Eagle* and
the *Times*.[46] Quite possibly he wrote it with George's trunk sitting in
Mrs. Whitman's front room. George's diary, with its impassive recording of skirmishes and miles marched, may have given birth to Walt's un-
ruly eloquence, the reserve of one brother sparking the outcry of the
other.

Knowing the frailty of the suffering soldiers; knowing their exceeding
vulnerability in many cases, as they lay weakened by dysentery and
other infections, with the attentions, often, of a single caregiver making
all the difference; Walt made as much noise as he could. He submitted
his prison exchange letter widely, hoping for more exposure than just

the *Eagle* and the *Times* could provide, and he sought meetings with officials who might intervene on George's behalf, including even the commissioner, Hitchcock, whom he had treated so roughly in his screed.

Earlier that month, he had acted decisively for another brother, in even sadder circumstances. On December 5, exactly a year after brother Andrew's death, Jesse Whitman had become an inmate of the Kings County Lunatic Asylum in Flatbush, Brooklyn.[47] Mrs. Whitman did not give up her ailing sons easily, and Jesse's outbursts and other symptoms of disorder must have further intensified in the year just past—Walt, in the commitment document, noted that Jesse often woke in the middle of the night, entirely deranged. The tension and fear that had obtained for everyone in the house at times must have found relief with his removal. Jeff, father of two little girls and his main antagonist, made no comment about Jesse's commitment, other than to note, in a letter to Walt mailed in February, "Jess I have not heard from since you went away   I suppose I ought to go see him but they are taking such quantities of small pox patients out to that hospital . . . that I am almost afraid to."[48]

On December 30, Walt heard from William O'Connor in Washington. The news was that O'Connor and J. Hubley Ashton, an assistant attorney general and Whitman admirer, had found Walt a position in the bureaucracy if he wanted it—a regular position, with steady pay and duties by no means onerous. This sinecure (for that was what it was: an artist's classic well-feathered berth) would make him financially comfortable for the first time since the 1850s, while leaving many hours in the day for writing or visiting soldiers. Walt wrote back, "Your welcome letter of December 30 came safe . . . I am most desirous to get the appointment, as enclosing, with the rest of the points, my attentions to the soldiers & to my poems, as you intimate." And he added, "Mother & all home are well . . . Not a word for over three months from my brother George—the probabilities are most gloomy. I see [friends in New York] now & then. I am well, but need to leave here—need a change."[49]

O N JANUARY 19, Walt recorded, "We have just heard from George after a blank of four months. He is in the Confederate Military Prison at Danville."[1] In a note dated November 23, George had written that he was "well & hearty," but the claim was now two months old, and much could have happened since. The next day, a second message arrived from George, this one dated November 27 and "written in good spirits," Walt recorded. It listed the officers of the 51st being held at Danville and their status.

Walt paid a visit to Colonel Shepard, the regiment's friend, to convey the news in George's note. Shepard, whose offices were at 18 Wall Street, does not appear to have been able to help the men, despite all his connections. The New York papers had been reporting for a year on the shocking situation at Andersonville Prison, and early in 1865 a New York journalist and Union spy, Albert D. Richardson, had become the subject of equally sensational coverage about Salisbury Prison, from which he had recently escaped. Richardson testified before Congress that Union captives were dying there at a rate of twenty-eight per day, or 13 percent a month.[2] Jeff wrote Walt on January 31, "I feel very sad and downhearted to-night—I have just been reading about the prisoners as detailed before the committee . . . I begin to think that after all that it is quite likely that Gen Grant is the one that does not want to give an exchange . . . can it be that he is willing to let the men starve and die without result."[3]

Jeff had also read about "special exchanges every now and then" when the right person knew how to pull the right string. He wanted Walt to consider a scheme that would exploit their network of connections (not a large network, but not inconsiderable, either) to gain George's release. Jeff mentioned "our friend John Swinton," the managing editor of the *New York Times*, and the fact that Swinton had been one of Grant's earliest supporters. During a visit to New York, Grant had sent for Swinton and given him "a long interview"—Jeff's source for this information was his good friend Dr. Ruggles, who was likewise a friend of Swinton's (who was a champion of Walt's writing as well as his sometime employer). "Now I am positive," Jeff wrote, "that a letter could be got from Swinton to Grant signed as Editor of the Times asking that a special exchange might be made in George's case—and I believe it would have effect."[4]

Jeff had been following the political maneuvering around the issue of responsibility for the exchange breakdown. General Butler, recently sacked by Grant, had accused the general in chief of being the one to halt all exchanging—according to Butler, his own good work, which had won many a merciful release, had been cut short by a heartless telegram from Grant that said, "Do not give the rebels a single able-bodied man."[5] Jeff reasoned that the Union leader would be anxious not to be left holding the bag: "Grant is just now in the position when a few words of censure in a print like the Times would do him great injury—I know he is in no danger of getting it from the Times yet he would . . . like to make it sure by doing a supposed favor to its editor."[6]

"Poor mother," Jeff added, "reads about the treatment of the prisons and will set with her head in her hand for an hour afterward . . . Think the matter well over," he advised Walt, "you can think of it in more bearings than I can," although the evidence is that Walt's younger brother, after ten years in the highly politicized Brooklyn waterworks world, needed no mentoring in the deployment of influence and favor.

Walt had been groping for a plan of his own for weeks, meeting with New York influentials and sending out feelers in hopes of arranging his own exchange. His sense of urgency was heightened by two letters he received as soon as he returned to Washington, on January 23—two young officers of the 51st wrote that George and the other captives were in desperate straits, and one letter urged the sending of "Salt Pork and hard tack" and hoped earnestly that Walt "would look out for all hands."[7]

His new clerkship, in the Indian Bureau, paid him $1,200 per year.* He was gratified to have a solid position again; as he wrote his mother, "My work . . . is quite easy—I am through by 4 . . . I am very glad I have employment (and *pay*)—I must try to keep it."[8] This change in fortunes allowed him to spend the impressive sum of $28 to send a box of provisions to George from City Point, Virginia, with the help of a soldier friend of Jeff's, Julius Mason, who was stationed at the army depot there.[9] Jeff was sending provisions, too, from Brooklyn; he wrote Walt on January 26, "I got some hoop iron and straped the box up strong . . . I had in it a ham piece of smoked beef can of milk (condensed) coffee can of peaches—crackers—potatoes—salt," plus items of clothing.[10]

None of the boxes got to George when he most needed them. On February 3, Walt wrote Swinton asking him to do what Jeff had suggested, to "write a brief letter, not filling more than one page . . . to Lt. Gen. Grant. Date it from the office of the *Times*."[11] Walt wanted "one of the special exchanges . . . of which they are now making quite a number . . . in favor of my brother . . . and also another officer same regiment [Pooley]." Swinton, Walt instructed, should mention George's battle record and that he had "an aged widowed mother in deepest distress."

At almost the same moment, Swinton heard from Dr. Ruggles, carrying water for Jeff and urging Swinton to do the right thing by the Whitmans. Swinton's personal letter to Grant received an immediate response. Before he learned of this happy outcome, Walt went to see E. A. Hitchcock, presumably hat in hand. That recent object of Whitmanian censure also smiled on the request for an exchange, directing his executive officer to hand carry the necessary papers to Petersburg as soon as possible.

Walt had written at least twenty letters to George in prison, on the chance that one might get through.[12] On January 19, having heard from George for the first time in months, he submitted an article to the *Brooklyn Daily Union* called "A Brooklyn Soldier, and a Noble One." Again it

---

*Walt's salary put him in the same financial class as his two competent younger brothers. George, although an acting major, was still being paid a captain's wages, $115.50 per month, or $1,386 per annum. Jeff's yearly earnings in the mid-1860s increased from about $1,100 in 1863 to $4,000 in '67, when he became chief engineer of the Saint Louis waterworks.

rehearsed George's valorous service in hopes of keeping the plight of the glorious 51st before the public. Walt's journalistic profile was high this season—a month before, he had published a six-thousand-word article in the *Times*, with the appropriately long title "Our Wounded and Sick Soldiers. Visits Among Army Hospitals, at Washington, on the Field, and here in New-York." It recounted his entire experience since Fredericksburg and summed up, in phrases that would appear, unchanged, in *Memoranda During the War*, all that he had learned about the suffering of men. O'Connor said that he read the piece "with a swelling heart and wet eyes. It was very great and touching to me. I think I could mount the tribune for you on that and speak speech which jets fire . . . it filled me with infinite regrets that there is not [yet] a book from you, embodying these rich and sad experiences."[13]

In the end, larger forces were at play than Walt's journalistic eloquence. The war was at last being won by the North, and Lincoln had triumphed electorally, following Sherman's victory at Atlanta and Sheridan's triumph in the Shenandoah Valley, September–October 1864. At the time of George's near-death from pneumonia, the South was retreating from its violent policy toward black captives, thus allowing the Union leadership to soften its position. A general exchange of prisoners began on February 17, 1865—no doubt Grant's and Hitchcock's capitulations to the Whitman insider onslaught reflected their awareness of this impending change, and everyone's desire to look magnanimous.[14]

Jeff does not appear to have had a starry-eyed opinion of Walt's writerly influence. He was himself a canny weigher of opportunities and degrees of sway, but he was also a close and longtime reader of Walt's journalism, and he felt that it might really accomplish something. On February 3, he asked, "Did you see the Tribune of to-day—It had [another article by Richardson, the recent Salisbury escapee] . . . to-night's Evening Post extracts quite a long passage from it." In case Walt did not get the hint, Jeff added, "I wish you could write upon the same subject and keep it before the reading public."[15] Four days later he wrote, "Do talk it up—Walt— write it up if you have a chance," and his insistence reflected his own fears for George's survival but also a frank estimate of Walt's ability to command attention. Together, they just might save their brother. "I wish you would write me quite often," he wrote at the height of the crisis. "[S]omehow since you went away . . . I have felt lonely—I suppose its because I dwell so much on the thought that something ought to be done [for] George. Oh if we only could it seems to me it would be worth almost a life time."[16]

As the crisis mounted, Walt settled into another Washington boarding-house, this one at 468 M Street, west of Twelfth. He told Jeff, "I am quite comfortable . . . with a wood stove, & a pile of wood in the room, a first rate . . . big bed, & a very friendly old secesh landlady" whose husband and son were serving with the rebels.[17] He began visiting hospitals again. Jeff imagined that there would be few wounded now, with no recent big battles, but Walt found the hospitals crowded. There were "quite a good many bad old lingering wounds, & also a good many down with sickness," he wrote, and the army seemed to be breaking up its field hospitals, sending the invalids north.[18]

The Indian Office, of the Interior Department, was in the northeast corner of the Patent Office Building, basement floor. This structure that he loved for its architecture and as a temple of American practical inge-nuity, a hospital in the first years of the war, had been returned to mostly civilian uses and would serve as the site of the Second Inaugural Ball, held on March 6. About that gala celebration, Walt would write in *Mem-oranda*, "To-night, beautiful women, perfumes, the violins' sweetness, the polka and the waltz; but [two years before], the amputation, the blue face, the groan, the glassy eye of the dying, the clotted rag, the odor of wounds and blood."[19]

February 17, the day the general exchange began, he made some notes while in his room:

> A heavy sulky night, & beating snow storm. I have just opened the window & looked out. It is bleak & silent & dim. Off in a distant camp the drums beat . . . I heard to-day from Head-quarters of the armies, at City Point, by official letter from Lt-Gen'l. Grant's Mili-tary secretary. He writes that [Grant] has directed a special exchange for George & also for Lt. Pooley. This is an addition to the order al-ready given by Maj-Gen. Hitchcock.[20]

Nevertheless, he remained worried. No word had come from George more recent than November 27, and a news article had reported "an

immense fire" at Danville on about February 10 that had caused "unpar-
alled destruction." Furthermore, George's name was missing from a
printed list of Danville prisoners he had seen.[21]

There had been an attempted escape at Danville on December 10. In the
coming days, as prisoners began arriving from down south, but never
George or other officers of the 51st, Walt began to fear that his brother
was being punished for playing a role in the escape. General Hitchcock,
whom Walt visited at least twice, thought that unlikely, and talking to the
chief commissioner "relieved me a good deal," Walt noted, although "for
a couple of days & nights I was deeply, deeply deprest."[22]

Walt may have gone to Annapolis, hoping to see his brother among the
returnees brought there by boat.[23] *Memoranda* contains a description of
a group of several hundred prisoners debarking from a steamer, and
"out of the whole number only three individuals" were strong enough
to walk onto the dock—the rest had to be carried. "Can those be *men*—
those little livid-brown, ash-streak'd, monkey-looking dwarfs ?—are
they really not mummied, dwindled corpses ?"[24] George arrived there
on February 23, in a group of five hundred officers. He later told his
mother that, among his group, twenty died upon arrival, some from
gorging themselves to death. But Walt was in Washington on February
23, watching a procession of ill-clad rebel deserters saunter up Pennsylvania Avenue, according to *Memoranda*. And on the twenty-fifth, the
date he attached to the arrival of the monkey-looking men, he was again
in Washington, torn by worry over George—aware that the general exchange was soon to be completed, he was still unable to find George's
name on any list, including the list of those safely returned.[25]

Thus, the description of men so shrunken they look like monkeys, and
the account of several hundred former prisoners unable to walk a few
steps off a boat, may repeat stories he heard or accounts he read that
were written by actual eyewitnesses. One of the most vivid eyewitness
passages in *Memoranda*—the chapter called "Murder of President
Lincoln"—conveniently locates a skillful professional writer inside
Ford's Theatre on the very night of the assassination. That professional
writer—Walt—was actually at home in Brooklyn on the day in question. His eyewitness account depends entirely on details provided him
by a real attendee, Peter Doyle, a young man who in this period of
worry over George's fate became a special friend. Doyle had gone to the

theater on Good Friday, April 14, after reading in the *Washington Evening Star* that the president planned to take in *Our American Cousin*, the popular farce written by Tom Taylor. "[W]hat I felt then, or saw . . . is all put down in Walt's piece," Doyle told an interviewer many years later, adding, "that piece is exactly right," in other words, it reproduced Doyle's own experience.[26]

Walt failed to see George's name when at last it appeared in the papers. George does not appear to have been in a monkey-looking dwarf condition upon his arrival—his comrades and he "sang away the night aboard the boat" that took them from Libby Prison, Richmond, down the James River and up the Chesapeake to Annapolis, Walt later wrote.[27] Walt's box of expensive provisions had caught up with George in Richmond, as had Jeff's box from Brooklyn. "[T]he way we went into the eatables . . . was a caution," George told Mrs. Whitman, adding, "I am perfectly well Mother although I am in the Hospital Buildings . . . The reason that I am quartered here is that the Hotels and Boarding Houses in town are cramed full,   I stay here for one dollar and a half a day while the Hotels charge three or four dollars."[28]

George drew two months' pay and bought himself a new suit of clothes. Someone trembling on the edge of starvation would be unlikely to have the energy for acquiring clothes, not to mention enough flesh on him to make the fitting useful. George was careful to address his mother in the same can-do, hail-fellow tone of most of his other letters. That he had seen grave and disturbing things can be surmised only from his breezy promise, "I have lots of yarns to tell you Mother but will wait untill I get home as I cant do justice to the darn Rebs, in a letter."[29]

When she heard those stories of starvation and savagery, Mrs. Whitman advised her soldier son to stop thinking about them. George had made a success of being a prisoner, as he had of being an officer, in the sense that he had survived and that his comrades had also survived, at least one of them in part because of the protection he provided. No doubt he had been unusually lucky. When he fell sick, a doctor noticed his distress and cared enough about it to remove him to an infirmary— this was a kindness not to be taken for granted at Danville, where, according to prisoners' reports, soldiers dying of smallpox were left to die on the floor of the tobacco warehouses among the other men, despite the risk of wider infection.[30]

George attracted devotees, as brothers Walt and Jeff did also. Dr. Wilson may have been one of those who responded to something stalwart but unstuffy about him, a good-natured reluctance, as if for reasons of style, to plead his own case. Sam Pooley told Mrs. Whitman that he was "very much attached to George," adding, "When the Captain was sick he was A great mind to play sick to get in the hospital" with him.[31] Pooley and Colonel John Wright, who ran into Walt some months later, in Washington, only wanted to talk to him about George. They bent his ear out on Pennsylvania Avenue and then "we adjourned to a place where we could sit down & continued the conversation," Walt noted. Pooley repeated what he had told Mrs. Whitman on a night in early March, when he stayed with her on his way home to Buffalo on leave, that he was "attached" to George and that when George was put in the Danville hospital, Pooley "took the separation pretty hard."[32] Walt's notes about George on this occasion were proud and exact, but not effusive. As if borrowing George's reserve, he recorded what George's brother-officers had to say about him and left it at that.

He had recently written an article, for the *Brooklyn Daily Union,* about George's career, and he would publish another in midsummer, without a signature.[33] The situation of singing a brother's praises dictated a certain restraint, as did conventions at least as old as the Greeks about allowing acts of martial valor to speak for themselves. But George's character may have in some ways eluded his brother. The tendency to accept, even to prefer, being overlooked ("[W]e don't get much credit for what we doo," George wrote about serving with Burnside, "but I don't care much . . . as long as the work is done") suggested an attitude not seen much of in Walt's conduct of his career as a writer.[34] Even in his hospital work, Walt's instinct was to make his efforts widely known. Performance without publicity was for him incomplete as a gesture. He had good reasons to promote himself as a young poet, to boost himself out of the obscurity that attended him and his family and other striving members of his class—probably without a healthy instinct for self-advertisement, he would never have emerged at all. The "Americanness" of his loud, sometimes playful sounding of his own horn is now taken for granted, and his example has not been lost on other American artists, but there was an "Americanness" about George's demeanor, too.

Almost Walt's only recorded observation about his brother's basic character was the fond report to their mother in April 1864, that George was "the same good & noble fellow he always was." This undoubtedly captured something about him, but it tended to play down the Civil War as an influence. If three years of massed battles and the deaths of comrades, along with the responsibilities of leading men in combat, had not changed him, then George was probably unique as a man.

Our literature's ablest recorder of one kind of change among soldiers—the change into medical subjects, helpless, pathetic—Walt was less sure about the inner changes that sometimes attend soldiering. He was quick to register surface alterations, the access of confidence, of an attractive rude manliness, but the idea that deeper changes might result, fundamental ones, either puzzled or repulsed him.

He was anxious about war's effect on America. On the one hand, he wished the military minutia to be promptly forgotten and the humane caregiving made the focus of all future remembrances; but on the other, he recognized that the nation had been profoundly militarized, and that the fighting heritage of the Revolutionary generation had now been made nearly universal. In *Specimen Days*, he speaks of this new reality hopefully; after once again reciting the remarkable accomplishments of the 51st ("Went out early—march'd, fought everywhere"), he declares, "I strengthen and comfort myself much with the certainty that the capacity for just such regiments . . . is inexhaustible in the United States, and that there isn't a county nor a township . . . nor a street in any city" unable to turn out just such groups of citizen-heroes.[35]

On the whole, though, the war for him was a horror. It had tested the character of Americans and found it to be made of the truest, deepest stuff, and the precious Union had been preserved at last; but to talk about the war was to talk about an amassing of corpses, fundamentally. In a chapter of *Specimen Days* called "The Million Dead, Too, Summ'd Up," he addressed "the dead in this war":

[T]here they lie, strewing the fields and woods . . . Virginia, the Peninsula—Malvern Hill and Fair Oaks—the banks of the Chickahominy—the terraces of Fredericksburgh . . . the varieties of the *strayed* dead, (the estimate of the War department is 25,000 national soldiers kill'd in battle and never buried at all . . .)—Gettysburgh . . .

Vicksburgh . . . Petersburgh . . . the crop reap'd by the mighty reapers, typhoid, dysentery, inflammations—and blackest and loathesomest of all, the dead and living burial-pits, the prison-pens of Anderson-ville, Salisbury, Belle-Isle.[36]

Overwhelmed, like Lear near the end of Shakespeare's tragedy, trying to reckon with the loss of a beloved child ("Thou'lt come no more / Never, never, never, never, never"), Walt declaimed,

the dead, the dead, the dead—*our* dead—or South or North, ours all, (all, all, all, finally dear to me)—or East or West—Atlantic coast or Mississippi valley—some where they crawl'd to die, alone, in bushes, low gullies, or on the sides of hills . . . our young men once so hand-some and so joyous . . . the son from the mother, the husband from the wife . . . the clusters of camp graves, in Georgia, the Carolinas, and in Tennessee—the single graves left in the woods or by the road-side . . . corpses floated down the rivers, and caught and lodged . . . the infinite dead—(the land entire saturated, perfumed with their im-palpable ashes' exhalation in Nature's chemistry distill'd, and shall be so forever, in every future grain of wheat and ear of corn, and every flower that grows . . .).[37]

The very worst incidents of killing had come, he believed, at the pris-ons. At Salisbury, North Carolina—a site indelibly associated for him with the fate of the enlisted men of the 51st—"the known are only 85, while the unknown are 12,027, and 11,700 of these are buried in trenches." The terrible word "Unknown" capped the vast tragedy—to die in youth, consumed by the bloody-mawed monster War, was bad enough, but to die unmarked and unnamed was for him almost beyond contemplation.

The enlisted men had not, in most cases, served for four full years, as George finally managed to do. If not wounded or killed or sickened and sent to a hospital, they usually retired after their enlistment ran out; some few became officers; some reenlisted late in the war to win a bounty, or to be in on the final battles. The muster-out roll of George's Company K, dated July 1865, included only 9 men who had served from 1861 until the end (out of 121 men listed).[38] One of these rare long-serving soldiers, Charles Appenzeller, entered at age twenty-seven as a private; he mustered out a private still. Another, Augustus Ellsie, was twenty-five when he signed up on August 26, 1861, just a few days before George did, and by the end of the war he had become a sergeant.

Company K's final muster-roll lists many soldiers still missing in action, a full ten months after the events at Poplar Springs Church. Private John Quinn, for instance, had still not been heard from nor his body recovered—the nineteen-year-old had served only twenty-eight days in the regiment before his capture. Other men taken at Poplar Springs Church, sent to Salisbury Prison, and never seen again included Richard Coleman, George R. Dickson, August Denzel, Juan Gomez, Carl V. Gensang, Frederick Holden, Henry Logan, Andrew Paul, and John Regan.[39] Most had been in the 51st only a short time. Their average age was twenty-three, and they had been doubly unfortunate in being sent to a prison like Salisbury, as foul an abyss as Andersonville, and sent there as recent recruits, with few of the survival skills that men like George had acquired over time. From October 1864 to February 1865, 3,479 prisoners died at Salisbury out of the 10,321 known to be held there in that period—a mortality of over 33 percent. The regiment that had served everywhere—in the west, in the final titanic campaign against Petersburg and Richmond, for four years traveling "a long and dark and bloody road of battle and death," as Walt put it memorably—had largely melted away.

George and his fellow officers had been sent to Salisbury, too, to begin with. As war-hardened men used to finding ways to get on, they might have fared better there than did the regiment's new recruits, but even they would likely have fallen victim, in some measure, to the lack of adequate food, water, shelter, and clothing, not to mention the violence of some guards and prisoners and the conditions of appalling filth. After two weeks, they were sent on to Danville, where at least they could sleep in out of the weather. The success of this small cohort of officers at organizing extra food at Danville raises at least the possibility that they were able to influence the decision to get them sent on from Salisbury. One of the officer-group, Lieutenant William Ackerson, kept a detailed list of the items he purchased while in prison; the entries run from October 15, 1864, to January 26, 1865, and suggest a regular commerce between prison officials and prisoners with money or other useful resources.[40]

Outside the prisons, field officers died at a considerably higher rate than did enlisted men. But both classes of soldier were familiar enough with the oblivion that threatened them. Walt's concern for the fate of the unknowns is as telling a sign of his identification with the soldiers of the war as are his countless acts of bedside caring. What he called "the significant word Unknown" presided over the whole affair, threatening the least fortunate of those who had served their country with a second, yet more somber, extinction.

THE WORD "UNKNOWN" referred to the soldiers who died without a name, swept on in the "melancholy tide" of war. But there was another meaning to the word. Some years after the war was over, in a puff piece he wrote about himself, Walt asserted that his poetry was about "the expression, more decidedly than before, of that combination in which Death and the Unknown are as essential and important to the author's plan . . . as Life and the Known."[1] The great mystery—the dark realm of nonbeing—was now to be at the heart of his poetic project, if it had not been before.

What becomes of us when we die—where do we go—what sort of home do we find after death, if we do find one? These basic questions, arising for many people in childhood, were central concerns of some of his earliest poems, for instance, "We All Shall Rest at Last," first published in the *Long Island Democrat* on July 14, 1840, when he was twenty-one:

> On Earth are many sights of woe,
>   And many sounds of agony,
> And many a sorrow-withered cheek,
>   And many a pain-dulled eye.
>
> The wretched weep, the poor complain,
>   And luckless love pines on unknown,
> And faintly from the midnight couch
>   Sounds out the sick child's moan.

But,

> . . . dread ye not the fearful hour;
>   The coffin, and the pall's dark gloom;
> For there's a calm to throbbing hearts,
>   And rest, down in the tomb.
>
> Then our long journey will be o'er,
>   And throwing off this load of woes,
> The pallid brow, the feebled limbs,
>   Will sink in soft repose.[2]

The popular literature of death, burial, and consolation circulating in America before the war encouraged such doleful lines from a young printer who hoped to become known as a man of letters. But other of his early writings, such as the story that mentions "God's angels," volunteers who served the poor during a cholera epidemic, testify to what was probably an authentic interest in human suffering and death, driven not entirely by the desire to break into print. His early concern for the victims of accidents and diseases may be less prophetic of the role that he would play in the Civil War than evidence of a vivid apprehension of tragic reality. Not every man or woman who becomes a doctor can be called a farseeing prophet; still, life uncannily fulfills the expectation that there will be suffering and dying enough to justify every effort of preparation taken.

Had he not become the poet Whitman, Walt might have become a doctor; he formed friendships with several medical men before the war, admiring and applauding the work they did. In the larger sense, he was an enthusiastic participant in one of the central hygienic improvements of his era, the building of better sewers and water-delivery systems. His younger brothers partook of the same progressive enthusiasm. Whether influenced by Walt or for their own reasons, they made careers as builders of infrastructure, and the three Whitmans displayed a kind of familial fondness for tasks of hydraulic betterment.

Although he made fun of George for believing in "pipes, not poems," Walt was himself a believer in them—and in a poetry equivalent to new water pipes, fulfilling a health-related function. Replete with sublime aesthetic effects, his poems push one agenda or another, at their best arriving at problematic, unexpected destinations, but seeking always to arrive somewhere useful. Thus he addressed himself to a real need born of the war. "The Million Dead," as he estimated them, required mourning. For each soldier slain there was a family plunged in sorrow, "women, parents, orphans" in need of consolation. How to think of the dead; how to arrive at some acceptance of a loss. These were legitimate questions for millions of his countrymen, as he saw it.

He was confident that he could provide answers simple enough to soothe unlettered hearts and also profound enough to honor the dead. His hospital work was his education; the bedside sitting as thousands of young men ventured over, not a one displaying terror or even much reluctance (according to Walt), had instructed him. In late September 1865—the war now well over, but Walt still visiting hospitals—he found "an old acquaintance . . . a rebel prisoner, in a dying condition. Poor fellow, the look was already on his face," Walt recorded. And that look, and all it signified, remained of interest to him:

> He gazed long at me. I ask'd him if he knew me. After a moment he utter'd something, but inarticulately. I have seen him off and on for the last five months. He has suffer'd very much . . . I placed my hand lightly on his forehead and face, just sliding it over the surface. In a moment or so he fell into a calm, regular-breathing lethargy or sleep, and remain'd so while I sat there.[3]

Often, Walt remained at bedside even though a dying soldier was entirely comatose, to keep faith with the man but also because something thrilling was going on. By lightly touching the face of the dying rebel while it bore "the look," he made contact with the old soul-traveling miracle yet again. "It was dark," he continued, "and the lights were lit . . . A Sister of Charity, dress'd in black, with a broad white linen [cowl] around her head and under her chin, and a black crape over all and flowing down from her head in long wide pieces, came to him, and moved around the bed. She bow'd low and solemn to me."[4]

He had an abiding interest in—an attraction toward—death. D. H. Lawrence, a literary descendant of Whitman's, called him a "very great postmortem poet" who took "the last steps and looked over into death."[5]

The soldiers in their final moments were portals upon the Unknown, and Walt's study of them would seem to suggest something almost exploitive, except that his placing of his hand "lightly on . . . forehead and face" was also an entirely characteristic gesture of loving connection and soothing sympathy, and few could have wished the poet not to have been there at that moment.

His interest in death did not trail off into spirit rapping or a Poe-ish fascination with the grave's corruptions. It was a philosophical interest and a practical one. The childish questions were not beneath his notice—they continued to perturb him. They deserved useful answers so that an American mother and father who had lost someone in the war could begin to live with that, their sadness not blunted or denied but beginning to be assuaged. He did not, in fact, arrive at a doctrine of the afterlife to be invoked in all cases. His letters to families avoided statements on the order of, "Although your son is gone he died for a good cause," the cause on balance insufficient or irrelevant in his eyes. By the same token, his condolence letters did not often describe a heavenly home the dead man was headed for, and the absence of Christian terminology is noteworthy considering its wide use in other writers' literature of consolation.

On May 1, 1865, Corporal Frank Irwin, of the 93rd Pennsylvania Volunteers, died at Armory Square, and Walt's letter to Irwin's mother, written the same day, shows his approach to the problem of what to say. "I will write . . . as a casual friend that sat by his death-bed," he began, establishing from the outset a standard of simple truth. Corporal Irwin had been wounded near Fort Fisher, Virginia, March 25. Three days later he arrived at Armory Square Hospital, where he received competent care: "[T]he wound became worse, and on the 4th of April the leg was amputated a little above the knee—the operation was perform'd by Dr. Bliss, one of the best surgeons in the army." Walt adds that a great deal of pus had gathered in the wound, and that the bullet was found inside the knee joint.[6]

These medical details, unsettling as they may have been to read, further ground the experience; for a few precious moments, Mrs. Irwin sits in the presence of her son, near enough to hold his hand. No doubt Walt had met relatives unable to countenance graphic medical information. But as evidenced by those few of his letters that survive, he had found that most people preferred, even needed, to know. He was not in fact at the hospital when Frank Irwin arrived. He was home in Brooklyn, celebrating George's return from captivity, thus the details of Frank's surgery had to be gathered from Dr. Bliss or the nurses, and Walt took the trouble to gather them. "For a couple of weeks afterwards," he continued, "[Frank] was doing pretty well. I visited and sat by him frequently, as he was fond of having me." Walt was still in Brooklyn as the corporal began to succumb, but he did sit with Irwin occasionally between April 21, when he returned to Washington, and the young man's death on May 1. "The last ten or twelve days of April," he specified, "I saw that his case was critical":

He previously had some fever, with cold spells . . . The actual cause of death was pyaemia . . . Frank, as far as I saw, had everything requisite in surgical treatment, nursing, &c . . . I myself liked him very much. I was in the habit of coming in afternoons and sitting by him, and soothing him, and he liked to have me—liked to put his arm out and lay his hand on my knee—would keep it so a long while.[7]

Not knowing Mrs. Irwin personally, Walt assumed she would appreciate hearing of Frank's good deportment:

Toward the last he was more restless and flighty at night—often fancied himself with his regiment—by his talk sometimes seem'd as if his feelings were hurt by being blamed . . . for something he was entirely innocent of . . . All the time he was out of his head not one single bad word or idea escaped him. It was remark'd that many a man's conversation in his senses was not half as good as Frank's delirium . . . I do not know his past life, but I feel as if it must have been good . . . he behaved so brave, so composed . . . it could not be surpass'd.[8]

Traversing, finally, the religious realm, but lightly, Walt wrote,

He seem'd quite willing to die . . . had become very weak and had suffer'd a good deal, and was perfectly resign'd, poor boy . . . And now like many other noble and good men, after serving his country as a soldier, he has yielded up his young life at the very outset in her service. Such things are gloomy—yet there is a text, "God doeth all things well"—the meaning of which, after due time, appears to the soul.[9]

On March 6, Walt learned that he would not have to mourn his own brother. George's letter from Annapolis arrived, forwarded from Brooklyn ("Walter I should have sent you this [before] but thought of course you knew," Mrs. Whitman scribbled on the back).[10] George had shown up the morning of March 5, sent home to Brooklyn on medical leave. That night Mrs. Whitman wrote about his condition ("looks quite thin . . . feels pretty well considering") and his incarceration, noting that George had "brought home a peice of the corn bread" made from corncobs on which the men had at times subsisted.[11]

Walt now yearned to be in Brooklyn, too. He wanted to lay eyes on his heroic brother, but he also wanted to take another pass at publishing *Drum-Taps*, to see if he could finally carry through on the project. The war was coming to a close. Punishing Southern defeats in Tennessee and Georgia at the end of 1864 had left Lee's army the only sizable force still in the field on the Southern side. Still tied down in defense of Richmond and Petersburg, Lee's men were dependent for supplies on what could be brought up the Cape Fear River on blockade-running boats; Fort Fisher, where Frank Irwin had suffered his fatal wound, defended the mouth of the river against Yankee warships, but the giant fort would fall on January 15.[12]

Now, surely, was the hour to publish. The war was in him if it was in any man; bathed in the blood of the nation, lover of the suffering sons of families North and South, he had seen the first and the last. In a letter to William O'Connor in January he declared, "['Drum-Taps'] is in a state to put right through, a perfect copy being ready for the printers—I feel at last, & for the first time without any demur, that I am satisfied with it—content to have it go to the world."[13] Then, sounding like a man trying to convince himself, he added, "It is in my opinion superior to Leaves of Grass—certainly more perfect as a work of art, being adjusted in all its proportions, & its passion having the indispensable merit that though to the ordinary reader let loose with the wildest abandon, the true artist can see it is yet under control."[14]

Infinitely smaller, in every poetical way, than the 1860 edition of

Leaves, *Drum-Taps* nonetheless seemed to him to embody his dearest, deepest ideas about art, delivering on

> my ambition of the task that had haunted me, namely, to express in a poem . . . the pending action of this *Time & Land we swim in*, with all their large conflicting fluctuations of despair & hope, the shiftings, masses, & the whirl & deafening din . . . with the unprecedented anguish of wounded & suffering, the beautiful young men, in wholesale death & agony, everything sometimes as if in blood color, & dripping blood.[15]

The new book worked by a kind of symphonic method, he told O'Connor; the parts of it that were sad yielded to "the blast of the trumpet, & the drum . . . then [sounded] an undertone of sweetest comradeship & human love, threading . . . inside the chaos," with "clear notes of faith & triumph."

By mid-March, flush with government pay, he was able to underwrite the printing of his little book—and maybe its littleness had been the real impediment all along: only fifty-two poems, many of them brief, several with the look of mere page fillers.[16] The book was so small and the war so large. He wanted, as any writer would, to post a substantial response to the times, large in conception if not in pages. In one of those short poems he commanded,

> Shut not your doors to me, proud libraries,
> For that which was lacking among you all, yet needed
>   most, I bring;
> A book I have made for your dear sake, O soldiers,
> And for you, O soul of man . . .
> The words of my book nothing, the life of it everything.[17]

It was an idea borrowed from *Leaves*, that the intimacy offered by his poems overleaped mere printed words on a page. But it was also a confession, that the book as a book was less important than the sentiment that had given birth to it. Now, inside the proud libraries, there would be a book about the nation's tragic war, permanent testimony to the "wholesale death & agony" of the soldiers he had loved.[18]

Walt saw President Lincoln on Saturday, March 4, the day of the second inaugural, passing along Pennsylvania Avenue in a carriage. He appears to have missed the famous inaugural address, but his advice to Mrs. Irwin, to bethink herself of the biblical verse "God doeth all things well," recalls Lincoln's advice that afternoon to the American people: that "the judgments of the Lord, are true and righteous altogether," no matter the grave destructions of the war.

Walt probably read the president's speech when it appeared in the papers. He was much taken with Lincoln, finding his figure and demeanor immensely suggestive. "He has a face like a hoosier Michael Angelo," he wrote in 1863, "so awful ugly it becomes beautiful, with its strange mouth . . . deep cut, criss-cross lines, and . . . doughnut complexion." To Walt's way of thinking—not a common way in 1863—Lincoln had the mystic lineaments of greatness. "I do not dwell on the supposed failures of his government," he wrote to some New York friends, for, notwithstanding such failures, "he has shown . . . an almost supernatural tact in keeping the ship afloat at all, with head steady . . . and flag flying in sight of the world [as] high as ever."[19]

Walt thought he could detect an "idiomatic western genius" in the raw rail-splitter, "careless of court dress or court decorums." Two years further along as steward of the nation in its near-suicidal war, the president looked "very much worn and tired," Walt noted on Inauguration Day. "[T]he lines, indeed, of vast responsibilities . . . and demands of life and death, cut deeper than ever upon his dark brown face," which showed however "goodness, tenderness, sadness, and canny shrewdness, underneath the furrows."[20]

Somewhat repulsed by the carnival atmosphere of the inaugural afternoon, Walt took a closer look at Lincoln that night, at a White House reception. He had a "notion to go," he wrote, "was in the rush inside with the crowd," surging down the elegant interior passageways. There had been much rain recently in Washington and the crowd, including many "country people, some very funny," would not have been careful of the carpets. He heard "fine music from the Marine Band," and then "I saw Mr. Lincoln, drest all in black, with white kid gloves, and a claw-hammer coat, receiving . . . looking very disconsolate, and as if he would give anything to be somewhere else."[21]

That afternoon, as Lincoln stepped forward at the Capitol, the sun had burst through the clouds, in a dramatic effect of the recent weather. Newspaperman Noah Brooks had felt the "meridian splendor" with its hint of divine sympathy for the affairs of men, and he wrote afterward that Lincoln, a personal friend, inquired of him, "Did you notice that sunburst? It made my heart jump."[22]

The second week in March, the skies clearing, Walt enjoyed the sight of Venus in the evening hours, consorting with the moon along the western horizon. Sometime after the middle of the month, he took a train to New York, finding George to be in moderately good shape, considering. Walt wrote the O'Connors that George "would be in what I would almost call fair condition, if it were not that his legs are affected . . . rheumatism, following the fever that he had . . . goes to bed quite sleepy & falls to sleep—but then soon wakes, & frequently little or no more sleep that night." George was in "first rate spirits" in any case and inclined to go out "most every day . . . He is going to report to Annapolis promptly when his furlough is up—I told him I had no doubt I could get it extended, but he does not wish it."[23]

George "says little," Walt informed the O'Connors. No one had ever complained before that George was too taciturn, nor was Walt really complaining now; it may be that the war had encouraged a tendency in him, or, like many veterans returning from many wars, he may have felt that the effort needed to make himself understood was a little too much. The reunion was joyous, no matter how much he spoke. "I . . . never enjoyed a visit home more than I am doing this," Walt told Washington friends. Still living in the house on North Portland, the Whitman family looked as if it had survived the war. They had lost Andrew, and Jesse had been put away, but the others were doing fairly well. Jeff and his daughters, aged almost five and almost two, were thriving; Jeff liked to take rides out on the Island with his wife, Mattie, and their older daughter, leaving the baby home with Mother Whitman, who Jeff persuaded himself "rather likes to have [the little one] all to herself" for a few hours.[24] Mattie was now in another period of prodigious sewing of shirtfronts for New York manufacturers. She was mortally ill, probably with tuberculosis, but showing few signs of it; she cooked for Mrs. Whitman and her son Eddy, cooked and cleaned for her own family, and worked her machine. The ingathering of family to celebrate George's return was a glad version of the somber gathering at Andrew's dying fifteen months before, when the moribund son had had on hand not only his mother, his brother Jeff, sister Mary Elizabeth, sister-in-law Mat, and wife Nancy, but also, symbolically, his brothers George and Walt, whose photographs he had gazed at just before he died.

Walt's letter to the O'Connors hinted that he had been approaching people about *Drum-Taps*. He complained, "All the printers tell me I could not pick a more inopportune time—that in ten days prices of paper, composition &c will all be very much lower &c."[25] But he went ahead anyway. On April 1, he signed a contract for the stereotyping of his poems for $254, paying $138 up front. The strictly worded contract mentioned a book of 120 pages. Peter Eckler, printer, managed to fit all of Walt's work on a mere 72, and he submitted a revised total bill on April 12 of $192.85.[26]

The plates next went to Coridon A. Alvord, at another shop, to be press-run. The book, "small & not thick at all," Walt told O'Connor, was ready to be bound on Monday, May 1. But the world had convulsed meanwhile. In the month or so it took to create *Drum-Taps* as a physical object, it became inadequate—in Walt's eyes, possibly, only more inadequate—to "the pending action" of his times. The woeful events of April 14 in Ford's Theatre, combined with the glorious events (to Northerners) of five days earlier, when Lee had surrendered to Grant in the town of Appomattox Court House, diminished it. Writing in a hurry, Walt stuck in a fifty-third poem, "Hush'd Be the Camps To-day," acknowledging the death of Lincoln. But it was only a sketch—a raw outline of a response:

No more for him life's stormy conflicts;
Nor victory, nor defeat—No more time's dark events,
Charging like ceaseless clouds across the sky.

But sing, poet, in our name;
Sing of the love we bore him—because you, dweller in camps, know
    it truly.[27]

Self-conscious—enjoining the singer to sing, while providing only snippets of song—the twelve short lines were, however, pregnant with a larger response. The poet counsels the soldiers "each, with musing soul" to retire and think on their lost commander. To muse and "celebrate"—not mourn. In passing, he also registers the portentous skies of the season, racing clouds counterpoised to "shovel'd clods" of earth that fill a grave.[28]

The idyll in the house on North Portland Avenue modulated, darkened. Walt was home with Mrs. Whitman and probably the rest of the household, when church bells began tolling on Saturday, April 15. It was the day before Easter, and as they read in the papers, Abraham Lincoln had been murdered. "Mother prepared breakfast—and other meals afterwards—as usual," Walt later remembered, "but not a mouthful was eaten all day by either of us. We each drank half a cup of coffee; that was all."[29]

The children would have been underfoot; the Brown family, still sharing the modest house, probably contributed some creakings and poundings through the walls and ceilings. "Little was said" between Walt and his mother, he noted, and they read every newspaper they could get, including "the frequent extras of that period, and pass'd them silently to each other."[30]

It had always been a special pleasure for him to be at home, quietly reading with his mother. George may also have been home this day, and Eddy surely was at home, attached to his mother, as usual; but Walt edits them out of the picture. She was a "stately sensible matron," in Bronson Alcott's description of Mrs. Whitman from the 1850s, "a spry, vivacious, handsome old lady, worthy of her illustrious son," according to John Burroughs, who described her ten years later. Walt makes Lincoln's death an occasion of special silent communion between them, and it may be that there was no one with whom he preferred to share such ill-boding and epic news, if shared it had to be.

Jeff's description of her, at the time of George's captivity, sitting with head in hand after reading of the treatment of the prisoners, sitting that way for a whole hour, may be an exaggeration, but it captures a quality of comprehending compassion. George and Walt had run almost the entire war past her by then, via graphic letters, and she had taken in and understood. To witness her reaction to this tragic turn, untutored, homebound woman that she was, moved Walt. He mentions no tears, no macabre flights of fancy. Only dignified silence; an urge to know; a Quakerish reciprocity.

Around noon the weather changed. "[H]eavy moist black weather," Walt wrote; "the rain sent the women from the street & black clothed men only remained." He stayed with his mother till around four P.M., then took the ferry to Manhattan. Out on the streets he could sense "the horror, fever, uncertainty, alarm" animating the public.[31] One of the very few pocket notebooks, bound with a pin, that survives intact to this day—not torn apart by time or eager scholars—dates from this afternoon; the writing on its small pages is a scrawl, as if Walt had written mostly in the street. He went up vibrant, colorful Broadway, America's oceanic thoroughfare, the scene now "solemn . . . The stores were shut, & no business transacted, no pleasure vehicles, & hardly a cart—only the rumbling base of the heavy Broadway stages" rolling over cobblestones.[32]

He noticed "one large and fashionable picture store, all shuttered up close," that showed nothing through its plate-glass front but a small picture frame, "vacuous of a picture." The weather went on sympathizing, "sulky, leaden, & dripping continualy moist tears." In his notebook he wrote, "The blood of Abraham Lincoln was permitted by the," then could not complete the thought, or did not need to. He also noted, "The tragedy of the last five years has risen to its climax," and, "When a great event happens, or the news [of] some signal solemn thing spreads out among the people, it is curious to go forth and wander awhile in the public ways."[33]

These first scribbled notes seem aimed at an article he might submit to the papers, but the city and the harbor with its "shipping densely crowding the docks" instead would make their way into "When Lilacs Last in the Door-Yard Bloom'd," a poem otherwise given over mostly to images from nature.[34] In "Lilacs," Walt notes "Mighty Manhattan, with spires, and the sparkling and hurrying tides, and the ships," also the busy streets, "how their throbbings throbbed . . . the cities pent." He noticed the city because his elegy for the first assassinated American president was intended to play out against the largest backdrop he could suggest, the whole of the nation. In the streets crowded with black-clad men, who mobbed bulletin boards for the latest news, he took the temper of his people; took solace from their nearness and their shared grief; and in hints he gathered of their "fury, tenderness, & a stirring wonder brewing," began to formulate something other than a newspaper response.

He did not rush back to Washington. He had taken the trouble to get his short leave of absence from the Indian Office extended, just as, despite George's reluctance, he had intervened on George's behalf ("My brother . . . has sulkily permitted me to get an extension of his leave," he wrote O'Connor on April 7).[35] Dr. Ruggles signed George's request for twenty days' more rest and recuperation, but Walt had drafted the letter, writing, in his bold hand, in the person of the agreeable family doctor, "I have carefully & several times examined this Officer and find that he has Rheumatism, with swelling & weakness of legs, & Debility—resulting from six months incarceration in Rebel prisons at Salisbury and Danville."[36] On April 19, he took his first short poem about the assassination to the printer. It was the beginning of an extraordinary interlude of national mourning, the president's casket, accompanied by the casket of his son, Willie, who had died of typhus three years before, circuiting by train from Washington to Springfield, Illinois, by way of Northern cities large and small.

The wet season had nourished lilacs. Also apple blossoms, hyacinths, daffodils, and early tulips.[37] But "by one of those caprices that enter and give tinge to events," Walt wrote in *Memoranda*, ". . . I find myself always reminded of . . . that day by the sight and odor" of lilacs. "I remember where I was stopping at the time . . . were many lilacs in full bloom."[38] The newspaper accounts, too, stressed the abundance of lilacs when the presidential casket was taken from the White House, following the first funeral rites, to the Capitol, where it lay in state for two days; great sprays of lilacs there banked the caskets of the president and his young son.[39]

Lincoln's body had been carefully embalmed by Henry P. Cattell, of the Washington embalming firm of Brown & Alexander.[40] Staff workers accompanied the casket as the train left Washington on April 21, bound first for Baltimore. Still in New York, Walt made an advance payment for the binding of *Drum-Taps* ($20) to J. M. Bradstreet & Son, 8 Spruce Street, on the twenty-first, then entrained for Washington; possibly he passed the president's train en route, since the casket lay in state in Baltimore for five hours.[41] Early viewers of Lincoln's remains noted his pale complexion, and one recorded that the expression on his face was "calm as an infant's in unutterable sweet peace . . . bathed in a blessed . . . supreme sereneness shed from heaven."[42]

Letter drafted by Walt Whitman, signed by Dr. Ruggles, requesting an extension of George Whitman's leave, April 1865.

By the time the cortège had reached Manhattan, on April 24, the president's complexion had gone a deep gray-brown. In Philadelphia, more than one million mourners had crowded into the city, many of them hoping to file closely by the casket, to peer in. The embalmers cleaned dust and pollen from the president's face, but the eyes were soon sunken, the cheeks hollow and pitted.[43]

Abraham Lincoln's funeral procession, New York City, April 24, 1865.

In "Lilacs," Walt seems to speak of a personal encounter with the funeral cortège:

> Coffin that passes through lanes and streets,
> Through day and night, with the great cloud darkening the land,
> With the pomp of the inloop'd flags, with the cities draped in black,
> With the show of the States themselves, as of crape-veil'd women . . .
> With the waiting depot, the arriving coffin, and the sombre faces,
> With dirges through the night, with the thousand voices rising strong
> and solemn[44]

Almost surely, though, he read about the funeral train, and the astonishing turnout of mourners, rather than witnessed them personally. There were countless news articles, and he would have seen lithographs of the open casket (as, for example, one that appeared May 6 in *Harper's Weekly*, depicting the viewing in New York, when a half million mourners passed through City Hall). In some towns a number greater than the town's known population awaited the train, the surrounding countryside having emptied out.[45] The people appeared despite storms; they waited through the night in places; some cities greeted the arrival of the train with a tolling of bells or with cannon fire, the people themselves tending to crowd alongside the tracks in reverent silence.

Eulogies were not rare or spare. In New York, George Bancroft, former secretary of the navy, former minister to Great Britain, and close adviser to newly installed president Andrew Johnson, spoke to a throng in Union Square. This speech, a kind of rehearsal for Bancroft's official memorial address, delivered to Congress ten months later, moves with bracing swiftness from words on Lincoln's goodly temperament to thoughts on how best to honor the slain leader:

> There can be but one answer. He was struck down when he was highest in [the nation's] service, and in strict conformity with duty was engaged in carrying out principles affecting its life . . . and its relations to the . . . progress of mankind. Grief must take the character of action . . . The standard which he held in his hand must be uplifted again, higher and more firmly.[46]

Bancroft was concerned lest the South, in the current confusion, reinstall slavery somehow. He recognized the grief of the nation ("the crime . . . wounded the affections of the whole people"), but grief in its own right had small claim on his attention. Another soldier had gone down—Soldier Number One—but that death would prove instrumental, as had the hundreds of thousands of others:

> The country may have needed an imperishable grief to touch its inmost feeling. The grave that receives the remains of Lincoln receives the costly sacrifice to the Union; the monument which will rise over his body will bear witness to the Union . . . He was happy in his life, for he was the restorer of the republic; he was happy in his death, for his martyrdom will plead forever for the Union.[47]

Other eulogies also put Lincoln's death to use. Indeed, not to invoke Union and emancipation as noble causes was to court offense to the memory of the 360,000 dead of the North. The obviousness of the argument—that, because a man died in a meaningful fight, his death had some meaning—did not disprove it. Even Walt sometimes implied as much in his letters to grieving parents.

The more emotional strain in the observances attending the progress of the two caskets expressed, powerfully, horror and sadness. Commentators compared the outpouring to the observances when George Washington had died, but there was really nothing American that it resembled. The Reverend Henry Ward Beecher, of Plymouth Church, Brooklyn, likened Lincoln's death to the death of Moses, since both leaders had been vouchsafed only glimpses of the Promised Land before being cut off. Beecher was the most famous preacher in America. His sermon on Sunday, April 23, answered an extraordinary need that the correspondent for the *Daily Eagle* tried to suggest by describing the crush of listeners into the church:

> [There] we never saw so great a throng . . . Rushing by the sextons, they surged in like a mighty stream, occupying seats without regard to order or arrangement . . . in the course of which several ladies were pretty roughly handled by the crowd, injuring one or two . . . while others fainted away.[48]

Beecher—perhaps a little unnerved himself—ordered the sextons not to enforce the usual rules, declaring that at such an anguished time, "pewholders must take their chances."

Unlike Bancroft, Beecher did not hurry to invoke Unionism and emancipation as causes. He elaborated the comparison with the death of Moses, asserting, "Never did so many hearts in so brief a time touch two such boundless feelings [joy and sorrow] . . . It was so terrible that it stunned sensibility . . . Men were bereaved and walked for days as if a corpse lay in their house." Lincoln was the nation's savior because of his extraordinary capacity for feeling but also his emotional control:

> Through toil, and sorrow, and wars . . . [he] came near to the promised land of peace . . . Who shall count the work of our martyr? Never rising to the enthusiasm of your impassioned natures in hours of hope; never sinking into despondency with more mercurial

natures . . . he wrestled with all the trials of time. At last, the watcher beheld the gray dawn of the morning; the mountains began to give their forms forth out of the darkness, the east came rushing toward him with arms full of joy.[49]

Beecher's was well-known as a ministry of emotion. As he once declared, "I never knew how to worship until I knew how to love," an assertion that opened him to mockery when he was revealed later as an adulterer. Now he went straight to what he imagined was most troubling for many of his parishioners, the awfulness of the actual murder, and declared, "We need not fill our minds with horror . . . They that go wide awake and watching as a bridegroom to the wedding, and not they that waste . . . are blessed."[50]

If the manner of death were not so terrible—a simple death by enemy bullet, such as many soldiers had found—where was the sting? Where the horror? Indeed, "the martyr is [now] moving in triumphal march," Beecher declaimed, "mightier than one alive. A nation rises up at every stage of his coming, cities and states are as pallbearers." Lincoln is not really dead, he insists:

> He yet speaketh. Is Washington dead? . . . Is David . . . ? Is any man that ever was fit to live dead? Disinthralled of the flesh and risen to the unobstructed sphere [of pure spirit], he begins his illimitable work. His life now is grafted upon the infinite, and will be fruitful, as no earthly life can be.[51]

Clearly, Beecher's talk of feelings was closer to Walt's orientation. Still, Walt's ruminations on Lincoln's death did not lead him to visions of a higher sphere. But the funeral train in its slow, vagrant progress from Washington to Springfield by way of Harrisburg, Trenton, Jersey City, Albany, Syracuse, Buffalo, Cleveland, Columbus, Indianapolis, and Chicago, not to mention dozens of lesser places, captivated him. The stately pace and eccentric route would find form in the poem he would soon write. The apparent uncertainty of its destination would also influence "Lilacs," which wends its way to no easily predicted poetic or emotional terminus.

His decision to suspend *Drum-Taps* came fairly soon but not instantly. In another notebook scrap from the same time, "For Funeral piece A. L.," he laid plans for more writing; he admonished himself to make "a list of things, sights, scenes, landscapes, rivers, &c peculiar to the west, & bring it in / also in dim perspective, the large & varied future," and then he added a bit of new poetry:

> No mourning drape hang
> I about my song,
> But these I hang &
> plant about my
> song.[52]

He may already have been planting lilacs in his mind. Nor, to judge from this scrap, was anguished grief to be the keynote of whatever he would have to say. Mourning, yes, but mourning as he understood it— more in line with the fond brooding on the recently dead of "Vigil Strange" or of his response to the death of Charles Chauncey, his one-time drinking companion.

He was back in Washington and back in the hospitals as the train pressed on in its journey. On May 3, the papers reported, the cortège arrived in Springfield. On May 4, Matthew Simpson, a Methodist Episcopal bishop, sermonized at the burial service that "the conviction has been growing on the nation's mind . . . that, by the hand of God, [Lincoln] was especially singled out" to guide America through its dark ordeal.[53] The signs of sublime influence abounded: the storms of winter, Venus in the evening, and the awesome coincidence of the forbearing redeemer suffering his fatal wound on the same day as the martyrdom of the Son of Man. Although Walt was no churchgoer, he was imbued with the tropes of Protestant Christianity, and by his close association with thousands of Christian young men who had suffered their own ordeals he had learned to mute his agnostic iconoclasm. "I [had] come to adapt myself," he wrote in *Memoranda*, ". . . not only washing and dressing wounds . . . but [reading] passages from the Bible, expounding them, [with] prayer at the bedside." (Then he added, "I think I see my friends smiling at this confession, but I was never more in earnest in my life.")[54]

The trinity of images in "Lilacs" is its most manifestly Christian element—maybe its only one. Words such as "soul" and "psalm" also appear, but only occasionally, and they are pre-Christian. More telling as a religious key to the poem—more than the threefold character of lilac, bird, and star—is the remarkable absence of any mention of dying for the good or the redemption of others. This is an act of singular poetic forbearance, given the identification between Lincoln and Christ so prominent in the popular response to the murder.

Lincoln, never mentioned by name, is not savior or redeemer but simply "him I love," as well as "the large sweet soul that has gone" and "the sweetest, wisest soul of all my days and lands."[55] The poem works no images of crucifixion into its pattern. There is no talk of resurrection, nor is there in a general sense a movement "upward"—the poet more often extends his thoughts outward, to encompass all his broad nation, and downward, as he seeks an essential encounter with death:

> Then with the knowledge of death as walking one side of me,
> And the thought of death close-walking the other side of me,
> And I in the middle, as with companions, and as holding the hands
>   of companions,
> I fled forth to the hiding receiving night, that talks not,
> Down to the shores of the water, the path by the swamp in the
>   dimness,
> To the solemn shadowy cedars, and ghostly pines so still.[56]

Lincoln's death evoked all the others. In its own right shocking and saddening, it opened the door on the overspilling crypt of the war—on the dead in their "Million," known and unknown. The profound disturbance to the national spirit caused by the assassination was something that Walt was sensible to as a Union man and a Lincoln lover, but it was as the writer of thousands of kindly, specific letters of reassurance and condolence that he framed a response. This death like all the others was of this world, significant mainly in worldly terms; attended by a visible star in an actual sky, and by the pastel odor of spring flowers, it did not find its meaning elsewhere. Lincoln had been embalmed like any one of the young officers—Captain Sims, perhaps—slain in their thousands and processed using the solution of zinc chloride patented by Charles R. Brown, of Brown & Alexander, for the hygienic shipping home of the dead. A greater soul, a mightier and more historic figure than an ordinary soldier, perhaps, but no more beloved—and to reconcile with the loss of him would require the same kind of inner journey.

On May 11, the poet received a promotion to clerk second class in Indian Affairs.[57] Two days later, George became officially a major of infantry, with an increase in pay of nearly 50 percent.[58] A general sense of financial improvement may have contributed to Walt's willingness to pull *Drum-Taps* back from distribution, despite an investment already of more than two hundred dollars. Some copies did make it out into the world, by accident or plan—he sent two to John Swinton at the *Times* and five to his mother in Brooklyn, as well as a few elsewhere. But Lincoln's death could not be hurriedly sketched in, he had decided. The book would miss the propitious war-ending moment. Now, it would become larger.

G EORGE HAD BEGUN to think beyond the war. The 51st was bar-racked in Alexandria, Virginia, within shouting distance of Walt's haunts in Washington, and at the end of April the soon-to-be major took up a new assignment, as commandant of the Prince Street Military Prison.[1] This facility housed "thieves, Bounty jumpers and Deserters," plus about twenty rebel officers, George wrote his mother; he assured her that "they are used very different from what we were, when we were in Rebeldom."[2]

George saw his brother when he could. Walt came over for dinner with the regiment, and George hoped to hunt him down when his duties took him across the Potomac, but he was serving on a court-martial in early summer and had few free hours. He issued an open invitation, "Walt come over and see us, the stage leaves Willards twice every day and brings you right to Camp, so jump in and come over."[3]

Walt was more likely to walk to Alexandria than take the stage. One of his great enjoyments at this time was to go on nature jaunts along the river with Pete Doyle or John Burroughs, sometimes heading south out of Washington via the Navy Yard Bridge and then across by ferry to the Virginia side. Doyle remembered that the poet was in these days still "an athlete—great, great. I knew him to do wonderful lifting, running, walking."[4] On May 7, on one of those hikes near Alexandria, Walt came upon a crowd of men from Sherman's army, most of them sick or disabled, on their way to a hospital camp. "These fragmentary excerpts," he wrote in *Specimen Days*, "with the unmistakable Western

Walt Whitman and Pete Doyle.

physiognomy and idioms, crawling along slowly—after a great campaign, blown this way, as it were, out of their latitude—I marked with
curiosity."[5]

Doyle had grown up in Alexandria. Sometimes Walt and he would
go for a long distance without speaking, then Walt would break out in
poetry—he favored quotations from Shakespeare. Walt was also a
whistler and a singer in the woods. He recalled late in life, "We would

walk together for miles and miles, never sated . . . It was a great, a precious, a memorable experience."[6] Doyle decades later also remembered something deeply pleasurable about these wanderings.[7] With the nearness to water, a shady forest, and a fresh and warming season of the year, the conditions were entirely Calamus-like. "I will plant companionship thick as trees along all the rivers," Walt had written in Calamus 5, and in Calamus 10 he enjoined "You bards of ages hence!" to think of him as one "Whose happiest days were far away, through fields, in woods, on hills, he and another, wandering hand in hand."[8]

If he was working on "Lilacs" at this time, he was doing so under the influence of a love affair. That odd juxtaposition (love al fresco, exited new love, with focused thoughts of death) was also familiar from the Calamus cluster of poems. In Calamus 2 he wrote, "I am not sure but the high Soul of lovers welcomes death most," meaning, possibly, that the exaltation of being with a lover was a finished sensation, a ne plus ultra, like death. The cast of mind that sometimes accompanies sexualized love—slowed down, dreamily alert—seems to preside over a number of passages in "Lilacs," including this one, with its use of love's simplest tokens:

> In the door-yard fronting an old farm-house, near the white-wash'd
>   palings,
> Stands the lilac-bush, tall-growing, with heart-shaped leaves of rich
>   green,
> With many a pointed blossom, rising, delicate, with the perfume
>   strong I love,
> With every leaf a miracle . . . . . . and from this bush in the door-yard,
> With its delicate-color'd blossoms, and heart-shaped leaves of rich
>   green,
> A sprig, with its flower, I break.

The mood of love was not so far from the mood of mourning. An important influence on the poem Walt was writing or soon to write, William Cullen Bryant's "Thanatopsis" (1814–21), another fluent meditation on death, also does most of its reflecting out in nature.[9] Bryant tells anyone concerned about mortality, "Go forth, under the open sky, and list / To Nature's teachings," secure in the knowledge that the hills

> Rock-ribbed and ancient as the sun,—the vales
> Stretching in pensive quietness between;
> The venerable woods—rivers that move
> In majesty, and the complaining brooks
> That make the meadows green . . .
> . . . Are but the solemn decorations all
> Of the great tomb of man.[10]

Bryant's Nature is welcoming—venerable and good, but not really a place for kisses, or for fondly offering someone a heart-shaped leaf. But Walt's nature is such a place, no matter how many corpses it harbors. Nature as a place for lovers lies behind the song the thrush inspires in the swamp in the hiding night in "Lilacs," a song of seduction and surrender, almost a sex song,

> Come, lovely and soothing Death,
> Undulate round the world, serenely arriving, arriving,
> In the day, in the night, to all, to each,
> Sooner or later, delicate Death.
>
> Prais'd be the fathomless universe,
> For life and joy. . . .
> And for love, sweet love . . . O praise and praise,
> For the sure-enwinding arms of cool-enfolding Death.

Death is like an overmastering lover; in Death's presence, the poet can only surrender, and sing praise:

> Have none chanted for thee a chant of fullest welcome?
> Then I chant it for thee—I glorify thee above all. . . .
> . . . .
> From me to thee glad serenades,
> Dances for thee I propose, saluting thee—adornments and feastings
>   for thee

Trysts in the forest with a young friend: These were not necessarily inspiration for his presidential elegy but a reminder, a conduit back to the wellsprings of his early, greatest poetry. And the cheekiness of a confident lover seems to flavor his song for death. Feasts and dances not for Lincoln, but for the thief Death itself: This was a nonstandard approach, at the least, grieving in a new key.

George, in the course of the war, had ascended in class; he had become one of an honored cohort of men from which America traditionally drew its political leaders and heads of business. His wish to remain a soldier looks, therefore, like a sensible calculation of advantage. Jeff was sanguine about his chances to continue in the regular army as an officer; he began scheming on how to help George overcome the usual requirement that an officer be a graduate of a military academy, and in response to a letter from George early in May, spelling out his professional ambitions, Jeff wrote Walt declaring that "I have though[t] considerably about it and have made up my mind if we all go to work it could be done."[11] Jeff consulted his friend Julius Mason, who had helped when George was in prison, and Mason declared that he "could help us a good deal" because "in his duties he was brought . . . in [close] intercourse with General Grant." Jeff lined up other potential helpers in such number—Moses Lane, his boss; Congressman John Bidwell of California; New York congressman Tunis G. Bergen; John Swinton; Secretary Stanton—and with such relish that the suspicion arises that his gifts as an engineer were at least equaled by his instincts for institutional maneuvering. "[B]ut for God-sake don't let him think of enlisting" in the army in the ordinary way, starting out at the bottom again, he advised Walt; "that is too dangerous."[12]

Soon, though, George was backing off from his plan. Despite Jeff's willingness to pull many strings (and Walt no doubt would have helped all he could), George began thinking of a nonmilitary future for himself. On May 23, he paraded through Washington with the rest of the 51st, his honored regiment allotted a special place in the grand review that for two days sent soldiers and cavalrymen flooding down Pennsylvania Avenue. The triumphal review signaled both war's end and war's promise—as the Prussian ambassador said admiringly, an army of this size and prowess could stand against any in the world.[13]

"I still think if [George] wishes he could get in the regular army," Jeff wrote Walt July 16, which suggests that the push through influential friends was never tried. The huge army—more than one million men at war's end—would soon shrink to a mere twenty-seven thousand, but such fluctuations in number occurred within a context of authentic military legacy.[14] Now American sons and grandsons had images and stories of heroic campaigns to call upon when they thought of war; the nation had mobilized itself as no other had yet done, and millions of American families had had direct experience of a soldier son or brother.

Now there was a vast army of veterans, too. Its needs and attitudes would shape American politics for many decades, and may be said to shape them still, in the legacy of military responses to crises and in the doctrine of state responsibility for the welfare of ex-soldiers, and by extension, for other needful citizens.[15] Unlike many of his friends in the 51st, George never filed for a pension for age or medical disability; he was skeptical of some soldiers' claims but, more to the point, he was successful in the postwar years and never needed a pension.* The rise in fortune hoped for by his parents had come to pass. It had come to pass on almost the same scale for Jeff, and even Walt, the head-in-clouds poet, died solidly in the black.[16]

George may have sensed, with the war's end, an economic tide he would be wise to float his boat upon. And just possibly his brother's offer of help rankled. He was older than Jeff, and unlike him he had fought a war. To have strings pulled for him in the peacetime army when he had been proud to earn advancement with his own blood and daring may have put him off, and he appears to have responded the same way to yet another attempt by Jeff to finagle him a position, as Jeff communicated to Walt in a letter in September:

George has started in his building business—he is in hopes of getting a pretty large job in New York—will know to-day—Mr. Lane offered him a first rate berth [at the waterworks, where Jeff had a lead

---

*After his death in 1901, George's estate was appraised at $59,349.14, a goodly sum equivalent to millions of dollars today. A housing contractor, a pipe inspector, a private investor who held mortgages on many properties and wisely spread his cash holdings among many banks, he was solidly a member of the moneyed and comfortable middle class. Source: Surrogate's Office of the County of Burlington, Mount Holly, NJ.

position]—he thought at first he would take it but afterwards declined—perhaps he did better in going on with his venture[17]

George struggled for several years. Proud, and not averse to cutting a dashing figure—he "wore his new sword and sash looked very good," Mrs. Whitman reported about one postwar celebration—he had hopes of winning a position in the customs service, then, when that failed to happen, he concentrated on speculative building. Mrs. Whitman noted that he was "very restless . . . i tell him not to be in a hurry but rest but i can see he is very uneasy."[18] When Fred McReady, George's wounded friend (still with a bullet in his hip), came to visit, Mrs. Whitman reflected, "I gess they are all sorry i dont know as they are sorry the war is over but I gess they would much rather staid in camp."[19] George had amassed capital from his wages, and he formed a partnership with a man named Smith to buy vacant lots and put up new housing, as his father and older brother had done. He lived at home meanwhile, feeding up at his mother's table; she had "fixed up georges room," she told Walt, "and put a carpet on so he can take his friends up when he has them come."[20]

Smith turned out to be an unreliable partner. The problem was not dishonesty but limited capital, thus difficulty in riding out shortages of funds when new units failed to sell, or when anticipated rises in value were slow in coming. Still, the two speculators did acquire properties and did build in both New York and Brooklyn. Mrs. Whitman's letters to Walt for the five years after the war offer an insider's vigilant view of George's efforts with Smith and with a third partner, a man named French, whom they soon took on. "George comes home to dinner mostly every day," she wrote in December 1865, "he is very busiley engaged buying timber and materials for finishing their building in new york i believe they have hired one or two carpenters there is plenty to be got . . . since the great discharge in the navy yard."[21] For thirty years, Mrs. Whitman had attended her husband while he pursued schemes for building in Brooklyn, and she was savvy about all aspects of the enterprise, not only the benefit to a contractor of having thousands of nearby men out of work, but also the strain of small-time entrepreneurship, the way even promising projects were always anxious. "[G]eorge is building his shop and he gets very tired," she reported in March 1866; "he had never ought to have commenced to work at his trade he says . . . and if his money was not invested he would go south."[22]

She wanted him to have something to show for having fought the war, for dutifully saving his wages, therefore she encouraged him to buy properties and build. But she was not a completely disinterested party. One of those new houses, she dearly hoped, would be hers. Seventy years old in September 1865, she was tired of living in rented places. Soon the family would have to decamp from North Portland at Myrtle, their longtime residence, for a worse house at a high rent, with "hard stairs" where "the going up and down . . . tires me more than it ever did," she complained to Walt.[23] This house was also shared, and the only piped water was in the basement. It was with a special concern of her own, then, that she watched how her veteran son fared in the business that had mostly defeated her husband.

"[G]eorge has paid the rent he dont like it very well here," she told Walt about the new house, then added, "[I] dont know what his ideas are probably he will get married who its too we dont know but he appears to be very much taken with some one." If George married, he would likely set up housekeeping with his wife, with Mrs. Whitman and Eddy to be disposed who knew where. "[I] said something to him about it the other day," she continued, "partly in joke and partly in earnest he said he dident know but he should [marry] when he got time."[24] This was a distant worry, if even a worry. Whether her son succeeded in building on his capital was the main concern, with his future and her own security intertwined, as they had been ever since he went away to war.

Jeff and Mattie contributed, but responsibility for Mrs. Whitman's part of the rent for the new house as for the old fell on George and Walt.[25] Walt was dependable with small gifts of money in almost every letter he mailed, and his sudden dismissal from the Indian Bureau on June 30, 1865, the incident that William O'Connor, in *The Good Gray Poet*, turned into a minor cause célèbre, did not slow him down financially, as he was hired anew in the attorney general's office the very next day. But George's contribution was central. During the war, he had prided himself on his openhandedness with his mother, telling her to spend freely out of the wages he sent home; now he had to watch every cent. George "has got to be very economical," she told Walt, "very different from when he was in the army . . . every body changes some for the better some for the worser."[26] That other point of pride—not having Jeff pull strings for him—soon took on a different complexion. By early 1867 he was taking jobs at the waterworks, as Jeff had proposed he do. He was a troubleshooter on a water main, and Mrs. Whitman reported that Moses Lane depended on him implicitly, assigning him to stop a major leak in the system. Entrenchment under fire at Petersburg and other great battles may have been good preparation, and hard, muscular work had never put him off, but to end up "mud from head to foot," as Mrs. Whitman described him at the end of one workday, may not have comported with his largest idea of himself.[27]

He was entitled to be called "colonel," and so he was often called.* To create a life equal to that title became his quiet study. "George and smith and french . . . has bought 5 lots on portland ave opposite the arsenal," Mrs. Whitman reported in June 1866, "950 a lot going to put up brick houses." Walt came home to Brooklyn a few weeks after getting this news, and no doubt George's efforts with his partners were the subject of kitchen-table discussions. After Walt returned to Washington, his mother wrote him, "George says if you will buy smiths half of that lot he will fix the shop for me . . . i would not mind its setting back from the street he says there is about 70 dollars worth of lumber there he wont take less than 900 dollars."[28] Cautiously, Walt replied, "George, how would it do for you to put up a couple of small houses, to be worth about $2000 a piece, in some good spot, outer part of the city—one of the two for *us* . . . I could raise $800 cash."[29] He was offering to invest, but not in any of the properties George already had under title. A few months later, in January 1867, he renewed the offer, but slightly reduced in amount: "Ask George whether any thing could be done with $500 cash about getting a lot & moderate-sized two story house to have say 15 or $1600 [left] on mortgage?"[30]

Walt wanted to help—but did not want to lose money. That spring, the maneuverings grew more complex still. Mrs. Whitman reported that

---

*Upon his retirement from the army in 1865 George was a lieutenant colonel by brevet, one of only six (out of one hundred seventy-seven) officers of the regiment recommended for an honorary increase in rank. The description of his service, in a letter sent to Secretary of War Edwin M. Stanton, noted that he had fought in seventeen major battles, that he had been wounded by a shell at Fredericksburg, that his canteen had been shot away at Spotsylvania, and that his "clothes [had been] shot through about twelve times in all." Source: National Archives.

George, who had bought property on Putnam Avenue at her urging, had later decided not to build on it. Instead, "he and smith went to look at some lots yesterday they liked very much on the corner of tomkins aven and lafaett st george says it is very fine . . . and the price is 3000 dollars cash." She added, "George says he knows you would like it it is within one block of the decalb aven cars if they could get it they would build a number of smallish houses."[31]

In addition to working on the mains, George was soon serving as an inspector of pipe for the city of Camden, New Jersey. The work had come to him via his Brooklyn connections; a close friend of Jeff's, Samuel Probasco, an assistant engineer, moonlighted as an inspector, and he advised George on the ins and outs of the lucrative work. But it was Moses Lane who had "done it for his good will to george as there will be work [in Camden] all winter and this where he was will stop and it was very bad cold ugly work."[32] Lane arranged for George to be taken on, and Probasco showed him how to leverage his connections even further. "[P]erbasco says Jeff [now chief water engineer of Saint Louis] is having a great quantity of pipe made about 20 miles from Camden," Mrs. Whitman reported, "and george could just as well inspect that and not neglect [his city of Camden work] in the least."[33] A critical mass in connectivity had been reached. Sounding much like Jeff, who grew excited strategizing over how to get George in the peacetime army, Mrs. Whitman observed, "Mr lane has wrote to Jeff and george wanted matt to write to him that george was there [outside of Camden] if he could put any thing in his way . . . but whether she mentioned it to Jeff or not she said mr Lane had wrote." And she concluded, "Walt if you write to Jeff you can speak about it," too.[34]

In the same way—by a coming together of enough resources and supporters—George's building efforts became, after a struggle, a solid success. By filling up the family coffers from several revenue streams, there was at last capital enough to weather the downs of the short-term market cycle. Those sources were Jeff, George, and Walt's salaries (abetted by Martha's earnings from sewing), pooled to provide a fund out of which George paid for and protected his speculations. Walt did finally invest, in a scheme that fulfilled another long hope of the Whitman family, to build a place for Mrs. Whitman that she would not be quickly dispossessed of. "George has been home came on saturday," she wrote Walt on November 2, 1868; he "staid untill to day to vote he got me two tons of coal . . . and he wished me to say to you walter that the 1 of next month he thought he could pay you all up."

Walt had put money in George's enterprise, which that fall had completed a three-story house, with a storefront at street level. Even as the cellar was being dug, though, in July, George told his mother that he was afraid that he would run out of money.[35] It may have been to alleviate that fear that Walt became an investor. In late September, George moved his mother to the new house; Walt, visiting New York at the time, helped with the move.[36] Possibly for reasons of space, or because Smith needed to sell his share, George almost immediately started on another house, on "portland ave opposite the arsenal," intending this one to go to his mother more permanently. Jeff was also an investor, and late that fall he helped George draw up plans for the new place.[37] Jeff's investment soon became very large: On September 6 he contributed $510 via a draft on a New York bank; by June 23, 1869, George owed him a total of $3,400.[38]

Jeff provided such sums, representing much of his net worth, at a time when he was relocating to a distant city with his wife and school-age daughters. He would struggle in Saint Louis to find decent housing for his family and to pay for the girls' education, his wife Matt now a semi-invalid, suffering pulmonary hemorrhages and at times unable to walk. But Jeff had faith in George as a builder and a wage earner, and he also had faith in his own expanding career and long-term ability to provide. One of his loans to George took the form of a mortgage on the Portland Avenue property, an arrangement that Walt stipulated for the protection of all concerned.[39] George "is dooing very well now," Mrs. Whitman declared late in November 1868; she showed uncharacteristic optimism by using money that Walt sent her to buy a horsehair sofa, "something i have always wanted but never was able to get," and by ordering a new stove "on georgeys credit."[40]

Spec building was nothing if not uncertain, though, and a credit squeeze in early 1869 put everything at risk.* "Georgey has had trouble enoughf . . . owing to not getting a loan on smiths house," Mrs. Whit-

---

*In March, Mrs. Whitman wrote, "[G]eorge says this building without money is a bad business," tersely summing up two generations' worth of disappointment in her aspiring family.

man wrote, "the houses is . . . insured and no mortgage or nothing on smiths it seems almost incredible to tell but so it is."[41] Writing two weeks later, she gave a sense of a deepening crisis:

[T]he houses is pretty well along but george hasent got any loan on [the one intended for Smith] yet he expected to get three thousand dollars on it but hasent got any yet the agents for loaning money say they never knew such a time . . . georgey has . . . I think about 2000 dollars of Jeff but he is in hopes of getting a loan on smiths house if he don't get disappointed.[42]

Creditors were putting their money in government bonds instead of construction. George and partner were in danger of defaulting because George "has paid all along for both [of them] as they went on dident think he would have any difficulty in getting [a] loan on such security."[43]

A week and a half later, Mrs. Whitman wrote Walt on a Monday, not her usual day:

My dear Walt dont be frightened at getting this unseasonable letter there is nothing more than usual the matter [but] the cause of my writing george has got disappointed and dont hardly know what to doo in the money matters the masons he contracted to doo the work lumped out the plaistering and they have got it all done but the last coat and smith says they wont finish it till they have the payment.[44]

The masons were owed $600. They were serious about holding the project hostage. Why George did not write or telegraph to Walt directly—why he made his request for a bailout through their mother—may have had something to do with embarrassment, but just as likely it had to do with Mrs. Whitman's central role in the family communication, her position, as during the war, at the nexus of all concerns. She knew what was going on and knew its meaning, and her personal interest in the outcome made her an advocate George could depend on. "[G]eorge says if it would be a trouble for you to get it he will doo the best he can," she added, "but if you could send him a draft for five or six hundred it would accommodate him very much . . . he wants you to telegraph to him when you get this letter . . . he feels sure of getting the money [back to you] by the first of may."[45]

Walt Whitman after the war, early 1870s.

Walt did provide the needed funds.[46] The plasterers went back to work, and Mrs. Whitman was able to occupy her new house that spring—the last house she would live in in Brooklyn. And soon, George had succeeded in securing a loan on partner Smith's behalf, for $3,200. "[S]mith works," Mrs. Whitman commented, "but seems to depend wholly on George . . . smith wouldent have got the money if . . . george hadent applied."[47] George's sheer competence was the determining factor, in the scrambling to get a loan in a tight market as in his work for Moses Lane and others. "[H]e and mr Lane seems to get along very well," Mrs. Whitman told Walt. "Jeffy wrote . . . that george would not be discharged as long as . . . Lane was [chief engineer in Brooklyn]."[48] Within a few years, George was inspecting for the Metropolitan Water Board of New York City in addition to Camden, where he moved, with his new wife (Louisa Orr Haslam), in the spring of 1871. Mother Whitman came to live with them the next year, bringing Eddy, and Walt came to live there in 1873, after he suffered the cerebral hemorrhage that crippled him. Walt would live on in George's house, and eat at Louisa's table, for the next eleven years.

Mrs. Whitman's last season of life was difficult, to judge from what she told Walt:

> [I] couldent sleep for the pain in my face saturday night . . . i got quite down while I was sick it dont take much to get mama discouraged in these days . . . i am not feeling very well walter dear i am very nervous and have such a trembling in my whole system my appetite is very poor.[49]

At first grateful to George and his wife for taking her in, Mrs. Whitman began to write from Camden complaining about George's stinginess, his new wife's coolness, the food, the wife's other relatives, being old. "[L]ou has had quite a run of company this week," she wrote about three months before her death on May 23, 1873:

> mostly girls from the place where she used to work all have to be taken up in my room I stayed down in the kichen part of the time their discourse was not interesting to me . . . every body that comes has to be taken up [to my room] I don't like it sometimes there is no fire any where else to take any one.[50]

She hated how everything seemed to be about money in George's house. "[T]o hear the talk about money you would think their means was limited," she wrote, adding, "i get quite tired of hearing of money matters . . . i havent felt lately as if i cared much about it."[51]

That year was one to take her mind off money and focus it on final things. Mattie Whitman died in February, her last months agonized, saddening—she left her two daughters and Jeff in a state of profound bereavement, and Mrs. Whitman, so near the end herself, took the loss hard. She had often complained to Walt about Mattie's gadding about, talking too much, selfishness, and uppityness, but now she wrote,

[T]he weather here is very disagreeable dark and dreary just so i feel . . . i have been writing to Jeff and speaking about matty makes me always feel so down hearted she was so good to me i cant never get reconciled to her loss never shall i find her kindness from daughter or daughter in law.[52]

Unlike Mattie, George's wife had never lived in Mrs. Whitman's house, had never acquired—never needed to acquire—the attitude of grateful deference of a dependent daughter-in-law. Louisa was "english" in manner, and an aunt of hers who came to stay that winter was also "english," Mrs. Whitman wrote, which may have meant to the mother-in-law a steady diet of condescension.[53] She told Walt, "Little things cuts sometimes . . . and I am very sensitive."[54]

In April she noted, "The other day Lou was saying how much butter we used in a week and it was so dear she said she was sure aunt libby dident eat much butter." Mrs. Whitman understood herself and Eddy to be the accused parties, and as she wrote, "I said . . . I dont think edd and i together eats a quarter of a pound in a week he dont [like] it to eat the aunty is helpt to the best and the largest sometimes I feel bad enoughf if I was younger I should show . . . my dignity."[55]

Mrs. Whitman stayed in a second-floor room with a fireplace. Sometime in March, Louisa thought that she might be pregnant, and George became highly attentive, carrying her up and downstairs in his arms; for further comfort and protection, Lou sometimes spent the day in bed in Mrs. Whitman's heated room. Mrs. Whitman, seventy-seven years old and disabled by rheumatism, was displaced to less cozy and less private rooms in the house. "[I] am writing this downstairs all alone," she reported one day in April, "i have been on my feet all day and now i can hardly walk." She had made a breakfast of Indian cakes and also "cooked the dinner and made a pie and made some cake i was very tired when I washed the dinner dishes."[56]

She complained that Eddy was being used like a servant ("Lou . . . sends and eddy goes the errands").[57] They were both being used, but at the same time, "she could dispense with me very easily," she said of Louisa, who preferred the company of her aunt. The situation was genuinely bitter. That George would countenance such arrangements for his mother added to the bitterness. She was skeptical about Lou's claim of pregnancy (rightly so), and she resented what she saw as a change in George, her independent soldier-son now so broken to harness as to give "the strictest account of every thing and if he goes out [he] wont be gone more than 10 minutes."[58]

"[I] havent been out except next door in ten weeks," she wrote pitifully, adding that she had caught cold from getting her feet wet visiting the privy. The pileup of complaints became almost comical, Mrs. Whitman herself sometimes aware of going too far, of letting go—her explanation, and it was a true enough explanation, was that she was weak, sick, old, and divested of authority. The life of the family no longer flowed through her. Her intelligence and character would shape it no more, except as they found expression in her children.[59] George was working a whirlwind of well-paying jobs, excited about building a new house, an extravagantly grand house, Mrs. Whitman implied, and in the old way she interested herself for a while in the details of the project:

> [G]eorge is up to his eys in business . . . his house is begun the cellar is dug and the foundation laid he is going to build a three story brick house with an extention parlor and dining room and kitchen . . . the [contractor] does it all for i believe its 38 hundred dollars puts in a range in the kitchen and bath and . . . prive and water closet there is no fireplaces except in the kitchen . . . george says [the contractor] will lose money on it.[60]

But this house, at 431 Stevens Street, would belong to Lou, not her. With a touch of Quakerish disdain for the nonsimple, Mrs. Whitman commented on all the getting and spending, "So you see walt the more we have the more we want."[61]

She was also saddened that spring by what had befallen her faultlessly loyal, ever-corresponding poet-son. Walt's regular letters softened her hurts while reporting on his own grave, very nearly life-ending stroke and his attempts to recuperate. His letters of the time did not minimize his incapacity, but they treated his return to full functioning as guaranteed, which it was decidedly not. His left leg and arm were paralyzed. He was grateful that his "mind is just as clear as ever," as he wrote, but he was weak and "liable to dizziness & nausea . . . on trying to move."[62] His letters to his mother display an odd cheeriness—but then, it had always strengthened him to tell her his story, no matter what that story was.

"I am certainly over the worst of it, & *really*—though slowly—*improving*," he wrote just six days after falling ill.[63] He told her to disregard what she read about him in the papers. He was not at death's door, and he was being taken care of by close friends, Peter Doyle and Charles Eldridge among them. These young men "come in & do whatever I want, & are both *very helpful* to me," he wrote, "one comes day time, & one evening."[64] Doyle had described him eight years before as a great athlete. Eldridge provided a sobering, undoubtedly accurate account of the change in him due to the stroke in a letter to John Burroughs:

> Walt returned here [after Mrs. Whitman's May funeral] in a very depressed condition . . . He still has those distressed spells in the head quite often, and his locomotion is no better . . . I begin to doubt whether [he] is going to recover, and I am very apprehensive of another attack . . . He is a mere physical wreck to what he was . . . It is a terrible misfortune, one of the saddest spectacles I have ever seen . . . Such vigor, health, and endurance to be so changed, is a melancholy thing.[65]

Walt described the death of his mother as the one loss never to be gotten over.* But the death of Mattie also hit him hard. He wanted to go to

---

*Mrs. Whitman died after several weeks of progressive weakening, during which she described bad feelings in her head and complained of trembling spells and a "nervous system . . . very much out of order." Hearing that she had taken a turn for the worse, Walt traveled to Camden by train and was with her for her last three days. A friend of the family's, Helen E. Price, recalled the funeral in George's house in a newspaper article published in 1919: "On taking my seat among [the mourners], I noticed a curious thumping at intervals that made the floor vibrate beneath my feet. I was so absorbed in my own grief that at first I was hardly conscious of it. I finally left my chair, and going to [another room] . . . I saw the poet all alone by the side of his mother's coffin. He was bent over his cane, both hands clasped upon it, and from time to time he would lift it and bring it down with a heavy thud on the floor."

Saint Louis to see her in her last days, but his paralysis prevented travel. After her death on February 19, he was visited by thoughts of her, a flood of irresistible thoughts. He wrote his mother on February 23:

[M]other dear, here I sit again in the rocking chair by the stove—I have just eat some dinner, a little piece of fowl & some toast . . . I have been sitting up all day—have some bad spells, but am decidedly gaining upon the whole—think I have fully recovered where I was a week ago [after a sharp setback in strength] . . . went down stairs yesterday and out into the street.

After explaining that a "first-rate" doctor came to see him every day, he confessed that

yesterday was a very serious day with me here—I was not so very sick, but I kept thinking all the time it was the day of Matty's funeral— Every few minutes all day it would come up in my mind—I suppose it was the same with you—Mother, your letter came Friday afternoon— it was a very good letter, and after reading it twice, I enclosed it in one to [sister Hannah] . . . Mother, I have just been down & out doors— walked half a block . . . *went all alone* . . . this is the most successful raid yet—& I really begin to feel something like myself.[66]

WALT ATTENDED THE next funeral, Mrs. Whitman's, hobbling on a cane. He had gone back to work by that time, on a part-time basis. Shortly before he traveled to Camden to be with his mother, he wrote to John Burroughs that he was in a "pretty bad way," walking clumsily and often feeling oppressed in the head. In his room in Washington, he had "a big bunch of lilacs in a pitcher," he told his good friend—this recurrence to lilacs in spring may have rung a bell for Burroughs, who had written in his *Notes on Walt Whitman as Poet and Person* that Walt's elegy on Lincoln, a "piece of importance which deserves to be specially analyzed," displayed no ordinary "development of plot, but a constant interplay—a turning and re-turning of images and sentiments."[1]

Burroughs had coached Walt while he wrote that particular piece of importance. Walt learned from the young naturalist about the hermit thrush, that it was a "moderate sized grayish brown bird / sings oftener after sundown . . . is very secluded / likes shaded, dark places." They had walked the Potomac woods together that spring/summer of 1865, after Walt had withdrawn *Drum-Taps* from distribution; in a pocket notebook, he recorded that the thrush was often to be found in swamps, that its song was "clear & deliberate—has a solemn effect," and that its call was heard only in "the solemn primal woods . . . of Nature pure & holy."[2]

The thrush of "Lilacs" recalls the hypnotic songbird of "A Word Out of the Sea," a poem that Walt first published in 1859. In "A Word Out of the Sea," a young boy is enraptured to hear the call of a mockingbird that has lost its mate; the boy, a poet-to-be, is awakened to song himself, becoming in time a "chanter of pains and joys," a "uniter of here and hereafter."[3]

The commonalities of "A Word Out of the Sea" with "When Lilacs Last in the Door-Yard Bloom'd" are so marked that the earlier poem reads like a trial run for the later. Not only are there magical songbirds in both, there are celestial bodies, emblematic trinities, and the "fierce old mother" the sea (which becomes, in "Lilacs," the "Dark Mother" death). "A Word" shows Walt putting to use the structural breakthrough that had come to him, probably, as a result of being a devotee of Italian opera. Passages of intense poetic song—arias—alternate with longer passages of less heightened poetic recitativo; as in many of the operas Walt saw performed in the 1840s and '50s, the arias in his verse correspond to points of dramatic crisis or revelation in the overall narrative flow. Again as in opera, the principal images in "Lilacs"—the bird, the star, the flower— appear and disappear and reappear, the poem's "I" holding forth about each as he follows a twisting, questing path toward some sort of understanding.

There is an impression of waywardness in the poem. The grieving singer ambles as he will; his interior impulses guide him, not quite randomly but with as high a degree of unpredictability as is consistent with the making, eventually, of some kind of forward progress. Certain encounters nearly overwhelm him. "O great star disappear'd! O cruel hands that hold me powerless! O helpless soul of me!" he cries out, anguished because of the death of "him I love." Dark thoughts cascade over the stricken heart— there is no avoiding that, and one of the poem's subjects is how to experience anguish and yet not be undermined, morally and spiritually enfeebled.

The narrator asks a series of reasonable questions:

O how shall I warble myself for the dead one there I loved?
And how shall I deck my song for the large sweet soul that has gone?
And what shall my perfume be, for the grave of him I love?
. . . .
O what shall I hang on the chamber walls?
And what shall the pictures be that I hang on the walls,
To adorn the burial-house of him I love?[4]

The poem offers sane, plausible answers to these questions. For a memorial perfume, American sea winds, blowing from east and west and meeting over the prairie; for memorial pictures, images of America in the "Fourth-month," the month of Lincoln's assassination. The faithful hospital visitor, his pockets full of tobacco and oranges, his mission always to be of use, here continues his responsible labor. For the most tragic losses, those that seem utterly beyond consolation, there are yet steps to take and rituals that avail. Begin with what can be done most simply. Prepare an appropriate house of burial; do so with quiet respect; proceed from there.

As he composed "Lilacs" over a period of weeks or months, Walt could not have been unaware of its formal resemblance to "A Word Out of the Sea," which he was soon to republish in the fourth, 1867, edition of *Leaves*. Both poems offer up "carols" to death. "I float this carol with joy, with joy to thee, O Death!" the poet declares in "Lilacs," and in "A Word Out of the Sea" he sings of

> *. . . the night's carols!*
> *Carols of lonesome love! Death's carols!*
> *Carols under that lagging, yellow, waning moon!*
> *O, under that moon, where she droops almost down into the sea!*
> *O reckless, despairing carols!*[5]

In "Lilacs," the poet describes a "harsh surrounding cloud that will not free my soul"—an emblem of his despair. Yet particles of goodly life—sweet-scented lilacs, the transfixing star of evening—impinge on his senses as well, and fate ironically arranges for sorrow to arrive with greenest spring. The lilac sprig, whimsically plucked, disappears from mention as the poet goes on ambling, then reappears at the moment when it finds a special use:

> Coffin that passes through lanes and streets,
> Through day and night, with the great cloud darkening the land . . .
> With all the mournful voices of the dirges, pour'd around the
>   coffin,
> The dim-lit churches and the shuddering organs—Where amid
>   these you journey,
> With the tolling, tolling bells' perpetual clang;

> Here! coffin that slowly passes,
> I give you my sprig of lilac.[6]

This promises a journey not quite entirely aimless. At an unhurried pace, and stopping to notice this, then this, the poem introduces its symbols. Already the problem of being overwhelmed by grief begins to have a sort of answer: If we can smell this lilac, see this magical star, then perhaps we will not be overthrown entirely.

The poem discusses, and at the same time embodies, a way of grieving. There is a balance between waywardness and progress, between vulnerability before the most devastating feelings and the performance of useful gestures. Mourning has a larger dimension, as well:

> (Not for you, for one, alone;
> Blossoms and branches green to coffins all I bring:
> For fresh as the morning—thus would I chant a song for you,
>   O sane and sacred death.

> All over bouquets of roses,
> O death! I cover you over with roses and early lilies;
> But mostly and now the lilac that blooms the first,
> Copious, I break, I break the sprigs from the bushes:
> With loaded arms I come, pouring for you,
> For you and the coffins all of you, O death.)[7]

Even as the poet's view widens, to the thousands and the tens of thousands of the dead, the poem remains specific:

> O western orb, sailing the heaven!
> Now I know what you must have meant. . . .
> As we walk'd up and down in the dark blue so mystic,
> As we walk'd in silence the transparent shadowy night,
> As I saw you had something to tell, as you bent to me night after night,
> As you droop'd from the sky low down, as if to my side[8]

Likewise, the encounter with the songbird remains specific, if mysterious. It begins like a quotation from the homely field notes that Burroughs had given him:

In the swamp, in secluded recesses,
A shy and hidden bird is warbling a song.

Solitary, the thrush,
The hermit, withdrawn to himself, avoiding the settlements,
Sings by himself a song.

Song of the bleeding throat!
Death's outlet song of life (for well, dear brother, I know,
If thou wast not gifted to sing, thou would'st surely die).[9]

The bird, at first only one of three symbols, becomes a little more than the other two. The poet makes his way down, into the swamp in the deep night. Birdsong transports him, but he needs to go beyond the consolations of this mesmerizing sound:

From deep secluded recesses,
From the fragrant cedars, and the ghostly pines so still,
Came the singing of the bird.

And the charm of the singing rapt me,
As I held, as if by their hands, my comrades in the night;
And the voice of my spirit tallied the song of the bird.[10]

In "A Word Out of the Sea," the transporting song of the lovelorn mockingbird opened the young poet's soul to another, darker song:

Answering, the sea,
Delaying not, hurrying not,
Whispered me through the night, and very plainly before daybreak,
Lisped to me constantly the low and delicious word DEATH,
And again Death—ever Death, Death, Death,
Hissing melodious.[11]

Just so now, the poet of "Lilacs" goes beyond what he hears. And the words he attaches to the bird's song are the aria that welcomes "lovely and soothing Death," death that undulates 'round the world, "serenely arriving, arriving / In the day, in the night, to all":

Approach, encompassing Death—strong Deliveress!
When it is so—when thou hast taken them, I joyously sing the dead,
Lost in the loving, floating ocean of thee,
Laved in the flood of thy bliss, O Death.

. . . .

The night, in silence, under many a star;
The ocean shore, and the husky whispering wave. . . .
And the soul turning to thee, O vast and well-veil'd Death,
And the body gratefully nestling close to thee.

Here is the paradoxical consolation—the ritual that works. The poet recommends surrender—a fearless descent into a sovereign vastness. Embrace death, know death, he enjoins, for death is an aspect of God's infinitude, the form of His merciful all-enfoldingness. The body returns to death, and the soul also returns. Do this, surrender in this way, and then will come an end to anguish. The poem, like the thrush's song, has arrived somewhere after following a "varying, ever-altering" course, first "low and wailing" then "rising and . . . flooding the night . . . sinking and failing . . . and yet again bursting with joy."[12] The poem and the poet have arrived.

Finishing by early fall, Walt went home to Brooklyn, bearing with him copies of a thin new pamphlet, "Sequel to *Drum-Taps*," printed in Washington. His plan was to sew the new pamphlets, which contained "Lilacs" and seventeen lesser poems, into the preexisting copies of *Drum-Taps*, the ones printed the previous spring but held back from distribution. A shop in Manhattan did the binding for him, and on October 28 Bunce & Huntington, New York publishers, halfheartedly announced the expanded book with small notices in two papers.[13] Walt had assumed all production costs; five hundred copies became available to the public, which did not hurry to buy them.

The reviews were not many, and they included Henry James's savage slam of Whitman as war poet—indeed, as any kind of poet at all. Mrs. Whitman, who paid close attention to any and all reviews of her son's work, commented,

[I] have got a [*Brooklyn Daily*] union with an article about your book
i told Jeff to take it and send it to you would you like to have it or

dont you care about it, it is not so severe as the one in the nation of the 16th November [Henry James's] . . . i should like for mr Oconnor to see that in the nation it is a long piece with flourishes.[14]

James's attack on *Drum-Taps* followed a similarly damning notice by William Dean Howells, in the *Round Table*, and preceded by a few days a violent snub of the book in the *New York Times*. Walt's friend John Swinton was no longer managing editor at the *Times*, and without his guiding hand a reviewer had been assigned who forthrightly declared that the author

has no ear, no sense of the melody of verse. His poems only differ from prose in the lines being cut into length, instead of continuously pointed. As prose, they must be gauged by the sense they contain, the mechanism of verse being either despised by, or out of the reach of the writer . . . we find in them a poverty of thought, paraded forth with a hubbub of stray words, and accompanied with a vehement self-assertion in the author.[15]

Other reviewers admitted to being moved by the book. A writer identified only as "F." in the *Saturday Press* accused Whitman of gross materialism but granted him a "picturesqueness of phrase unsurpassed in literature, and a powerful rhythm, whose long musical roll is like . . . the waves of the sea." "B.," writing in the *Radical*, said that one could not open the book without catching "the soft and sweet strains of a sublime tenderness," evidence of a talent "more purely permeated with the subtile essence of poetry than almost any" contemporary's.[16] Bunce & Huntington had "finally printed it," charged an anonymous reviewer for the *Commonwealth*, "but without their name [displayed anywhere on the volume], and without taking any of [the] customary steps to introduce the book to the reading public." As a result, "it is scarcely to be got at a bookstore . . . and, though full of the noblest of verses, is utterly unknown to the mass of readers."[17]

Time would cure *Drum-Taps* of its obscurity. The strongest review, and the best and wisest reading of "Lilacs," came a year after its official publication in the fall of 1865, from Walt's good friend John Burroughs. Undoubtedly coached in part by Walt, but an elegant writer himself, therefore in no need of a ghost, Burroughs took aim at this poem that he loved and meanwhile warmed up for the following year's *Notes on Walt*

Whitman as Poet and Person, producing a ten-page article that ran in the *Galaxy* on December 1, 1866. Walt Whitman, Burroughs declared, was a "rejected and misinterpreted poet." For ten years he had been "sneered at and mocked and ridiculed . . . cursed and caricatured and persecuted," notwithstanding the "beautiful benevolence . . . shown during the war in nourishing the sick and wounded soldiers."[18]

About the anguish of the war's survivors—those left to mourn as well as those with lingering wounds—Burroughs commented, "[Walt] has looked deeper into the matter than the critics are willing to believe."[19] The poem that best displays his transcendent art is "like intricate and involved music, with subtle and far-reaching harmonies," Burroughs said of "Lilacs."

By that curious indirect method which is always the method of nature, the poet makes no reference to the mere facts of Lincoln's death—neither describes it, or laments it, or dwells upon its unprovoked atrocity [but instead] seizes upon three beautiful facts of nature which he weaves into a wreath for the dead President's tomb. The central thought is of death, [and] around this he curiously twines . . . the early blooming lilacs . . . the song of the hermit thrush . . . and . . . the evening star, which, as many may remember . . . hung low in the west with unusual lustre.[20]

Burroughs granted that Walt's poem was so unusual that at first it might confuse a reader.

It eludes one; it hovers and hovers and will not be seized by the mind, though the soul feels it. But it presently appears that this is precisely the end contemplated by the poet. He would give us as far as possible the analogy of music, knowing that in that exalted condition of the sentiments at the presence of death . . . the mere facts or statistics of the matter are lost sight of, and that it is not a narrative of the great man's death done into rhyme . . . that would be the most fitting performance on an occasion so august and solemn.[21]

As in symphonic music, voices mix and contend; if one becomes prominent, the others seem to drop away, only to return later. Read it again and again, Burroughs advised America; "It is a poem that may be slow in making admirers, yet it is well worth the careful study of every student of literature."

And about *Drum-Taps* the book, he added,

> The gravity and seriousness of [it] . . . are entirely new in modern literature: With all our profuse sentimentalism, there is no deep human solemnity—the solemnity of a strong, earnest affectionate, unconventional man—in our [poetry]. There are pathos and tears and weeds of mourning; but [I] would indicate an attitude or habit of the soul which is not expressed by melancholy . . . [and] not inconsistent with cheerfulness and good nature . . . a state or condition induced by large perceptions, faith, and deep . . . sympathies. It may be further characterized as impatient of trifles and dallyings, tire[d] even of wit and smartness, [disliking] garrulity and . . . but one remove from silence itself. The plainness and simplicity of the biblical writers afford the best [prior] example.[22]

One can see Walt, perhaps, standing behind Burroughs, stooping low to whisper this last observation, this likening of himself to the Bible's holy scribes—those anonymous poets who transmitted, it is said, the very word of God—into Burroughs's ear, as the young man's pen flies swiftly down the page. To be forward in one's own cause is to be immodest and even undignified on occasion, but not necessarily to be presumptuous or incorrect—no, not if that cause be true.

Afterward

WALT'S ELEVEN YEARS living under George's roof, in the handsome new house at 431 Stevens Street, Camden, were life saving, but at the same time they were not entirely agreeable. Illness had humbled the poet. He would never again venture forth with the freedom that had once delighted him, and that was a great loss. Two years after coming to live with George, he wrote, "I feel yet about as cheerful and *vimmy* as ever . . . though my days of active participation, & ganging about in the world, are over."[1]

The extent of his suffering is shocking to consider—and the degree of his eventual recovery astonishing. He continued to have strokes, some of them crippling.[2] As he wrote Charles Eldridge, "My head does not get right . . . the feeling now being as if it were in the centre of the head, heavy & painful & quite pervading," and he reckoned that a fatal stroke might come at any time. Therefore he spoke plainly, to Pete Doyle, for example: "I still think I shall get over this, & we will be together again & have some good times—but for all that it is best for you to be prepared for something different—my strength cant stand the pull forever, & if continued must sooner or later give out."[3]

He received no useful medical treatment. "My saving points are pretty good nights' rest," he told Nelly O'Connor, "and a fair appetite . . . Still I can see I am gradually being pulled, and, though I have not at all given up hope . . . I do not shut my eyes to the other termination."[4]

What pulled him did not frighten him. The deaths of his mother and sister-in-law, and the thorough immersion in mortality of the war, had made him as stoic as any man. Still, he was "quite feeble," he told Nelly, so challenged by the simple problems of locomotion that to leave George's house was beyond him.[5] The rooms he occupied in the first house, before the move to 322 Stevens, were a "north & south one, second floor"—they were his mother's old rooms, the ones she had hated to leave in the cold, and "with all her nice & homely furniture & bed & chairs" in place, so that he lived "day & night in her memory & atmosphere."[6]

When the family did move, Walt again found a spot he liked, "up in the 3rd story . . . fronting south—the sun [shines] in bright . . . My brother had a large room, very handsome, on 2d floor, with large bay window fronting west built for me, but I moved up here instead, it is much more retired, & has the sun."[7]

Unable to work in Washington but able to send a substitute, so that he continued harvesting part of his salary for a while, he feared, for good reason, that he might go blind or lose his mind. "Don't be alarmed—but I am worse to-day," he wrote Eldridge, "having a bad spell—a succession of those *blurs* . . . only far more intense and persistent."[8] Sometimes he was too weak to read or to dispel the confusion.[9] He wrote a new will. "What little I have . . . I have left mainly to my lame brother Ed, poor man," he told Doyle, adding, "I have left you $200 & my gold watch."[10]

The move out of Brooklyn does not seem to have awakened nostalgia. It was Washington and the life there that he missed—"My *heart* is blank and lonesome utterly," he told Doyle, adding, "I don't know a soul here . . . sometimes sit alone & think, for two hours on a stretch—have not formed a single acquaintance here."[11]

When able, he went about remedying that aloneness. George's house was close to a railroad depot. There were "trains rumbling continually, night & day, & lots of RR men living near . . . if only I felt just a little better, I should get acquainted with many of the men."[12] That was in August 1873. In October he wrote, "I have just been talking with a young married RR man . . . he stood by the open window, 1st floor, & talked with me, while I sat in an arm-chair inside . . . you could tell by the cut of his jib [that he was a railroad worker] . . . dark complexion, and hard dark hands."[13]

Soon he ventured outside. In a reprise of his Brooklyn Ferry–riding days, he took a streetcar to the Delaware River crossing, then ferried back and forth to Philadelphia several times. One day he went up Market

Street after stopping first at the Mercantile Library on Tenth—"There is a large reading room," he told Doyle, "they have all the papers from every where—have the Wash. Chronicle, Capital, &c."[14]

Until a stroke killed him or drove him mad, he would be himself. "The Camden free masons marched by here this morning," he reported, "about 250, the finest collection of men I thought I ever saw, but poor music, all brass, a lot of fat young Dutchmen, blowing as if they would burst."[15] From appreciating a noisy parade, he moved in the old way to affectionate sympathy for one vulnerable young man; "I am feeling quite bad to-day about a 13 year old boy," he wrote, "[who lives] next door but one—he has had his eye very badly hurt, I fear it is put out . . . by an arrow yesterday, the boys playing."[16]

He could not get around as he once had, but that new dependency brought young men close to him. In 1876, he was well enough to visit the offices of the *Camden New Republic*, where he met a young worker, Harry Stafford, who soon became a warm friend. Six months later, Walt gave Harry a ring to express his commitment.[17] Often he stayed over at Harry's family's farm outside Camden; a creek there became the site of self-administered nude nature therapies. In *Specimen Days*, Walt described stripping down to just his shoes and a hat, thrashing himself with wild bristles, and immersing himself in the cool waters.

In these same years of infirmity, of worry about a possible fatal stroke, Walt may also have had an affair with Edward Cattell, a farmworker. Edward worked along the same creek that ran through the Stafford farm. Harry knew of Edward and was jealous. "[I] Cant get of[f] a day now for we are so Bisse . . . husking Corn," Cattell wrote Walt in October 1877, but "i Would like to Com up to town. i think of you old man think of the times down on the Creek."[18]

George's protectorship was liberal; the two brothers knew each other well and got along. George was "full of work," Walt wrote to Pete Doyle, "is in splendid health, a great stout fellow—weighs more than I do." Jeff visited Camden one fall, and Walt wrote that "both my brothers are stout & hearty, & full of business, & interested in it thoroughly—& doing well."[19]

Walt's own stoutness stood him in good stead. With no effective medical treatment for strokes, he weathered the years of greatest jeopardy on the basis of his solid constitution. He wrote some new poetry, published

Walt Whitman and Bill Duckett, Camden, New Jersey, 1886.

Memoranda During the War (1876) and *Specimen Days* (1882), the former published a second time in the latter, and oversaw the spread of his poetic reputation. In 1868, William Michael Rosetti, brother of the poet Dante Gabriel Rosetti, published a selection from the 1867 *Leaves* in England, calling it *Poems by Walt Whitman.* It was successful, and by the 1880s Walt was more honored as a poet overseas than in America, although the idea that he was sustained mainly by handouts from literary Englishmen, a tale that was sometimes told about him, was false. He was sustained by handouts from Englishmen but also by handouts from Americans—and the Americans contributed more.[20]

He supported himself on the sales of books, on those handouts, and on sales of articles and poems. Sometimes he placed items in newspapers describing his semidestitution, to stimulate further contributions. A study of his finances during his last seventeen years reveals that he was never truly destitute, and that over the period from 1876 to 1892 he earned in excess of $20,000.* His records of his book sales are meticulous, almost penny-perfect. At the end, his estate was valued at almost $6,000, despite his having recently spent about $4,000 on a mausoleum in Harleigh Cemetery, Camden, where he was buried with most of his family.[21]

There came a breach with George. George, unstoppably, built another new house for the family, this one on a handsome farmstead twelve miles outside Camden. Never thinking that Walt would not want to join them there, George built Walt a special room on the third floor; and when Walt elected to stay on in Camden, in a neighborhood full of coal smoke and trains, George's feelings were hurt.

Walt bought a house of his own. To his rudely furnished, manuscript-choked cottage on Mickle Street came admirers both foreign and American; soon the place was a kind of shrine. George's wife visited regularly, bringing Walt gifts out of her farm kitchen—in 1882, a bottle of Louisa's elderberry wine had oiled an affectionate meeting between Walt and Oscar Wilde, an English admirer of the new generation. But George and Walt probably did not see each other again, or communicate directly, until Walt lay on his deathbed.[22]

By building another house and moving to the country, George fulfilled an old dream of the family's, one mentioned in some of his Civil War letters. Once the Whitmans had been Long Island gentry, with extensive holdings; now, wealthy with the earnings of a modern economy, George returned to the land, although not to practice market

---

*Probably Walt earned considerably more, since the principal evidence of his earnings comes from his bank records, and on occasion he must have cashed checks and spent the money without creating a deposit record.

agriculture. George and Louisa were childless, as was George's sister Hannah.* A son born in 1875, whom they named Walter, not after the child's grandfather but after his poet uncle, died eight months later; a second son, "the most beautiful, perfect, and well-developed babe," according to Walt, was stillborn.[23] In 1892, a few months after Walt's death, George's Louisa also died; Eddy died that same year, Jeff Whitman having died two years before in Saint Louis.

Jeff was survived by a single daughter, and she, Jessie Louisa, inherited George's estate as well as her father's.[24] She had been but a babe in arms when George was campaigning behind Vicksburg; he saw her for the first time in January 1864, while home on leave, and over the years Jessie often visited him in Camden and out on the farm. She was a loving and intelligent young woman. She traveled several times in Europe. Unmarried, she lived in Saint Louis until the late 1940s, when, having broken her hip in a fall, she went to live with a Mrs. Rudolph J. Blome, a private-duty nurse she had met in a rest home.[25]

The Blome family moved to Roswell, New Mexico, in 1956. They brought Jessie Whitman along. Now in her nineties, she rode west in a station wagon fitted out with a mattress. She adapted easily to New Mexico in the fifties, where the "beautiful days and leisurely living" pleased her, according to her nurse. Mrs. Blome recalled of their first years together, "She responded to me very openly and enjoyed my family . . . very much . . . Miss Whitman was a lovely woman and became a regular family member. She enjoyed our friends, neighbors, television and family life; however, she was very ugly whenever Miss Taylor came to visit"— Miss Taylor being the guardian who had first put her in a rest home.[26]

Under western skies, ten years after the famous UFO events at Roswell, the last direct heir of the Whitman family's hard-fought material ascent died, on May 5, 1957, surrounded by people she had won to her by her openness and charm. She was buried in Saint Louis.

---

*Hannah died in 1908. George and Walt's other sister, Mary Elizabeth, who married young and to a great degree escaped the ambit of the family, died in 1899. A Whitman scholar in the 1940s found a grand-niece of the poet in Greenport, Long Island, whom she described as a "tall, handsome, white-haired" elderly lady, "grey-eyed and altogether resembling the poet in startling fashion."

ACKNOWLEDGMENTS

A few years ago, the distinguished Whitman scholar Ed Folsom wrote, "The Whitman *Collected Writings* project is now hopelessly scattered, fragmented, and incomplete. It is difficult even to keep track of the number of volumes that have appeared."

All the original members of the advisory board of the project, which began in the 1950s, then continued for half a century, had died. So had the general editors, Gay Wilson Allen and Sculley Bradley. Hoping to put Whitman and his massive output of poetry, prose, journals, and personal letters between covers once and for all, the *Collected Writings* project had produced a series of indispensable volumes but had somehow failed to come to the end of Walt.

The poet seemed to be toying with his devoted scholarly protectors from beyond the grave. More private letters and journalistic manuscripts kept turning up; the poet who had called himself a "kosmos" and claimed to "contain multitudes" seemed to be making good on his promise.

Granting that the mystic, world-bestriding Walt will never finally be contained, a humble late-arrival at the feast of Whitman scholarship can still assert that wonderful, essential work has been done and continues to be done, and that the large group of men and women who have studied and interpreted Walt for the last century and more has yielded a literature Whitmanesque in its amplitude.

I am a late arrival at a second feast of scholarship as well, that on the Civil War. My debts are too many to acknowledge easily. For the current book, I found particular inspiration in work by George M. Frederickson,

Charles Royster, William Frassanito, James M. McPherson, William Matter, Reid Mitchell, John Michael Priest, George C. Rable, and Gordon C. Rhea. Among Whitman scholars, my debts are again too many to name, but work by these writers was especially suggestive for my purposes: Gregory Eiselein, Roy Morris Jr., Jerome Loving, Harold Aspiz, Martin G. Murray, Peter Coviello, Gary Schmidgall, Jonathan Ned Katz, Patricia Cline Cohen, Charley Shively, and Paul Zweig.

To the U.S. National Park Service, and those among its friends who keep it from the brink, many thanks for protecting access to the American battlegrounds. A curious citizen can still walk them and feel, with pity and awe, the meaning of the topography. At Fredericksburg and Spotsylvania National Military Park, staff historians Donald Pfanz, Mac Wyckoff, and Frank A. O'Reilly were unusually generous with their time and insight, as was ranger Kris White. At the Antietam Museum Library, Ted Alexander steered my investigations wisely and with humor. At the New York State Archives in Albany, I found answers to questions about the 51st New York Volunteers with the guidance of Dan Lorello, Bill Gorman, and Christine Karpiak. At the National Archives, Lucy Barber and Mike Meier helped me work out a research strategy, and Trevor Plante opened inner doors.

Barbara Bair was warmly encouraging of my project when I spoke with her at the Library of Congress. When I visited the Trent Collection of Whitman manuscripts at Duke University, I found a true treasure in the form of Mrs. Whitman's letters for the period 1860–73; these and other documents at Duke helped shape my sense of the inner life of the family Whitman, and I wish especially to thank Eleanor Mills, Zachary Elder, Elizabeth Dunn, and Janie Morris for their generosity.

Looking for evidence of the real life of Jesse Whitman, the eldest Whitman son and reputedly an ordinary seaman, I found some among the crew lists stored at the National Archives regional facility in Manhattan. Two assistants, Petrina Crockford and Caitlin Roper, worked hard for me and in the end handled more of the original documents than I did.

My loyal and astute agent of many years, Michael Carlisle, presented my book proposal to several excellent editors. But all along, I think, he was hoping the project would end up where it did, with Walker & Co., publishers of works of history both meticulous as to scholarship and friendly to general readers. Here it was my excellent good fortune to be edited by George Gibson, that rare head of a publishing house who reads and rereads the manuscripts he acquires, and who gets down in the trenches with his wary authors, colored pencils in hand.

This book took shape in many conversations with close friends, some of them also writers. Those who offered the gift of their intelligent interest include Michael Vitiello, Andrew Moss, Robert Spertus, Bill Pearson, Betty Pearson, Ward Little, Paul Gruber, Seymour Moscovitz, Bert Hansen, Jean McGarry, Avery Rome, and David Cohen. Another stroke of wonderful luck was to have married an American historian of the highest accomplishments, Mary Ryan—she, calming me in my dark moments, advising me on matters relating to research and historiography, and seeming not to care as I crudely poached on her territory, has made the writing of this book the deepest sort of fun.

Chapter One

1. Thompson, "In the Ranks," 558.
2. Priest, *Before Antietam*, 197.
3. Loving, *Civil War Letters*, 71.
4. Parker, *History of the 51st*, 226–27.
5. Priest, *Before Antietam*, 218.
6. Styple, *Writing*, 128.
7. Loving, *Civil War Letters*, 66.
8. Ibid., 67.

Chapter Two

1. Gould, Antietam Collection, letter of Corporal Elmer Bragg, September 17, 1862.
2. Loving, *Civil War Letters*, 42–43.
3. Ibid., 44.
4. Ibid., 44–45.
5. Whitman, *Complete Poetry and Prose*, 710.
6. Ibid.
7. Kolata, "So Big and Healthy," 18.
8. Dowe, "A Child's Memories," 3.
9. Loving, *Civil War Letters*, 44.
10. Gohdes and Silver, *Faint Clews*, viii.
11. Miller, *Correspondence*, 1:111.
12. Ibid., 1:123, 102.
13. Ibid., 1:112.
14. Ibid, 1:59.
15. Whitman, *Memoranda*, 8–9.

16. Ibid., 9–10.
17. Ibid., 11.
18. Miller, *Correspondence*, 1:60.

Chapter Three

1. Berthold and Price, *Dear Brother*, 189, 191.
2. Quoted in Loving, *Civil War Letters*, 8.
3. Van Sinderen, Yale Collection, Beinecke Library.
4. Kennedy, *Battlefield Guide*, 283.
5. Loving, *Civil War Letters*, 118.
6. On cholera, Grier, *Notebooks*, 1:10n32. "God's angels" quoted in Aspiz, *So Long!*, 17.
7. Aspiz, *So Long!*, 17.
8. Feld, *Brooklyn Village*, 59.
9. Ibid., 3.
10. Trent, Whitman pocket notebook, November 23, 1862.
11. Feld, *Brooklyn Village*, 92.
12. Traubel, *In Re*, 38.
13. Wilentz, *Chants Democratic*, 116.
14. Blumin, *Emergence of the Middle Class*, 110.
15. Trent, pocket notebook, November 23, 1862.
16. Allen, *Solitary Singer*, 598.
17. Whitman, *Complete Poetry and Prose*, 698.

18. Papers of Walt Whitman, Barrett Library, University of Virginia.
19. Berthold and Price, *Dear Brother*, 5.
20. Ryan, *Cradle of the Middle Class*, 113–14.
21. Berthold and Price, *Dear Brother*, 5.
22. Ibid., 3–4.
23. Allen and Bradley, *Collected Writings*, 6:256.
24. Applegate, "Henry Beecher," 110. Wilentz, *Chants Democratic*, 128.
25. Blumin, *Emergence of the Middle Class*, 1.

Chapter Four

1. Grier, *Notebooks*, 1:11.
2. Allen, *Solitary Singer*, 599.
3. Loving, *Song of Himself*, 32–33.
4. Wilentz, *Chants Democratic*, 129.
5. Feld, *Brooklyn Village*, 220–23. Loving, *Song of Himself*, 31.
6. Loving, *Song of Himself*, 36.
7. Traubel, *In Re*, 38.
8. Molinoff, "Some Notes on Whitman's Family," 11. Allen, *Solitary Singer*, 22.
9. Katz, *Love Stories*, 45.
10. Wilentz, *Chants Democratic*, 265.
11. Whitman, *Complete Poetry and Prose*, 700.
12. Molinoff, "Whitman's Teaching at Smithtown, 1837–1838," in *Monographs*, 19.
13. Genoways, *Correspondence*, 1.
14. Ibid., 2–3.
15. Molinoff, "Whitman's Teaching," 19.
16. Allen, *Solitary Singer*, 32.
17. Molinoff, "Whitman's Teaching," 29.
18. See http://www.longislandernews.com.
19. Allen, *Solitary Singer*, 34.
20. Ibid., 43.
21. Zweig, *Making*, 68.

Chapter Five

1. Allen, *Solitary Singer*, 41.
2. Cohen, *Murder of Helen Jewett*, 69.
3. Ibid., 68.

4. Whitman, *Complete Poetry and Prose*, 1189–91.
5. Ibid., 1190, 1189.
6. Allen, *Solitary Singer*, 43.
7. Ibid., 46.
8. Rubin and Brown, *Walt of the Aurora*, 44.
9. Ibid., 110–11.
10. Allen, *Solitary Singer*, 55.
11. Loving, *Song of Himself*, 57.
12. Rubin and Brown, *Walt of the Aurora*, vii.
13. Ibid., 50.
14. Ibid., 51.
15. Ibid.
16. Ibid., 31.
17. Ibid., 33.
18. Ibid., 32.
19. Allen, *Solitary Singer*, 35.
20. Traubel, *In Re*, 34.
21. Rubin and Brown, *Walt of the Aurora*, 20–21.
22. Ibid., 45.
23. Ibid., 53–54.

Chapter Six

1. Cohen, *Murder of Helen Jewett*, 203.
2. Ibid., 69.
3. Ibid., 63.
4. Katz, *Love Stories*, 55.
5. Cohen, *Murder of Helen Jewett*, 191–92.
6. Rubin and Brown, *Walt of the Aurora*, 140.
7. Katz, *Love Stories*, 54.
8. Rubin and Brown, *Walt of the Aurora*, 47.
9. Katz, *Love Stories*, 36.
10. Whitman, *Complete Poetry and Prose*, 1115.
11. Ibid., 1112–20. Loving, *Song of Himself*, 53.
12. Whitman, *Leaves* (1855), 47.
13. Ibid., 52.
14. Ibid., 119.
15. Miller, *Correspondence*, 5:73.
16. Zweig, *Making of the Poet*, 190, on

Walt as sexually inactive; Morris, *Better Angel*, 210–11, on Walt as unfulfilled until settling down.

17. See, for informed and persuasive discussions of Walt's intimate life, Katz, *Love Stories*, Schmidgall, *A Gay Life*, and Shively, *Calamus Lovers*.

18. Grier, *Notebooks and Unpublished Prose*, 1:248–49.

19. Ibid., 2:487, 497.

20. Katz, *Love Stories*, 148–49.

21. "Calamus 18," in Schmidgall, *Selected Poems*, 239.

22. Schmidgall, *Selected Poems*, 266.

23. Ibid., 66.

24. Traubel, *In Re*, 35.

25. Ibid., 34–35.

26. Ibid., 36.

Chapter Seven

1. Grier, *Notebooks*, 1:11.

2. Feinberg, "A Whitman Collector," 75–76. Allen, *Solitary Singer*, 599.

3. Feinberg, "A Whitman Collector," 75.

4. Ibid., 77.

5. Allen, *Solitary Singer*, 75.

6. Pessen, "Jacksonian Brooklyn," 319.

7. Schmidgall, *A Gay Life*, 15.

8. Ibid., 16.

9. Grier, *Notebooks*, 1:4.

10. Feinberg, "A Whitman Collector," 81.

11. Ibid., 80.

12. Feinberg Collection.

13. Feinberg, "A Whitman Collector," 82–83.

14. New York State Census, 1855.

15. Allen, *Solitary Singer*, 106.

16. Grier, *Notebooks*, 1:11.

17. Feinberg, "A Whitman Collector," 84.

18. Feinberg Collection.

19. Ibid.

20. Feinberg, "A Whitman Collector," 86.

21. Ibid., 87–88.

22. Ibid., 86.

23. Trent Collection, Louisa Van Velsor Whitman letter, November 1863.

24. Trent Collection.

25. "A Sketch," quoted in Loving, *Song of Himself*, 84.

26. Whitman, *Leaves* (1855), 43.

27. Ibid., 42.

28. Allen, *Solitary Singer*, 112.

29. *Brooklyn Advertizer*, October 4, 1849, in Zweig, *Making of the Poet*, 101.

30. Zweig, *Making of the Poet*, 124.

31. Whitman, *Leaves* (1855), 93–95.

Chapter Eight

1. Letter of Jessie Louisa Whitman (daughter of Jeff), March 8, 1940, in Molinoff, "Some Notes on Whitman's Family," *Monographs*, 19.

2. Molinoff, "Some Notes," 22.

3. Ibid., 19.

4. Heflin, *Melville's Whaling Years*, 4.

5. Ibid., 8–13.

6. The author has found Jesse Whitman listed as a crewmember on two ships: in 1839, on the *Carroll of Carrollton*, arriving in New York from Liverpool, and in 1841 on the *Eagle*, outward bound for Veracruz, Mexico. National Archives and Records Administration, Northeast Region, Record Group 36.

7. Heflin, *Melville's Whaling Years*, 11. Allen, *Solitary Singer*, 106. "Sun-Down Poem," Schmidgall, *Selected Poems*, 135.

8. Berthold and Price, *Dear Brother*, 84.

9. Ibid., 84–85.

10. Ibid., 85.

11. Hutto, "Syphilis," 453–60.

12. Miller, *Correspondence*, 1:189n75.

13. Berthold and Price, *Dear Brother*, 85–86.

14. Trent, Louisa Van Velsor Whitman letter, December 10, 1865.

15. Ibid., April 7, 1869.

16. Miller, *Correspondence*, 1:179.

17. Loving, *Song of Himself*, 276.

18. Trent, Louisa Van Velsor Whitman letter, November 1863.

19. Ibid.

20. Ibid., December 1863.

21. Berthold and Price, *Dear Brother*, 81.

22. Molinoff, "Some Notes," 11.

23. Ibid., 12.

24. Ibid.

25. Howey, "Weaponry."

26. Ibid.

27. Trent, Louisa Van Velsor Whitman letter, December 5, 1863.

28. Ibid., December 25, 1863.

29. Ibid., March 28, 1867.

30. Waldron, *Mattie*, 1.

31. Trent, Louisa Van Velsor Whitman letter, August 29, 1865.

32. Waldron, *Mattie*, 23.

33. Berthold and Price, *Dear Brother*, 28.

34. Shryock, *Medicine in America*, 143–44.

35. Dale, *Medical Biographies*, 205.

36. Trent, Louisa Van Velsor Whitman letter, December 5, 1863.

37. Waldron, *Mattie*, 34–35.

38. Ibid., 36.

39. Trent, Louisa Van Velsor Whitman letter, December 5, 1863.

40. Ibid.

41. Ibid.

Chapter Nine

1. Rubin and Brown, *Walt Whitman of the Aurora*, 41.

2. Berthold and Price, *Dear Brother*, 118n12. Allen, *Solitary Singer*, 216. The Whitman family lived in two houses at this location, numbers 107 and 109, moving to the second in May 1860. Holloway, *Uncollected Poetry and Prose*, 2:88n8. This second house was "the 4th door north of Myrtle," according to Walt. Miller, *Correspondence*, 1:130.

3. Trent, Louisa Van Velsor Whitman letter, March 30, 1860.

4. Ibid., May 3, 1860.

5. "Brooklyn in the Civil War," http://www.brooklynpubliclibrary.org.

6. Kirkwood, "Report," 5.

7. Zweig, *Making of the Poet*, 99.

8. Holloway, *Uncollected Poetry and Prose*, 1:254.

9. Berthold and Price, *Dear Brother*, xviii.

10. Ibid., xvi.

11. Ibid., xviii.

12. Ibid., 11.

13. Ibid., 9.

14. Ibid., xxv–xxvi.

15. Ibid., xxvi.

16. Allen, *Solitary Singer*, 211.

17. Traubel, *In Re*, 37.

18. Berthold and Price, *Dear Brother*, 51.

19. Ibid., 49–50.

20. Ibid., 46.

21. Miller, *Correspondence*, 1:87. Berthold and Price, *Dear Brother*, 47n13.

22. Genoways, *Correspondence*, 7:13.

23. Waldron, *Mattie*, 34.

24. Berthold and Price, *Dear Brother*, 32.

25. *Brooklyn Daily Eagle*, random selection of "To Let" advertisements, 1859–61. Houses made of brick, with about ten rooms or more, often of three stories plus a basement, with water and gas piped in, commonly rented for $350 to $700 in the early war years and just before. For instance, a house offered in the *Eagle* for February 15, 1859, was described as "THE THREE STORY BRICK house No. 34 East Baltic street, containing 9 rooms, front and back basement and sub cellar . . . gas throughout the house, good grape vines in the yard." Rent was $375. A house offered the same day for $650, at Baltic and Clinton, had four stories and a stable, and was said to be "very suitable for a doctor" because it was large and "finished in good style." Another, offered two years later, was "THE 3 STORY, BRICK" dwelling at 59 Carroll Street, with twelve rooms, gas, and piped water. Rent: $410. And another, advertised May 1, 1861, had fourteen rooms "newly painted and papered throughout; range, and cistern

water in kitchen and laundry; furnace, good fruit trees and shrubbery," and, again, a stable. Given their expenditures on rent, the Whitmans would have occupied houses roughly of this type.

26. Berthold and Price, *Dear Brother*, 24–25.

27. Loving, *Civil War Letters*, 49. Boatner, *Civil War Dictionary*, 624.

28. Loving, *Letters*, 77n2. Boatner, *Civil War Dictionary*, 624.

29. Loving, *Letters*, 61n4.

30. Ibid., 71, 73.

31. Ibid., 77.

32. Trent, Louisa Van Velsor Whitman letter, November 1, 1863.

33. Ibid., December 1863.

34. Loving, *Civil War Letters*, 27–28.

35. Trent, Louisa Van Velsor Whitman letter, March 1863.

36. On presence of sewing machines in the home, Loving, *Civil War Letters*, 50. On Hattie's fall, Berthold and Price, *Dear Brother*, 41.

37. Trent, Louisa Van Velsor Whitman letter, December 25, 1863.

38. Miller, *Correspondence*, 1:56.

39. Allen, *Solitary Singer*, 240.

40. Trent, Louisa Van Velsor Whitman letters, March 1863 and March 19, 1863.

41. Ibid., March 19, 1863.

42. Waldron, *Mattie*, 36. Berthold and Price, *Dear Brother*, 52.

43. Trent, Louisa Van Velsor Whitman letter, March 1863.

44. Loving, *Civil War Letters*, 49–50.

45. Ibid., 50.

46. Berthold and Price, *Dear Brother*, 71.

47. Ibid., 81–82.

48. Ibid., 30, 32.

49. Ibid., 67.

50. Miller, *Correspondence*, 1:117–18.

51. Loving, *Civil War Letters*, 104, 101.

52. Ibid., 129.

53. Ibid., 104.

54. Ibid., 130. On the number of men who survived imprisonment, Bateman, "A Few Facts," 5. See also chapter 25.

55. Loving, *Civil War Letters*, 127n3.

56. Ibid., 130.

57. Ibid., 131–32.

Chapter Ten

1. Miller, *Correspondence*, 1:171.

2. Alcott, *Hospital*, xlii.

3. Morris, *Better Angel*, 94.

4. Miller, *Correspondence*, 1:168.

5. Morris, *Better Angel*, 104. Morris claims that Walt invariably wore a necktie when visiting the hospitals. Many photos from the 1860s show him without a necktie. Some show him wearing a loosely knotted cravat, the collar beneath it unbuttoned—a way to have it both ways.

6. Calder, "Personal Recollections," 199.

7. Ibid., 211.

8. Roberts, "A Map," 23.

9. Leech, *Reveille*, 5.

10. Ibid., 10.

11. Ibid., 5–7.

12. Ibid., 10.

13. Ibid., 207.

14. Ibid., 261–77.

15. Ibid., 264.

16. Miller, *Correspondence*, 1:62, 75. Holloway, *Uncollected Poetry and Prose*, 2:26–29.

17. Whitman, *Leaves* (1855), 71.

18. Ibid., 63–67.

19. Schmidgall, *Selected Poems*, 237.

20. Ibid., 238.

21. Ibid., 246.

22. Grier, *Notebooks*, 2:487–89.

23. Ibid., 2:492–93. Another of Walt's notebooks gives evidence that he slept with a Daniel Spencer on September 3. If this was also under Mrs. Whitman's roof, conditions may have been crowded.

24. Schmidgall, *A Gay Life*, 194.

25. Ibid., 195.

26. Reynolds, "Nineteenth-Century Views," 39.

27. Alcott, *Journals*, 290.

28. Ibid., 286.

29. Ibid.

30. Ibid., 287.

31. Schmidgall, *Selected Poems*, 236.

32. Ibid., 234.

33. Ibid.

34. Ibid., 232.

35. Schmidgall, *A Gay Life*, 196.

36. Ibid.

37. Miller, *Correspondence*, 1:61.

Chapter Eleven

1. Loving, *Song of Himself*, 189.

2. Allen, *Solitary Singer*, 179.

3. Miller, *Correspondence*, 1:61.

4. Grier, *Notebooks*, 2:488.

5. Miller, *Correspondence*, 1:58.

6. Ibid., 1:63.

7. Morris, *Better Angel*, 50.

8. Loving, *Civil War Letters*, 80.

9. Warner, *Generals*, 57.

10. McPherson, *Battle Cry*, 569.

11. Styple, *Writing*, 145.

12. Parker, *History of the 51st*, 259.

13. Loving, *Civil War Letters*, 78.

14. McPherson, *Battle Cry*, 571.

15. Ibid., 572.

16. Ibid., 571.

17. Parker, *History of the 51st*, 267.

18. Ibid., 268.

19. Ibid., 269.

20. On number of men in Company E, National Archives, 51st New York Infantry Morning Reports.

21. Styple, *Writing*, 150.

22. Loving, *Civil War Letters*, 66–67. Henry W. Francis letter, September 20, 1862.

23. Henry W. Francis letter, December 18, 1862.

24. Loving, *Civil War Letters*, 78.

25. McPherson, *Battle Cry*, 572.

26. Rable, *Fredericksburg!*, 242.

27. Styple, *Writing*, 148.

28. Rable, *Fredericksburg!*, 218–44.

29. Ibid., 218–19.

30. Ibid., 233.

31. Parker, *History of the 51st*, 271.

32. Grier, *Notebooks*, 2:502.

33. Ibid., 477.

34. Ibid., 504.

35. Williams, *Clara Barton*, 82.

36. Morris, *Better Angel*, 54. Williams, *Clara*, 71.

37. Williams, *Clara*, 84.

38. Morris, *Better Angel*, 63.

39. Williams, *Clara*, 73.

40. Ibid., 71.

41. Ibid., 72.

42. Miller, *Correspondence*, 1:61n8.

43. National Archives, New York Regimental Descriptive Book.

44. Walt Whitman Collection, Beinecke Library, Yale.

45. Miller, *Correspondence*, 1:60n6.

46. National Archives, Office of the Board of Examination report, June 22, 1864.

47. Henry W. Francis letter, April 10, 1862.

48. Ibid., May 18, 1862.

49. S. P. Olds letter to H. W. Francis, New York State Archives.

50. Miller, *Correspondence*, 1:60.

51. Ibid., 1:59.

52. Grier, *Notebooks*, 2:502.

53. *Brooklyn Daily Eagle*, January 5, 1863.

54. Loving, *Civil War Letters*, 60.

55. Ibid., 127–28.

56. Ibid., 78.

57. Ibid., 54.

58. Henry W. Francis letter, June 1, 1862.

59. Ibid.

Chapter Twelve

1. Grier, *Notebooks*, 2:513.

2. Whitman, *Complete Poetry and Prose*, 441.

3. Grier, *Notebooks*, 2:504.

4. Ibid., 2:506.

5. Ibid., 2:507.

6. Ibid., 2:503, 508, 504, 509.

7. Loving, *Civil War Letters*, 83.

8. Ibid., 137.

9. Ibid., 141–42.

10. Ibid., 143.

11. Ibid., 149.

12. Ibid., 154.

13. Ibid., 152.

14. Ibid.

15. Ibid., 144.

16. Grier, *Notebooks*, 2:501.

17. Loving, *Civil War Letters*, 152. Grier, *Notebooks*, 2:506.

18. Grier, *Notebooks*, 2:512.

19. *Brooklyn Daily Eagle*, January 5, 1863.

20. Styple, *Writing*, 10.

21. Traubel, *In Re*, 35–36.

22. Berg Collection.

23. Traubel, *With Walt*, 1:227.

24. George's "work writing" may also refer to the elaborate records he was required to keep as a regimental officer. When Hannah wrote him, however, he was on leave, presumably relaxing from such labors.

25. Henry W. Francis letter, April 10, 1862.

26. Ibid., June 1, 1862.

27. Ibid., December 23, 1862.

28. Ibid., January 19, 1863.

29. Ibid.

30. Ibid.

31. Ibid.

32. Grier, *Notebooks*, 2:508.

33. Loving, *Civil War Letters*, 79. Report of Col. Robert B. Potter, *Official Records*, series 1, vol. 21, part 1, 330.

34. Miller, *Correspondence*, 1:68.

35. Grier, *Notebooks*, 2:508–9.

36. Rable, "It Is Well," 55–56.

37. Linderman, "Embattled," 436–55.

38. Grier, *Notebooks*, 2:509.

39. Rable, "It Is Well," 63.

40. Grier, *Notebooks*, 2:515–16.

41. These are the names by which the poems were known in the final, "Deathbed" edition of Whitman, *Leaves*, 1892.

42. Alcott, *Hospital*, 44.

43. Ibid., 45.

44. See Feldman, "Remembering a Convulsive War."

45. Henry W. Francis letter, January 14, 1863.

Chapter Thirteen

1. Morris, *Better Angel*, 76.

2. Miller, *Correspondence*, 1:59.

3. Ibid., 60.

4. Loving, *Whitman's Champion*, 22, 7.

5. Ibid., 29.

6. Ibid., 75.

7. Loving, *Song of Himself*, 245.

8. Morris, *Better Angel*, 72.

9. Loving, *Whitman's Champion*, 157–62.

10. Ibid., 56–65.

11. Morris, *Better Angel*, 77.

12. Leech, *Reveille*, 226.

13. Miller, *Correspondence*, 1:62.

14. Berthold and Price, *Dear Brother*, 20.

15. Ibid., 18.

16. Ibid., 19–20.

17. Ibid., 25.

18. Ibid., 26, 23.

19. Miller, *Correspondence*, 1:86.

20. Ibid., 1:72, 100.

21. Ibid., 1:71.

22. Ibid., 1:63.

23. Ibid., 1:63–64.

24. Lowenfels, *Whitman's Civil War*, 89–90.

25. Ibid., 90.

26. Ibid., 90–91.

27. Ibid., 91.

28. Morris, *Better Angel*, 92.

29. Author's visit to the Lacy House (Chatham Manor), Fredericksburg and Spotsylvania National Military Park, Falmouth, VA.

30. Grier, *Notebooks*, 2:519–20.

31. Ibid., 2:499.

Chapter Fourteen

1. Lowenfels, *Whitmans's Civil War*, 91.

2. Miller, *Correspondence*, 1:126.

3. Ibid., 1:68.

4.   Ibid., 1:69.

5.   Ibid.

6.   Ibid., 1:69–70.

7.   Ibid., 1:70.

8.   Emerson, *Essays*, 260.

9.   Ibid., 261.

10. Rubin and Brown, *Walt of the Aurora*, 105.

11. Emerson, *Essays*, 264.

12. Ibid., 18.

13. Miller, *Correspondence*, 1:68.

14. Journal of James Bryce, 1870, quoted in Loving, *American Muse*, 186.

15. On Emerson's dates, Loving, *American Muse*, 124. On a six-year prime, ibid., 134. F. O. Matthiessen coined the term "American Renaissance," referring to the period 1836–55, and specifically including the writers Emerson, Whitman, Thoreau, and Melville, ibid., 16.

16. Schmidgall, *Selected Poems*, 267.

17. Ibid., 267–68.

18. Miller, *Correspondence*, 1:185.

19. Ibid., 1:105.

20. Ibid., 89.

21. Aaron, *Unwritten War*, 75.

22. Ibid., 333.

23. Schmidgall, *Selected Poems*, 281.

24. Grier, *Notebooks*, 2:518.

25. Loving, *Civil War Letters*, 83, 89.

26. Ibid., 107.

27. James, "Mr. Whitman."

28. Loving, *Song of Himself*, 306. Savoy, "Reading Gay America," 9–12.

Chapter Fifteen

1.   Burroughs, *Notes*, 12.

2.   Ibid.

3.   Allen, *Solitary Singer*, 300.

4.   Morris, *Better Angel*, 151.

5.   Ibid., 153.

6.   Ibid., 154.

7.   Burroughs, *Notes*, 13. Morris, *Better Angel*, 151.

8.   Glicksburg, *Walt and the War*, 137.

9.   Ibid.

10. Miller, *Correspondence*, 1:149.

11. Ibid., 1:149n49.

12. Loving, *Whitman's Champion*, 50–51.

13. Grier, *Notebooks*, 2:621.

14. Berg Collection.

15. Ibid.

16. Miller, *Correspondence*, 1:187.

17. Ibid., 1:186-87n70.

18. Ibid., 1:187.

19. Ibid., 1:176–77.

20. Ibid., 1:177n40.

21. Ibid., 1:229.

22. Ibid., 1:69.

23. Ibid., 1:103.

24. Ibid., 1:110.

25. Ibid., 1:74–75.

26. Leech, *Reveille*, 278–79.

27. Ibid., 279–82.

28. Grier, *Notebooks*, 2:592.

29. Ibid., 2:592–93.

30. Shively, *Drum*, 55–56.

31. Ibid., 154.

32. Miller, *Correspondence*, 1:153.

33. Ibid., 1:165–66.

34. Ibid., 1:173.

35. Trent, Louisa Van Velsor Whitman letter, November 1863.

Chapter Sixteen

1.   Miller, *Correspondence*, 1:102.

2.   Ibid., 1:103.

3.   The soldier was Livingston Brooks— see chapter 2.

4.   Miller, *Correspondence*, 1:112–13.

5.   Ibid., 1:113.

6.   Whitman, *Memoranda*, 41.

7.   Ibid., 40–41.

8.   Peter Coviello, introduction to Whitman, *Memoranda*, xliii–iv.

9.   Traubel, *With Walt*, 1:227.

10. Miller, *Correspondence*, 1:107.

11. Ibid., 1:105–6.

12. Ibid., 1:114–15.

13. Ibid., 1:115.

14. Ibid., 1:117–18.

15. Lowenfels, *Whitman's Civil War*, 133.

16. Trent, Louisa Van Velsor Whitman letter, August 1, 1867.

17. Allen, *Solitary Singer*, 383.

18. Trent, Louisa Van Velsor Whitman letter, March 1863.

19. Ibid., March 19, 1863.

20. Ibid., June 3, 1865.

21. Linderman, "Embattled," 94, cited in Shively, *Drum*, 49.

22. Trent, Louisa Van Velsor Whitman letters, November 1 and March 19, 1863.

23. Ibid., November 1, 1863.

24. Ibid., October 26, 1863.

25. Miller, *Correspondence*, 1:144–45.

26. Trent, Louisa Van Velsor Whitman letter, September 3, 1863.

27. Miller, *Correspondence*, 1:140.

28. Lowenfels, *Whitman's Civil War*, 133.

29. Whitman, *Complete Poetry and Prose*, 754–55.

30. Calder, "Personal Recollections," 198.

31. Miller, *Correspondence*, 1:183.

32. Ibid., 1:185.

Chapter Seventeen

1. Miller, *Correspondence*, 1:63.

2. Loving, *Civil War Letters*, 87–88.

3. Ibid.

4. Berthold and Price, *Dear Brother*, 35.

5. Miller, *Correspondence*, 1:79.

6. Trent, Louisa Van Velsor Whitman letter, March 19, 1863.

7. Miller, *Correspondence*, 1:93.

8. Ibid.

9. Katz, *Love Stories*, 370n54.

10. Ibid.

11. Miller, *Correspondence*, 1:92–93.

12. Ibid., 1:91.

13. Berg Collection.

14. Miller, *Correspondence*, 1:106.

15. Berg Collection.

16. Miller, *Correspondence*, 1:106.

17. Katz, *Love Stories*, 153.

18. Miller, *Correspondence*, 1:186.

19. Whitman, *Memoranda*, 15.

20. Ibid., 15–16.

21. Grier, *Notebooks*, 2:573.

22. Whitman, *Memoranda*, 16.

23. Stearns, *Lady Nurse*, 42, cited in Murray, "Traveling," 63.

24. Murray, "Traveling," 63.

25. Glicksberg, *Walt and the War*, 44.

26. Whitman, *Memoranda*, 11–12.

27. Ibid., 18. Murray, "Traveling," 62.

28. Miller, *Correspondence*, 1:120.

29. Ibid.

30. Rutkow, *Bleeding*, 155.

31. Miller, *Correspondence*, 1:154.

32. Ibid., 1:155.

33. Grier, *Notebooks*, 2:549.

34. Ibid., 2:556–57.

35. Ibid., 2:557.

36. Ibid., 2:557–58.

37. Ibid., 2:558.

38. Ibid., 2:560.

39. Ibid., 2:565.

40. Ibid.

41. Ibid., 2:544.

42. Ibid., 2:605.

43. Ibid., 2:606.

44. Ibid., 2:606–7.

45. Ibid., 2:604.

46. Miller, *Correspondence*, 1:108.

47. Grier, *Notebooks*, 2:566.

48. Ibid., 2:554–56. Miller, *Correspondence*, 1:365.

Chapter Eighteen

1. Miller, *Correspondence*, 1:82.

2. Ibid.

3. Ibid., 1:81.

4. Ibid., 1:85–86.

5. Whitman, *Memoranda*, 19.

6. Shively, *Drum*, 53.

7. Katz, *Love Stories*, 158. Shively, *Drum*, 53.

8. Katz, *Love Stories*, 158.

9. Shively, *Drum*, 128.

10. Ibid., 128–29.

11. Miller, *Correspondence*, 1:332.

12. Shively, *Drum*, 125.

13. Miller, *Correspondence*, 1:330–31n80.

14. Stearns, *Lady Nurse*, 69.

15. Ibid., 57.

16. Ibid., 74–75.

17. Ibid., 19.

18. Wardrop, "Nursing Narratives," 32.

19. Ibid., 35–38.

20. See Schmidgall, *A Gay Life*, 143–52. Schmidgall amusingly tracks the disappearance from later editions of *Leaves* of many of Walt's most libidinous and/or homoerotic passages. Whole poems disappeared, among them some of Walt's most affecting love lyrics (e.g., "Calamus 9"). These lines, from "Song of Myself," disappeared after the 1860 edition: "Thruster holding me tight, and that I hold tight! / We hurt each other as the bridegroom and the bride . . ." Likewise disappearing, from "A Song of Joys:" "O love branches! love-root! love-apples! / O chaste and electric torrents! O mad-sweet drops!" After the 1860 edition, Walt "ceased to be the singer of the 'bedfellow's song' and the celebrator of the cruiser's life," Schmidgall concludes. "[Whitman] became, instead, a diplomat, a poet/prophet, an America-boosting master of ceremonies . . . His relationship with the reader was no longer figured as an intimate one-on-one nocturnal encounter. Rather, one thinks of the bully pulpit or the orator's platform."

21. Erkkila, "Homosexual Republic," 162–64.

22. Murray, "Traveling," 66.

23. Whitman, *Memoranda*, 32.

24. Miller, *Correspondence*, 1:143.

25. Whitman, *Memoranda*, 29.

26. Stearns, *Lady Nurse*, 17–18.

27. Ibid., 102–3.

Chapter Nineteen

1. Miller, *Correspondence*, 1:80.

2. Grier, *Notebooks*, 2:591.

3. Whitman, *Memoranda*, 3–4.

4. Ibid., 5–6.

5. Ibid., 7.

6. Grier, *Notebooks*, 2:581.

7. Whitman, *Memoranda*, 7.

8. Whitman, *Complete Poetry and Prose*, 778.

9. Whitman, *Memoranda*, 7.

10. Grier, *Notebooks*, 2:580.

11. Whitman, *Memoranda*, 6.

12. Burroughs, *Notes*, 97–98.

13. Ibid., 98.

14. Ibid., 106.

15. On fifty thousand books to date: McPherson, *Battle Cry*, 865.

16. Burroughs, *Notes*, 107.

17. Huddleston, *Killing Ground*, 3.

18. Loving, *Civil War Letters*, 46.

19. Ibid., 46n1.

20. Ibid., 67.

21. Ibid., 62.

22. Ibid., 62–63.

23. Whitman, *Complete Poetry and Prose*, 740.

24. Whitman, *Leaves* (1855), 60.

25. Schmidgall, *Selected Poems*, 300.

26. Ibid., 272.

27. *Putnam's Magazine*, January 1868. Cited in Allen, *Solitary Singer*, 364.

28. Schmidgall, *Selected Poems*, 271–72.

29. Ibid., 272.

30. Miller, *Correspondence*, 1:231.

31. Schmidgall, *Selected Poems*, 273.

32. Ibid., 271.

33. Miller, *Correspondence*, 1:130.

34. Loving, *Civil War Letters*, 97–98.

35. Ibid.

36. Ibid., 98.

37. Ibid., 98–99.

38. Ibid., 99.

39. Royster, *Destructive War*, 110–15.

40. Loving, *Civil War Letters*, 99–100.

41. Ibid., 99n8. Another family member could have done this marking out, but in all likelihood it was Walt.

42. Miller, *Correspondence*, 1:128.

43. Ibid., 1:131.
44. Morris, *Better Angel*, 127.
45. Miller, *Correspondence*, 1:127.
46. Ibid., 1:128.
47. Ibid.
48. Ibid., 1:129.
49. Ibid.
50. Ibid.
51. Ibid.

Chapter Twenty

1. Miller, *Correspondence*, 1:123.
2. Ibid., 1:134.
3. Whitman, *Memoranda*, 22.
4. Miller, *Correspondence*, 1:154.
5. Ibid.
6. McPherson, *Battle Cry*, 482. The quote is from Frederick Law Olmsted.
7. Rutkow, *Bleeding*, 161–62.
8. Ibid., 78.
9. Frederickson, *Inner War*, 136.
10. McPherson, *Battle Cry*, 482.
11. Morris, *Better Angel*, 193.
12. Rutkow, *Bleeding*, 206.
13. McPherson, *Battle Cry*, 485.
14. Rutkow, *Bleeding*, 215–16.
15. Miller, *Correspondence*, 1:63.
16. Ibid., 1:100.
17. Rutkow, *Bleeding*, 235–36.
18. Ibid., 236.
19. Ibid., 319.
20. Civil War surgeon W. W. Keen, quoted in Morris, *Better Angel*, 96.
21. Freemon, *Gangrene*, 48.
22. Rutkow, *Bleeding*, 238.
23. Grier, *Notebooks*, 2:669.
24. Ibid.
25. Ibid., 2:119n70.

Chapter Twenty-one

1. McPherson, *Battle Cry*, 718.
2. Ibid., 718–19.
3. Papers of the 51st Regiment New York State Volunteers, New York State Archives, Albany.
4. *New York Times*, October 29, 1864.

5. Ibid.
6. Bateman, "A Few Facts," 10–11.
7. "51st N.Y. Infantry," Antietam Museum.
8. Bateman, "A Few Facts," 10.
9. Gallagher, *Confederate War*, 29.
10. *New York Times*, October 29, 1864.
11. Ibid.
12. Warner, *Generals*, 382–83.
13. Loving, *Civil War Letters*, 46–47.
14. Priest, *Antietam*, 230.
15. Ibid., 237–39.
16. Loving, *Civil War Letters*, 145.
17. Smith and Judah, *Life in the North*, 79–80.
18. "Quarter Century Banquet," 32, 12.
19. Fowler, *Memoirs*, 36–39.
20. Ibid., 8–9.
21. Ibid., 42–43.
22. Ibid., 11.
23. Ibid., 12.
24. Ibid., 14–15.
25. Loving, *Civil War Letters*, 68.
26. Fowler, *Memoirs*, 15, 53.
27. McPherson, *Battle Cry*, 544, 539.
28. Frassanito, *Antietam*, 17.
29. Ibid., 27–28.
30. Cox, *Military Reminiscences*, 1:165–71.
31. Muster Rolls, 51st Regiment New York Volunteers, Record Group 94, National Archives.
32. Loving, *Civil War Letters*, 46.
33. Military report of Capt. John G. Wright, August 8, 1864, in Loving, *Civil War Letters*, 162–63.
34. Loving, *Civil War Letters*, 106.
35. Ibid., 163.
36. Sims, Pension Record, National Archives.
37. Loving, *Civil War Letters*, 24.
38. Sims, Consolidated Military Service Record.
39. McPherson, *Battle Cry*, 472.
40. Miller, *Correspondence*, 1:100.
41. Loving, *Civil War Letters*, 118.
42. Miller, *Correspondence*, 1:223.

43. Ibid., 222–23.

44. LeGendre, Pension Record, National Archives.

45. Miller, *Correspondence*, 1:223.

46. Ibid., 227.

47. McReady, Pension Record, National Archives.

48. Ibid.

49. McReady, Consolidated Military Service Record.

50. McReady, Pension Record, National Archives.

Chapter Twenty-two

1. Miller, *Correspondence*, 1:193.

2. Morris, *Better Angel*, 167.

3. Whitman, *Complete Poetry and Prose*, 741.

4. Grier, *Notebooks*, 2:725.

5. Miller, *Correspondence*, 1:199.

6. Whitman, *Complete Poetry and Prose*, 740.

7. McPherson, *Battle Cry*, 718.

8. Miller, *Correspondence*, 1:211.

9. Ibid., 1:213.

10. Ibid., 1:207–8.

11. Ibid., 1:205.

12. Ibid., 1:203.

13. Ibid., 1:211–12.

14. Ibid., 1:212.

15. Ibid., 1:212–13.

16. De Forest, *Volunteer's Adventures*, 58.

17. Ibid., 68–69.

18. Congdon, *Combat*, 290, 294.

19. Thompson, "With Burnside," 661.

20. Ibid., 661–62.

21. Ibid., 662.

22. Miller, *Correspondence*, 1:210. Loving, *Civil War Letters*, 114.

23. Grier, *Notebooks*, 2:611–21.

24. Ibid., 2:612–13. Grier, whose explanatory notes to the poem drafts are very helpful, himself expresses a debt to Shannon Drews Rayl, who edited the manuscript for her senior honors essay in English at the University of Kansas.

25. Ibid., 2:493.

26. Congdon, *Combat*, 473–74.

27. Schmidgall, *Selected Poems*, 276.

28. Miller, *Correspondence*, 1:123–24.

29. Ibid., 1:124.

Chapter Twenty-three

1. McPherson, *Battle Cry*, 400. Royster, *Destructive War*, 103.

2. McPherson, *Battle Cry*, 330.

3. Catton, *Grant Moves*, 229.

4. Royster, *Destructive War*, 103.

5. Ibid., 34–40.

6. Ibid., 40.

7. Ibid., 41.

8. Ibid., 46.

9. McPherson, *Battle Cry*, 414.

10. Priest, *Nowhere*, 19.

11. Wheeler, *Fields of Fury*, 120.

12. Loving, *Civil War Letters*, 118.

13. Ibid., 114.

14. *Official Records*, series 1, vol. 36, part 1, 351.

15. Priest, *Victory*, 37–38.

16. Ibid., 141.

17. Ibid., 140.

18. *Official Records*, series 1, vol. 36, part 1, 928.

19. Priest, *Victory*, 140.

20. Wheeler, *Fields of Fury*, 129.

21. Ibid., 122.

22. Ibid., 127.

23. *Official Records*, series 1, vol. 36, part 1, 928.

24. Priest, *Victory*, 144.

25. *Official Records*, series 1, vol. 36, part 1, 948. Priest, *Victory*, 144.

26. Loving, *Civil War Letters*, 121–22.

27. For a listing of regimental histories, see http://www.mosocco.com/regiment.html.

28. Priest, *Nowhere*, xvi.

29. Priest, *Victory*, 242.

30. Rhea, *Spotsylvania*, 6.

31. Matter, "Federal High Command," 46.

32. Ibid., 47–51.

33. *Official Records*, series 1, vol. 36, part 1, 928.

34. Ibid. Rhea, *Spotsylvania*, 254.

35. Rhea, *Spotsylvania*, 254.

36. Matter, "Federal High Command," 51.

37. Rhea, *Spotsylvania*, 311.

38. Loving, *Civil War Letters*, 119. For average size of the regiment, "Morning Reports of Capt. George W. Whitman," National Archives.

Chapter Twenty-four

1. Miller, *Correspondence*, 1:233. Roberts, "A Map," 24.

2. Miller, *Correspondence*, 1:229.

3. McPherson, *Battle Cry*, 733.

4. Morris, *Better Angel*, 181.

5. Miller, *Correspondence*, 1:229, 233.

6. Loving, *Civil War Letters*, 118.

7. Whitman journal, May 9, 1865, 8, Yale Collection, Beinecke Library.

8. Ibid., 7.

9. Loving, *Civil War Letters*, 124. *Official Records*, series 1, vol. 40, 734.

10. Loving, *Civil War Letters*, 124.

11. McPherson, *Battle Cry*, 733.

12. Rhea, *Cold Harbor*, 150.

13. Ibid., 149.

14. *Official Records*, series 1, vol. 36, part 1, 929.

15. Ibid.

16. Ibid., 930.

17. Rhea, *Cold Harbor*, 370.

18. Ibid.

19. Ibid.

20. Loving, *Civil War Letters*, 120–21.

21. McPherson, *Battle Cry*, 735–42.

22. Ibid., 735.

23. Loving, *Civil War Letters*, 122.

24. McPherson, *Battle Cry*, 734–35.

25. Ibid., 740.

26. Loving, *Civil War Letters*, 124.

27. Ibid., 125.

28. Ibid., 123.

29. McPherson, *Battle Cry*, 758–60.

30. Loving, *Civil War Letters*, 128.

31. Ibid., 127.

32. Ibid., 162–63.

33. Grant message to Halleck, quoted in McPherson, *Battle Cry*, 760.

Chapter Twenty-five

1. Miller, *Correspondence*, 1:238.

2. Berthold and Price, *Dear Brother*, 103–4.

3. Miller, *Correspondence*, 1:236.

4. Loving, *Civil War Letters*, 123.

5. Miller, *Correspondence*, 1:236, 239.

6. Grier, *Notebooks*, 2:761, 761n13. Allen, *Solitary Singer*, 577n55.

7. Grier, *Notebooks*, 2:702.

8. Miller, *Correspondence*, 1:238, 241–42.

9. Grier, *Notebooks*, 2:693.

10. Miller, *Correspondence*, 1:243.

11. Ibid.

12. Whitman, *Complete Poetry and Prose*, 777.

13. Morris, *Better Angel*, 189–90.

14. Glicksberg, *Walt and the War*, 40.

15. Personal communication of Donald Pfanz, Staff Historian, Fredericksburg and Spotsylvania National Military Park, October 2, 2007.

16. Grier, *Notebooks*, 2:686.

17. Glicksberg, *Walt and the War*, 178–79.

18. Grier, *Notebooks*, 2:745.

19. McPherson, *Battle Cry*, 755.

20. "When captured," McPherson, *Battle Cry*, 794. Kean quoted ibid., 792.

21. Glicksberg, *Walt and the War*, 179.

22. Grier, *Notebooks*, 2:699.

23. Ibid. Loving, *Civil War Letters*, 131.

24. Thomas B. Marsh, Consolidated Military Service Record, National Archives.

25. Grier, *Notebooks*, 2:702.

26. Ibid., 701.

27. Loving, *Civil War Letters*, 132.

28. P. Mitchell, " 'Truly Horrible,' " 12.

29. Ibid., 13.

30. Ibid., 12.

31. Small, *Road to Richmond*, 17.

32. Miller, *Correspondence*, 1:244.

33. Grier, *Notebooks*, 2:743.

34. Trent, Louisa Van Velsor Whitman letter, March 5, 1865.

35. See http://www.censusdiggins.com/prison_danville.html.

36. Trent, Louisa Van Velsor Whitman letter, March 5, 1865.

37. Ibid.

38. See http://www.censusdiggins.com/danville_prisoners.html.

39. Grier, *Notebooks*, 2:716.

40. William T. Ackerson, an officer of the 51st New York imprisoned at Danville, kept a list of items purchased from prison staff during his incarceration and the prices paid. Collection 109, Ackerson Papers, Monmouth County Historical Society. See also Small, *Road to Richmond*, 245–51.

41. Trent, Louisa Van Velsor Whitman letter, March 5, 1865.

42. Whitman notebook, May 9, 1865, Yale Collection, Beinecke Library.

43. Miller, *Correspondence*, 1:242n31.

44. Whitman notebook, December 26, 1864, Yale Collection, Beinecke Library.

45. Ibid.

46. Miller, *Correspondence*, 1:244.

47. Six days after committing Jesse to the asylum, Walt published an article in the *New York Times*, "Our Wounded and Sick Soldiers," that described the many hospitals he had visited in Washington and New York and "on the Field." In passing he mentioned the insane asylum at Flatbush, singling it out for extraordinary praise ("I have deliberately to put on record about the profoundest satisfaction with professional capacity, completeness of house arrangements, and the right vital spirit animating all."). Jesse's institutional home was a decent, hopeful place, Walt implied. Mrs. Whitman, who was sad and perhaps tormented by guilt to have committed her firstborn son, may have been somewhat consoled. The doctors in charge of the institution, reading Walt's generous praise of their professionalism, may have become more kindly disposed toward any inmates named Whitman.

48. Berthold and Price, *Dear Brother*, 104.

49. Miller, *Correspondence*, 1:246–47.

Chapter Twenty-six

1. Grier, *Notebooks*, 2:747.

2. Berthold and Price, *Dear Brother*, 97.

3. Ibid., 100.

4. Ibid., 101.

5. Ibid., 100n3.

6. Ibid., 101.

7. Miller, *Correspondence*, 1:249n13.

8. Ibid., 1:251.

9. Grier, *Notebooks*, 2:762.

10. Berthold and Price, *Dear Brother*, 98.

11. Miller, *Correspondence*, 1:252.

12. Grier, *Notebooks*, 2:750.

13. Miller, *Correspondence*, 1:256n32.

14. Loving, *Civil War Letters*, 23.

15. Berthold and Price, *Dear Brother*, 102–3.

16. Ibid., 104.

17. Miller, *Correspondence*, 1:250.

18. Ibid., 1:253.

19. Whitman, *Memoranda*, 79.

20. Grier, *Notebooks*, 2:749.

21. Ibid., 2:750.

22. Ibid., 2:752.

23. Morris, *Better Angel*, 204.

24. Whitman, *Memoranda*, 89.

25. Grier, *Notebooks*, 2:751–52.

26. Murray, "Pete," 15.

27. Grier, *Notebooks*, 2:753.

28. Loving, *Civil War Letters*, 134.

29. Ibid.

30. See http://www.censusdiggins.com/prison_danville.html.

31. Trent, Louisa Van Velsor Whitman letter, March 5, 1865.

32. Whitman notebook, May 9, 1865, Yale Collection, Beinecke Library.

33. Loving, *Civil War Letters*, 27.

34. Ibid., 132.

35. Whitman, *Complete Poetry and Prose*, 775.

36. Ibid., 776–77.

37. Ibid., 777.

38. This list of 121 men for Company K was swollen by the recent transfer of the 109th New York Volunteers into the 51st New York.

39. Final Muster Roll, Co. K, 51st New York, National Archives.

40. Ackerson Papers.

Chapter Twenty-seven

1. Grier, *Notebooks*, 2:874.

2. Holloway, *Uncollected Poetry and Prose*, 1:10–11.

3. McElroy, *Sacrificial*, 145–46.

4. Ibid., 146.

5. Aspiz, *So Long!*, 1.

6. Miller, *Correspondence*, 1:258–59.

7. Ibid., 1:259.

8. Ibid.

9. Ibid.

10. Loving, *Civil War Letters*, 134–35n1.

11. Trent. Louisa Van Velsor Whitman letter, March 5, 1865.

12. McPherson, *Battle Cry*, 819–20.

13. Miller, *Correspondence*, 1:246.

14. Ibid.

15. Ibid., 1:246–47.

16. Loving, *Song of Himself*, 286.

17. Ibid., 287.

18. Allen, *Handbook*, 113.

19. Miller, *Correspondence*, 1:82–83.

20. Whitman, *Memoranda*, 76.

21. Ibid., 76–77.

22. Abraham Lincoln Online, http://show case.netins.net/web/creative/lincoln/speeches/inaug2.htm.

23. Miller, *Correspondence*, 1:256–57.

24. Berthold and Price, *Dear Brother*, 109.

25. Miller, *Correspondence*, 1:257.

26. Ibid., 1:260n39.

27. Schmidgall, *Selected Poems*, 284.

28. Ibid.

29. Allen, *Solitary Singer*, 332.

30. Ibid.

31. Grier, *Notebooks*, 2:763.

32. Ibid., 2:764.

33. Ibid., 2:765.

34. Ibid., 2:762.

35. Miller, *Correspondence*, 1:258.

36. National Archives.

37. Allen, *Solitary Singer*, 332. Apple blossoms are mentioned in Whitman, *Memoranda*, 83, and in "When Lilacs Last in the Door-Yard Bloom'd," line 30.

38. Allen, *Solitary Singer*, 334.

39. Ibid.

40. Lee, "Undertaker's Role," 22.

41. On the binding of *Drum-Taps*, Miller, *Correspondence*, 1:260. On the president's train, Harris, *Lincoln's Last*, 235.

42. Harris, *Lincoln's Last*, 235.

43. Ibid., 236.

44. Schmidgall, *Selected Poems*, 292.

45. Harris, *Lincoln's Last*, 236.

46. *New York Times*, April 11, 1915.

47. Ibid.

48. *Brooklyn Daily Eagle*, April 24, 1865.

49. Ibid.

50. Ibid.

51. Ibid.

52. Grier, *Notebooks*, 2:769.

53. Harris, *Lincoln's Last*, 237.

54. Whitman, *Memoranda*, 54.

55. Schmidgall, *Selected Poems*, 291, 293, 298.

56. Ibid., 295.

57. Allen, *Solitary Singer*, 336.

58. Miller, *Correspondence*, 1:262n43.

Chapter Twenty-eight

1. Loving, *Civil War Letters*, 26.

2. Ibid., 135.

3. Ibid., 136.

4. Murray, "Pete," 19.

5. Whitman, *Complete Poetry and Prose*, 769.

6. Murray, "Pete," 20.

7. Ibid., 19–20.

8. Schmidgall, *Selected Poems*, 229, 233.

9. Aspiz, *So Long!*, 20.

10. Bradley et al., *American Tradition*, 264.

11. Berthold and Price, *Dear Brother*, 109.

12. Ibid., 110.

13. Morris, *Better Angel*, 224, 226.

14. McPherson, *Battle Cry*, 853.

15. Skocpol, *Protecting*, 7–11, 102.

16. Miller, "Whitman's Income," xix. See Afterward.

17. Berthold and Price, *Dear Brother*, 116.

18. Trent, Louisa Van Velsor Whitman letter, August 8, 1865.

19. Ibid.

20. Ibid., August 29, 1865.

21. Ibid., December 3, 1865.

22. Ibid., March 1866.

23. Ibid., May 31, 1866.

24. Ibid.

25. Loving, *Civil War Letters*, 28.

26. Trent, Louisa Van Velsor Whitman letter, May 31, 1865.

27. Ibid., April 27, 1865.

28. Ibid., October 10, 1866.

29. Miller, *Correspondence*, 1:293.

30. Ibid., 306.

31. Trent, Louisa Van Velsor Whitman letter, May 3, 1867.

32. Ibid., November 19, 1867.

33. Ibid.

34. Ibid.

35. Ibid., July 1, 1868.

36. Miller, *Correspondence*, 2:46, 51.

37. On Jeff as investor, Berthold and Price, *Dear Brother*, 131. On house plan, Trent, Louisa Van Velsor Whitman letter, November 11, 1868.

38. Berthold and Price, *Dear Brother*, 131, 128n1.

39. Trent, Louisa Van Velsor Whitman letter, February 17, 1869.

40. Ibid., November 2, 1868; March 13, 1868; December 28, 1868.

41. Ibid., February 17, 1869.

42. Ibid., March 4, 1869.

43. Ibid.

44. Ibid., March 15, 1869.

45. Ibid.

46. Berthold and Price, *Dear Brother*, 136.

47. Trent, Louisa Van Velsor Whitman letter, April 14, 1869.

48. Ibid., spring 1869.

49. Ibid., January 19, 1973; "From Camden 1873."

50. Ibid., "February or March 1873."

51. Ibid., "February or March 1873;" February 28, 1873.

52. Ibid., "Shortly after Mattie's death."

53. Ibid., "Letter #137."

54. Ibid., undated, probably May 1873.

55. Ibid., April 21, 1873.

56. Ibid., "Spring of 1873."

57. Ibid., April 21, 1873.

58. Ibid., April 12, 1873.

59. Walt paid George twenty dollars per month for the support of Mrs. Whitman and her disabled son, their brother, Eddy. Other than contributions from George, Walt, and Jeff, Mrs. Whitman was now without resources, in a society that made no provision for the old.

60. Trent, Louisa Van Velsor Whitman letter, April 8, 1873.

61. Ibid., April 12, 1873.

62. Miller, *Correspondence*, 2:193.

63. Ibid.

64. Ibid., 194.

65. Allen, *Solitary Singer*, 452–53.

66. Miller, *Correspondence*, 2:200–201.

Chapter Twenty-nine

1. Price, *Contemporary*, 129.

2. Grier, *Notebooks*, 2:766.

3. Schmidgall, *Selected Poems*, 208.

4. Ibid., 293.

5. Ibid., 211.

6. Ibid., 292.

7. Ibid.

8. Ibid., 293.

9. Ibid., 291.

10. Ibid., 295.

11. Ibid., 213.

12. Ibid., 297.

13. Miller, *Correspondence*, 1:270n64. Price, *Contemporary*, 120–21.

14. Trent, Louisa Van Velsor Whitman letter, November 25, 1865.

15. Price, *Contemporary*, 118.

16. Ibid., 122, 121.

17. Ibid., 120.

18. Ibid., 123.

19. Ibid., 127.

20. Ibid., 129.

21. Ibid.

22. Ibid., 129–30.

Afterward

1. Miller, *Correspondence*, 2:343.

2. Ibid., 2:323.

3. Ibid., 2:223, 229.

4. Ibid., 2:230.

5. Ibid., 2:230, 227.

6. Ibid., 2:230.

7. Ibid., 2:248.

8. Ibid., 2:246.

9. Ibid., 2:247.

10. Ibid., 2:248.

11. Ibid., 2:248, 245.

12. Ibid., 2:231.

13. Ibid., 2:248.

14. Ibid., 2:239.

15. Ibid., 2:245.

16. Ibid., 2:249.

17. Schmidgall, *A Gay Life*, 214–15.

18. Ibid., 393n216. Shively, *Calamus Lovers*, 156.

19. Miller, *Correspondence*, 2:242.

20. Miller, "Whitman's Income," xix.

21. Ibid., xxii.

22. Loving, *Song of Himself*, 411–12.

23. Miller, *Correspondence*, 3:91.

24. George also made handsome provision in his will for his sister Hannah, who was therefore financially secure in her last years.

25. Waldron, *Mattie*, 96.

26. Ibid.

BIBLIOGRAPHY

Aaron, Daniel. *The Unwritten War: American Writers and the Civil War.* New York: Alfred A. Knopf, 1973.

Ackerson, William T. Papers, 1861–1914. Collection 109. Monmouth County (NJ) Historical Association Library and Archives, Freehold, NJ.

Alcott, Bronson. *The Journals of Bronson Alcott.* Boston: Little, Brown and Company, 1938.

Alcott, Louisa May. *Hospital Sketches.* Edited by Bessie Z. Jones. Cambridge: Belknap Press, 1960.

Allen, Gay Wilson. *The New Walt Whitman Handbook.* New York: New York University Press, 1975.

_____. *The Solitary Singer: A Critical Biography of Walt Whitman.* New York: Macmillan, 1955.

Allen, Gay Wilson, and Sculley Bradley, general eds. *The Collected Writings of Walt Whitman.* New York: New York University Press, 1961–67.

Antietam Museum. "51st N.Y. Infantry." Antietam National Battlefield, Sharpsburg, MD.

Applegate, Debby. "Henry Ward Beecher and the 'Great Middle Class': Mass-Marketed Intimacy and Middle-Class Identity." In *The Middling Sorts: Explorations in the History of the American Middle Class,* edited by Burton J. Bledstein and Robert D. Johnston, 107–24. New York: Routledge, 2001.

Aspiz, Harold. *So Long! Walt Whitman's Poetry of Death.* Tuscaloosa, AL: University of Alabama Press, 2004.

Clifton Waller Barrett Library of American Literature. Papers of Walt Whitman. Albert H. Small Special Collections Library. University of Virginia, Charlottesville.

Bateman, James S. "A Few Facts About the 51st New York Vet Vols." Yale Collection of American Literature, Beinecke Rare Book and Manuscript Library.

The Henry W. and Albert A. Berg Collection of English and American Literature. New York Public Library.

Berthold, Dennis, and Kenneth Price, eds. *Dear Brother Walt: The Letters of Thomas Jefferson Whitman.* Kent, OH: Kent State University Press, 1984.

Blumin, Stuart M. *The Emergence of the Middle Class: Social Experience in the American City, 1760–1900.* New York: Cambridge University Press, 1989.

Boatner, Mark Mayo. *The Civil War Dictionary*. New York: D. McKay and Company, 1959.

Bradley, Scully, Richmond Croom Beatty, E. Hudson Long, and George Perkins, eds. *The American Tradition in Literature*. 4th ed. New York: Grosset & Dunlap, 1974.

Brooks, Noah. *Washington, D.C., in Lincoln's Time*. Chicago: Quadrangle Books, 1971.

Burroughs, John. *Notes on Walt Whitman, As Poet and Person*. New York: Haskell House, 1971.

Calder, Ellen (O'Connor). "Personal Recollections of Walt Whitman." In *Whitman in His Own Time*, edited by Joel Myerson, 194–211. Detroit, MI: Omnigraphics, 1991.

Carman, Ezra Ayres. Papers of Ezra Ayres Carman, 1861–1909. Washington, D.C.: Library of Congress, Manuscript Division.

Catton, Bruce. *Grant Moves South*. Boston: Little, Brown, 1960.

Cohen, Patricia Cline. *The Murder of Helen Jewett : The Life and Death of a Prostitute in Nineteenth Century New York*. New York: Alfred A. Knopf, 1998.

Congdon, Don, ed. *Combat: The Civil War*. New York: Delacorte Press, 1967.

Cox, Jacob Dolson. *Military Reminiscences of the Civil War*. New York: Charles Scribner's Sons, 1900.

Dale, Philip Marshall. *Medical Biographies: The Ailments of Thirty-three Famous Persons*. Norman, OK: University of Oklahoma Press, 1952.

De Forest, John William. *A Volunteer's Adventures: A Union Captain's Record of the Civil War*. New Haven: Yale University Press, 1946.

_____. *Miss Ravenel's Conversion from Secession to Loyalty*. New York: Holt, Rhinehart and Winston, 1964.

Dowe, Amy Haslam. "A Child's Memories of the Whitmans." Private collection of Jerome M. Loving.

Dyer, Frederick H. *A Compendium of the War of the Rebellion*. Vol. 2. New York: Thomas Yoseloff, 1959.

Eiselein, Gregory. "Whitman and the Humanitarian Possibilities of Lilacs." *Prospects* 18 (1993): 51–79.

Emerson, Ralph Waldo. *Selected Essays*. New York: Penguin Books, 1985.

Erkkila, Betsy. "Whitman and the Homosexual Republic." In *Walt Whitman: The Centennial Essays*, edited by Ed Folsom, 153–71. Iowa City: University of Iowa Press, 1994.

Faust, Drew Gilpin. *This Republic of Suffering*. New York: Alfred A. Knopf, 2008.

Feinberg, Charles E. "A Whitman Collector Destroys a Whitman Myth." *The Papers of the Bibliographical Society of America*. Vol. 52. Chicago: University of Chicago Press, 1958.

The Charles E. Feinberg Collection of the Papers of Walt Whitman, 1839–1919, Library of Congress, Washington, D.C.

Feld, Ralph Foster. *Brooklyn Village, 1816–1834*. New York: Columbia University Press, 1938.

Feldman, Mark B. "Remembering a Convulsive War." *Walt Whitman Quarterly Review* 23, 1/2 (Summer/Fall 2005): 1–25.

Fowler, Andrew L. *Memoirs of the Late Adjutant Andrew L. Fowler of the 51st New York Volunteers*. Washington, D.C.: Library of Congress, Manuscript Division.

Francis, Henry W. "Letters to His Wife, 1861–1864." New York State Archives, Albany.

Frassanito, William A. *Antietam: The Photographic Legacy of America's Bloodiest Day*. New York: Scribner, 1978.

Frederickson, George M. *The Inner Civil War: Northern Intellectuals and the Crisis of the Union*. New York: Harper & Row, 1965.

Freemon, Frank R. *Gangrene and Glory: Medical Care During the American Civil War*. Madison, NJ: Fairleigh Dickinson University Press, 1998.

Gallagher, Gary W. *The Confederate War*. Cambridge: Harvard University Press, 1997.

Genoways, Ted, ed. *Walt Whitman: The Correspondence*. Vol. 7. Iowa City: University of Iowa Press, 2004.

Glicksberg, Charles I. *Walt Whitman and the Civil War*. Philadelphia: University of Pennsylvania Press, 1933.

Gohdes, Clarence, and Rollo G. Silver, eds. *Faint Clews & Indirections: Manuscripts of Walt Whitman and His Family*. Durham, NC: Duke University Press, 1949.

Gould, John M., ed. The Antietam Collection. Dartmouth College Library, Dartmouth, NH.

Grier, Edward F., ed. *Walt Whitman: Notebooks and Unpublished Prose Manuscripts*. Vols. 1 and 2. New York: New York University Press, 1984.

Harris, William C. *Lincoln's Last Months*. Cambridge: Belknap Press, 2004.

Heflin, Wilson. *Herman Melville's Whaling Years*. Nashville, TN: Vanderbilt University Press, 2004.

Hesseltine, William B. *Civil War Prisons*. Columbus, OH: Ohio State University Press, 1930.

Holloway, Emory, ed. *The Uncollected Poetry and Prose of Walt Whitman*. Vols. 1 and 2. Garden City, NY, and Toronto: Doubleday, Page & Company, 1921.

Howey, Allan W. "Weaponry: The Rifle-musket and the Minie Ball." *Civil War Times Magazine*, October 1999.

Huddleston, John. *Killing Ground: Photographs of the Civil War and the Changing American Landscape*. Baltimore: Johns Hopkins University Press, 2002.

Hutchinson, George. "Race and the Family Romance: Whitman's Civil War." *Walt Whitman Quarterly Review* 20 (Winter/Spring 2003): 134–50.

Hutto, Burton, M.D. "Syphilis in Clinical Psychiatry: A Review." *Psychosomatics* 42 (December 2001): 453–60.

James, Henry. "Mr. Walt Whitman." *The Nation* 1 (November 16, 1865).

Katz, Jonathan Ned. *Love Stories: Sex Between Men Before Homosexuality*. Chicago: University of Chicago Press, 2001.

Kennedy, Frances H., ed. *The Civil War Battlefield Guide*. 2nd ed. Boston and New York: Houghton Mifflin, 1998.

Kirkwood, James P. "Report Descriptive of the Construction of the Brooklyn Water Works." *The Brooklyn Water Works and Sewers. A Descriptive Memoir*. New York: D. Van Nostrand, 1867.

Kolata, Gina. "So Big and Healthy Nowadays, Grandpa Wouldn't Know You." *New York Times*, July 30, 2006.

Lawrence, D. H. *Studies in Classic American Literature*. New York: Viking Press, 1964.

Lee, James C. "The Undertaker's Role During the American Civil War." *America's Civil War Magazine* (November 1996): 20–24.

Leech, Margaret. *Reveille in Washington, 1860–1865*. New York and London: Harper and Brothers, 1941.

Linderman, Gerald F. "Embattled Courage." In *The Civil War Soldier: A Historical Reader*, edited by Michael Barton and Larry M. Logue, 436–55. New York: New York University Press, 2002.

Loving, Jerome M., ed. *Civil War Letters of George Washington Whitman*. Durham, NC: Duke University Press, 1975.

_____. *Emerson, Whitman, and the American Muse*. Chapel Hill: University of North Carolina Press, 1982.

_____. *Walt Whitman: The Song of Himself*. Berkeley: University of California Press, 1999.

_____. *Walt Whitman's Champion: William Douglas O'Connor*. College Station, TX: Texas A&M University Press, 1977.

Lowenfels, Walter, ed. *Walt Whitman's Civil War*. New York: Da Capo Press, 1989.

Matter, William. "The Federal High Command at Spotsylvania." In *The Spotsylvania Campaign*, edited by Gary W. Gallagher, 29–60. Chapel Hill: University of North Carolina Press, 1998.

McElroy, John Harmon, ed. *The Sacrificial Years: A Chronicle of Walt Whitman's Experiences in the Civil War*. Boston: David R. Godine, 1999.

McPherson, James M. *Battle Cry of Freedom: The Civil War Era*. New York: Oxford University Press, 1988.

Melville, Herman. *Battle-Pieces and Aspects of the War*. Amherst: University of Massachusetts Press, 1972.

Miller, Edwin Haviland, ed. *Walt Whitman: The Correspondence*. Vols. 1 and 2. New York: New York University Press, 1961.

_____. "Walt Whitman's Income, 1876–1892." In *Walt Whitman: The Correspondence*, vol. 6, edited by Edwin Haviland Miller, xi–xxxvi. New York: New York University Press, 1977.

Mitchell, Patricia B. " 'Truly Horrible' Danville Civil War Prisons." *The Pittsylvania Packet* (Spring 1993): 12–13.

Mitchell, Reid. *Civil War Soldiers*. New York: Viking, 1988.

Molinoff, Katherine. *Monographs on Unpublished Whitman Material*, no.1–3. Brooklyn: Comet Press, 1941.

Moon, Michael. "Rereading Whitman Under Pressure of AIDS: His Sex Radicalism and Ours." In *The Continuing Presence of Walt Whitman*, edited by Robert K. Martin, 53–66. Iowa City: University of Iowa Press, 1992.

Morris, Roy, Jr. *The Better Angel: Walt Whitman in the Civil War*. New York: Oxford University Press, 2000.

Murray, Martin G. "Traveling with the Wounded: Walt Whitman and Washington's Civil War Hospitals." *Washington History: Magazine of the Historical Society of Washington, D.C.* 8 (Fall/Winter 1996–97): 58–73, 92–93.

_____. " 'Pete the Great': A Biography of Peter Doyle." *Walt Whitman Quarterly Review* 12 (Summer 1994): 1–51.

National Archives and Records Administration. "Record of Events, 51st Regiment New York Veteran Volunteers." NARA Microfilm Publication. Washington, D.C.

National Archives and Records Administration. Record Group 94. Office of the Adjutant General, Volunteer Organizations, Civil War Returns. Washington, D.C.

National Archives and Records Administration, Northeast Region. Record Group 36. U.S Customs Service and New York Customs House crew lists. New York, NY.

New York State Archives, Albany, NY.

Parker, Thomas H. *History of the 51st regiment of P.V. and V.V., from its organization, at Camp Curtin, Harrisburg, Pa., in 1861, to its being mustered out of the United States service at Alexandria, Va., July 27th, 1865*. Philadelphia: King & Baird, Printers, 1869.

Perkovich, Mike. *Nature Boys: Camp Discourse in American Literature from Whitman to Wharton*. New York: Peter Lang, 2003.

Pessen, Edward. "A Social and Economic Portrait of Jacksonian Brooklyn." *New-York Historical Society Quarterly* 55 (1971): 318–53.

Phisterer, Frederick. *New York in the War of the Rebellion, 1861 to 1865.* 3rd edition. Albany: J. B. Lyon Company, 1912.

Price, Kenneth, ed. *Walt Whitman: The Contemporary Reviews.* New York: Cambridge University Press, 1996.

Priest, John Michael. *Antietam: The Soldiers' Battle.* Shippensburg, PA: White Mane Publishing Company, Inc., 1989.

_____. *Before Antietam: The Battle for South Mountain.* Shippensburg, PA: White Mane Publishing Company, Inc., 1992.

_____. *Nowhere to Run: The Wilderness, May 4th & 5th, 1864.* Shippensburg, PA: White Mane Publishing Company, Inc., 1995.

_____. *Victory Without Triumph: The Wilderness, May 6th & 7th, 1864.* Shippensburg, PA: White Mane Publishing Company, Inc., 1996.

"Quarter Century Banquet of the 51st Regiment N.Y. Volunteers." Washington, D.C.: Library of Congress, Manuscript Division.

Rable, George C. *Fredericksburg! Fredericksburg!* Chapel Hill and London: University of North Carolina Press, 2002.

_____. "It Is Well That War Is So Terrible: The Carnage at Fredericksburg." In *The Fredericksburg Campaign: Decision on the Rappahannock,* edited by Gary W. Gallagher, 48–79. Chapel Hill & London: University of North Carolina Press, 1995.

Reynolds, David S. "Whitman and Nineteenth-Century Views of Gender and Sexuality." In *Walt Whitman of Mickle Street: A Centennial Collection,* edited by Geoffrey Sill, 38–45. Knoxville: University of Tennessee Press, 1994.

Rhea, Gordon C. *The Battle of the Wilderness, May 5–6, 1864.* Baton Rouge: Louisiana State University Press, 1994.

_____. *The Battles for Spotsylvania Court House and the Road to Yellow Tavern, May 7–12, 1864.* Baton Rouge: Louisiana State University Press, 1997.

_____. *Cold Harbor.* Baton Rouge: Louisiana State University Press, 2002.

Roberts, Kim. "A Map of Whitman's Boarding Houses and Work Places." *Walt Whitman Quarterly Review* 22 (Summer 2004): 23–28.

Robinson, Armstead L. *Bitter Fruits of Bondage: The Demise of Slavery and the Collapse of the Confederacy, 1861–1865.* Charlottesville: University of Virginia Press, 2005.

Royster, Charles. *The Destructive War: William Tecumseh Sherman, Stonewall Jackson, and the Americans.* New York: Vintage Civil War Library, 1993.

Rubin, Joseph Jay, and Charles H. Brown, eds. *Walt Whitman of the New York Aurora: Editor at Twenty-two.* State College, PA: Bald Eagle Press, 1950.

Rutkow, Ira M. *Bleeding Blue and Gray: Civil War Surgery and the Evolution of American Medicine.* New York: Random House, 2005.

Ryan, Mary P. *Cradle of the Middle Class: The Family in Oneida County, New York, 1790–1865.* Cambridge: Cambridge University Press, 1981.

Savoy, Eric. "Reading Gay America: Walt Whitman, Henry James, and the Politics of Reception." In *The Continuing Presence of Walt Whitman,* edited by Robert K. Martin, 3–15. Iowa City: University of Iowa Press, 1992.

Schecter, Barnet. *The Devil's Own Work: The Civil War Draft Riots and the Fight to Reconstruct America.* New York: Walker & Company, 2005.

Schmidgall, Gary. *Walt Whitman: A Gay Life*. New York: Dutton, 1997.

_____, ed. *Walt Whitman. Selected Poems 1855–1892*. New York: St. Martin's Press, 1999.

Sherman, William Tecumseh. *Memoirs of William T. Sherman, by Himself*. Westport, CT: Greenwood Press, 1972.

Shively, Charley. *Calamus Lovers: Walt Whitman's Working-Class Camerados*. San Francisco: Gay Sunshine Press, 1987.

_____, ed. *Drum Beats: Walt Whitman's Civil War Boy Lovers*. San Francisco: Gay Sunshine Press, 1989.

Shryock, Richard Harrison. *Medicine in America: Historical Essays*. Baltimore: Johns Hopkins University Press, 1966.

Skocpol, Theda. *Protecting Soldiers and Mothers: The Political Origins of Social Policy in the United States*. Cambridge: Belknap Press, 1992.

Small, Abner R. *The Road to Richmond: The Civil War Memoirs of Major Abner R. Small of the Sixteenth Maine Volunteers. Together with the Diary Which He Kept When He Was a Prisoner of War*. Berkeley: University of California Press, 1959.

Smith, George Winston, and Charles Judah, eds. *Life in the North During the Civil War: A Source History*. Albuquerque: University of New Mexico Press, 1966.

Stearns, Amanda Akin. *The Lady Nurse of Ward E*. New York: Baker & Taylor Company, 1909.

Styple, William B., ed. *Writing and Fighting the Civil War: Soldier Correspondence to the New York Sunday Mercury*. Kearny, NJ: Belle Grove Publishing Company, 2000.

Thompson, David L. "In the Ranks to the Antietam" and "With Burnside at Antietam." In *Battles and Leaders of the Civil War*, vol. 2, edited by Robert Underwood Johnson and Clarence Clough Buel, 556–58, 660–62. New Jersey: The Century Co., 1887–88.

Traubel, Horace. *With Walt Whitman in Camden*. New York: Rowman and Littlefield, 1961.

Traubel, Horace L., Richard Maurice Bucke, and Thomas B. Harned, eds. *In Re Walt Whitman*. Philadelphia: David McKay, 1893.

Josiah P. Trent Collection of Walt Whitman Manuscripts. Duke University Rare Book, Manuscript, and Special Collections Library, Durham.

Trowbridge, John. "Reminiscences of Walt Whitman." *Atlantic Monthly*, February 1902.

Waldron, Randall H., ed. *Mattie: The Letters of Martha Mitchell Whitman*. New York: New York University Press, 1977.

War of the Rebellion: A Compilation of the Official Records of the Union and Confederate Armies. Volumes 19, 21, 36, 40, and 44. Washington, D.C., 1880–1901.

Wardrop, Daneen. "Civil War Nursing Narratives, Whitman's *Memoranda During the War* and Eroticism." *Walt Whitman Quarterly Review* 23 (Summer/Fall 2005): 26–47.

Warner, Ezra J. *Generals in Blue: Lives of the Union Commanders*. Baton Rouge: Louisiana State University Press, 1964.

Wheeler, Richard. *On Fields of Fury: From the Wilderness to the Crater, an Eyewitness History*. New York: HarperCollins Publishers, 1991.

Whicher, Stephen E. "Whitman's Awakening to Death." In *The Presence of Walt Whitman*, edited by R. W. B. Lewis, 1–18. New York: Columbia University Press, 1962.

Whitman, Walt. *The Gathering of the Forces*, edited by Cleveland Rodgers and John Black. New York: G. P. Putnam's Sons, 1920.

_____. *Leaves of Grass: The First (1855) Edition*. New York: Penguin Classics, 1986.

_____. *Leaves of Grass: Facsimile Edition of the 1860 Text*, edited by Roy Harvey Pearce. Ithaca and London: Cornell University Press, 1961.

_____. *Leaves of Grass: A Textual Variorum of the Printed Poems*, edited by Sculley Bradley, Harold W. Blodgett, Arthur Golden, and William White. New York: New York University Press, 1980.

_____. *Memoranda During the War*, edited by Peter Coviello. Oxford: Oxford University Press, 2004.

_____. *Walt Whitman: Complete Poetry and Collected Prose*. New York: The Library of America, 1982.

Wilentz, Sean. *Chants Democratic: New York City and the Rise of the American Working Class*. New York: Oxford University Press, 1984.

Williams, Blanche Colton. *Clara Barton: Daughter of Destiny*. Philadelphia: J. B. Lippincott Company, 1941.

Wilson, Edmund. *Patriotic Gore: Studies in the Literature of the American Civil War*. New York: Oxford University Press, 1966.

Yale Collection of American Literature. Walt Whitman Collection. Beinecke Rare Book and Manuscript Library, Yale University, New Haven.

Zweig, Paul. *The Making of the Poet*. New York: Basic Books, 1984.

INDEX

Note: page numbers in *italics* refer to illustrations; those followed by "n" refer to notes.

A NOTE ON THE AUTHOR

Robert Roper has won awards for his fiction and nonfiction alike. His most recent book, *Fatal Mountaineer*, a biography of American climber-philosopher Willi Unsoeld, won the 2002 Boardman Tasker Prize given by the British Alpine Club. His works of fiction include *Royo County*, *On Spider Creek*, *Mexico Days*, *The Trespassers*, and *Cuervo Tales*, which was a *New York Times* Notable Book. He has won prizes or grants from the NEA, the Ingram Merrill Foundation, the Joseph Henry Jackson competition, and the Royal Geographical Society of London. He teaches at Johns Hopkins and lives in Maryland and California.